THE CAMBRIDGE COMPANION TO
THE EPIC

Every great civilization from the Bronze Age to the present day has produced epic poems. Epic poetry has always had a profound influence on other literary genres, including its own parody in the form of mock-epic. This *Companion* surveys over four thousand years of epic poetry from the Babylonian Epic of Gilgamesh to Derek Walcott's postcolonial *Omeros*. The list of epic poets analysed here includes some of the greatest writers in literary history in Europe and beyond: Homer, Virgil, the poets of *Beowulf* and the Norse *Eddas*, Dante, Camões, Spenser, Milton, Wordsworth, Keats, and Pound, among others. Each essay, by an expert in the field, pays close attention to the way these writers have intimately influenced one another to form a distinctive and cross-cultural literary tradition. Unique in its coverage of the vast scope of that tradition, this book is an essential companion for students of literature of all kinds and in all ages.

CATHERINE BATES is Professor of Renaissance Literature at the University of Warwick. Her previous publications include *The Rhetoric of Courtship in Elizabethan Language and Literature* (Cambridge, 1992) and *Masculinity, Gender and Identity in the English Renaissance Lyric* (Cambridge, 2007).

A complete list of books in the series is at the back of the book

THE CAMBRIDGE
COMPANION TO
THE EPIC

EDITED BY
CATHERINE BATES

University of Warwick

CAMBRIDGE
UNIVERSITY PRESS

CAMBRIDGE UNIVERSITY PRESS
Cambridge, New York, Melbourne, Madrid, Cape Town, Singapore,
São Paulo, Delhi, Dubai, Tokyo

Cambridge University Press
The Edinburgh Building, Cambridge CB2 8RU, UK

Published in the United States of America by Cambridge University Press, New York

www.cambridge.org
Information on this title: www.cambridge.org/9780521707367

First published 2010

Printed in the United Kingdom at the University Press, Cambridge

A catalogue record for this publication is available from the British Library

Library of Congress Cataloging-in-Publication Data

The Cambridge companion to the epic / edited by Catherine Bates.
p.   cm. – (Cambridge companions to literature)
Includes bibliographical references and index.
ISBN 978-0-521-88094-7 (Hardback) – ISBN 978-0-521-70736-7 (pbk.)
1. Epic poetry–History and criticism.   I. Bates, Catherine, 1964–   II. Title.   III. Series.
PN1303.C36 2010
809.1′32–dc22

2009051399

ISBN 978-0-521-88094-7 Hardback
ISBN 978-0-521-70736-7 Paperback

4772273668

CONTENTS

CONTENTS

CONTRIBUTORS

CATHERINE BATES, University of Warwick

JOHN FRECCERO, New York University

A. R. GEORGE, School of Oriental and African Studies, University of London

JASPER GRIFFIN, University of Oxford

ROBERT HAMNER, Hardin-Simmons University, Texas

DAVID LOEWENSTEIN, University of Wisconsin, Madison

GIUSEPPE MAZZOTTA, Yale University

PAUL MERCHANT, The William Stafford Archives

GEORGE MONTEIRO, Brown University

MICHAEL O'NEILL, Durham University

CLAUDE RAWSON, Yale University

KARL REICHL, University of Bonn

PETER TOOHEY, University of Calgary

JOHN WHITTIER-FERGUSON, University of Michigan, Ann Arbor

PREFACE

The endurance of the epic tradition is an extraordinary literary phenomenon: a form of writing that has recognizably survived – for all the hazardous vicissitudes of transmission and in spite of historical changes themselves of historical proportions – from *Gilgamesh*, which dates back to the second millennium BC, to *Omeros*, which won its author the Nobel Prize for Literature in 1992. Nor does epic as a genre show any signs of decay, for it is constantly being updated and revived for a modern audience, a flood of new, often celebrated, translations making the texts newly available and accessible to a general readership, while cinematic remakes and the perpetuation of epic motifs in contemporary blockbusters and computer games ensure that the form remains ever present in the popular consciousness. The spate of essays and monographs recently published on the epic tradition – many of them by contributors to this volume – clearly indicates that the topic continues to attract a current and very lively interest within the academy, and it is with this ongoing intellectual engagement with the subject that the present volume identifies itself.

In first mooting the contents of this book, it was originally suggested that the essays collected might most usefully focus on a particular historical period, such as antiquity or the Renaissance. However, since it is a quintessential if not defining characteristic of epic to refer back to and revise what went before, too exclusive a focus on one particular period risks removing texts from a literary continuity to which they belong and within which they consciously position themselves. In order to understand Renaissance epic texts, for example, it is necessary to see them as speaking to and commenting upon a millennia-long tradition that stretches back as far as Homer if not beyond; while they, in turn, set up new (Christian or romance) agendas that are crucial to understanding the development of epic in texts of later periods. This is the rationale, therefore, behind the inclusiveness and scope of the present volume, which seeks not only to look closely at the epic productions of particular periods but also – perhaps above all – to locate those productions explicitly within a literary tradition that they at once constitute, continue, and change. The essays that follow, therefore, look in chronological sequence at the epic tradition as a whole. A series of fully contextualized essays considers, in turn: the Epic of Gilgamesh; the tradition of Greek epic (both Homeric and Hellenistic); the classical Latin epic (including Virgil, Ovid, Lucan, Statius); the tradition of heroic song in the Dark and early Middle Ages (including the Norse sagas, *Beowulf*, the *chansons de geste*); *The Divine Comedy* as a late medieval Christianization of the epic genre; the Italian Renaissance chivalric epics of Boiardo, Ariosto, and Tasso; the *Lusíadas* of Camões as an example of the Renaissance epic of empire; the epics of Spenser, Milton, and Lucy Hutchinson as exemplifying the Renaissance Protestant epic; the period during which epic might be said to be 'in crisis' (roughly from Dryden to Byron); Romantic re-appropriations of epic by Shelley, Wordsworth, Blake, Keats, and others; the creative interface between epic and modernism that might be found in the poetry of T. S. Eliot and Ezra Pound; Derek Walcott's *Omeros* as a revisionist, postcolonial epic; and, in a final, synoptic essay, translations of epic and the theme of cultural 'translation' generally as central to the epic mode.

Although there are many other texts and cultural productions – such as Joyce's *Ulysses* or contemporary fantasy – which this more expansive survey of the epic tradition might be thought obliged to include, the present volume restricts itself to a working definition of the epic as texts that were written in verse and that, in length, content, and style, clearly make reference to their predecessors, thereby constituting and situating themselves within a distinctive literary tradition. In each case, the contributors to the volume historicize the texts under discussion and explore those aspects that pointedly repeat, develop, critique, or revise what went before. The advantage of this is that the reader can 'dip in' and enjoy individual accounts of some of the greatest works of the literary canon while at the same time being given an opportunity to trace the unfolding of a culturally central and remarkably persistent literary genre.

I would like here to extend my thanks, first and foremost, to the contributors of this volume, all of whom have stuck heroically to their impossible brief of discussing the infinite riches of these great texts in the very little room allowed them. For the original inception of the project, I thank Sarah Stanton, and for its ongoing progress and finalization, Linda Bree and Maartje Scheltens. Finally, I would like to dedicate this volume to the memory of G. K. Hunter (1920–2008), who forty years ago made a course on The Epic Tradition foundational to the English curriculum he was designing for what was, then, the new University of Warwick. That the course is still going strong is testament to the enthusiasm of generations of students whose appetite for reading epic poetry remains, it seems, undiminishable.

Catherine Bates

CHRONOLOGY

Dates marked with an asterisk are approximate or speculative

BC

*2200	Oral Gilgamesh poems
*2000	Oldest copy of a Sumerian Gilgamesh poem
*1750	Old Babylonian Gilgamesh epic
*1300	Middle Babylonian versions of the Gilgamesh epic
*1100	Standard Babylonian Epic of Gilgamesh
*800	Possible oral origins of the *Mahabharata*
*750	Possible oral origins of the *Ramayana*
*700–675	Homer, composition of the *Iliad* and the *Odyssey*
*700–650	Hesiod, *Theogony, Works and Days*
*650	Copies of the Gilgamesh epic from Assyria
*400	Copies of the Gilgamesh epic from Uruk and Babylon
*300	Core sections of *Mahabharata* written
*300	Original version of the *Ramayana* written
*270	Apollonius of Rhodes, *Argonautica*
*220	Livius Andronicus, Latin translation of the *Odyssey*
*200	Gnaeus Naevius, *The Punic War (Bellum Punicum)*
*170	Ennius, *Annales*
*150	Last copies of the Gilgamesh epic
*50	Lucretius, *On the Nature of the Universe (De rerum natura)*

1590	Spenser, *The Faerie Queene*, Books I–III
1594	Tasso, *Discourses on the Heroic Poem*
1596	Spenser, *The Faerie Queene*, Books I–VI
1614	Cervantes, *Don Quixote*
1623	Marino, *L'Adone*
1667	Milton, *Paradise Lost*, ten-book version
1671	Milton, *Paradise Regained*
1674	Milton, *Paradise Lost*, twelve-book version
1674	Boileau, *Le Lutrin*, four-canto version
1679	Lucy Hutchinson, *Order and Disorder*
1682	Dryden, *Mac Flecknoe*
1683	Boileau, *Le Lutrin*, six-canto version
1697	Dryden, translation of the *Aeneid* into English
1699	Samuel Garth, *The Dispensary*
1704	Swift, *The Battle of the Books, A Tale of a Tub*
1714	Pope, *The Rape of the Lock*
1715–20	Pope, translation of the *Iliad* into English
1726	Pope, *et al.*, translation of the *Odyssey* into English
1728–9	Pope, *Dunciad*, early versions
1743	Pope, *Dunciad*, four-book version
1749	Samuel Johnson, *The Vanity of Human Wishes*
1751	Richard Owen Cambridge, *Scribleriad*
1781	William Hayley, *The Triumphs of Temper*
1782	William Hayley, *Essay on Epic Poetry*
1785	William Cowper, *The Task*
1796	Southey, *Joan of Arc*
1799	Wordsworth, *The Prelude*, two-book version
1801	Southey, *Thalaba the Destroyer*
1804–20	Blake, *Jerusalem*

I

A. R. GEORGE

The Epic of Gilgamesh

Introduction

The name 'Epic of Gilgamesh' is given to the Babylonian poem that tells the deeds of Gilgamesh, the greatest king and mightiest hero of ancient Mesopotamian legend. The poem falls into the category 'epic' because it is a long narrative poem of heroic content and has the seriousness and pathos that have sometimes been identified as markers of epic. Some early Assyriologists, when nationalism was a potent political force, characterized it as the 'national epic' of Babylonia, but this notion has deservedly lapsed. The poem's subject is not the establishment of a Babylonian nation nor an episode in that nation's history, but the vain quest of a man to escape his mortality. In its final and best-preserved version it is a sombre meditation on the human condition. The glorious exploits it tells are motivated by individual human predicaments, especially desire for fame and horror of death. The emotional struggles related in the story of Gilgamesh are those of no collective group but of the individual. Among its timeless themes are the friction between nature and civilization, friendship between men, the place in the universe of gods, kings and mortals, and the misuse of power. The poem speaks to the anxieties and life-experience of a human being, and that is why modern readers find it both profound and enduringly relevant.

Discovery and recovery

The literatures of ancient Mesopotamia, chiefly in Sumerian and Babylonian (Akkadian), were lost when cuneiform writing died out in the first century AD. Their recovery is one of the supreme accomplishments in the humanities; the process began in the middle of the nineteenth century and continues today. In 1850 the gentleman adventurer Austen Henry Layard tunnelled through the remains of an Assyrian palace at Nineveh, near Mosul in modern Iraq, extracting the limestone bas-reliefs that lined its rooms. He stumbled across a chamber knee-deep in broken clay tablets bearing cuneiform writing. This was part of the archive of the Neo-Assyrian kings, who ruled most of the Near East in the seventh century BC. Layard was unable to read the tablets, but shipped them back to the British Museum with the bas-reliefs.

Sixteen years later a young man called George Smith began to read the tablets. By 1872 he had sorted many into categories. Already discrete literary compositions were emerging, among them what he called the Poem of Izdubar. This was the Epic of Gilgamesh; the hero's name was not correctly read until 1899. Smith's translation gained wide readership because the poem included a story of the flood very similar to that of Noah in Genesis.[1]

Smith died soon afterwards, but his translation led German scholars to study the Assyrian tablets. Within fifteen years Paul Haupt published the cuneiform text of Gilgamesh, which he called the Babylonian 'Epic of Nimrod'.[2] The title was a reference to the great hunter of the Bible, who many supposed was based on the Babylonian hero. Alongside the Assyrian tablets this book included a single Babylonian tablet. This was the first of many Babylonian manuscripts of Gilgamesh to be identified among the huge number of tablets that the British Museum acquired by purchase and excavation in Babylonia, south of Baghdad, in the 1870s–90s.

Haupt's cuneiform text did nothing to make his discoveries known to the larger public, but in 1900 Peter Jensen's anthology of Akkadian narrative poetry transliterated the text into Roman characters and translated it into German.[3] Another early translation, by Arthur Ungnad, publicized the existence of the poem more widely and finally brought it recognition as a masterpiece of world literature.[4]

Meanwhile, more pieces of the poem had been identified in the British Museum, both Assyrian tablets from seventh-century Nineveh and slightly later pieces from Babylonia. Much older tablets soon began to appear on the antiquities' market but the British Museum had ceased collecting so voraciously and the bulk of tablets offered for purchase went elsewhere. These included three Gilgamesh tablets of Old Babylonian date (eighteenth century BC) from Babylonia, which ended up in Berlin, Yale and Philadelphia. At the same time archaeological exploration increased dramatically. German expeditions found a Gilgamesh tablet of the late second millennium at Hattusa (Boğazköy), the Hittite capital in central Anatolia, and a Neo-Assyrian tablet at Asshur, on the Tigris downstream of Nineveh. Both the market and excavations also began to yield tablets that contained poems about Gilgamesh in the Sumerian language. Thus the decade before the First World War saw a growing diversity in the provenance and period of tablets of Gilgamesh, and their diaspora to Europe and America.

The sources for the Babylonian poem were next collected by R. Campbell Thompson, who published a verse translation in English in 1929, and cuneiform and transliterated texts a year later.[5] The second book fell short of the highest contemporaneous standards in Assyriology but, despite its poor reception, endured for more than seventy years as the only critical edition of the Babylonian Gilgamesh. By the 1960s the lack of a modern and authoritative treatment was everywhere deplored. By the end of that decade thirty-four pieces were known in addition to those edited by Thompson, twenty of them in cuneiform only. By the turn of the millennium any scholar wishing to read the poem from original sources had to consult a dossier of over thirty different publications.

The absence of an up-to-date critical edition of the Epic of Gilgamesh in the latter part of the twentieth century produced a boom in translations. Some of these translations were faithful renderings by people who could read Babylonian; others were less authoritative. At present, only three translations include the Babylonian poem in its most complete form: my own (1999), and those of Benjamin Foster (2000) and Stefan Maul (2005).[6] Foster's and my books also include the Sumerian poems of Gilgamesh.

In 2003 I brought together all the known sources of the Babylonian poem then accessible. The progress made in the recovery of the text across the preceding seven decades can be measured in the number of sources: where Thompson's edition was based on 112 manuscripts, mine utilizes 218 pieces. Another improvement in knowledge can be seen in the division of the material. Thompson interpolated the four second-millennium sources then extant into his edition of the first-millennium poem. I separate the sources into four periods and treat the versions of each period as distinct stages in the poem's evolution, showing that there is no single Epic of Gilgamesh: parts of different versions survive, spread across eighteen hundred years of history.

The recovery of the Epic of Gilgamesh continues, as does the recovery of Babylonian literature generally. Since 2003 no fewer than ten pieces of the poem have become available.[7] Some have already been published. It is certain that more will accumulate, adding to our knowledge in ways unsuspected as well as suspected, and eventually necessitating another critical edition.

Literary history

The oldest literary materials about the hero-king Gilgamesh are five Sumerian poems. These are known from tablets of the Old Babylonian period, especially the eighteenth century BC, but they probably go back to a period of intense creativity under the patronage of King Shulgi of Ur (2094–2047 BC).

The Sumerian poems report some of the same legends and themes as parts of the Babylonian poem, but they are independent compositions and do not form a literary whole. The Sumerian and Babylonian poems shared more than just a common literary inheritance, whether that was oral (as seems likely) or written. They are products of a bilingual literary culture that displayed a high degree of intertextuality even between compositions in different languages; neither, however, is a translation of the other.

The oldest Babylonian fragments of the epic are contemporaneous with the Sumerian tablets. Would-be scribes demonstrated their competence by copying out texts from the scribal curriculum. The Old Babylonian curriculum consisted almost entirely of Sumerian compositions, and we possess multiple copies of most of them. Literary compositions in Babylonian were not then copied in the same numbers, so many fewer fragments are extant. Eleven pieces of Gilgamesh survive from this period, all from Babylonia itself. Some of them are fine copies of large sections of the poem; prominent among these are a pair of tablets now in Philadelphia and Yale (OB Tablets II–III), and a tablet from northern Babylonia (OB VA + BM). Other pieces are short excerpts, some poorly executed, and were the work of juniors, either as set exercises or as extemporized writing.

Altogether these eleven Old Babylonian manuscripts provide several disconnected episodes in a little over six hundred lines of poetry. Some of these lines are from passages that describe the same episode slightly differently, so it transpires that the eleven manuscripts are not witnesses to a single edition of the poem, but to at least two and probably more. There is not enough shared text to determine how extensive the differences are, but it is already clear that we can fairly speak both of distinct recensions (where the differences are minor) and of distinct versions (where the differences are major).

The version represented by the tablets in Philadelphia and Yale (OB Tablets II–III) went by the name of its opening phrase, 'Surpassing all kings'. We do not yet know whether the titles of other Old Babylonian versions differed. The complexity of the written tradition in the eighteenth century suggests that by then the poem was a composition of some antiquity; in the absence of older written sources it seems justified to postulate an oral prehistory extending over several generations of singers. There is therefore no sign of any one author who might have been responsible for the poem's original creation.

The recensional situation is even more complex in the later second millennium (1600–1000 BC). From this intermediate or Middle Babylonian period twenty-three fragments survive. The oldest fragment is probably sixteenth-century, and probably from south-east Babylonia, which makes it very rare (MB Priv$_1$). It is also remarkable because the names of the poem's heroes, Gilgamesh and Enkidu, are replaced by the gods Sîn and Ea. The fragment provides the text of an episode already well known from an Old Babylonian tablet and the first-millennium text, but with very significant differences.

Other tablets of the intermediate period are Middle Babylonian pieces from Ur and a group from Nippur, probably from the thirteenth and twelfth centuries. The former tablet (MB Ur) is closely related to the Standard Babylonian epic of the first millennium. The latter group (MB Nippur) reveals the poem's use as a pedagogical tool in the training of scribes; by this time a Babylonian curriculum had replaced the Sumerian one. Roughly contemporaneous with these Babylonian tablets are manuscripts from Syria, Palestine and Anatolia. Cuneiform writing and the languages of southern Mesopotamia were exported to the west from the third millennium BC. Discoveries of tablets from the fourteenth to twelfth centuries reveal that cuneiform writing was taught from Egypt to Anatolia using a modified version of the Babylonian scribal curriculum. The Epic of Gilgamesh was part of this modified curriculum, and parts of it have turned up at Megiddo in Palestine, Ugarit and Emar in Syria and Hattusa in Anatolia. One of the oldest pieces of this material (MB Boğazköy from Hattusa) is remarkably close to the text of the Old Babylonian tablet now in Yale (OB Tablet III). Among the youngest are two (MB Emar) that are much more like the Standard Babylonian text of the first millennium. Several pieces are notable for corruption so severe that in places the text is no longer meaningful. At this time prose paraphrases of the epic were made in languages of the north Mesopotamian periphery, including Hurrian and Hittite.

Most sources for the poem come from the first millennium BC: to date about 190. This material can be divided by period into three groups: (a) early Neo-Assyrian manuscripts, (b) Neo-Assyrian manuscripts from Nineveh, and (c) Neo- and Late Babylonian manuscripts from Babylon, Uruk and other cities of Babylonia (sixth to second centuries BC).

To start with group (a): recent study in Berlin of tablets excavated at Asshur one hundred years ago has revealed two fragments of early Neo-Assyrian date, probably ninth century, that belong to a version of the poem clearly older than that known to the overwhelming majority of first-millennium manuscripts. This version was probably a Middle Babylonian text imported to Assyria in the intermediate period, perhaps in the reign of Tukulti-Ninurta I (1243–1207 BC), who is known to have carried off Babylonian scribal learning after sacking Babylon. Other tablets from Asshur and Kalah (also known as Nimrud, a city south of Nineveh) show that other remnants of old editions of the poem survived into the seventh century.

By far the majority of tablets and fragments of the Babylonian Epic of Gilgamesh belong to groups (b) and (c), and are witness to a single version of the poem called after its opening phrase, 'He who saw the Deep'. This composition was divided into twelve tablets, also called the 'Series of Gilgamesh'. It was associated in Babylonian tradition with the name Sîn-leqi-unninni, a scholar-exorcist who was claimed as an ancestor by scribes of Uruk. Their view that he was the advisor of a historical King Gilgamesh immediately after the flood is anachronistic. His name is typical of the late Old Babylonian and Middle Babylonian periods. This was a time when scholars compiled standardized versions of many traditional compositions, bringing order to the multiple versions then extant. It is assumed that Sîn-leqi-unninni was responsible for producing the standardized text 'He who saw the Deep'. He probably lived towards the end of the second millennium BC.

Pioneers called the Akkadian language 'Assyrian', in reference to the Greeks' name for the land where the cuneiform tablets of Nineveh were discovered. Thompson employed this adjective in his edition, and the first-millennium poem is often still called the 'Assyrian' or 'Neo-Assyrian' version. Only the script of the Nineveh tablets is Assyrian; the language of 'He who saw the Deep' is a literary dialect of Akkadian now called Standard Babylonian. Accordingly, I use the term Standard Babylonian (SB) Epic of Gilgamesh.

The SB poem was soon adopted as the authoritative text, and after the seventh century no copies of variant versions survive. Nevertheless, the text of 'He who saw the Deep' was not completely fixed. Variants occur in grammatical form, vocabulary and line-order, even in contemporaneous manuscripts. More substantial changes, such as the omission and interpolation of lines, are uncommon but the point of division between Tablets IV and V altered over time. Textual variants do not allow us to distinguish recensions that accord with provenance and date (e.g. Neo-Assyrian v. Late Babylonian, Babylon v. Uruk). On present evidence, the text was remarkably stable.[8]

At present the SB poem is about two-thirds recovered; it must once have extended to about 3,600 lines of poetry. Some episodes are well preserved, others less so, but the narrative sequence is now certain. It is unlikely that future discoveries will much alter the placing of those sections of text that remain disconnected. Because the SB text is comparatively well established, the fragments of the second millennium can be properly situated in the story. But it is not possible to be sure of the full extent of any second-millennium version of the poem. A synopsis of the poem therefore relies almost entirely on the SB version.

Synopsis

Tablet I. The poem begins with a prologue that introduces the hero as a man made wise, but also weary, by his unique experiences. The prologue is a late addition, being followed by the praise poem that introduced the Old Babylonian poem, 'Surpassing all kings'. Thus the SB poem has two prologues, old and new, contrasting a wise but worn-out man with a mighty and glorious king. Next it tells of the hero's semi-divine origins and miraculous size and beauty. Then begins the narrative proper, as Gilgamesh struts about his city, Uruk, tyrannizing his people. The people's complaints reach the gods of heaven, who create Gilgamesh's counterpart, the wild man Enkidu. Enkidu grows up with the animals of the steppe, but an encounter with a hunter starts his transition to the role the gods chose for him. The hunter goes to Gilgamesh in Uruk, who advises him to have a woman seduce Enkidu. The woman, a prostitute, sates Enkidu's newly awakened sexual desire over six days and seven nights. The animals no longer accept him but he has gained self-awareness. This is the first step in Enkidu's humanizing and civilizing by the woman, which continues as she tells him how Gilgamesh has dreamed of his coming.

Tablet II. Enkidu is led to a shepherds' camp, taught to eat bread and drink beer, shaved, clothed and given a club to defend the sheepfold. A passing stranger tells him of Gilgamesh's tyranny in Uruk, and Enkidu's destiny calls him there to confront Gilgamesh. They fight and become friends, as the gods planned. Enkidu is next found in misery, perhaps because of a realization that he has no family (damage to the text prevents certainty). Gilgamesh proposes an expedition to the Cedar Forest and is not put off by Enkidu's first-hand knowledge of its terrible guardian, the ogre Humbaba. They equip themselves with mighty weapons and Gilgamesh seeks the blessings of the young men and the elders of Uruk. The latter try to dissuade him but he laughs off their advice.

Tablet III. The elders give their blessing and entrust their king's safety to Enkidu. The heroes go to see Gilgamesh's mother, the goddess Ninsun. From her roof she addresses a long monologue to the rising sun, the god Shamash, asking his protection for Gilgamesh and calling for the winds to come to his aid in battle. She reveals to Shamash Gilgamesh's final destiny as divine king of the shades in the netherworld, then summons Enkidu and adopts him as Gilgamesh's brother. Further rituals are lost in damaged passages, and the tablet ends with the heroes' departure from Uruk, as the people commend their king into Enkidu's safekeeping.

Tablet IV. Gilgamesh and Enkidu travel for three days, camp for the night and conduct a ritual to bring a dream. Gilgamesh wakes in terror and tells his nightmare to Enkidu, who explains it as a favourable portent. This happens five times, related in passages that in the SB poem are repeated word for word, save for the dreams and their explanations. As they near their goal Gilgamesh and Enkidu hear Humbaba bellowing from afar. Shamash urges them to attack before the ogre can cloak himself with his mysterious auras of power. The Ugarit fragments reveal that Gilgamesh or Enkidu (or both) are temporarily incapacitated, probably by contact with one of Humbaba's auras. They recover and the tablet ends with a dialogue in which Gilgamesh exhorts Enkidu to 'forget death' and go fearless into battle.

Tablet V. The heroes arrive at the forest and marvel at the cedar, the mountainous terrain and the ominous tracks left by Humbaba. A damaged section follows, in which they enter the forest and encourage each other with proverbial wisdom. When the text resumes Humbaba is challenging them. Gilgamesh and Humbaba meet in single combat and the winds blind Humbaba so that Gilgamesh can overcome him. Then begins a parley that ends when Enkidu, insulted by Humbaba, cuts off his head. But Humbaba has already laid a curse on him. Gilgamesh and Enkidu then cut timber in the forest, which Enkidu wants to turn into a huge door for the god Enlil. They make a raft of cedar, and return home down the river Euphrates with Humbaba's head.

Tablet VI. Back in Uruk Gilgamesh washes and changes. His renewed beauty captures the heart of the goddess Ishtar, who proposes marriage to him. Gilgamesh refuses, recalling the unhappy ends of her previous lovers. His plain speaking infuriates her. She rushes up to heaven to persuade her father, Anu, to give her the fiery Bull of Heaven with which to take revenge. She leads the bull to Uruk, where it causes mayhem. Enkidu grabs it by the tail and Gilgamesh pierces its neck with his knife. Enkidu insults Ishtar as she establishes rites of mourning over the bull's carcase. Gilgamesh dedicates its horns to his father's memory, the heroes parade in Uruk and hold a feast. That night Enkidu has a dream.

Tablet VII. The dream is not preserved in the SB poem. According to the Hittite paraphrase Enkidu sees Enlil and other gods in assembly; for the wrongs he and Gilgamesh have done the gods, they sentence him to death. The SB text resumes with Enkidu lying delirious on his deathbed, cursing first the door of cedar he had made for Enlil, then the hunter and the prostitute, both indirect agents of his misfortune. Shamash bids him also bless the prostitute, because she brought him the love of Gilgamesh. Enkidu has a terrible dream in which he is dragged captive to the netherworld. The passage in which he describes to Gilgamesh what he saw there is largely missing. He sickens and dies.

Tablet VIII. Gilgamesh utters a great lament for his friend. The funeral lasts several days: a funerary statue is made, the grave goods are displayed in public, and prayers are spoken for Enkidu's well-being in the netherworld. The tablet is poorly preserved; it must have ended with Enkidu's burial.

Tablet IX. Gilgamesh abandons his city and royal duties. In fear of death he takes to wandering the world, searching for his remote ancestor, Uta-napishti, the one man in human history who became immortal, whose secret he covets. The journey brings him to the mountain where the sun sets, guarded by a monstrous couple, half human, half scorpion. Eventually they allow him to pass, and he races the sun along its hidden path under the mountain, emerging just in time in a fabulous garden where trees bear gemstones for fruit.

Tablet X. There, in her tavern by the shore of the world-ocean, lives the wise Shiduri. Terrified by the newcomer's haggard and menacing appearance she bars her gate and quizzes him from her roof. Gilgamesh tells her of his quest and begs her assistance. She tells him that only the sun crosses the ocean but he should seek aid from Uta-napishti's ferryman, Ur-shanabi, who is to be found by the shore with his magic crew of Stone Ones. Without thinking, Gilgamesh rushes down on them, overcomes Ur-shanabi, smashes the Stone Ones and casts them into the water. Ur-shanabi asks who his assailant is and Gilgamesh answers, in a long passage that repeats much of Gilgamesh's dialogue with Shiduri. Ur-shanabi reveals that smashing the Stone Ones has hindered Gilgamesh's quest; he will have to cut three hundred enormous punting poles to cross of the Waters of Death. This done, they set off in Ur-shanabi's boat and reach the Waters of Death. But the punting poles run out too soon, and Gilgamesh is driven to hold Ur-shanabi's garment aloft as a makeshift sail. He is spied by Uta-napishti and lands on his shore. In a third repetition, Uta-napishti asks Gilgamesh his business and the hero again tells of his quest, wishing at last to put his sorrows behind him. Uta-napishti counsels him on the un-wisdom of his behaviour, and apparently admonishes him for neglecting his kingly duties. Then he voices a beautiful elegy on the fragility of human life and the unpredictability of death. On an Old Babylonian fragment similar sentiments are expressed by Shiduri.

Tablet XI. Gilgamesh interrupts Uta-napishti, demanding to know how he came to be immortal. Uta-napishti tells his story, how he alone was chosen to survive the great flood that long ago destroyed mankind, how he had built a strange boat and taken on board his family, men skilled in every craft, and animals of all kinds. A great storm had then swamped the world, drowning all left behind. After the boat had run aground Uta-napishti had sent out birds to determine that the waters were receding, disembarked and burnt incense to the gods, who had gathered 'like flies' around the 'sweet savour'. Enlil had made him immortal in unique circumstances. Who could do the same for Gilgamesh? Can he even resist sleep? He cannot. Uta-napishti gives him a magic white garment and orders Ur-shanabi to take him home. At the last moment, he takes pity and tells Gilgamesh how to obtain a magic plant of rejuvenation. This secured, Gilgamesh leaves with Ur-shanabi. But on the way home, while Gilgamesh is bathing in a pool, a snake catches scent of the plant and steals it, sloughing its skin as it goes. All has ended in bitter failure; Gilgamesh wishes he had never reached his goal. Returning to Uruk he shows Ur-shanabi the view of the city from the wall: one part city, one part date-groves, one part clay-pits, one part the temple of Ishtar. All humanity is there: domestic life, agriculture, industry, and spiritual and mental activity.

Tablet XII. This prose appendix comprises a translation of the latter part of one of the Sumerian poems of Gilgamesh. It is related to the epic but not in form and structure. The hero tyrannizes his people with playthings fashioned from a primordial tree, and at their outcry the playthings fall into the netherworld. Enkidu goes to retrieve them but is taken captive. Gilgamesh raises his ghost and questions him about conditions in the realm of the dead.

Cultural context and genre

No evidence survives for the Babylonian Epic of Gilgamesh before its emergence in the eighteenth century BC. We know that Babylonian courts employed singers and it seems likely that the poem took shape as a courtly entertainment, a function for which its topic, the exploits of the greatest king of old, made it suitable. The mood of the Old Babylonian poem, most clearly expressed in the prologue embedded in SB Tablet I, is one of praise and glory. This is epic not far removed from its 'primary' or oral stage, in C. S. Lewis's distinction.[9]

The moment a text enters the scribal tradition we begin to lose sight of any oral version; we can only chart the poem's evolution as a piece of written literature. Written texts were largely an outcome of scribal training, but fine copies were kept by scholars. During the Old Babylonian period the poem already appears in a pedagogical environment, although it was not yet part of the scribal curriculum of set texts. The few surviving apprentices' tablets present parts of the long episode that relates the expedition to the Cedar Forest. The Sumerian poem that tells the same story (Bilgames and Huwawa) was one of a group of ten standard texts of the Old Babylonian scribal curriculum. Routine study of the Sumerian poem was evidently accompanied by, or generated, a less intense engagement with its Babylonian analogue.

The late second-millennium school tablets from Nippur show that study of the poem was by that time embedded in the scribal curriculum. During the first millennium two uses for it were found in teaching. Beginners occasionally studied excerpts, probably because it was such a good story. More advanced students copied out individual tablets of the poem as part of a deeper engagement with the text. Many scholars probably knew it by heart as a classic text of the old literature inherited from the second millennium; some were able to quote lines of it in glosses to demonstrate the meanings of words in other texts.

The new prologue prefixed to 'He who saw the Deep' aligned the poem with what is known as *narû*-literature, a didactic 'wisdom' genre typified by compositions in which an ancient king counselled his successors.[10] The prologue addresses the reader in the singular, which reveals an intention to speak to the individual. This is the 'secondary' or literary stage of epic, in C. S. Lewis's analysis. The poem had evolved from a celebration of fame and glory to a meditation on the human condition. This evolution speaks for a move out of the public arena, such as court entertainment, into a more solitary and personal context. By the middle of the first millennium the language of the epic was undoubtedly archaic, and this also makes it doubtful that the poem known to us was any longer a performed work. That is not to say that there were no oral songs about Gilgamesh at this time; very probably there were, in Aramaic as well as Babylonian and Assyrian, but the oral tradition is an unknown quantity. We know the poem only because it entered the written tradition and became a scribal copybook.

There have been several attempts to demonstrate the influence of the Epic of Gilgamesh on other literature. Some have written in terms of lineal descent. It would be surprising if a masterpiece of such distinction and wide diffusion left no imprint on literatures other than Hittite and Hurrian. However, most attestations of Gilgamesh in later literatures know him as an ancient king or a demon, and echo not the epic but Babylonian divinatory and religious traditions. In literary study we have to reckon with a common fund of stories and motifs; lineal descent can be determined only by more rigorous methodology than hitherto applied.[11] Aelian's story of the infant Gilgamos, conceived in secret, cast from a tower, saved by an eagle and brought up by a gardener, eventually to succeed his grandfather as king, is probably related to Mesopotamian literary traditions; it is clearly no lineal descendant of the written poem, but may offer a glimpse of an oral version transported to the Mediterranean through Aramaic or Phoenician intermediaries.

The written poem was not so easily transmitted. By the Parthian period the cuneiform tradition was intelligible only to a small number of families in

Uruk and Babylon. When cuneiform finally expired in the first century AD, the written poem's only remaining social context – scribal training – disappeared, and the Babylonian Epic of Gilgamesh was lost for eighteen centuries.

NOTES

1 G. Smith, *The Chaldean Account of Genesis* (London: Low, Marston, Searle and Rivington, 1876).

2 P. Haupt, *Das babylonische Nimrodepos*, 2 vols. (Leipzig: J. C. Hinrichs, 1884–90).

3 P. Jensen, *Assyrisch-babylonische Mythen und Epen*, Keilinschriftliche Bibliothek, 6, 1 (Berlin: von Reuther and Reichard, 1900).

4 A. Ungnad, *Das Gilgamesch-Epos neu übersetzt* (Göttingen: Vandenhoeck and Ruprecht, 1911).

5 R. C. Thompson, *The Epic of Gilgamish: A New Translation* (London: Luzac, 1929); and *The Epic of Gilgamish: Text, Transliteration and Notes* (Oxford: Clarendon Press, 1930).

6 See Further reading for the translations by George and Foster; Maul's translation is available in German only: Stefan M. Maul, ed. and trans., *Das Gilgamesch-Epos* (Munich: C. H. Beck, 2005).

7 A. R. George, 'The Gilgameš Epic at Ugarit', *Aula Orientalis* 25 (2007): 195–212; and 'The Civilizing of Ea-Enkidu: An Unusual Tablet of the Babylonian Gilgameš Epic', *Revue d'Assyriologie* 101 (2007): 59–80.

8 A. R. George, 'Shattered Tablets and Tangled Threads: Editing Gilgamesh, Then and now', *Aramazd: Armenian Journal of Near Eastern Studies* 3,1 (Yerevan, 2008): 7–30.

9 C. S. Lewis, *A Preface to Paradise Lost* (London: Oxford University Press, 1942), 12.

10 A. R. George, 'The Epic of Gilgameš: Thoughts on Genre and Meaning', in *Gilgameš and the World of Assyria*. Proceedings of a Conference Held at Mandelbaum House, the University of Sydney, 21–23 July 2004, ed. J. Azize and N. Weeks, Ancient Near Eastern Studies Supplement 21 (Leuven: Peeters, 2007), 37–65.

11 J. H. Tigay, 'On Evaluating Claims of Literary Borrowing', in *The Tablet and the Scroll: Near Eastern Studies in Honor of William W. Hallo*, ed. M. E. Cohen, D. C. Snell, and D. B. Weisberg (Bethesda, MD: CDL Press, 1993), 250–5; W. F. M. Henkelman, 'The Birth of Gilgameš (Ael. *NA* XII.21): A Case-Study in Literary Receptivity', in *Altertum und Mittelmeerraum: Die Antike Welt diesseits und jenseits der Levante: Festschrift für Peter W. Haider*, ed. R. Rollinger and B. Truschnegg, Oriens et Occidens 12 (Stuttgart: F. Steiner, 2006), 807–56, esp. 815–16.

2

JASPER GRIFFIN

Greek epic

Like other Indo-European peoples, the Greeks of the early period delighted in poetry and song which glorified the deeds and destinies of great heroes, their predecessors and, as they often believed, their ancestors. Such songs illustrated the nature of the world and showed their own connection with the gods. In most traditions, once literacy comes in, such oral poems look old fashioned. They lose favour, they are not written down, and soon they are forgotten. Sometimes a revival of interest may lead antiquarians to search and to rediscover some of them. That was the fate of the Old English epic of *Beowulf,* which was rescued, surviving in a single manuscript, from the wreck of a larger oral literature. Most of the old heroic songs, however, simply disappear. When learned men come to search for them, they are not to be found. That is what happened to the epic poems that were sung in early Rome, before the impact of Greek literature from the third century BC. Cicero already knew only a vague tradition that they had existed; he wished, vainly, that he could read them. Macaulay's *Lays of Ancient Rome* were meant as an attempt to recreate a couple of those lost martial songs.

The Greek tradition was importantly different. When literacy came in, many of the old songs were lost; but the *Iliad* and the *Odyssey* – the two long oral epic poems ascribed to 'Homer' – did not fall from favour. They always continued to be recited, read and highly valued. Familiarity with Homer was expected of any Hellene not utterly illiterate. The epics are characterized by the regular repetition of formulaic phrases and verses, originally a mnemonic device for the singer, who performs by constant re-creation from memory.

Both epics, but particularly the *Iliad,* which was always thought the greater and the more important of the two, survive in a large number of manuscripts. We possess a very substantial body of ancient commentaries, grammars, and dictionaries on the poem; and, to a much lesser extent, on the *Odyssey,* too. That illustrates the *Iliad*'s central position in ancient education and culture. All Greeks shared in the inheritance of Homer, often called simply 'the poet', and the epic is fundamental, both for the development of Attic tragedy and for the *Histories* of Herodotus.

Since the decipherment, in the last two centuries, of some of the ancient languages of the Near East, we have been able to read the Epic of Gilgamesh. Dating from about 2000 BC, and current in half a dozen languages for hundreds of years, the poem tells of King Gilgamesh and his friend Enkidu. Together, they kill the monstrous Bull of Heaven, sent by the goddess Ishtar to ravage the world; but Ishtar takes her revenge on Enkidu, who dies, plunging Gilgamesh into a grief that reminds us of Achilles's mourning for his friend Patroclus. He almost succeeds in reviving Enkidu. From the bottom of the sea he fetches the plant of immortality, but the serpent manages to steal and swallow it. That is why snakes can do what men cannot: cast off their old skin and be young again. Enkidu cannot be brought back to life.

The poem has no comfort to offer for the cruel fact of mortality. Its discovery and decipherment drew attention to the existence, in the second millennium BC, of extensive and sophisticated literature, in a number of languages, all over the Near East. Both Homer and the Hebrew Old Testament descend from provincial branches of that literature, which centred on the ancient cities of Mesopotamia.

In time, the languages of Sumer, Assyria, Babylon, Egypt, and the rest were lost to sight and knowledge: all except Hebrew and Greek, which, in different ways, remained alive. In both those languages, the old texts became the subject of intense and continuing study. Among the Hebrews, textual criticism and exegesis arose from study of the Old Testament. Among the Greeks, they began with scholarly work on the *Iliad*; and an impressive bulk of learned material from later antiquity, notably Homeric commentaries and dictionaries, still survives. The *Odyssey*, always regarded as the lesser of the two poems, received much less of this work than the *Iliad*.

Iliad and *Odyssey* were each divided by scholars, probably in the third century BC, into twenty-four Books. That is the number of letters in the classical Greek alphabet, and those Greek letters were often used as a shorthand way of referring to the different Books of the two epics: 'Alpha' means Book One, 'Beta' means Book Two, and so on. The division works well enough for the *Iliad*, but some Books of the *Odyssey*, a shorter poem, are undeniably rather slight. Virgil's decision that his epic poem should be divided into twelve Books, just half the number of *Iliad* or *Odyssey*, is a self-conscious gesture of modesty. At the same time, in his own epic he was exploiting, and using up, not one but both Homeric poems: a procedure of supreme self-confidence.

The presence and influence of the Homeric epic can be seen everywhere, in Greek lyric poetry, in Attic tragedy, and even in the *Histories* of Herodotus, whom later Greek critics call 'most Homeric'. Serious Greek poetry of the Hellenistic period (*c.* 323–31 BC) maintains a constant dialogue with the epic of Homer, on every question of style, metrics, myth, vocabulary, geography, history, genealogy, and theology.

Outside Hellas, Homer had a crucial impact on the high literature of Rome. As later Romans believed, it actually began with a translation into Latin of the *Odyssey*, made by an ex-slave of Greek origin: Livius Andronicus (*c.* 220 BC). His would be almost the sole Greek name, as it turned out, in the whole history of Latin literature. As for his work, it was extinguished by the masterpieces of the late Republic and the Augustan period. Only a few short, isolated, and tantalizing quotations survive, mostly cited for their archaic quaintness.

In time, a literature in Latin struggled into existence, always suffering under the daunting quality, enormous range, and over-powering influence of Greek. Whatever had been produced before that influence was dominant, came to be felt as barbarous and unworthy of serious attention. Unread and unlooked for, it soon faded from memory and disappeared. Homer, the fountainhead of Greek literature, remained the ultimate standard and model, and Romans did not feel that their own literature was fully mature until it possessed a great epic poem in Latin.

After two hundred years of various attempts, including the daring claim by the archaic poet Ennius (239–169 BC) that he actually reincarnated Homer's soul, it was Virgil who succeeded finally in creating the longed-for Latin epic. He found the only truly Roman subject for such a poem: the history and destiny of Rome itself, seen and interpreted in the perspective and context of the purposes of heaven, and written in a style which could stand comparison with Homer.

Virgil's epic *Aeneid* presents the struggle of a Trojan survivor, providentially saved from the final disaster of Troy, to sail west, to reach Italy, and to found Lavinium, the mother city of Rome. The tradition of Romulus as founder of the Imperial city itself was too strong to be displaced, but now Rome was firmly sited in the ever memorable, and truly significant, mythical history of Greece and of Greek literature. The hero is Aeneas, son of the goddess Venus (in Greek, Aphrodite), who appeared as a Trojan warrior and a character in the *Iliad*.

The *Aeneid* would show that the lessons of Greek technique and Greek sophistication had now been fully learned and assimilated. It is a poem greater than any that had been produced in Greek for several centuries past; but the Greeks, not unnaturally, refused to notice. It was bad enough to have been conquered, oppressed, and looted by these Roman barbarians. To be expected to take seriously a poem in their uncouth language: that, for a Hellene of any culture, was altogether too much to ask. It would remain true that, even in the days of the Roman Empire, Greeks almost never refer to any Latin author, Virgil included, as literature. At most, they can be cited as evidence for some historical fact or argument.

The rise of the Greek epic

When the ancestors of the Greeks had first entered the Mediterranean world, in the second millennium BC, they encountered various peoples – Cretans, Egyptians, Babylonians, Phoenicians, and others – who had their own traditions of divine and heroic legend. In poetry, as in the visual arts, some of those traditions influenced the productions of early Greece. Like them, the Greek epics present a pantheon of gods and goddesses, who quarrel and make love, and who are involved, interested, and active in the careers of great heroes. The epic songs were performed by bards: sometimes with musical accompaniment on a lyre, sometimes simply chanted by a performer leaning on a staff, called in Greek a *rhabdos*. That provided an imaginative ancient etymology for the Greek word for such a performer: a 'rhapsode' – supposedly, a singer with a staff.

The subject matter of these songs is summarized by the early Greek poet Hesiod (lived *c.* 700 BC) as 'the glorious deeds of men of old and the blessed gods who inhabit Olympus' (*Theogony*, 100–1). We see at once that heroic song implies the participation of gods in certain human stories, which therefore possess special stature, dignity, and interest. They are exemplary for the understanding of human life, in a world where, nowadays, the actions of the divine are harder to discern and to interpret, and where human history often seems to lack either shape or meaning.

The events described in epic poetry are set in the past, when such supernatural intervention could be found credible. At that time, men were closer to the gods. They were greater than they are nowadays, in the degenerate present. Gods joined in the battles of mortal men; they engendered splendid children with mortal women. Occasionally, a goddess might bear a child to a mortal man. Above all, the gods took part visibly in certain human actions and undertakings, which therefore possess special and timeless significance.

It follows that no one has ever actually lived in an heroic age. That is a perspective reserved for posterity, looking back with admiration, or with envy, at the truly great and memorable actions of the past. It is a universal experience that the men and women of one's own generation are less impressive, somehow, than the adults whom we saw with the magnifying gaze of childhood, when we ourselves were young. We can never catch them up. The heroes and heroines of legend, and of epic, stand in something like the same relation to later generations.

In the early period of Greece, we hear of a number of epic songs. Two were never lost to sight, and they survive: the *Iliad* and the *Odyssey*. Both are very substantial in length, the *Iliad* being the longer of the two. Together, they amount to some 27,000 lines. We cannot be sure how many other epic poems there were, and about their authors – even about the poet of the *Iliad* – we know nothing at all. Later on, to fill what came to be felt as a painful void, romantic tales were invented of a blind singer earning his living by his songs. Minstrelsy was, of course, one of the few careers open to a blind man, and blind singers do recur in other traditions besides the Greek. In the *Odyssey* we meet Demodocus, a blind singer. The Muse, we hear, gave him both good and bad: she took away his eyes, but she gave him sweet song.

The stories that were told in the epic contained some real historical memories. The greatness of Mycenae, stronghold of King Agamemnon, and of Tiryns and Pylos, palaces connected with the famous names of Heracles and Nestor; the wealth of Troy, the city of King Priam, and of Cnossos, the capital of Cretan King Minos: they all lived on in memory, long after those places had fallen into ruin. Now ruins, naturally, breed myths to answer the obvious questions: what great people lived here, where we now see these impressive remains, and what happened to them?

The ancient sites of Troy and Mycenae and Cnossos, famous in the myths, awaited their systematic excavation by modern archaeologists in the far distant future. In the last hundred and fifty years, the evidence of the spade has shown that in the heroic epics of Greece, as in the Germanic *Nibelungenlied*, the French *Chanson de Roland* and the Spanish *Canto de Mio Cid,* there lie – re-shaped, re-ordered, and variously transformed – some nuggets of historical fact.

The songs also contained material that was not historical. In the first place, the events are pervaded, and largely dictated, by the interventions of a pantheon of personal gods. In the *Iliad*, some gods favour Troy; others – the stronger party – support the Achaeans. Above them all, the impressive figure of Father Zeus broods on events and, when he chooses to intervene, determines their outcome. He has, reluctantly, assented to Troy's eventual fall. In the *Odyssey*, the homecoming of Odysseus is opposed and delayed by Poseidon but favoured and assisted by Athena. In the Homeric poems, we see in action both gods and, no less importantly, goddesses. Athena, daughter of Zeus, virgin and warrior, is the most dynamic and effective divine figure in both *Iliad* and *Odyssey*, as she is in the literature and cult of classical Athens.

The heroes were mortal men. We are repeatedly told in the *Iliad* that even Achilles, the greatest hero to fight at Troy, will die there, although he is the son of a goddess and supreme in strength and beauty. The victorious son of Atreus, Agamemnon, Lord of Men, returning home in triumph, will be murdered by his unfaithful wife and her lover, a cowardly draft-dodger who skulked at home when the Achaeans sailed away to Troy.

Not all the characters in heroic myth were merely mortal. A number of stories and reminiscences of Heracles, for example – his labours, and his eventual apotheosis – have made their way into the Homeric poems. The characters love to hear them narrated. But the heroes of the Theban and Trojan Wars were mortal men, even though some of them were the off-spring of gods by human partners, and though the *Iliad* emphasizes that they were all stronger, greater, and altogether of more significance and more interest than their feebler modern successors.

Heracles represents a different and more primitive type of heroism than the great armies, commanded by kings, and fighting in formation, which we find attacking and defending the cities of Thebes and Troy. Achaeans and Trojans, in Homer, fight on a regular battlefield, wearing armour of glittering bronze, or sometimes – more anachronistically – of iron; mention of that metal, in principle alien to the age of heroes, creeps in when the singer is off his guard. There are constant attempts, too, at regular military discipline.

Heracles was a hero of a very different type. A solitary superman, he led no army. Rather than a panoply of shining metal, he wore the skin of a lion, which he had throttled with his bare hands and skinned with its own claws. He was armed with the most primitive of weapons: with a massive club, and with bow and arrows, envenomed with the poison of an uncanny creature that he had killed. Solitary slayer of lions, of wild boars, and of monsters, antagonist and conqueror of Old Age and even of Death itself, Heracles is the universal Averter of Evils (*Alexikakos*), who could be invoked for protection in any moment of sudden shock or alarm – as, in another tradition, people invoke a saint, or cry 'God between us and harm!' He belongs out in the wild, not in the city, and most of his great exploits have no relation to city life. The people in the Homeric epics loved to hear them repeated.

There were other heroes, too, who contended single-handed with monsters. Perseus, son of Zeus, beheaded the snaky-haired Gorgon, whose gaze turned men to stone. Theseus, greatest of Athenian heroes, slew the Minotaur, half man, half bull, a nightmare at the heart of a bewildering labyrinth at Cnossos: here we see preserved a distorted memory of the bull-leaping games depicted, centuries earlier, on the frescoes of the enormous palaces of Minoan Crete.

These heroes performed their great deeds single-handed, or with the aid of Athena, divine patron of brave young men. Oedipus, too, delivered his people. He solved the riddle of the Sphinx and so ended her deadly career; but his terrible destiny drove him on, to kill his own father and to beget children with his own mother. He affirmed and ratified the limits of human life and action by transgressing them and suffering for it, a blinded outcast.

Like Heracles himself, such heroic figures proved hard to fit into the normal life of the family, or into the regular human scale appropriate to citizens of a city. There was, indeed, a sense of deep unease about these supermen. It was said of Heracles that, in a fit of madness sent by his jealous stepmother, Hera, he killed his own wife and children. Oedipus, the incestuous parricide, brought ruin on all his family, and his curse destroyed his sons.

Theseus caused his own father's death, when he forgot to hoist the white sail on his ship, as the signal that he was returning alive from his peril with the Minotaur. He also condemned his son Hippolytus, falsely denounced by his stepmother, Phaedra, to an undeserved death. We even find it claimed that Theseus tried to carry off Persephone herself from the Underworld. Having failed in that sacrilegious attempt, he must sit for ever on a rock, down there in the world of the dead.

That is what is said of Theseus by Virgil. It was not what the Athenians believed about their own greatest hero, the mythical founder of their democracy. If they admitted the story at all, they added that he had been pulled from the rock and brought up from Hades by Heracles. That illustrates an important point: there never was a single or standard version of these heroic myths. Local patriotisms, family pedigrees, and pure poetic inventions, all constantly intervened, to shape, develop, change, and colour them.

The myths might serve an additional purpose. They can illustrate the nature of women, with the dangers, temptations, and deceptions that are involved with that problematic sex: fascinating, but inscrutable and dangerous. For instance, the hero might be assisted in his perils by a woman of his enemy's own kin. Young Jason was saved from death at the hands of King Aeetes by the king's daughter, Medea; later on, he would abandon her. Young Theseus, condemned by King Minos to wander in the labyrinth and be slain there by the Minotaur, was given the vital clue by the king's daughter, Ariadne, along with a sword to kill the monster; on the way home, he abandoned her on an island. Both Medea and Ariadne, after their abandonment, went on to have spectacular careers.

These princesses acted from love. A young woman, we see, may suddenly reject her father, and all his plans and intentions, to follow a glamorous stranger, especially if she sees him in deadly peril. These stories both end badly, with the dashing hero betraying and abandoning the exotic bride who had saved him in his hour of danger. A warning to potentially susceptible girls, and also to their parents, is clearly part of the point, but only a part: it is the adventurous young hero, naturally, who engages our sympathy and our interest. But both Jason and Theseus must suffer for their breach of faith. Otherwise, presumably, the tale would have been unacceptable.

The stories are conceived, as a rule, from a masculine point of view. The inscrutable hearts of women, those strange and alluring creatures, were evidently a constant source of interest and anxiety. Women were seen as capable of passion, and of a violence that might lead to infidelity or to crime. Medea took a fearful revenge on Jason, killing the children that she had borne him, as well as his new bride. It was the adultery of Helen, running off with a glamorous Oriental, which triggered the disasters of the Trojan War; it was the folly and disobedience of Pandora, like Eve in another tradition, that brought suffering and death into the world in the first place. And disloyalty and division within the family were an ever-present anxiety. They must not be shown as prospering in the end.

Epic poems varied greatly in length. The *Iliad* seems to have been exceptionally long: it certainly could not be performed in a single evening, which might seem, from the point of view of an audience, the naturally attractive and desirable duration. The *Iliad* thus implies an exceptional singer, whose prestige was great enough to bring the listeners back, day after day, in the confidence that so long a recital would be well worth their while. The singer, not the audience, is now in control. The *Odyssey*, in all probability, attained its comparable length under the influence, and perhaps in emulation, of the *Iliad*. All genuine information about the great singer, or the two great singers, was lost, and, to fill the tantalizing gap, the figure of blind Homer was invented.

A number of early epic songs were collected into a consecutive 'Cycle' on the story of Troy: all the way from Paris's fatal judgement of the three goddesses, to the sack of the city and the adventures of the victorious Achaeans on their way home. It ended only after the *Odyssey*'s conclusion, with the tragic story of Telegonus, Odysseus's son by Circe. A person unknown to the *Odyssey*, he will kill his father in ignorance.

We know disappointingly little about those epics that have not survived. It appears that they were much shorter than *Iliad* and *Odyssey*. As noted above, these were each divided into twenty-four Books around the third century BC. Most other epics seem to have been much shorter, consisting of two Books, or of four. The longest recorded, the *Cypria*, on events before the Trojan War, was apparently divided into eleven. That is a poem which we should very much like to possess, although it seems to have been episodic, lacking the true unity which Aristotle singles out in his *Poetics*, rightly, as characteristic of the two great Homeric poems.

Another epic cycle, now completely lost, dealt with the tragic history of Thebes in the mythical period. There was the sin of Laius: it appears that he invented paederastic love, an offence against marriage, for which he was punished with childlessness. Recklessly, he defied the warning and fathered a son, Oedipus. The epic dealt with the exposure and return of that son, predestined to a career of horrors, killing his father and bedding his mother. It went on to the war between Polynices and Eteocles, the doomed sons of his incest. That culminated in their death at one another's hands, in the denial of burial to Polynices's body, and in the heroic defiance and death of Oedipus's daughter Antigone. The Seven (the group of champions who attack Thebes, led by Polynices) were, in due course, avenged by their sons, more successful but less interesting; that was narrated in the epic *Epigoni*.

Those Theban epics, all lost to us, lie behind many Attic tragedies, including both the earliest to survive: Aeschylus's *Seven Against Thebes* (472 BC), and one of the very latest: Sophocles's *Oedipus at Colonus* (406 BC). It appears that the Theban cycle had a notably darker atmosphere, and a more guilt-laden theology, than the two extant Homeric epics, which come from a different set of songs. We possess the Latin *Thebaid* of Statius, (*c.* 100 AD), on the war of the Seven: a skilful poem, and admired by Dante, in modern times it is little read. It is dark in atmosphere and rich in the uncanny and the sinister.

The Homeric epics deal with the greatness, the offence, and the ruin, of the city of Troy, beloved of Zeus, and with the varied fortunes of its Achaean conquerors. In the *Iliad* and the *Odyssey*, violent deaths are numerous; but both perversity and monstrous actions within the family are carefully excluded or marginalized. Attic tragedy, by contrast, would make them central. The epic also strictly excludes homosexual love.

It was perhaps inevitable, human nature being what it is, that the high seriousness and elevated style of the heroic epic should evoke a satirical counter-form: the epic burlesque. Tragedy, similarly, would be shadowed by another disreputable genre, that of the satyr play, and constantly burlesqued in Old Comedy.

We do not have the archaic *Margites* (literally 'madman'), a poem of unknown date and authorship about an anti-hero, who 'possessed many skills, but possessed them all wrong'. We do have a comic *Batrachomyo-machia (Battle of the Frogs and the Mice)*, dating apparently from the time of the Roman Empire, but coming from a much older tradition. It presents, in exaggerated heroic form and metre, the great war between these tiny creatures, complete with grandiose names, heroic duels, high-flown speeches, and divine interventions. More effective, perhaps, as well as funnier, are the burlesque heroic episodes – the fights, soliloquies, threats of suicide, and so on – in Attic comedy and in the Latin *Satyrica* of Petronius.

For us, the *Iliad* is the beginning of European literature, which opens with a cosmic bang. There lived heroes before Agamemnon, says the Augustan poet Horace, but they are lost in oblivion, because they had no great epic poet to make them immortal. There lived poets before Homer, too; we can sometimes make inferences about their lost works, but we can know virtually nothing about them.

While most of the enormous Greek literature that once existed has long since vanished from the world, the two great Homeric epics, the *Iliad* and the *Odyssey*, have never ceased to be read, admired, studied, and imitated. Archaic works, set in a distant past, when heroes were the sons of gods, they are composed in an artificial dialect, and in a style which belongs to oral, pre-literate, composition and performance; but they never went out of fashion and were lost, or needed to be rediscovered and rescued from oblivion by scholars, like the *Nibelungenlied* in Germany, or like *Beowulf* in Britain. That is a cardinal fact about the literature of Hellas.

The *Iliad*

The *Iliad* was always regarded as the greater of the two epic poems: in fact, as the greatest work in all Greek literature. It deals with an episode near the end of the long siege of Troy by the Achaeans, who are demanding the return of the abducted queen Helen 'and', rather unromantically, of 'the treasures that were taken with her'.[1] A quarrel over a captive woman between two leading Greek chieftains, Agamemnon the supreme commander and Achilles the greatest warrior, causes Achilles to withdraw from the fighting in anger. Implored by her son, Achilles's goddess mother persuades Zeus to grant success to the Trojans and defeat to the Achaeans, until they shall be forced to plead for his return to battle.

Throughout the poem, the gods play an active and highly visible role in events. Father Zeus tells us, at the beginning of Book 4, that he loves the city of Troy; he grieves for its coming ruin, and for the fated death of Hector, its greatest warrior. In Homer, Zeus is never shown coming down to earth. He sits on high and ultimately decides the course of events from afar. Other gods do join in, except when Zeus explicitly forbids them, and fight with the heroes on the battlefield. Most active, and most effective, is the warrior maiden Athena.

Some of the immortals favour the Achaeans. Their party is led by the great goddesses Hera and Athena, whose implacable hatred for Troy is left unexplained. Behind it, although never narrated in the *Iliad*, must lie the story of their defeat in the fatal Judgement of Paris, the play-boy Trojan prince. He foolishly took Helen, as a bribe to choose Aphrodite (sensual pleasure), above kingly rule (Hera) or heroic prowess (Athena). Other gods, a less effective group, support the Trojans. It is a striking fact that two goddesses, Hera and Athena, both on the Achaean side, are the most determined and the most effective of the immortals in the fighting.

We see many men killed in the course of the poem, both Achaeans and – in greater numbers – Trojans. Hundreds of warriors appear and are named only at the moment of their death. Splendid and god-like in life, their bodies are fought over, once they are dead; they are stripped of their precious armour, trampled under foot, crushed under the wheels of chariots. There is nothing in the way of a consoling after-life, and no Valhalla, even for heroes: the souls of the slain go down into darkness, lamenting the youth and manhood they are leaving behind. In the next world, they are pallid and senseless. It is repeatedly emphasized that the dead, once they have been given a funeral, never return. In the *Odyssey*, when the hero must voyage to the very edge of the world, there to call up the spirits of the dead, we hear that they need the offering of fresh sacrificial blood, if they are to regain sense and speak to the living.

The gods watch the fighting with intense partisanship, although they have other interests, and at times they turn away their shining gaze and look elsewhere. Except for Zeus, who remains on high, they come down at times to the battlefield and intervene directly in the fighting; in Books 5 and 21, in fact, they fight there among themselves. The pro-Achaean party, generally, is the stronger and has much the best of the conflicts. It was a Trojan offence that started the war, and we know that, ultimately, Troy will fall.

At other times, there are lively disputes on Olympus. In Book 14, Hera seduces her husband Zeus, to distract his attention from events on the Trojan plain, where the Trojans are suffering a day of defeat. First, we hear, 'she looked at him, and she hated him in her heart'; then she carefully made herself irresistible to the King of gods and men, a typically gullible male, with triumphant results. Concealed with her in a golden cloud, first in love and then in sleep, he leaves the war at Troy, and indeed the whole world, to manage by itself. When he wakes (Book 15) he will be memorably angry at the deception.

The divine involvement in events is an important fact. Homer presents, not just a thrilling story, but a vision of the world and its hidden workings, to which the singer is given privileged access by the divine Muse who inspires him. That world contains not only mortals but also immortals, and watching them helps us to understand the position and the destiny of mankind. We see that we are not, ultimately, so very important to the gods. At times, they simply turn away their shining gaze, even from the destiny of mighty heroes, who are far greater and more interesting than any of us moderns, and contemplate something in the far distance (Book 13). Or they may go off on a pleasure trip to the land of the Aethiopians, leaving Europe and Asia, for a few weeks, to get along without them (Book 1).

In Achilles's absence from the battlefield, the Achaeans suffer heavy losses, as gradually they are pushed back to the sea and face annihilation. Hector, the greatest Trojan hero, over-confident with temporary success, is threatening to burn their ships and cut off their return home. At the last minute, after incurring, through his own stubbornness, the death of Patroclus, his dearest friend, Achilles returns to battle in fury. He drives the Trojans before him and kills Hector beneath the walls of Troy (Book 22). The city is now doomed.

Achilles then holds funeral games in Patroclus's honour (Book 23): he is generous and charming to the comrades whom he was allowing to die without him, and we see his true nature. But he still pursues his revenge beyond death, refusing to surrender Hector's body for burial. This breach of the divine law is only ended (Book 24) when the gods guide Priam, the aged Trojan king, through the night, into the Achaean camp. He comes in secret, to meet Achilles and to ransom Hector's body. He must bring himself to kneel and kiss the hand that slew his best and dearest son.

The poem ends with the two great enemies appreciating each other's stature, as they recognize a kind of companionship in the suffering to which mortal men are born. Together they weep for the hard lot of human kind. Achilles has returned to true humanity – just in time for his death. They foresee that the fighting will start again: Achilles's death is very close; then Troy will fall, and Priam's body will be mauled by his own dogs, as his city is looted, its men are killed and its women are dragged away into slavery. We are very far from any happy ending, and very far, too, from any patriotic rejoicing in the imminent defeat of the guilty barbarian foe. Evidently 'poetic justice', at this supreme moment, is not the poet's chief concern.

The many brilliant similes, drawn both from human activities and from non-human nature, add to the poem's vividness and to its scope: the poet contrives to comprehend the whole world in his action, including scenes of farming and hunting, of forest fires and of storms at sea, of women weaving and children crying until they are picked up. Homer was so influential that the picture given in the epic proved very hard for later generations to escape.

Those passionate gods and goddesses, striving, competitive and all too human, would remain vivid, offering an irresistible target to philosophers, to satirists, and – in time – to Christian propagandists, too ('Just look at what your own writers say about your gods!').

The *Odyssey*

A second great epic poem, the *Odyssey*, also goes under the name of Homer. In antiquity, everyone but a few eccentrics, known as 'the separators', believed that the *Iliad* and the *Odyssey* were the work of a single poet; but nowadays many scholars stress their differences, in vocabulary, theology, and world-view. The question is, in fact, unanswerable: we cannot estimate the potential of a great oral singer. The *Odyssey* tells the story of the homecoming of Odysseus, the last Achaean hero to get back from Troy. He had farthest to go, right round Hellas to the Western island of Ithaca. The Greeks, unanimously, regarded the *Iliad* as the greater poem; modern taste has often preferred the *Odyssey*, with its feminine interest, its fantastic incidents, its variety of place, and its happy ending. Historically, it is the ancestor of the Greek novel, and so of the novel in Europe.

The *Odyssey* falls into three parts. In the first four Books, we see the situation on the island of Ithaca, in the prolonged absence of the king. The ambitious young men of the neighbourhood, assuming his death, are competing for the hand of Odysseus's wife, the prudent Penelope, still beautiful. She is desperately fending them off. It appears, although the constitutional position is not made entirely clear, that the palace and the kingship will go with the hand of the queen: they will not necessarily pass to the hero's son, Telemachus. That was never the custom in historic Hellas, and the motif is perhaps Oriental, or perhaps merely poetical: if he does not return home in time, Odysseus risks the loss of everything.

When his father sailed away to Troy, Telemachus was a babe in arms. Now, twenty years later, he is maturing into a man and, potentially, a hero. The epic is, among other things, the story of his development: he must change, from a passive and demoralized adolescent, into a man who can stand beside his father in the final battle with the Suitors. The *Odyssey* may be called the first *Bildungsroman* in European literature.

The Suitors, more than a hundred in number, have decided to wear down Penelope's stubborn resistance by eating her out of house and home. They are pressing her to choose one of them as her husband, haunting the palace, consuming the royal wealth, and abusing the servants. When Telemachus, for the first time, asserts himself, disrupts their greedy idyll, and orders them out, they immediately decide to kill him.

Athena sees that Telemachus must be got away. He is to travel, grow up, and meet his social equals. He goes off to find news of his father, and is entertained and encouraged by two of Odysseus's old friends: by the aged Nestor, in Pylos (Book 3), and by Menelaus, in Sparta (Books 4 and 5). They tell him stories of Troy and of his father's deeds. In Sparta he meets Queen Helen, still beautiful, and completely in control of the situation, despite having been brought back from Troy – one might think – in deepest disgrace. Helen and Menelaus and Nestor all have good stories to tell: of the last days of Troy, of the resourcefulness of Odysseus, and of their own return home. They bridge the gap between the *Iliad* and the *Odyssey*, and they keep the absent hero before the eye of the audience.

Odysseus, meanwhile, is far away. The poem, to avoid disastrous anti-climax, needs him to return home, not with shiploads of loyal warriors at his back, but disguised and alone. The *Odyssey* insists that, on their way back from Troy, the hero's men were lost through their own fault: while Odysseus slept, they opened the forbidden bag, in which a friendly god had given him all the winds except the one he needed for his homeward journey. The ship was promptly blown off course and off the map, into the realms of fable. The disobedient sailors perished in one misadventure or another. Like the rebellious Suitors, they serve to point the moral: be faithful to the King! The theme of loyalty and disloyalty runs right through the poem. Like the Suitors, the sailors pay for their offence with their lives.

At last, Odysseus is able to build a raft and sail away. He has marvellous tales to tell of his experiences after leaving Troy. At first, he has his fleet of six ships; then they are reduced to a single one; then both ship and sailors are lost, and the hero, after surviving the menaces of exotic monsters, must confront the insolent Suitors alone. He was blown far off course, to unknown lands; he raided in Egypt, with initial success but eventual disaster; he passed the whirlpool Charybdis, and Scylla the six-headed monster, who took six of his crew; he was tempted to linger forever in the land of the Lotus Eaters, eating the lotus and forgetting all about his home. He got into, and out of, the cave of a man-eating giant, the one-eyed Cyclops. He met the charming young princess Nausicaa, and Circe, the glamorous vamp who turned his men into swine but whose magic failed against the prepared and resolute hero.

At last he is marooned on an island with the beautiful nymph Calypso, without a ship, and lost to human knowledge. Her name seems to mean 'Hider'. A loving character, in contrast to the hard-boiled Circe, she has been hoping that the hero would stay with her forever; but he tactfully declines her offer of immortality, as the gods intervene, telling her to send him on his way home.

There was an earlier epic, now lost, which narrated the quest of Jason and the Argonauts for the Golden Fleece. It lies behind our *Odyssey*, to which it has contributed two important things: the figure of Circe the enchantress, and the adventure of Odysseus with the Laestrygonians, who smash up his fleet and reduce him, from a commander of Iliadic type, with a contingent of ships and men, to the captain of a single vessel.

That is vital. His encounters with Scylla and Charybdis, for instance, need him to have one ship only: a whole flotilla sailing past them would be a hopeless anticlimax. Then the hero must be further reduced. The scene of parting with Calypso is conceived as one between two individuals, with no impatient crew of sailors in the background. Then, a solitary survivor, he must cling to a spar of his wrecked ship, build himself a raft, and return at the last moment to Ithaca unarmed, unrecognized, and alone.

The hero faces various perils. His curiosity gets him into the cave of the Cyclops: he escapes by his wits, making the monster drunk and burning out his one eye. That act of self-defence earns him the resentment of the sea god Poseidon, the Cyclops's father, who delays and impedes the hero's home-coming. Odysseus evades the devouring whirlpool Charybdis and escapes, not without losses, from the six-headed monster Scylla, who snatches passing sailors and devours them outside her cave. He must even visit the world of the dead: he has touching encounters there with his dead mother and with other friends, and he contemplates the punishments of a few choice mythical sinners, but there is little of the gruesomeness or the terror which often mark such visions, and much scope was left for the more grandiose inventions of Virgil and Dante.

He passes the Clashing Rocks unscathed. The *Odyssey* actually refers to the only ship ever to have sailed that way: 'the Argo, interesting to everyone' (Book 12.70). That is an acknowledgement of a poetic source, the first in European literature. The adventures of Jason and the Argonauts were set in the East and reflected the difficulties and perils of entering the Black Sea to trade at its furthest Eastern end. In the *Odyssey*, some of those adventures have been transferred to Odysseus, who at other times seems to be wandering in the far West. That is where Scylla and Charybdis and the Cyclops were traditionally placed.

These stories are presented by the poet as sailors' yarns, narrated to spellbound listeners, after dinner, by the hero himself. Odysseus is even complimented by the Phaeacians in highly ambiguous terms: 'Many men are liars, but you have told your story well and skilfully, like a professional bard' (Book 11.368). If a listener to the *Odyssey* chooses not to believe every word of Odysseus's tale, that is up to them – the singer has not personally vouched for its truth. But every time the epic is performed, the present occasion is glorified by this implicit identification with a more splendid one: we are hearing a recital given by the hero himself, to an audience who are closer than we to the gods.

The *Argonautica* and later epics

On the story of the Argonauts, no early epic poem survives. It seems likely that originally it followed the widespread folk pattern of the Hero and his Magic Helpers, each possessing a special skill, which in some crisis will turn out to be just what is needed. The two sons of the North Wind could fly: they chased off the attack of the winged Harpies ('Snatchers'). Polydeuces was the great boxer: he knocked out brutal King Amycus, who forced strangers to box with him and killed the losers. Orpheus with his divine music defeated the Sirens, whose deadly song lured sailors to destruction: chagrined at defeat, they hurled themselves down the rocks to death – which explains why, nowadays, travellers no longer encounter them.

The only extensive early source that survives for the Argo myth is Pindar's Fourth *Pythian* Ode, dating from 462 BC. At some three hundred lines, it is by far his longest extant poem. In the regular manner of the choral lyric, it gives an unconnected series of brilliant vignettes from the story, making no attempt at a systematic or complete narration.

From a later period, we possess the conscientious *Argonautica* of Apollonius of Rhodes, scholar-poet of the third century BC, which introduces into epic, with considerable success, the motif of romantic love. His treatment of Medea, and of her passion for Jason (Books 3 and 4), is quite new in its depiction of the passion of love as it dawns, grows and dominates her, turning her from an *ingénue* to a formidable and forceful woman, capable of violent emotions and drastic actions. It strongly influenced Virgil's creation of Dido, Queen of Carthage. We also have the exhaustive, and exhausting, Latin epic on the theme, from the second half of the first century AD, by Valerius Flaccus.

Euripides's tragedy *Medea* (431 BC), famous, disturbing and influential, deals with the dark aftermath of the story. Once safely back home, Jason is anxious to get rid of Medea, the exotic foreign bride to whose help, in rather un-heroic style, he owed the achievement of his heroic quest for the Golden Fleece. She is now an embarrassment to the middle-aged hero, who wants to settle down, marry a Greek princess, and be conventionally respectable. That has a terrible outcome, as jealous Medea kills her rival and her own children, too, leaving Jason alone in his misery. It is one of the most powerful and most celebrated of Attic tragedies. Seneca's tragedy *Medea* is a very free version in Latin.

Epic poems continued to be composed in Greek, and in considerable numbers. Almost all are lost, and information about them is scanty. In the third century BC, the prickly scholar-poet Callimachus declared that the day of full-scale epic was now past. The future belonged to poems that should be short, exquisitely chiselled and ostentatiously learned: to poems, in fact, like his own. We are told that Apollonius was among Callimachus's targets.

Callimachus did compose a short epic poem, *Hecale*, of which only fragments now survive. It told of a youthful exploit of Theseus, centring on his entertainment, one stormy night, by Hecale, an aged widow now living in poverty. Next day, he fought and defeated the formidable Bull of Marathon. The emphasis was far more on the homely entertainment offered by an old woman, who has come down in the world, and who tells Theseus her story at length, than on the heroic exploit which he duly performs in the morning. Returning, he finds old Hecale dead, and he sets up a cult in her memory.

No later Greek epic poem survives – although we hear the names of some that are lost – until we reach the time of the Roman Empire. From dates hard to fix with any confidence, we possess the short and charming miniature epic by Colluthus, *The Abduction of Helen*, and – equally short but much less distinctive or distinguished – *The Fall of Troy*, by Tryphiodorus. Both are about five hundred lines long. The revealingly titled *Posthomerica* ('What Came After Homer'), by Quintus of Smyrna, fully extant in fourteen Books, finishes off the Trojan story, from the point where the *Iliad* ends. It attempts to reproduce the Homeric style and vocabulary. Posterity has not found it a gripping read. These poems filled in the beginning and the end of the Trojan War, which the *Iliad* and *Odyssey* had so unaccountably omitted to describe, in a manner as 'Homeric' as their authors could manage.

Other epic poems continued to be composed in Greek. There seems to have been a whole genre that celebrated the mythical foundations of cities. Most of that is now completely lost. The *Aeneid* of Virgil, on the mythical foundation of Rome, must owe it a certain debt. The story of the Greek epic ends with the elusive figure of Nonnus of Panopolis in Egypt (*c.* AD 500), who composed, drawing on a mass of earlier poetry, his enormous *Diony-siaca*, in forty-eight Books – as many as the *Iliad* and the *Odyssey* put together. Perhaps surprisingly, it survives complete. It tells the story of the god Dionysus, his birth, his career and his conquests, both of countries and of women.

The god is not born until Book 8; that gives an idea of the poem's scale. Florid and repetitive, it has a certain verve and energy, but there are many lost works of Greek literature for which we should be very happy to exchange it. Nonnus also versified, in much the same manner, the Gospel according to St John: that, too, is extant. The juxtaposition of two works, from the same pen and in much the same style, one so pagan, and the other so Christian, has set scholars an essentially insoluble puzzle.

But the victory of the new Christian religion was inimical to the creation of heroic epics. Their central qualities, of bravura, physical strength, justified pride and violent deeds, like the interaction of great heroes with the gods, were all alien to the new faith. Even death ceased to be properly tragic, in a world dominated by thoughts of resurrection and immortality; and the heroes of the Greeks, like those of the Teutonic legends, were eclipsed by tales of saints and martyrs. It is no surprise that the epic went into comparative retreat, until the time when it should be awakened in a Christian form: by tales of Charlemagne and his paladins, of the Reconquista of Spain and of the Crusaders and their deeds in the Holy Land.

NOTE

1 All quotations from Homer are my own. Where given, Book and line references relate to the Greek texts: the *Iliad* in *Homeri Opera*, ed. T. W. Allen and D. B. Munro, 2 vols. (Oxford: Oxford University Press, 1912–20), and the *Odyssey* in *Homeri Odyssea*, ed. P. Von der Mühll, 3rd edn (Stuttgart: Teubner, 1962).

3

PETER TOOHEY

Roman epic

What isn't epic? Very little it seems. This claim can be made confidently from a cursory contemplation of the range of the literature that is normally termed as epic and that is surviving from antiquity. Epic could vary in length from approximately 408 lines (Catullus's sixty-fourth poem) to approximately 9,894 lines (Virgil's *Aeneid*). Its themes could range from the comic or parodic (there is a whole subgenre in Greek devoted to this theme: the *Batrachomyomachia* or the *Margites* are typical) to the heroic (Homer's *Iliad* or Virgil's *Aeneid*, for example), from the 'religious' (such as the *Homeric Hymns*) to the philosophical (Lucretius's *On the Nature of the Universe*), from the annalistic historical epic (Ennius's *Annales*) to the didactic (Virgil's *Georgics* or Manilius's *Astronomica*), from the romantic (Virgil's *Aeneid* Book 4) to the militaristic (Silius Italicus's *Punica*). Epic, it seems, was the most capacious of genres. This simple observation is something that matches the occasional descriptions of the genre from antiquity, such as those of Quintilian (*Institutio oratoria*, 10.1.46–50) or Manilius (the beginning of the second book of his *Astronomica*).

Given the thematic diversity of these poems, it is very hard to be prescriptive about the timbre of Roman (or Greek) epic, let alone to pin down a precise essence of such ancient poetry. There would be little value in saying, for example, that Roman (or ancient) epic poetry was serious, or that it was very long, or that it was just about kings and battles. It clearly was not. And it certainly would be misleading to attempt to assimilate uncritically Roman or ancient epic poetry with that which is taken for granted in modern languages. Indeed, one could with some justification claim that ancient epic entailed just about anything in poetry that was not sung and that did not highlight the apparently individual voice of the poet (I stress the adverb apparently, for I am not suggesting that such sung poetry was personal in the modern sense). However, exceptions to such a rough and ready characterization could easily be found. Epic poetry could appear in different metres, and some epic literature could even appear in prose.

This chapter will focus on a limited number of epic poems that were written in the Latin language. Most of those to be discussed will fall into the category of 'narrative' epic – four have historical narratives, the remainder mythological narratives. This can include, as well, 'miniature epics' or *epyllia*, encomiastic epics and heroic epics. I will have next to nothing to say about didactic epics. It would be instructive to be able to include poems written in Greek under the Roman Empire (Quintus of Smyrna, for example, or Tryphiodorus, Colluthus and Nonnus), just as it would be instructive to include Roman epics from late antiquity (Prudentius's *Pyschomachia* or Corippus's *Johannis*). But, aside from swelling the size of this chapter to an unmanageable proportion, it is doubtful that the inclusion of this material would alter the conclusions suggested in the paragraphs above. Its value would reside primarily in providing a fuller picture of the contents and contexts of little-known works. It is almost impossible to discuss the nature of Roman epic without having frequent recourse to Greek epic. This is because Roman epic was (and this is said non-judgmentally) derivative of Greek epic. Roman poets seem to have viewed themselves as composing within the same poetical tradition as the Greek one. This is above all evident in the constant intertextual echoes of their Greek forebears.

Why or how does ancient epic come to be so different from the modern poetic type? The reason lies in the oral origins of epic poetry. We have, of course, no real evidence concerning the oral origins of Roman epic, but the oral origins of the earliest Greek epic poetry, Homer's *Iliad* and *Odyssey*, have been apparent since Milman Parry's publications of the 1930s. Epic at Rome was derivative of that Greek genre. Its first exemplar was Livius Andronicus, who published, in the first half of the third century BC, a translation of Homer's *Odyssey* into the strange Saturnian metre.[1] Roman epic, that is, seems to have by-passed its native oral traditions and to have begun anew in direct imitation of Greek oral models.

Orally based epic presupposes, at least in its early phases, that prose does not exist. To say that a prose literature did not exist within the oral medium implies that anything even remotely technical – material, that is, which we usually associate with prose – could be recorded only in verse. This provides some explanation for the existence of the large amount of didactic material that survives as epic poetry. This simple but unexpected fact colours the genre henceforth. This point also provides some explanation for one of the more interesting aspects of Roman epic: the extent to which what we might call the 'sub-genres' mentioned at the beginning of this essay, are blended, often imperceptibly, within a single text. Didactic elements within heroic or mythological epic, for example, are both common and pronounced. 'Miniature-epic' elements are apparent as digressions or interludes within all of the various forms of epic literature. Digression is as good a term as any for them, although they are usually quite close in thematic concerns to the poem as a whole – the Hypsipyle interlude in Statius's *Thebaid* provides one example within mythological epic; within didactic epic there is the Aristeas interlude in Virgil's *Georgics* 4; there are even didactic elements within Lucan's otherwise staunchly martial poem. On the face of it such digressions assault the generic integrity of Roman epic of whichever type it is, but, as we have observed and will observe, ancient, and in particular Roman epic, was a ragbag of a genre. 'Integrity' is more the characteristic of the epic of later eras.

Because the original epic poems are oral – that is to say, because they precede the ability to read and to write – they normally aim to affirm, perhaps to challenge, but never to undermine community values. This is no doubt because their performance relies on the good will and the interest of their target community. If such oral epics involve narratives, these narratives must strive both to sustain the interest and to address the values of its communal listeners. They do this by catering to one of the most basic of human drives, the love of orderly narrative. By orderly, I mean a narrative that sorts through and makes comprehensible important communal experience.

An allied aspect of the oral origins of Roman epic poetry relates to the duration and extent of performance. To judge from the length of surviving epic poetry, the length of the performance lasted between one and two hours (assuming that about 400 lines of poetry can be performed in approximately one hour). This is presumably one sitting. Long epics, such as Homer's *Iliad*, take contemporary readers approximately twenty-four hours to read aloud. One could imagine therefore that the *Iliad* would have taken twelve to sixteen sessions to perform. But there must have been many other epics that could be dealt with in an evening: the *Homeric Hymns* would fit into such a category, as would Hesiod's *Theogony* or *Works and Days*. At any rate, what epic survives from antiquity, both Greek and Roman, seems to mirror these possibilities, even when they are no longer oral, as is the case for all surviving Roman epic. We have surviving, as I have indicated, 'mini'-epics and the large-scale epics – poems, that is, which could fit comfortably into an evening's performance and those which would require a dozen or more evenings for recitation.

It hardly needs emphasizing that, once the primary needs and cravings have been assuaged, one of the most basic of human drives is to satisfy a desire for hearing or reading or viewing narrative. Perhaps we should say for *experiencing* narrative. This is catered for in most societies by a number of different media: in our own by books, oral story-telling, television, theatre and so forth. In Rome this natural human craving for narrative was catered for, primarily, by the theatre. There are rich literary remains of Roman theatre – works by Plautus, Ennius, Terence, and Seneca survive – and there is also a vast body of archaeological remains relating to theatre. But before the theatre there was epic. It is one of the most transportable of narrative genres and one of the easiest to experience, whether through public or private performance or recitation, or simply through reading oneself or being read to. So it is that we find that epic narrative becomes the major and most popular purveyor of narrative within most periods of the ancient world, and in particular the Roman world.

The pre-eminence of epic as a popular narrative medium can only have been assisted, for Romans, by writing. As literacy became more widespread (and, indeed, as the book trade increased to cater for this), the need for narrative was met also through reading. The major form of written narrative – and it is easy to forget this – was epic poetry. There was no comparable prose equivalent. The epic poem was the major literary source for extended narrative until it came into competition with the novel. It is doubtful, in antiquity at least, that the novel ever managed to displace the narrative epic from this societal role.

The type of Roman epic that I will be discussing is that which interests most people nowadays, namely, narrative epic. Epic narratives of this form, at least as they survive and relate to the longer poems to which I am alluding, tend to centre around mythological themes (such as Virgil's *Aeneid* or Statius's *Thebaid*) or historical themes (such as Lucan's *Bellum Civile* or Ennius's *Annales*). There is a tendency within these poems to focus on the reintegration of the outstanding individual within the community (themes of personal self-realization, the major preoccupation of the modern novel, do not of course figure strongly within the usual traditions of the ancient epic). That Roman epic narrative should take such an interest in this form of narrative is not surprising. Its key exemplars, Homer's *Odyssey* and *Iliad*, were both communal works of poetry and, it is fair to say, espouse communal values. The key narrative theme for early oral poetry was inevitably to be associated with the difficulty that group-orientated societies encounter with outstanding individuals, usually termed heroes, and, naturally, vice versa. At the root of the problems relating to epic heroes and their tendency to transgress the values of their communities is, usually, anger. Anger is a useful enough component of the warrior's make-up inasmuch as it can make him a better fighter. But it is easy to misuse, especially when it is combined with the self-confidence that such outstanding individuals usually require. Anger drives Achilles's worst excesses in the *Iliad* just as it drives Aeneas's most puzzling actions within the *Aeneid*.

Why emphasize this social role of narrative epic poetry? It is my contention that the main focus of attention, for those with an interest in narrative epic literature, should be on what it is that makes epic literature 'typical'. This is probably a more fruitful line of inquiry than the examination of politically embedded subtexts and the like.

Concerning definitions we can probably say little more, with any confidence, than that in its origins Greek and Roman epic literature was frequently orientated towards community concerns, that it generally, though not necessarily, favoured the hexameter or six-foot line as its medium, and that it was built from units of a minimum length of about 400–500 lines or of about one hour's recitation. Such a definition, we should take care to note, allows us to include within its ambit heroic or mythological epic (Virgil and Statius among others), didactic epic (Lucretius), encomiastic or annalistic historical epic (Ennius) and the other forms mentioned above such as the parodic or philosophical (as we shall see later on, however, this definition will have to be extended still further to take account of Petronius's 'inverse' or anti-epic, the *Satyrica*).

How did Roman epic evolve? This may seem like a vast and potentially amorphous question, but there are some simple responses that, while not answering all of the many issues relating to the question, can provide a straightforward model for understanding the major changes that take place in Roman epic. I hope to illustrate in the following paragraphs (and indeed within the remainder of this chapter) how we seem to witness a movement or an evolution (but not in the sense of a betterment) from what we might term a (1) collective narrative, one whose focus is on the community, and in Rome's case, on *empire*; to a type of narrative (2) which exploits the natural disjunction between words and their referents to produce, if you like, a *polyphonic* or multivalent text; to a type of narrative (3) which, seeming to eschew the public, collective role, places its focus on the individual or private emotion or *affect*; to a narrative (4) best entailing *evasion*: a literature that involves the suspension of the circumstances of normal human actions (usually in order to illustrate a simple moral point) and that aims, through the evocation of imaginary realms, to escape the real and the quotidian. I should stress of this movement or evolution that, like all periodizations, the change is not necessarily linear. Some elements move forward quickly while others are left behind; repetitions take place, and even reversions.

Stage 1: empire

For all that Virgil and Homer are different, what does bind the two together is that their primary focus is on the collective or the group. Virgil's vision of Aeneas's imperial mission may seem to be light years from the needs of the

Greeks at Troy, but the requirement for an outstanding individual who will eventually buckle under to the needs of the collective is paramount in both poems. Without Achilles, the Greeks cannot defeat the Trojans. Without Aeneas, Rome cannot be founded and there can be no empire. In a sense – through identification with Achilles and with Aeneas – the reader manages to work through emotionally and to understand his or her own place within the group or the collective. This is achieved through the reader's identification with the unfolding process of the epic narratives. But the Roman collective was not the warrior band of Homer. It was an organized and urbanized entity and, from the unfolding of the Punic Wars, its concern was not how to gain victory in a borderland skirmish such as the Trojan War, but rather how to maintain a large and diverse empire. When Zeus's will inclines to the Greeks at Troy, it is not quite the same thing as Jupiter vouchsafing a world empire in the *Aeneid*.

The earliest of Rome's epic writers make the link between the collective and poetry most evident. Gnaeus Naevius (*c.* 270–201 BC), who seems to have inspired his successor Ennius, may well have provided an ideational basis for Roman epic. Naevius wrote about the First Punic War (264–241 BC). His poem is therefore a national epic – a celebration, as it were, of this nascent nation. From the sense that can be gleaned from the sixty odd surviving lines of Naevius's annalistic poem, its audience was Rome, in the collective sense, and the epic represents and caters to the new nation's aspirations and sense of collective destiny.

Naevius's poem seems to have begun with an aetiological narrative that seeks to explain the cause of the Carthaginian war by going back to Aeneas's arrival in Italy via Dido's Carthage. These proto-historical events were either free-standing within the poem or part of a description of a pediment on the temple of Jupiter at Agrigentum (the first book of Naevius's poem may have concluded with a description of the capture of Agrigentum in 262 BC). What is important about this juxtaposition of the mythological with the historical – and these in the context of the approving presence of Jupiter – is that it seems to provide a template of sorts onto which Ennius (239–169 BC) builds his own annalistic poem, with its own juxtaposition of myth (Trojan myth in particular) with contemporary history. This is the very juxtaposition that, in a non-annalistic context and with different emphases, Virgil exploits in the *Aeneid*. The idea of mythological time as somehow providing a direct commentary on contemporary history is something exploited also by Catullus, Ovid, Valerius Flaccus, and Statius. Naevius's poem, therefore, may (with only sixty lines surviving we must say 'may') have provided a demonstration of the vital continuity of Roman history, namely that Aeneas and perhaps the early kings and their dilemmas provide prototypes for contemporary leaders. An additional element in this template is the significance of the divine machinery and in particular the will of Jupiter for the unfolding of Roman history. Jupiter, it appears, regulates and supports the development of the Roman Empire through history.

Naevius's model is just what we seem to see in the epic poem of Ennius on the Second Punic War (218–201 BC) and beyond (to the Istrian war and ending as late as 171 BC). To judge from the 600 odd lines that survive from the *Annales*, the narrative of Ennius's poem began with the sack of Troy and, in three-book units, narrated events down to two years before the poet's death. It is likely that Ennius's patron, M. Fulvius Nobilior, bulked large in the final books of the poem, thus forcing a juxtaposition between his actions and those of this parade of Roman heroes, both mythological and historical. But Ennius seems to have aimed to do more than just aggrandize his patron. Through the depiction of this series of Roman heroes that stretches from mythological time to the present, Ennius seems to have attempted to demonstrate the important position of the Roman Empire within world history. Each hero plays a role within a collective national endeavour that has been vouchsafed by Jupiter.

The pressures of the collective that so shaped Naevius's and Ennius's poetry are also crucial for Virgil. Virgil (70–19 BC), like Homer (fl. 750 BC), shares a focus on the collective, although the collective, as I have indicated, needs to be understood differently in these two contexts. In Homer the focus is more squarely on power and how this benefits the group. In Roman epic, however, and in Virgil in particular, the focus is on institutional power, which might also be described as empire. It would be difficult not to discount the influence of Naevius's and Ennius's vision here, for this seems to have been their focus as well. Virgil, like Naevius and Ennius, sees this institutional power or empire as stretching from Rome's Trojan founders, Aeneas in particular, right down to contemporary Romans, such as the emperor Augustus.

Just how it is that Virgil achieves this link between Aeneas and his contemporary society is well known, but a few of the more salient indicators deserve repeating here for the sake of clarity. The four most important of these follow. First, in Jupiter's prophecy (1.257–96), Virgil makes clear what Fate has in store for Aeneas and his descendants including Augustus (Virgil's patron and the Roman emperor for the last decade of his life). Roman civilization will be civilizing and pacific, Jupiter makes clear, and it will usher in a new Golden Age. Aeneas and Augustus will be party to this. Second, in Book 6, during Aeneas's visit to the Underworld, Anchises, Aeneas's late father, points out the souls of the great Romans who will follow on from Aeneas and, as well, propounds a theory of transmigration

(6.713–51 and 756–886), which provides an actual link between Aeneas and later prominent Romans such as Romulus and Augustus. The souls of the past great will pass into those of contemporary heroes such as Augustus. Third, the visit to the future site of Rome (Book 8) and Aeneas's shield (8.608–731) again look to the present: Aeneas's divine shield has Augustus and the Battle of Actium at its centre. On the edge of the shield is a series of vignettes that illustrate aspects of the Roman character. Fourth, the cessation of Juno's hostility to Aeneas and his descendants such as Augustus is urged and prefigured by Jupiter at 12.793–806. It was Juno's hostility that set the epic in chain. There are numerous other contexts where the destiny of Rome and with it Aeneas and Augustus are made plain, but these are perhaps the most obvious.

The point, however, is a simple one. Virgil's poem is, at one level, directed to illustrate the continuity of the empire from its beginnings to the present. Augustus is literally a reincarnation of Aeneas and all that he stood for. But the kernel of this idea is to be seen in the poems of Naevius and Ennius. The focus on empire and on Jupiter's acquiescence in this is peculiarly Roman.

Empire insinuates itself into most Roman epic. After Virgil its most uncritical display can be found in the *Punica* of Silius Italicus (AD 26–101). This poem seems to have been composed between the poet's fifty-sixth and seventieth year, presumably as a retirement project. It presents a seventeen-book epic on the Second Punic War. Silius has stolen Ennius's theme, but no doubt believes that he has brought the topic up to date with extensive research and Virgilian technique. Silius narrows the focus of Ennius to the years 218–201 BC and uses determinedly Virgilian language and, as one might expect, a much broader panoply of historical sources than those of Ennius, who wrote of course about events that he knew. It is also probable that Silius is offering his poem as a corrective of Lucan's (which will be discussed later in this chapter): the divine machinery is reintroduced, as is the privileged relationship of Rome with Jupiter (see 17.344–84 and Proteus's prediction at 7.435–93), and there are clear-cut heroes and villains. Silius's larger concept, however, is predictably derivative of Ennius. It seems likely that Scipio Africanus, the poem's epic hero, is to be understood, probably through the mythological hero Hercules who was associated with both Scipio and Domitian, as an imperial paradigm.

And what a hero! In *Punica* 15 the allegorical figures Virtue (*Virtus*) and Pleasure (*Voluptas*) compete for the general's allegiance, with the predictable outcome. Silius provides us with a very simple characterization. Scipio is peerless, Hannibal's father Hasdrubal is execrable, Hannibal is a gifted general, although very bloodthirsty, Flamininus, who precipitates the disaster at Cannae, is, like Hannibal, too prone to *dementia* and *furor*, and

Regulus is, well, Regulus. It follows that, because his heroes are monochromatic creations, there is no sense of the tragic or of pathos within this poem.

Silius chose to use a series of historical events and characters to provide the imperial paradigm (Scipio Africanus as the emperor Domitian), rather than the by now more predictable mythological paradigms chosen by Virgil (Aeneas as the emperor Augustus) and Valerius Flaccus (Jason as the emperor as Vespasian, Titus, or Domitian). In doing so, Silius is reviving the tradition established by two of the earliest surviving Roman epic poets, Naevius and Ennius. His motives are not hard to discern. Mythological epic had been worked almost to a standstill by Virgil and by his apparent imitators, Valerius Flaccus and Statius. Historical epic had been taken in a new and completely untraditional direction with Lucan's *Bellum Civile*, in which there are no clear imperial paradigms. It appears, then, that Silius was attempting to re-establish the viability of the imperial paradigm in the less used medium of historical epic. It was perhaps a good idea. That it is unsuccessful is primarily the result of the predictability of Silius's technique, but it is also the result of Silius's inability at any point in his poem to move us or, as does Statius, to provide us with a poem that is able to escape the real.

Stage 2: polyphony

In visual or written art there is often a tension that is deliberately exploited between the medium and the message, between words and their referents. In his *Metamorphoses*, Ovid might seem to be the obvious exemplar of this type of poetry. In the *Metamorphoses* there are the inevitable examples of wordplay, of incongruities, of anagrams, and of absolutely unnecessary ironies. As is well known, they tend to draw attention to the poetic medium rather than the narrative message. But Virgil's *Aeneid* may offer the most striking and innovative approach to this matter. He produces what I have termed elsewhere a polyphonic mode of composition, one which contrasts three voices, the imperial or collective (which we have just discussed), the tragic/empathetic or private, and the ludic (it seems to be almost inevitable, as the literary experience moves from listening to reading, that an element of play, a ludic element, enters into the poetic text).[2] The overall result of this polyphony can be a destabilizing of the relationship between the medium and the message – or at least the medium and any single message. This was a relationship that was much more secure in the oral or quasi-oral medium.

There is more to Virgil than empire. Virgil's imperial optimism (which we might have termed as the public register) is counter-pointed by a dour pessimism (a private register). It is customary to attempt to reconcile these registers: the private, it is sometimes said, *undercuts* or *subverts* the public.[3] Or the private exists primarily to stress the triumph of the public through a process of 'resurrection'.[4] What is this private register? This is the plangent private voice which so sympathizes with the victims of Aeneas's imperial destiny: Dido above all, but also Laocöon, Priam, Polydorus, Palinurus, Misenus, Pallas, Lausus, Evander, Camilla, or Turnus. All of these characters are depicted with an emotional sympathy such that it seems, for the time, to derail Virgil and Aeneas's aspirations to empire. That final duel between Aeneas and Turnus, with which the poem ends, represents the most prominent example. Who could not but sympathize with the fallen Turnus? What are we meant to think of the poem's imperial design? Virgil's poem treads, as it were, a tightrope between public and private. It is the resulting and seemingly unresolved tension which gives rise to such disparate readings of the *Aeneid*. The critic Christine Perkell speaks helpfully, in regard to this hermeneutical tightrope, of 'suspension'.[5]

But the suspension does not end with public and private. There is what we might term a ludic voice, although this is one that is given little attention. There is much that is ludic in the *Aeneid*: think of the bizarre description of Hercules ripping the top off the Aventine to display the monster Cacus lurking in the depths below. Gordon Williams points to the description of Mercury in 4.238–55, to the seduction of Vulcan by Venus at 8.370–453, and to the transformation of Aeneas's ships into nymphs at 9.77–122.[6] For Williams this is 'Hellenistic rococo' and, for another critic, it is 'intellectual irony'.[7] The *Georgics* are outside the brief of this chapter, but the ludic element within this four-book poem is probably even more prominent.

There is no easy reconciliation between the claims of these three voices. It is for this reason that I use the term polyphony. I doubt that Virgil ever intended us to hear all of his voices at once. His purpose, I believe, is to create a contextual (or affective or aesthetic) unity. The registers become intermittently audible, sometimes when Virgil makes one prominent, sometimes when the reader, almost the performer, makes another one prominent. Paradoxically, it is this suspension that sustains multiple exposures to this great art. The *Aeneid* resists easy claims to unity precisely in so far as the three voices that I have singled out become prominent. In the end, however, it is the blend that provides a unity for Virgil's poem. We should bear this in mind when attempting to take a position on the seemingly irresolvable debate waged between supporters of an imperially optimistic and an imperially pessimistic Virgil. Besides the fact that such views ignore a large portion of Virgil's programme (the ludic, Alexandrian pose), they also offer privilege to a voice that exists in a harmonic rather than a dominant mode. Reading Virgil means hearing the polyphony: allowing Virgil's imperial encomium (part of his Roman epic heritage), but this without losing sight of his poem's vision of human suffering, and this also without denying the poem its modicum of play and of irony (the avant-garde tradition of Alexandrian poetics).

Stage 3: affect

The most unexpected change to take place in Roman epic was that provided by Ovid in his *Metamorphoses*. The change wrought by Ovid entailed no less than an upending of the Homeric and Virgilian imperatives of the collective and their replacement with a new narrative loyalty: a loyalty to the private, to what was based in private emotion or *affect*. Ovid's interest is primarily on the emotional experience of individual gods and humans. In the 250 or so stories within the *Metamorphoses*, Ovid infuses affect into his narrative in a mode that Virgil anticipated (as did the Greek epic writer Apollonius of Rhodes before him) but has glossed over because of its incompatibility with the constraints of an imperial vision. The simple change that Ovid has wrought is almost too obvious to notice: narrative no longer presents human experience as it ought to be within the larger community, but rather as something that the private individual could experience and with which he or she could identify.

We can see this tendency in the work of Ovid's predecessor, Catullus, in his miniature epic, designated simply as Catullus 64. The miniature epic, of which Catullus's sixty-fourth poem is an example, was, because of its size, a less prepossessing form of epic, but it also seems to have been relatively free of the collective and imperial constraints to which the large-scale narrative epic was subject. Its interests seem to have been either experimental (in a technical sense, as in the blended stories within Catullus 64) or related to affect. It is common to compare Catullus's evocation of the emotional life of the heroine of his small-scale epic, Ariadne, to Virgil's Dido. Both women were abandoned by their lovers, and both lovers left by sea. In both instances it is hard not to sympathize with the female partners. Whatever Catullus 64 means (and it seems likely that it is an attack on contemporary Roman perfidy), it is probably safe to say that it is Ariadne who dominates our impression of the poem (v. 116–201 above all). The emotional intensity – the affect – of Ariadne's lament and cursing of Theseus is remarkable, powerful, and memorable. Catullus's interest in affect is probably typical of the epyllion. There are instructive parallels of treatment in Moschus's *Europa*, for example, in Callimachus's *Hecale*, or, in Latin, in the pseudo-Virgilian *Ciris*.

The *Metamorphoses* are a linear descendant of Catullus 64. The structure of Ovid's collection of approximately 250 miniature and affective epics runs as follows: prologue (1.1–4); introduction, the creation and flood (1.5–1.451); part 1, gods (1.452–6.420); part 2, heroes and heroines (6.421–11.193); part 3, 'historical' personages (11.194–15.870); epilogue (15.871–9). This structure is not immediately apparent, however: it is not something that provides, on first reading, a coherence to the fifteen-book poem. What does in fact hold this long chain of stories together, from a technical point of view, are: chronology (the poem begins with creation and concludes with the accession to power of the emperor Augustus); interweaving (the miniature epics are woven together in an interlinked style to prevent fragmentation); and the theme of metamorphosis (change from one form to another is found in many of the stories, and the theme is eventually enunciated in a theoretical manner as metempsychosis – the belief that the soul transmigrated from one body to another – by Pythagoras at 15.60–478). From a stylistic and thematic point of view what also holds the poem together are: voice (an ironic, humorous undercutting of anything that approaches the plangent); an interest in love (Ovid was also a famous love poet); a choice of story that is completely unexpected (in terms of topic and often in terms of ending); an avoidance of what one might call the trauma-and-recovery narrative – of the type that we see with Achilles or Aeneas, both tempted and failing, but drawn back into the fold as the narrative progresses (this is a characteristic that Ovid shares with Lucan); and, finally, evasion (I will postpone discussion of this topic until the next section of this chapter).

What matters most, however, is Ovid's fascination not so much with psychology as with the depiction of affect and pathos. This was the legacy of the miniature epic, but Ovid has taken it to a level that could well be described as monumental, at least in the sense of volume. Affect can take in anything from the macabre to the sentimental. Ovid is a master of both. The famous story of Procne, Tereus and Philomela (6.424–674) involves horror, tragedy, the macabre, and the comic in almost equal doses: Philomela is raped and incarcerated, has her tongue cut out by Tereus; the latter has his own children served up stewed for a meal by way of revenge from his wife, Procne. Yet in the end they are all turned fantastically into birds. The tale of Pyramus and Thisbe (4.55–166), on the other hand, has two sorrowful and separated young lovers forced first to speak through a chink in the wall, but then separated by accident, mistaken death and finally suicide.

Although Ovid was inspired by the tradition represented by Catullus 64, at the same time a large-scale epic, according to Roman epic genre, ought to make some form of a political statement. This is certainly the case with the *Metamorphoses*. Ovid uses Pythagoras's doctrines of metempsychosis in *Metamorphoses* Book 15 (universal change, 15.176–272, the predictions of Rome's greatness, 15.418–452, and the transmigration of souls,

15.15.453–78) to provide a link between mythological heroes and non-mythological heroes such as Hercules, Aeneas, Romulus, Julius Caesar, and Augustus. We have seen this in Naevius, Ennius, and Virgil – the last two authors used Pythagorean lore as well. There is in addition a reference to the apotheosis of Caesar at 15.745–851 and a climactic prediction of the apotheosis of Augustus at 15.852–70.

Does it follow, from these imperial allusions, that we can speak of polyphony in Ovid's epic? Do the *Metamorphoses* exhibit three voices, the affective, the ludic, and the public? I would say not, for Ovid seems to place little weight on his public protestations, as we can see from the remarkably curt section in the final book of the poem on Augustus' apotheosis (15.852–70). And Ovid's version of affect, furthermore, is an ironic one, not one that stands in contradistinction to the ludic. In the *Metamorphoses* Ovid focused on the emotional experience of individual gods and humans and, by infusing affect and pathos into his many-storied narrative, produced a poem that, by taking the miniature epic to an extreme point, was probably a one-off occurrence. It is very difficult to imagine where epic could have gone next, should it have followed Ovid's model. If it did go anywhere, it was into the sorts of interests that produced the Greek novel.

Stage 4: evasion

I have heard it claimed that Ovid's *Metamorphoses* was until recently the second most read book in Western literature after the Bible. The claim cannot be verified, of course, but it makes sense. In my opinion the *Metamorphoses* is the greatest work of Latin literature, not just of Roman epic literature. It is certainly not because Ovid moves us deeply, although he can do this occasionally, nor is it because he provides us with a compelling vision of human experience, although he can do this too occasionally, nor, paradoxically, is it because he is comic on the level of Petronius (to be discussed later), although he is frequently very comic. There are no easy Aristotelian categories to describe Ovid's abilities. Rather, what seems to have attracted readers is the combination of narrative, affect and pathos, humour, erotic interest, and the creation of a alternative world that is intriguingly real yet sufficiently other to allow the reader to escape the quotidian into an imaginary, mythological world.

Here, then, is the fourth stage. In this literature the interest of the author is more on the alternative world he is creating than on any deeply philosophical or even imperial vision. Ideas are not vitally important. In this form of narrative there tends to be an avoidance of moral ambiguities. Good and evil are clearly demarcated. There may even be allegory. And values are

clear-cut. In this type of evasive creation, pathos is replaced by the sentimental and, while violence and brutality are often common, they exist
primarily to highlight the evil of their perpetrators and the goodness of
their opponents. Too much realism would spoil the goal of evasion.

Consider the killing of Creon in the final book of Statius's *Thebaid*. This
death assumes little of the moral ambiguity or of the tragic status of Virgil's
Turnus. The death of Virgil's Turnus comes not just at the climax of the
poem but at the end of a string of the deaths of the *Aeneid*'s sympathetic
victims. His death in a sense echoes theirs. In the *Thebaid* there is no chain
of tragic deaths to prefigure empathetically that of Creon. Nor, in fact, does
Creon's portrait within the poem assume sufficient narrative status to
induce real reader sympathy. The puzzle of his death, if there is one at all,
is why a poem that advocates *clementia* should allow the quasi-judicial
killing of Creon. That is easy to answer, however: the Roman state, which
espoused *clementia*, found nothing strange in capital punishment.

The *Thebaid* is little interested in ideas. This is clear from the outset of the
poem: Jupiter proposes no moral vision of empire within the *concilium
deorum* ('council of gods') in Book 1, merely a pitting of two wicked cities,
one against the other. Furthermore, *pietas*, *clementia*, and *virtus* are important, albeit unsurprisingly positive values and these are contrasted with the
furor, *invidia*, and the *saevus amor regendi* ('a mad desire for rule') of the
two brothers, of Tydeus, of Creon, and a number of other characters. Moral
types are characterized as blacks and whites, and villains such as Tydeus,
Eteocles, or Polynices are given no chance to evoke reader sympathy. The
interest of the poem in allegorical figures such as *Virtus* and *Pietas* points to
comparable ideational simplicity. What is more, characterization in Statius
is so startlingly obvious – 'monochromatic' as David Vessey notes – that it is
very difficult to take it too seriously.[8] To this lack of concern for ideas
I would add a parallel theme: the *Thebaid* replaces Virgilian pathos with
sentimentality (in Maeon's death, for example, or that of Amphiaraus) or
simple affect (Tydeus generally). That there is a general lack of concern for
ideas within the *Thebaid* does not for a minute suggest that this is a poor
poem, but rather that its intent and interest lie elsewhere. It is usually the
case that, when sentimentality is prominent, narrative will take over, and
that seems to me to be the case with Statius. The interest of the *Thebaid*
resides in the exuberance, the colour, the unexpectedness, and the brio of the
narrative. It also resides, as many of the intertextual studies of the last few
years have shown, in the skill with which Statius can manipulate, within his
own text, the work of his generic predecessors.[9]

It is very easy to forget how much of the *Thebaid* is extraneous to
the main narrative theme of the poem – which we take to be the conflict

between the two brothers and the civic reconciliation of their conflict. The very long digression on Hypsipyle admirably reflects this point. The Hypsipyle narrative, constituting approximately one twelfth of the whole of the *Thebaid*, has just about everything that a romance narrative ought to contain: a murder plot, sexual infidelity, miraculous escape, abduction by pirates, a dragon, death threats, infant death, and the sudden appearance of long-lost children. One might also wish to include within the ambit of the Hypsipyle digression the funeral games for the unfortunate ward of Hypsipyle, Opheltes – which would mean that one sixth of the poem is given over to an apparently extraneous event. What really seems to interest Statius is the creation of a literature of imaginative evasion. That, rather than moralizing, is the great strength of his poem. There is nothing like this within extant Greek and Roman epic poetry.

Does Statius's poem have anything to say concerning contemporary Rome? Does Statius have a view of Domitian? No doubt the conflict between the brothers Eteocles and Polynices stands as an emblem for civil war and the corrupting nature of power. That the Theban myth acts as a commentary on Roman history is apparent. There is, however, no simple historical analogy made between this conflict and the civil wars of AD 69 or, more precisely, between the characters of the *Thebaid* and real life: Eteocles and Polynices no more represent Domitian and his brother Titus (whom he had poisoned) than Romulus and Remus. Civil conflict was as much a persistent theme of Roman literature as it was a real-life event. Unless a precise historical referent is made apparent, the theme remains just that.

Epic heroes?

Epic narratives – at least as we see them in the longer epic poems – tend to take as their focus the sometimes troubled relationship between the epic hero and his community. In most instances the narrative concludes with the reintegration of the hero with his community. Achilles, in Homer's *Iliad*, is an obvious example of such a figure. And so to a large extent is Virgil's Aeneas: the wavering devotion of this hero to his mission is an especially prominent theme of the first six books of the *Aeneid*, no more so than in Book 4. His loyalty to the values of his collective is also tested during his violent outbursts of Book 10. He is, however, thoroughly reintegrated by the end of the poem, whatever we may think of the community values that this may display. The heroic theme, as I have indicated, is the product of the concerns and values of the collective society. It might be expected, therefore, that such a narrative theme could come under fire when values shift away from the heroic and the heroic impulse (the hero's unthinking compulsion to fight).

It is certainly true that, over time, the values of the collective become less central to the concerns of ancient literature in general – we can see this in the case of Roman epic especially in Ovid's *Metamorphoses*. But genres are conservative things, and none more so than epic. Ovid is hardly typical of the Roman narrative epic that survives. What we do witness, however, is that this theme of the epic hero as exemplar of collective values seems to stay firm, although at the same time the more innovative of the narrative epics ring a variety of clever and often substantial changes upon this theme.

In this section of the chapter I will attempt to show how these changes are sometimes registered. To do this I will look at what I believe are three of the most problematic of texts of Roman epic literature, at least as regards to depictions of the epic hero: these are Valerius Flaccus's *Argonautica* (the unfinished state of which provides evidence for my theme), Petronius's *Satyrica* (a fragment of epic literature, rather than epic poetry), and Lucan's *Bellum Civile* (another unfinished poem). I would like to illustrate how these three texts, which display quite specific links with one another, have radically modified this pattern but without actually abandoning it.

But I am perhaps moving too quickly, for I have not yet made clear what I believe this heroic template to be. Here is one way of defining the epic hero, which can act as a basis for the discussion:

> An epic hero is of superior social station and physique, is pre-eminent in fighting, courage, and perhaps in intelligence. Usually, as a result of a crisis or a war or an enforced quest, this hero will undergo some form of a change in status. After a period of being at odds (emotionally, physically, or even geographically) with his human and divine community he will assume his responsibilities and his duties to both groups.[10]

It is quite surprising how often this admittedly schematized version of the epic hero and his troubles is actually played out in ancient epic literature. The best instance is to be found in Homer's *Iliad* with the character Achilles. But Homer's Odysseus might also be compared, if we assume that his piratical actions with Polyphemus and more generally in Book 9 display a lack of loyalty both to his crew and in turn to his family and to the gods. Aeneas, as I have already indicated, is another instance. In mythological legends the template is played out notably with Heracles and his slaughtering of his family (retold in Euripides's *Heracles* and in Seneca's play of the same name). The fracturing of the link with the human community is sometimes dealt with geographically, rather than emotionally, which we see, for example, in the wanderings of Perseus and to a lesser extent in those of Jason.

At the beginning of Valerius Flaccus's *Argonautica* Jason is certainly a typical epic hero. His lineage, although usurped by the brutal Pelias, is regal (his mission for the Golden Fleece, he expects, will restore his regal rights); he is clearly handsome (why else are Hypsipyle and Medea so drawn to him?); and his warrior attributes are repeatedly emphasized in a series of combats (notably in the Cyzicean trials of Book 2, the civil war of Book 6, and especially in his unfaltering guidance of the *Argo* through the Clashing Rocks, 4.637–710), as well as in several paradigmatic digressions (Hercules's rescue of Hesione, 2.451–578, is paralleled to the dealings between Jason and Hypsipyle). Jason's status as an epic hero is also coloured by his status as a paradigmatic Roman hero. When, in Book 1, Pelias imposes on him the mission, Valerius's Jason responds with enthusiasm, and is described as fired up by a desire for that sought-after Roman attribute *gloria* (1.77) and by a sense of *religio* (1.80, 'trust in god'). Jason's quest is of the most traditional sort: treacherous journeys to dangerous foreign lands where, amongst other things, he must overcome monsters. But this geographical 'alienation' is complemented by one from his family. His parents decide, after the departure of their son, to commit suicide rather than fall into the hands of the dire Pelias (1.693–851). The successful completion of Jason's mission will not only restore his regal inheritance, but also reintegrate the status of his deceased parents within their ancestral Colchis.

Jason is portrayed as an imperial paradigm: this becomes apparent from the very outset of the poem. His voyage is paralleled to that of Vespasian's with Claudius to Britain (1.8–9). Valerius seems to have begun the *Argonautica* under Vespasian's reign (AD 69–79), but to have finished what he could of this incomplete poem under Domitian (reigned AD 81–96). Jason's function as an imperial paradigm is evident also in the divine assembly in Book 1.498–573: Jupiter implies that the Argonautic expedition will not just open up the world through sea travel, but it will shift world power westward to Greece and then, later, further west, presumably towards Italy and Rome. Jason's function is made apparent in a number of other places in the poem: notably in his special relationship with Minerva (a tutelary goddess for the emperor Domitian as well as for Jason) and in the imperial-like manner that he puts an end to the civil war in Colchis (6.690–751).

The heroic template outlined earlier requires, for its completion, some form of reintegration with the hero's divine and human societies. Jason's integration with the will of Jupiter seems never to have been in doubt but, on the familial level, there is the matter of the throne at Iolcus, which he never regains. The reintegration is never achieved, and there are signs within Books 7 and, especially, 8, that all is not well with Jason's status as an epic hero. In Book 7 Valerius denounces Medea as lacking in *pudor* ('shame' or 'self-respect'), as given to *furor*, and as *nocens* ('guilty'). Jason, her companion, barely gets off the hook. He appears even less reputable in the final Book of the poem, where he is over-reliant on this *nocens* woman. The poem breaks off just before the murder of her brother Absyrtus, in which Jason is complicit. But we know from Apollonius's version what happens. We know even more from Euripides's play, *Medea*, and from Seneca's play of the same name. What has happened to Valerius's poem and to his epic hero?

I would suggest two things. First, Jason never was a suitable epic hero. His disreputable status was made clear five centuries earlier in Euripides's play. He is too weak to bear the mantle of empire. But more may be involved. I have suggested elsewhere that Valerius is attempting to provide an ideological and mythological basis for the Roman principate – Vespasian, as we saw above, but also Titus and then Domitian, under whom he ended this incomplete poem.[11] Domitian's special status in Books 6–8 is emphasized by Minerva's protective role of Jason (6.609). But what would Domitian (and Minerva) have made of the Jason who was about to become complicit in the murder in Book 8 of Medea's brother Absyrtus? The paradigm could hardly have been flattering.

Thus an answer presents itself as to why the heroic template is cut short and why the poem itself ends so puzzlingly incomplete. Valerius, I suggest, could not go through with it. He had picked the wrong imperial prototype and an unsatisfactory epic hero. Rather than continuing with an explosively insulting conclusion, he chose silence. Valerius's aim, therefore, was to produce a political encomium, along the lines of the *Aeneid*, and he chose Jason as his model. It was a bad choice. Jason, always a suspect figure in mythological writing, could not withstand the ideological pressure placed upon him. Valerius lost control of the poem as it progressed and as a result was unable to finish his *Argonautica*.

Petronius's *Satyrica*, as it is now termed, has a number of strong links with epic literature. One of these is its 'hero', Encolpius, who seems deliberately to stand for everything an epic hero does not. A useful way to express this relationship would be to say that Encolpius is a deliberate inverse of the epic hero. But before I attempt to show that this is the case, let us go through some of the reasons why Petronius's novel could be included in an essay on Roman epic. Elimar Klebs seems to have been the first to assert (in 1899) that Petronius's *Satyrica* was 'a sort of a parody of the *Odyssey* and epics like it'.[12] Klebs was right to use the phrase 'epics like it', for the *Satyrica* has epic elements that point beyond the *Odyssey*. So it is that the *Satyrica* details, like the *Odyssey* or the *Argonautica* (there survives a Greek version by Apollonius of Rhodes as well as by Valerius Flaccus), the picaresque wanderings of a persecuted hero. The links, however, are more precise: first, Encolpius, the protagonist of the *Satyrica*, is hounded across land and sea by the wrath of a god (Priapus, rather than Odysseus's Poseidon); second, when the young paramour of Encolpius, Giton, hides beneath the bed to escape the rivalrous attentions of Ascyltus, he is compared to Odysseus hidden under a sheep to escape from the cave of the Cyclops; third, Encolpius's tortured liaison with Giton plays off that of Odysseus with Calypso and Circe; and last, the whole of the Circe episode in the *Satyrica* is reminiscent of events in the *Odyssey* Book 10, where the real Circe dominates the narrative. On a more general level, although the storm and the shipwreck passage in the *Satyrica* mirror the *Odyssey* Book 5 (Croton, therefore, with its *femme fatale* must match and reflect the Nausicaa episode), we might just as well have drawn a parallel to the arrival of Aeneas in North Africa in the *Aeneid* Books 1 and 4. Trimalchio's banquet (the *Cena Trimalchionis*) may well recall the banquets on Phaeacia of the *Odyssey* Books 7–8, but they could also be compared to the banquet of the *Aeneid* Book 1. And, finally, there is the prominent miniature-epic within the *Satyrica*, the *Bellum Civile*, which is usually taken to be a jibe at Lucan's epic. These elements that the *Satyrica* shares with the epic generally – and with the *Odyssey* specifically – hardly suggest parody. The normal parody of the *Odyssey* by writers such as Archestratus is quite different in nature. These links indicate the easy generic relationship that novels such as Petronius's held with epic.

How, then, does Encolpius fit into the template of the epic hero? To follow are some of the links between the characterization of Encolpius and the heroic template as outlined earlier. Encolpius and his companions could hardly be described as being of superior social station and physique. They are of low social status and give no indications of having impressive physiques (this is especially so in the case of Giton). Nor are they pre-eminent in fighting and in intelligence. Encolpius and Giton and Ascyltus seem keen to avoid physical confrontation of all forms, except the amatory. The hero of the *Satyrica* embarks on some form of a quest as a result of a crisis, but the crisis in Encolpius's case seems to have involved the defilement of the rites of Priapus. Encolpius becomes impotent as a result and his quest and his wanderings seem to be driven by a desire to regain his potency – a reintegration of a sort. Encolpius certainly does undergo trials, usually physical, as part of this quest: these are numerous (the *Cena* itself, the sea voyage and shipwreck, the encounter with Circe, and so on). Does he, as a result, develop through his quest a deeper understanding of his duties to gods and humans (reintegration)? We do not have enough of the novel to be able to speak of reintegration with the community, but we can guess that Encolpius by its end ceases to be impotent. This represents a reintegration of a comic sort.

Part of the humour of the *Satyrica* resides in the clever way it has adapted and inverted the theme of the epic hero. It is as if the writer of this novel asked himself how he could write epic that was not epic: how could he preserve the motifs of epic but at the same time exploit the less formal opportunities that were provided by the prose medium and its audience? One simple way of understanding the *Satyrica* and its epic heritage is to suggest that it achieves its comedic status by inversing the template of the traditional heroic epic.

Is there a hero in Lucan's epic poem, *Bellum Civile*? That was a question that used to be a subject of intense debate and was thought to highlight a weakness in the *Bellum Civile*. In Lucan's epic there are three candidates for the title of hero: Caesar, Pompey, and Cato. Caesar, on the narrative's own admission, was a villainous, although occasionally generous-hearted individual. Pompey was probably on the right side, but was old, rigid, and vain. Cato, the Stoic sage, was altogether too unbendingly 'good', priggish, and almost too comical to be taken seriously as an epic hero. Were we to apply the template of the epic hero to Caesar, Pompey, or Cato, we would find that each of them displays admirable social standing, looks, and bravery. Each of them has a quest – furthering or hampering Caesar's designs. Each of these characters seems at various points to be at odds with their society. Whether their 'quests' produce any form of reconciliation, we cannot know. Lucan seems to have turned his back on the 'trauma and recovery' narrative that I have suggested is so typical of the characterization of the epic hero. But perhaps the most perplexing aspect of the status of these characters is that at various points in the narrative of the poem the 'author' seems to praise, and at other times to denigrate, each of them.

In *Poetry and Civil War in Lucan's 'Bellum Civile'*, Jamie Masters argues a convincing solution to this problem.[13] The author's voice becomes another actor within the poem: almost another epic hero, we could say. The author's voice – at times partisan, at times encomiastic – is as confused and as morally vacuous as the three competing heroes of the poem. The author's fractured indecision is captured, Masters argues, in the ending of the poem: he cannot properly evaluate his heroes' status or the war itself and so, rather like Valerius, he is driven to a silence (the incompleteness of the poem), which is, we might assume, the only honest and moral response. Caesar, Pompey, and Cato therefore display the same indecision and moral ambiguity as the poem's authorial voice, the fourth 'hero'. In fact the wavering sympathy displayed towards these 'heroic' characters reflects the degenerate state of Rome that the *Bellum Civile* wishes to project. Hence the lack of a clear epic hero in the poem can be understood as one of its ideational strengths. I doubt that Lucan's solution necessarily makes for satisfying reading, but it does make for clever reading and a reading that in its way is passionately committed to a course of political reaction.

Nostalgia, empire, and leisure

The emotional register of nostalgia – or of a desire for homecoming – is something very common in ancient mythology. Ancient literature, as a result, is crowded with representations of stories of return: the frequency of myths of the Golden Age or the Age of Saturn is typical, as are texts that summon up the possibilities of homecoming and the establishment of harmony. Homer's *Odyssey* is perhaps the most famous and satisfying example of this type. But we might also wish to compare Aeschylus's *Oresteia*. A great portion of such creative literature exists as a nostalgic re-evocation of a lost time. This theme is an especially prominent one within narrative epic as it developed in Rome. Consider, above all, Virgil's *Aeneid*. The present world is seen as an active embodiment (cemented by the will of Jupiter) of the values and aspirations of mythological time. Were we to believe in metempsychosis, Augustus would not merely be like the Trojan Aeneas, but he also would have become Aeneas. It is striking confirmation of this observation that Virgil views the arrival of Aeneas's Trojans in Italy not as an exile, but as a homecoming. Troy, Virgil believed, had been settled from Italy, from Corythus (*Aeneid* 7.209 and 3.167–8). Modern-day heroes such as Augustus validate their ultimate origins in Corythus by taking on the mantle of Aeneas. It is as if Virgil's vision of empire is grounded within the notion of homecoming and nostalgia. The same vision seems to have existed in Ennius's poetry, although the fragmentary nature of his *Annales* denies access to detail, but the narrative began with Aeneas, and Ennius, like Anchises in the *Aeneid* Book 6, seems to have subscribed to the theory of metempsychosis. So too does Ovid: Pythagoras explains this in *Metamorphoses* 15.60–478 where a link is asserted between the mythological and historical heroes. Nostalgia and empire are thus linked again and it is in a manner that could be said to resemble that of Virgil. Lucan has no Pythagorean lore in the *Bellum Civile* – he removed the mythological and divine substrate from his poem – but the link of empire and nostalgia remains a constant. What Lucan aspires to is a return or a homecoming to the values of the earlier Roman Republic. This, he imagines, embodied a less degenerate political system than that of the world in which he lives. Lucan, nostalgic through and through, longs for a Republican past where these epic heroes could finally achieve a satisfactory reintegration within their societies. The implication of the unfinished state of his poem is sure to indicate that such a homecoming is impossible and that the link of nostalgia and empire is a mendacious one.

Nostalgia seems to gain its efficacy insofar as it is capable of moving the reader or listener, almost in the cathartic Aristotelian sense. It is easy to see how this is achieved in Virgil's epic. The fraught struggles of Aeneas with his sense of duty – as we see it, for example, in his relationship with Dido or Pallas – brings this emotional register to life. I have linked this mode with Virgil's personal voice and have suggested that it forms part of the *Aeneid*'s polyphonic tonality.

It is instructive to compare Silius Italicus. Such a personal voice as that of Virgil does not exist within the *Punica*, yet Silius Italicus's narrative is no less nostalgia-driven than that of Virgil. As we have seen, Silius holds up the earlier Roman Republic as a political and social ideal. Like that of Virgil, his vision of the Roman principate is one that believes it re-embodies the virtues of heroes such as Hercules (also crucial for Virgil's vision as we see it in the *Aeneid* Book 8) and of course Scipio Africanus. But this imperial voice, which defines itself through a strategy of nostalgia, is nowhere linked within his narrative to an emotional register that is capable of moving us. Whether or not a narrative like Silius's succeeds (and I do not believe it does) will not invalidate the main point of this final section of the chapter: namely, that the theme of nostalgia and of homecoming is something that is at the very core of the Roman epic. This may well be the result of the template that Naevius and then Ennius laid down, a template that links the fulfilment of the imperial present with a fulfilment of the values of the mythological past. We might wish to contrast Greek epic, or at least later Greek epic from Apollonius down as far as the remarkable Nonnus. This tradition, by comparison with the Roman, seems to have been a whirlwind of experiment. Avant-garde poets such as Apollonius and Callimachus can at times move, but their concern for imperial aspirations, despite occasional arguments to the contrary, seems to be tenuous. I believe it may be easiest to place Catullus 64 within this Greek tradition. Catullus moralizes, but not in any convincing sense.

If it is true that the great Roman epics represent acts of nostalgia, what, then, are we to do with Ovid and with Statius? Their interest in empire is cursory and their willingness to move the reader or listener is minimal. But the *Metamorphoses* and the *Thebaid* are unquestionably great instances of epic literature. Perhaps we should include both poems within the Greek tradition, as I have termed it. But perhaps it may be more satisfactory to consider both poems rather as great artifices of leisure. I use the term leisure not in the sense of relaxation, but in the sense of how it is that free time may constructively be absorbed. This relates, I believe, to the choice that both poets make for an evasive, essentially apolitical narrative. Both narratives place a premium on pleasure rather than politics, and admirably offer texts designed to enhance free time. In a sense they may be said to have made a sacrifice in doing so: literary critics, habitually valuing life more than literature, search fruitlessly for the subversive in these texts. Does it make them any the less serious or less important? Is it the primary social role of a public literature such as epic merely to preach? Is it the role of the critic to affirm this?

NOTES

1 Saturnian metre is the oldest Latin verse form. Disagreement remains as to its exact form.

2 Peter Toohey, *Epic Lessons: An Introduction to Ancient Didactic Poetry* (London: Routledge, 1996), following John F. Miller, *Ovid's Elegiac Festivals: Studies in the 'Fasti'* (Frankfurt am Main: Peter Lang, 1991), 141.

3 See for example: Michael C. J. Putnam, *The Poetry of the 'Aeneid': Four Studies in Imaginative Unity and Design* (Cambridge, MA: Harvard University Press, 1965), and *Virgil's Poem of the Earth: Studies in the 'Georgics'* (Princeton: Princeton University Press, 1979); David O. Ross, *Virgil's Elements: Physics and Poetry in the 'Georgics'* (Princeton: Princeton University Press, 1987); and Richard F. Thomas, ed., *Virgil: Georgics*, 2 vols. (Cambridge: Cambridge University Press, 1988).

4 See Brooks Otis, *Virgil: A Study in Civilized Poetry* (Oxford: Clarendon Press, 1964); and Michael O'Loughlin, *The Garlands of Repose: The Literary Celebration of Civic and Retired Leisure: The Traditions of Homer and Vergil, Horace and Montaigne* (Chicago: University of Chicago Press, 1978).

5 Christine G. Perkell, *The Poet's Truth: A Study of the Poet in Virgil's 'Georgics'* (Berkeley: University of California Press, 1989), 16.

6 Gordon Williams, *Technique and Ideas in the 'Aeneid'* (New Haven: Yale University Press, 1983), 28–9.

7 *Ibid*; Kenneth Quinn, *Virgil's 'Aeneid': A Critical Description* (London: Routledge and Kegan Paul, 1968), 216.

8 David Vessey, *Statius and the Thebaid* (Cambridge: Cambridge University Press, 1973), 65.

9 See in particular Philip Hardie, *The Epic Successors of Virgil: A Study in the Dynamics of a Tradition* (Cambridge: Cambridge University Press 1993); and Randall T. Ganiban, *Statius and Virgil: The 'Thebaid' and the Re-interpretation of the 'Aeneid'* (Cambridge: Cambridge University Press, 2007).

10 Adapted from Peter Toohey, *Reading Epic: An Introduction to the Ancient Narratives* (London: Routledge, 1992), 9–10.

11 Peter Toohey, 'Jason, Pallas, and Domitian in Valerius Flaccus' *Argonautica*', in *Festschrift for Miroslav Marcovich*, ed. David Sansone, *Illinois Classical Studies* 18 (1993), 191–201.

12 E. Klebs, 'Zur Komposition von Petronius *Satirae*', *Philologus* 47 (1899), 623–35, cited in J. P. Sullivan, *The 'Satyricon' of Petronius: A Literary Study* (London: Faber and Faber, 1968), 92.

13 Jamie Masters, *Poetry and Civil War in Lucan's 'Bellum Civile'* (Cambridge: Cambridge University Press, 1992); see also John Henderson, *Fighting for Rome: Poets and Caesars, History and Civil War* (Cambridge: Cambridge University Press, 1998).

4

KARL REICHL

Heroic epic poetry in
the Middle Ages

In his biography of Charlemagne, Einhard (d. 840) speaks highly of the
emperor's educational programme and mentions among his achievements
that he ordered 'the age-old narrative poems, barbarous enough, it is true, in
which were celebrated the warlike deeds of the kings of ancient times' to be
written down and in this way preserved for posterity.[1] These native songs
from ancient times ('barbara et antiquissima carmina') were no doubt heroic
narrative songs in the vernacular, celebrating the deeds of past heroes and
ancestors. Almost 750 years earlier, in his *Germania*, the Roman historian
Tacitus had mentioned the 'ancient songs' of the Germanic peoples, which
according to him reached back into a mythic past and were their only kind of
historical tradition. Charlemagne's efforts to have these narrative songs
recorded in writing came at a time when native oral traditions were
still flourishing but when the predominant culture in the West was Latin,
Christian, and literate. Charlemagne, although illiterate himself, did much
for the spread of literacy, not least by gathering the leading minds of Latin
Christendom at his Palace School. One of them was Alcuin, an Englishman,
'the most learned man of his time' according to Einhard. In 797 Alcuin wrote
a letter to the bishop of Lindisfarne complaining that it had come to his notice
that the monks in the Northumbrian monastery preferred to listen to the
harpist singing vernacular heroic lays rather than to the reader of holy books
in their refectory. 'What has Ingeld to do with Christ?' he asks, and continues,
'The house of the Lord is narrow, it cannot hold both.'[2]

   Although the *Lay of Ingeld* has been lost, we have some evidence of the
heroic legend on which it must have been based from other sources, among
them the Old English epic of *Beowulf*. As to the manuscript of 'age-old
narrative poems' that Charlemagne had commissioned, it has, unfortunately, not come down to us. Some of Charlemagne's own scholars like
Alcuin were dubious about the worth of vernacular poetry, at least of a
heroic kind and in inappropriate contexts, and the Emperor's successor,
Louis the Pious, was openly opposed to pagan poetry. His ninth-century

biographer, Theganus, recorded that when minstrels and harpists made everybody laugh he never 'showed his white teeth in laughter'. Later in life he also disdained all the pagan songs he had learned in his youth. No wonder circumstances were adverse to the preservation of native heroic poetry.

There is another factor that explains the paucity of heroic poetry from the early Middle Ages. This type of poetry was, as a rule, oral. Only with the spread of literacy did it become possible to commit vernacular poetry to paper, or rather parchment, but even then it had to be thought worthy of recording in writing. Sometimes a space left empty on a page tempted a scribe to record a piece of vernacular poetry; sometimes a certain antiquarian interest on the part of a scribe prompted him to write down poetry which was otherwise transmitted only orally. Despite unfavourable conditions for the survival of heroic poetry, some texts have been preserved. They help us to gain an impression of the oldest stratum of medieval heroic poetry.

Germanic lay and *Poetic Edda*

Among the heroic songs salvaged from the Dark Ages is a poem of sixty-eight lines, in Old High German, extant in a ninth-century manuscript from Fulda. This is the *Hildebrandslied* (*Lay of Hildebrand*). Hildebrand, who had to flee from his country, returns after thirty years, together with a group of warriors, and is met at the border by his son Hadubrand and his men. Father and son do not know each other. When asked his name, Hadubrand reveals that his father Hildebrand had left him and his mother behind when he fled with Theoderic (Dietrich) from Odoacer's hatred to the realm of the Huns. Hildebrand says that Hadubrand has never talked to a more closely related man and indicates in this veiled manner that he is his father. When Hildebrand offers him golden rings as a present, Hadubrand spurns the gift, challenges Hildebrand and calls him a wily old Hun. Seafarers, he adds, told him that his father has lost his life in warfare: 'Dead is Hildebrand, Heribrand's son.' As Hadubrand refuses to recognize his father, Hildebrand has to prove his valour and take up Hadubrand's challenge. Soon after the beginning of the fight between father and son the poem breaks off. The lay is not only fragmentary at the end; there also seem to be lacunae, as well as transposed lines, in the transmitted text. Despite the truncated end, there can be no doubt that the poem ended tragically, with Hadubrand's death. This is implied by early references to the story, but also by parallels in other epic traditions.

The *Hildebrandslied* begins with the words 'Ik gihorta ðat seggen' (I heard it said).[3] This introductory line belongs to a common store of Germanic formulas. The Old English *Beowulf* begins with 'Truly, we have heard of the might of the Spear-Danes, of the kings of the people, in the days of yore', and the later *Nibelungenlied* still echoes this formula in its beginning verses: 'We have been told in old legends many wondrous things . . .' 'Saying' and 'hearing' suggest an oral tradition, which in the case of the *Hildebrandslied* can be safely assumed. The text of the poem, however, has been copied from a written version of the lay to the first and the last page of the manuscript (fols. 1^r and 76^v); its linguistic form attests to a complicated transmission history, probably going back to a poem in the Bavarian dialect of Old High German, which in turn might have originated among the Langobards of northern Italy.

The legendary background of the *Hildebrandslied* has become a favourite in Middle High German epic poetry, most notably in the poems of the Dietrich cycle. Dietrich of Bern (Verona) is the legendary transformation of the Ostrogoth King Theoderic (d. 526); while in history Theoderic wrested the rule over Italy from Odoacer and killed him in 493, the *Hildebrandslied* makes Theoderic flee from Odoacer. In the later Dietrich cycle, the place of Odoacer as Dietrich's enemy and usurper of his patrimony is taken by Ermanaric. Once again, history is twisted in legend. Ermanaric was King of the Ostrogoths, who committed suicide at the invasion of the Huns into his realm (*c.* 375). The epic cycle on Dietrich and his heroic deeds and adventures was very popular in medieval Germany; about a dozen poems, most of them composed in the thirteenth century, have been preserved. From North Germany the Dietrich legends also travelled to Scandinavia, where they were translated in the *Thidrekssaga* during the reign of the Norwegian King Håkon (1217–63). King Ermanaric makes a late appearance in a (Middle) Low German ballad, which was published in 1560 (*Ermenrikes Dot*). Its subject is Dietrich's march to Ermanaric's stronghold with eleven valiant companions and Ermanaric's death at Dietrich's hands.

In its treatment of historical and legendary material the *Hildebrandslied* is typical of Germanic heroic poetry. The poem refers to historical personages and events that go back to the period of migrations (fourth to sixth centuries), which has often been termed (by H. M. Chadwick, among others) the Germanic heroic age. History, however, is transformed, and what historical basis there might be for the characters or actions of heroic epic and song has become transmuted by the workings of oral tradition, legend building, myth making, and poetic licence. Folklorists and students of oral tradition have commented on this process of change. Mircea Eliade has pointed this out repeatedly; he writes on one occasion: 'The historical personage is assimilated to his archetypal model (the Hero, the Adversary), while the event is integrated into the category of mythic Deeds (fight against the monster, hostile brothers etc.).'[4]

In the *Hildebrandslied* the 'mythic pattern' into which the action has been integrated is the fight between father and son. This motif is probably best known in its Persian form, found in the *Shah-nama* of Ferdowsi (completed *c.* 1010). The tragic fight between Rustam and his son Sohrab has been made familiar to English readers by Matthew Arnold's 'Sohrab and Rustum'. Arnold follows the course of events of Ferdowsi's epic: as the Persian and Turanian armies confront one another, Sohrab volunteers to fight single-handedly against any Persian hero, in order to demonstrate his prowess and impress his father, whom he has never met and who is unaware of having a son among the Turanians. Rustam takes up the challenge without announcing his identity. Only after he has dealt the fatal blow does he realize to his immense sorrow that he has killed his own son. Other versions of this motif – most notably the Irish saga of Cúchulain's fight with his son and the Russian *bylina* (epic narrative) of the duel of Ilya Muromets with his son – show a similar tragic situation: neither father nor son realizes against whom they are fighting until it is too late. Here the *Hildebrandslied* is harsher and uncompromising to the point of cruelty. Hildebrand knows that he is fighting against his son and that the outcome will be fatal to one of them. We are in the presence of an archaic ethos which puts a code of values such as the duty to answer a challenge or to avenge an insult above all considerations of pity or love. We meet this ethos also in the heroic songs of the Old Norse *Poetic Edda*, in many Icelandic sagas, and in the Middle High German *Nibelungenlied*. It is to be noted that this attitude was later felt to be unbearable. The re-telling of the story, both in the *Thidrekssaga* and in the *Later Hildebrandslied*, a ballad preserved in sixteenth-century broadsides, ends happily with a recognition scene.

The *Hildebrandslied* gives a good idea of the style of the Germanic heroic lay. After the introductory formula the initial situation is sketched in a few lines: father and son oppose one another and, clad in their armour, are ready to do battle. Hildebrand asks for the young man's descent and, when he is answered, realizes that he is facing his own son. The action unfolds in the form of a dialogue, which is punctuated by formulaic phrases like 'Hadubrant gimahalta, Hiltibrantes sunu' or 'Hiltibrant gimahlata, Heribrantes suno' (Hadubrand/Hildebrand spoke, Hildebrand's/Heribrand's son), phrasepatterns which are also found in other Germanic traditions, most notably in the Old English epic of *Beowulf*. It is only at the end of the fragment, when the fierce fight between the two warriors is described, that third-person narrative resumes. This mixture of narration and dialogue is typical of the Germanic heroic lay (called 'doppelseitiges Ereignislied', 'double-faced lay of action', by Andreas Heusler), as are the swift narrative pace and the focusing on a situation of conflict.[5]

The heroic lay can be assumed to have been a form of heroic poetry that was common to all Germanic peoples. Outside Scandinavia it is only scantily preserved. Apart from the *Hildebrandslied* another representative of this genre is the *Lay of Finnsburh* in Old English. This song is interesting in that we have, in addition to a fragmentary poem of forty-eight lines, an episode in the epic of *Beowulf* that describes a performance context for this type of poetry. When Beowulf's victory over the monster Grendel is celebrated during a feast in King Hrothgar's hall, the king's *scop* or professional 'singer of tales' gets up and recites (probably to the accompaniment of the Germanic lyre) the *Lay of Finnsburh*. Like the *Hildebrandslied*, this is a dark tale of manslaughter and revenge. Although there are many unclear elements in the story, the basic plot is fairly straightforward. While the Danish chieftain Hnæf is on a visit to his sister Hildeburh, who is married to the Frisian King Finn, the Danes are attacked and Hnæf is killed. Among the victims of the ensuing fight is Hildeburh's son. A truce is agreed upon between Finn and the new Danish leader Hengest, but fighting breaks out again in the following spring and the conflict ends with the Danes' victory and Finn's death. Together with a rich booty, Hildeburh – who has lost her husband, her son, and her brother – is taken back by the Danes. The episode in *Beowulf* stresses Hildeburh's grief, but highlights also the role of Hengest with his dual obligation of keeping the treaty with Finn and revenging the death of his lord. The *Lay of Finnsburh* has therefore been interpreted as the tragedy of Hengest, but the textual evidence is unfortunately too uncertain to warrant such an interpretation.

The majority of heroic songs in an Older Germanic tongue are found in the *Poetic Edda*. Of the twenty-nine items in the famous Codex Regius (since 1971 kept in Reykjavik) eleven are devoted to topics of Germanic mythology and the rest to heroic legend. The manuscript is dated to about 1270, but many of its texts are of considerably older age. The precise dating and textual history of the various poems have been much discussed; it is generally assumed that the composition of the Eddic poems ranges from before 850 to well into the thirteenth century. A few additional heroic lays are also found in other manuscripts or can be extracted from sagas and other sources. A total of about two dozen Eddic heroic lays have come down to us, some in fragmentary form and some mixed with prose passages, generally of an explanatory nature.

The denomination of the collection of poems in the Codex Regius as *Edda* is due to a misunderstanding. Snorri Sturluson wrote (between about 1210 and 1230) a prose work entitled *Edda*, which consists of a mythological commentary (*Gylfaginning*), a treatise on the diction of skaldic poetry (*Skáldskaparmál*), and a description of Old Norse metres (*Háttatal*).

When the Codex Regius was discovered in 1643, it was wrongly believed that this was the poetical source for Snorri's book and the collection of poems was hence also called 'Edda'. This word is somewhat of a puzzle; it means 'great-grandmother' in Old Norse, but other etymologies have also been suggested, such as a derivation from Latin *ēdere* 'to bring forth, tell, utter'.

The Eddic poems are of varying length, some comprising less than a hundred (long) lines, others around two hundred lines; the *Greenland Lay of Atli* (*Atlamál*) is exceptional in running to almost four hundred lines. Eddic poetry – as distinct from the *Hildebrandslied* or Old English poetry – is strophic, with stanzas generally consisting of four long lines in the alliterative metre of early Germanic poetry. In its simplest and most regular form, a long line is made up of two half-lines; both halves have two stressed syllables and an irregular number of unstressed syllables (sometimes also syllables with a secondary stress). The initial sound of the first stressed syllable of the second half-line defines the alliteration of the line; it alliterates with one or both stressed syllables of the first half-line. The respective consonants alliterate with one another as well as any vowel with any other vowel. The third line of the *Hildebrandslied* can serve as an example:

> Híltibrant enti Háðubrant   untar hériun tuém
> (Hildebrand and Hadubrand   between two hosts)

Here every half-line has two stressed syllables (marked by an accent) and the alliterating sound is /h/ (doubly underlined). According to the sequence of stressed and unstressed syllables, various patterns can be distinguished. Although, when looked at in detail, Germanic metre presents a great number of complexities and correspondingly different interpretations, the five basic metrical patterns of the half-line elaborated by Eduard Sievers are still widely employed (with refinements) in the analysis of Germanic metre. These types can be recognized most clearly in Old English poetry and in the Eddic poems composed in the metre called *fornyrðislag*, which is used in most of the heroic lays. Other metres are, however, also found in Eddic as well as in skaldic poetry.

Although there are a number of poems on Scandinavian heroes, such as the Helgi poems (*Helgakviða Hundingsbana* I and II, *Helgakviða Hjörvarðssonar*), the subject matter of the majority of the Eddic heroic lays is taken from the South Germanic legendary tradition, in particular the legends that lie at the basis of the later *Nibelungenlied*. The last act of the drama of the Burgundians' fall is enacted in two poems bearing the name of Atli (Attila), the ruler of the Huns. The shorter and earlier *Lay of Atli* (*Atlakviða*) begins with a messenger sent by Atli to Gunnar to invite him to the land of the Huns to receive treasure. Gunnar despises the offer and ignores the warning sent by his sister Guðrún, married to the king of the Huns. He rides with his brother Högni to Atli's realm, where they are attacked and made prisoners by Atli. Gunnar is promised his life if he reveals the whereabouts of the Burgundian gold. He stipulates that Högni's heart be ripped out in order that no one share the secret of the gold's hiding place. At first the heart of Hjall is presented to Gunnar, who recognizes it as the heart of a coward. When Högni's heart is shown to Gunnar, he refuses to reveal the secret. Gunnar is thrown into a snake pit, where he faces death with courage, playing his harp defiantly. The lay ends with Guðrún's revenge of the death of her brothers: she kills her two sons and offers their hearts as food to their father, Atli. Then she kills Atli and sets fire to his residence, destroying everything in her reckless hatred.

The tale is told in a mixture of direct speech, put into the mouths of the protagonists, and third-person narration, the latter comprising somewhat over half of the poem; it is, like the *Hildebrandlied* a 'double-faced lay of action'. Another characteristic trait of the *Lay of Atli* is the concentration of the action on a decisive moment. The lay gives virtually no background information; it is assumed that the audience know not only who the characters are but also why they act in the way they do. The lack of circumstantial description, the allusive narration, and the focus on a critical situation endow these heroic lays with a tense and highly dramatic quality. Stylistically, the lays of the *Poetic Edda* exhibit a certain soberness, especially when compared to the polished style of skaldic poetry. Metaphors (*kenningar*) and epithets are used sparingly and there is little enjambement between the alliterative long lines.

While the 'doppelseitiges Ereignislied' can be considered the common form of the Germanic heroic lay, other subgenres of the lay are also found in Old Norse. Two examples will have to suffice. *Brynhild's Ride to Hel* (*Helreið Brynhildar*) is introduced by a short prose passage explaining that after their death Sigurd and Brynhild were burnt on two pyres. Brynhild's had a chariot, on which she rode to Hel (the Germanic Hades). On her way she encounters a giantess, who accuses her of having been the cause of Gunnar's and his brothers' death. In the remaining eleven stanzas of the poem Brynhild defends herself by telling her story. We find a similar account of a heroine's life in one of the Guðrún poems (*Guðrúnarkviða* II), where, after Gunnar's and Högni's death at Atli's court, Guðrún surveys her life in a long monologue. These retrospective poems, in which a hero or heroine's life is passed in review, are sometimes close in tone to laments, as when in another lay Guðrún grieves over Sigurd's death (*Guðrúnarkviða* I). Although these subgenres of the heroic lay are found only in Scandinavia, the elegiac mood characteristic of a number of Eddic poems also imbues the elegiac passages of *Beowulf* and the Old English elegies. There are, in fact, strong arguments in favour of the view that, in addition to the heroic lay, the elegy also belongs to the common heritage of Germanic poetic genres.

Beowulf and the heroic epic

This is not the case with the epic. Extended verse narratives – which in scope and style can be called 'epics' – have flourished only in Anglo-Saxon England. While there are a number of Old English epics on biblical and hagiographic topics, only one secular epic has survived the ravages of time, the epic of *Beowulf*. The text, comprising over three thousand alliterative long lines, is preserved in a manuscript dating from the beginning of the eleventh century (British Library, MS Cotton Vitellius A.xv). In the first two-thirds of the poem, the action takes place in the Danish King Hrothgar's court, where after dark a monster, Grendel by name, causes havoc in Heorot, the king's mead-hall, and kills the king's thanes, so that the hall has to be emptied at night. Beowulf, a young Geatish hero, comes to the king's rescue; he arrives with fourteen companions by sea from the land of the Geats (in southern Sweden). Beowulf wrestles with Grendel when the monster attacks the mead-hall after nightfall and wounds him mortally by pulling out his arm. His victory is celebrated on the next day, and after the feast the thanes spend the night again in Heorot. Their tribulations, however, are not yet over, as another monster makes its appearance, Grendel's mother, who takes revenge for Gendel's death by killing a Danish warrior and dragging him to her abode in a nearby mere. On the following day Beowulf follows her tracks, dives down into the mere and in the course of a fierce fight in an underwater cave manages to kill Grendel's mother with the help of a miraculous sword. Beowulf returns in triumph to the Danish court, is richly rewarded, and sets out on his journey home, where he reports his exploits at the Danish court to King Hygelac. In the last third of the epic, the narrative focuses on Beowulf's final battle. After the death of King Hygelac in the course of a raid among the Franks, Beowulf, Hygelac's nephew, becomes king of the Geats and reigns for fifty years in peace. Then suddenly a dragon, accidentally provoked by the theft of a vessel that belonged to the treasure he was guarding, begins to ravage the country with his fiery breath. Beowulf does battle with the dragon; with the help of Wiglaf, his loyal retainer, he manages to give the dragon the deathblow with his sword, but is mortally wounded nevertheless. The epic ends with Beowulf's funeral: a pyre is erected, on which Beowulf is burnt, then a mound is built on a promontory, in which Beowulf's ashes, together with the contents of the dragon's hoard, are buried. Twelve warriors ride round the mound, praise the hero's deeds of prowess and lament their lord's demise. The poem ends:

cwǣdon þæt he wǣre wyruldcyning[a]
manna mildust ond mon(ðw)ǣrust,
lēodum līðost ond lofgeornost.
(They said that he was of all the kings on earth / the mildest and kindest man, / most gracious to his people and the most eager to win fame.)[6]

Bare as this outline of the plot is, it nevertheless indicates a number of peculiarities of this epic. One is that the main protagonist rises to heroic stature by his fights against monsters and dragons. This is at odds with other Germanic heroic poetry, where the action generally centres on human conflicts and the fighting takes place among warriors. There is, in fact, plenty of this also in *Beowulf*, not in the main plot, but as incidents that are either only alluded to or form a subordinate part in the development of the story. The *Lay of Finnsburh*, which is performed by the king's *scop* during the festivities after Beowulf's victory over Grendel, is one of these 'digressions' in *Beowulf*. The tragic *Lay of Ingeld*, which, according to Alcuin, the monks of Lindisfarne preferred to more suitable spiritual nourishment, is alluded to in Beowulf's report to Hygelac, when he mentions the intended marriage of King Hrothgar's daughter to the Heathobard chieftain Ingeld in order to bring peace between the two peoples: a peace, Beowulf correctly foresees, that might be of only short duration. Hygelac's Frankish expedition, in which Beowulf also took part and excelled as warrior, is repeatedly mentioned. Other references to Germanic heroic legend appear also, but they stay very much on the periphery of the action. Some older scholars have regretted this shift in emphasis, aptly expressed by W. P. Ker, who complained about the epic's 'disproportion that puts the irrelevances in the centre and the serious things on the outer edges'.[7] Scholarly opinion has since changed. In an influential paper, first published in 1936, J. R. R. Tolkien not only took previous critics of the poem to task but also pleaded for an understanding of the epic as a literary work in which the monsters and dragons are not what Ker termed 'irrelevances': 'the monsters are not an inexplicable blunder of taste; they are essential, fundamentally allied to the underlying ideas of the poem, which give it its lofty tone and high seriousness', symbolizing the threat of death, disaster, and the forces of evil.[8] By the same token, the numerous deflections from the progression of the narrative, which have been collectively labelled as 'digressions', have in the wake of Tolkien's paper been reinterpreted as elements that enrich the epic by adding detail, depth, and a network of allusions to the legendary past. In a long tradition of close reading the epic has come to be viewed as a carefully crafted and subtle work of poetry.

A second distinctive mark of the epic easily recognizable in the summary above is its division into two quite separate parts: heroic deeds at the beginning of Beowulf's career and a final and fatal encounter with a fearsome adversary in old age. In the nineteenth century, when the analysts' view among Homerists was gaining weight (i.e. the belief that the *Iliad* and the *Odyssey* could be seen as composed of smaller heroic songs), the Old English *Beowulf* was similarly thought to have arisen by a concatenation of individual heroic lays by the proponents of the so-called 'Liedertheorie' (theory of songs). The bi-partite structure of the epic seems to support such a view. In fact, scholars have argued that the first part really consists of two lays, one told by the narrating voice, the other (with some differences from the first) by Beowulf himself when he informs Hygelac of his adventures in Denmark (lines 2000–151). Furthermore, there can be no doubt that *Beowulf* in its present form is impregnated with Christian ideas, ideas that seem to jar with the pagan past evoked in the epic. The narrator tells us that the Danes implored their heathen gods' help against Grendel with sacrifices (lines 174–82), but he lets Beowulf tell Hrothgar that at the critical moment when Grendel's mother was about to kill him he was 'shielded by God', the 'Ruler of men', who let him see a miraculous sword hanging on the wall (lines 1658–61). No doubt, terms like 'Ruler of men' refer here, as in many other places in the epic, to the Christian God. The early enthusiasts of the 'Liedertheorie' were busy cutting out all Christian elements in the epic, but with doubtful results. Readers of the epic have come to realize that the poem as we have it, whatever its prehistory, is the composition of a Christian rather than a pagan Anglo-Saxon. Furthermore, however tenuous the unity of the two parts of the epic, in the absence of any other versions *Beowulf* has to be read and interpreted as one poem, in accordance with the text the manuscript transmits.

There is a corollary to the Christian elements in *Beowulf*; it cannot have been composed in its present form before the Anglo-Saxons were Christianized. While this would allow a seventh-century date, it has been proposed (most convincingly by Dorothy Whitelock) that the eighth century, when Christianity had already taken firm roots, is more likely than the seventh. There might, of course, be a prehistory to our version of *Beowulf*. However, even for such earlier epic tales of Beowulf there is an earliest date. King Hygelac has been identified in medieval historiographic works as a Scandinavian king who lost his life in a raid against the Franks in 521. Clearly, the legend of Beowulf can only have originated after that date.

In recent years a number of scholars have advocated a late date of *Beowulf*, placing the composition of the epic in the tenth century. A great number of arguments have been presented for both an early and a late date of the epic, but the nature of the evidence is such that no proposal has as yet found universal acceptance. Should the epic have been composed as late as the tenth century, possibly motivated by an antiquarian interest, it is nevertheless true that in its orientation it is clearly directed towards the Germanic heroic past and that it has in language and diction preserved many archaic elements.

With regard to epithets and poetic diction, as early as 1912 H. M. Chadwick drew attention to many striking parallels between *Beowulf* and the Homeric epics. The Homeric metaphors for kings, for example, 'poimēn laōn' (the shepherd of peoples) and 'herkos Akhaiōn' (the protector of the Achaeans), are mirrored in 'folces hyrde' (the shepherd of the people) and 'eodor Scyldinga' (the protector of the Scyldings (Danes)).[9] Pervasive stylistic traits of *Beowulf* are the use of compounds, many found only in poetry, of formulaic diction and variation. The first three lines of the epic can illustrate these:

> Hwæt, wē Gār-Dena   in ġeārdagum,
> þēodcyninga   þrym ġefrūnon,
> hū ðā æþelingas   ellen fremedon.
> (Truly, we have heard of the might of the Spear-Danes, / of the kings of the people, in the days of yore, / how the noble men performed deeds of valour.)

The elements making up the three compounds of these lines are found in various combinations; to take just 'þēodcyning' (people's king) as an example: 'cyning' is combined with 'beorn', 'eorð', 'folc', 'lēod', 'gūð', 'hēah', 'sǣ', 'worold', 'sōð', and 'wuldur' in *Beowulf*, yielding nominal compounds meaning 'hero-king', 'king of the land', 'folk-king', 'people's king', 'battle-king', 'high-king', 'sea-king', 'earthly king', 'king of truth', and 'king of glory', with 'sōð-cyning' and 'wuldur-cyning' referring to God rather than to a worldly king. Similarly 'þēod' (people) is found in various compounds such as 'sige-þēod' ('victorious people') or 'wer-þēod' ('people of men'). Some of the compounds are metaphoric, usually classified as *kenningar*, such as 'swan-rād' ('swan-road') or 'hron-rād' ('whale-road') for the sea, or 'beado-lēoma' or 'hilde-lēoma' ('battle-light') for the (flashing) sword. The opening lines of *Beowulf* also furnish an illustration of variation, defined as 'syntactically parallel words or word-groups which share a common referent and which occur within a single clause'.[10] In the second line the 'kings of the people' is an alternative expression of the 'Spear-Danes' in the first line; similarly the third line is a varying repetition of the preceding idea. The frequent use of compounds in combination with variation (and also parenthetical structures) gives *Beowulf* a slow-moving pace which accords well with the epic breadth unfolded in the narrative, with its speeches, dialogues, and elaborate scenes.

The first lines are also formulaic. Within the corpus of Old English poetry (about 30,000 lines), we find similar lines for instance in *Andreas*, a saint's legend in epic form: 'Hwæt! We gefrunan on fyrndagum' (Truly, we have heard in the days of yore), and in the biblical epic *Exodus*: 'Hwæt! We feor and neah gefrigen habað' (Truly, we have heard far and near).[11] Formulas have long been recognized as constitutive elements of Germanic poetry, but only with the comparative studies of Milman Parry and Albert B. Lord has formulaic analysis been rigorously applied to epic poetry such as *Beowulf*.[12] In their studies of South Slavic oral epic poetry, Parry and Lord had noticed that these poems were highly formulaic and they came to the conclusion that the ability of the *guslari* (epic singers) to perform long epics was not actually based on memorization but rather on their skill to manipulate formulaic lines as well as formulaic motifs and scenes (called 'themes'). This enabled a narrator to sing an epic without hesitation or interruption, even when the memory failed him, and to lengthen or shorten his performance as the occasion demanded. Although formulaic diction is typical of oral epics – at least of many traditions of oral epic poetry – it is no certain indication of orality in the case of *Beowulf* and other medieval epic poetry that might be suspected of having flourished in an oral milieu. It can be shown that practically all Old English poetry is highly formulaic, even when it is demonstrably 'un-oral', as in the case of the Old English translations of the poems in Boethius's *Consolation of Philosophy*.

While there is no proof that *Beowulf* is basically a representative of oral poetry, there is equally no proof that *Beowulf* belongs to the sphere of written literature. The latter has been affirmed by such eminent Germanists as Andreas Heusler, who was of the opinion that only the heroic lay is the common heritage of the Germanic peoples; the heroic epic is an Anglo-Saxon invention, which came about through the influence of written epics such as Virgil's *Aeneid*. For Heusler, *Beowulf* and the various Old English hagiographical and biblical epic poems (*Andreas*, *Juliana*, *Genesis*, *Exodus*, *Judith*, etc.) were 'Buchepen' (book epics), works of written literature. Parallels to the *Aeneid* have indeed been spotted in *Beowulf*, and it is not unlikely that at some stage in the process of putting the poem on parchment (and transmitting the poem in writing) Virgilian echoes might have occurred to some learned scribe and possibly been amplified in scribal changes or additions. But this is not to say that the genre of the epic owes its origin to the influence of Virgil. As can be seen in the well-studied case of South

Slavic oral epic poetry, linguistically closely related traditions such as those of the Croats, Serbs, Montenegrins, and Bosnians, share a common heritage but also go their separate ways. Only among the Bosnians have longer narrative poems of epic breadth been composed orally, while in other South Slavic traditions shorter heroic songs (*junačke pjesme*) are sung, poems more on the scale of the heroic lay rather than the heroic epic. There is no reason to suppose that the Anglo-Saxon epic genius could have come about only through the influence of written epics.

However one interprets pointers towards orality (such as formulaic diction) or towards literacy (such as possible Virgilian echoes) in *Beowulf*, a scenario for a purely oral composition of the epic in its present form is just as difficult to substantiate as one for a composition with pen (or quill) in hand. It can be argued that behind the text in the Vitellius manuscript there lies some process of written transmission, although for how long and with what textual changes is unclear. The role scribes have played in the written transmission of the epic is controversial, in particular that of the second scribe of the manuscript text (thought by some to have been responsible for the final redaction of the poem). Although we cannot be sure of the extent to which the epic as we have it has undergone scribal changes in the course of time, most scholars see the epic in its transmitted form as the creation of a poet rather than the result of purely scribal combination, redaction, revision, or adaptation. When speaking about *Beowulf* we also speak about the *Beowulf* poet, however difficult the idea of an 'author' is, especially in the case of traditional poetry and not only from the point of view of modern critical theory. In an 'oralist scenario' we can imagine this poet to have been a traditional *scop*, though Christianized, who might have dictated his poem somewhat like the illiterate Caedmon, who according to Bede's account had been divinely inspired to become a poet and orally composed biblical epics on the basis of the stories told him, to be written down by literate monks. Although the view of *Beowulf* as an 'oral-derived' text can be defended, it is nevertheless clear that the epic is not a transcript of an oral performance, but has in the processes of being written down become both 'lettered' and literature. Textualization has eliminated the performance aspect of oral poetry, which can at most be imagined, as when the epic talks about the 'clear song of the *scop*' performing in the hall ('swutol sang scopes', line 90). In a written text, subtle textual relationships between different parts of the epics can be explored, which in an oral performance context would be inaccessible.

Beowulf criticism in the past decades has concentrated on interpreting *Beowulf* as a work of literature, a text of 'unlimited semiosis', as one critic has put it.[13] Doubts, however, have also been raised as to whether such an approach does justice to the poem. As early as 1965 Kenneth Sisam pointed out how an understanding of *Beowulf* as an orally composed and performed poem can throw light on inconsistencies in our text.[14] An oral poet focuses on the scene at hand, elaborating details that on another occasion might be omitted or presented at variance with the previous scene. Grendel is said to have had a *glof*, some kind of bag, for his booty in Beowulf's report, but no *glof* is mentioned in the actual fights. Hrothgar's daughter Freawaru is not present in the elaborate descriptions of the two banquets held at Heorot, but she plays an important role in Beowulf's account of his adventures among the Danes. Shifts of emphasis and variations of this kind seem to point to the composition of the epic in an oral milieu. Although such an oral milieu has been explored in a number of studies, both within and outside the framework of Parry's and Lord's oral theory, the absence of uncontroversial oral clues and in particular of other versions and variants of the epic leaves the oral background to *Beowulf*, which can certainly be presupposed, much vaguer than we would wish. On the other hand, if we imagine the *Beowulf* poet to have been a poet with antiquarian interests, who used traditional poetic material and style to tell his tale, his imitation of the oral epic was in its overall effect so successful that we might feel entitled to take *Beowulf* nevertheless as a good representative of the *scop*'s art.

There is one more interpretational problem I would like to touch upon briefly. With Alcuin, who asked what Ingeld had to do with Christ, we might ask what Beowulf has to do with England. Beowulf is a Geat, and the action of the epic takes place in Scandinavia. It is true that legends of the Germanic past circulated among different Germanic peoples; as pointed out above, a great number of the Old Norse heroic lays treat of South Germanic heroes and legends. There are, however, also heroic epics that celebrate most specifically the past of one's own ethnic or 'national' group; the *Chanson de Roland* is such an epic. Germanic heroic poetry has on the whole not been 'tribal' or 'national' in this sense. Nevertheless, there are links between *Beowulf* and Anglo-Saxon culture. One somewhat puzzling link is the inclusion of a number of Danish kings, also mentioned in *Beowulf*, in the West Saxon genealogies. Given Beowulf's closeness to King Hrothgar's heart and hence to the Danish royal line, it has been thought that an Anglo-Saxon audience could see in Beowulf one of their heroes, despite his being a Geat. This would make *Beowulf* into a formative epic, that is, an epic in which an answer is attempted to the question 'who are we?' While such an interpretation is tenuous, there can be little doubt that *Beowulf* can be viewed as a normative epic, a narrative in which the values of heroic behaviour are presented within the cultural value system of the society depicted in the epic. How far these values apply to the society the audience belongs to, however, has been answered very differently, depending on many variables, of which date and manner of composition are only two.

Later heroic epic poetry

In medieval Europe, heroic epic poetry is not confined to works composed in the older Germanic languages. There is a rich epic tradition in the Romance languages as well as in Middle High German. Heroic epics have also been composed in Latin, such as *Waltharius*, a ninth- or tenth-century epic about Walther of Aquitaine, who flees with Hildegund from Attila's court and on his way home has to fight against Hagen and Gunther's men. The topic is clearly related to the *Nibelungen* legend; interestingly, fragments from an Old English epic on the same subject (*Waldere*) have also been preserved. Closest to the heroic spirit are a number of historical Latin epics, such as the eleventh-century *Carmen de Hastingae proelio*, a poem on the battle of Hastings (1066), or the crusade epic by Henry of Pisa on the expedition of the Pisans to the Balearic Islands in 1114–15 (*Liber Maiorichinus*). Space does not permit a discussion of these epics; I will have to confine myself to a few very sketchy remarks.

While the Germanic heroic legends left virtually no trace in the Middle English romances, they survived in a flourishing epic poetry in Middle High German, of which the *Nibelungenlied* is doubtless the most accomplished and best-known representative. The *Nibelungenlied* was composed around 1200. It is extant in three versions in over thirty manuscripts (including fragments) and comprises thirty-nine *aventiuren* (episodes), running to a total of well over two thousand four-line stanzas (*Nibelungen* strophes). The *Nibelungenlied* develops legendary traditions which also lie at the basis of various poems of the *Poetic Edda* (among them *Atlamál*, *Atlakviða*, *Helreið Brynhildar*, and *Guðrúnarkviða* mentioned above) and has as ultimate historical nuclei events such as the victory of the Huns over the Burgundians in 436 and the annihilation of the Bugundians by the Franks in 538. It is the tale of Siegfried's (Old Norse Sigurd) treacherous murder, his wife's Kriemhilt's (Old Norse Guðrún) second marriage to Etzel (Attila) and the final act of vengeance, in the course of which Kriemhilt's brothers and her husband's murderer, Hagen, find their gruesome death at Etzel's court. In the inexorability of its dénouement this Middle High German epic is a glorification of the heroic ethos as it is familiar from the poems of the *Poetic Edda*; but it is also imbued with the new spirit of courtly romance, which finds expression in the soundings of the protagonists' feelings and in the courtly behaviour and ritual prevailing at the Burgundian court and in the castle of Ruedeger of Bechelaren on the Burgundians' way to Etzel's stronghold. In harking back to an older Germanic world and yet incorporating certain aspects of the chivalric code, the *Nibelungenlied* stands at the crossroads not only of poetic styles and conceptualizations but also of traditions. It is incontestable that the *Nibelungenlied* arises from a milieu of oral tradition, but it is also clear that the form of the epic as we have it is due to a process of literate composition.

Medieval French heroic poetry is represented by about one hundred *chansons de geste*, narrative poems, comprising between 1,000 and 20,000 lines, of which some are extant only in fragmentary form, others in over a dozen manuscripts, some also in different versions and redactions. Following medieval custom they are generally grouped into cycles, one of the cycles being the *Geste du Roi*, the Carolingian cycle, to which the *Chanson de Roland* belongs. The *chansons de geste* are as a rule composed in verses of ten syllables, which are arranged into *laisses*, stanzas of unequal length. The binding principle of these *laisses* is assonance, an imperfect 'rhyme' with identical vowels but not necessarily identical consonants (as in e.g. 'pai*ens*: cheval*er*'). Other metrical forms are also found, but these are generally later developments. The *chanson de geste* was not confined to the strictly French-speaking area; there are *chansons de geste* also in Provençal and Franco-Provençal, and the genre was particularly popular in northern Italy, from where a great number of Franco-Italian poems have been preserved. *Chansons de geste* were imitated in Italian, Welsh, Middle English, and Middle High German; there is also a thirteenth-century prose translation of the Carolingian cycle into Old Norse, the *Karlamagnus saga*.

The earliest recorded *chanson de geste* is the *Chanson de Roland*. It is found in MS Digby 23 of the Bodleian Library, Oxford; the manuscript was written by an Anglo-Norman scribe in the twelfth century (probably the second quarter of the century). In about 4,000 lines the *Chanson de Roland* tells the story of Charlemagne's Spanish campaign and the death of Roland and the other Twelve Peers. Within seven years, Charles has wrested Spain from Arabic dominion with the exception of Saragossa under King Marsile. In order to avoid defeat, Marsile sends an embassy with presents to the emperor, treacherously promising to come to Aix-la-Chapelle to accept the Christian faith. When Roland advises that the military campaign is continued – while his stepfather, Ganelon, advocates a peace treaty – a heated debate breaks out, in which, on Roland's suggestion, Ganelon is chosen as messenger. Angered, Ganelon is ready to plot Roland's death with Marsile. He returns from Saragossa with rich presents and confirms Marsile's good intentions. Despite a portentous dream, the Emperor departs with his army for France, while on Ganelon's advice Roland is made the commander of the rearguard. In Roncevaux Roland and his companions are attacked by an overwhelming majority of Marsile's soldiers. Oliver urges Roland to blow his horn in order to call back the Emperor, but Roland refuses:

> Oliver said: 'The pagans have a huge army,
> Our French, it seems to me, are in mighty small number!
> Comrade Roland, do sound your horn,
> Charles will hear it and the army will turn back'.
> Roland replies: 'I would be behaving like a fool!
> I would lose my good name in fair France.
> I shall immediately strike great blows with Durendal,
> Its blade will be bloody up to the golden hilt.
> The vile pagans shall rue the day they came to the pass,
> I swear to you, all are condemned to death'.[15]

Their situation, however, is hopeless. When Roland finally blows his horn it is too late. The *douze pairs* with Roland, Oliver, the Archbishop Turpin, and all the others perish, and when Charles returns he can only lament their death. By divine intervention the sun halts his course so that the Emperor can take vengeance on Marsile's army; only Marsile escapes to Saragossa. Meanwhile, however, a new foe has arisen for Charles: Baligant, the Emir of Babylon, with his innumerable host. A fierce battle ensues, which is finally decided in a duel between Charlemagne and Baligant. Charles is victorious and the pagans are utterly defeated. In the last three hundred lines, the tale is brought to a conclusion with Charlemagne's return to Aix-la-Chapelle, where Belle Aude, Roland's betrothed, dies of grief when she hears the sad news, where Ganelon is tried for treason and executed, where Bramimonde, King Marsile's wife, is baptized, and where the emperor has yet another dream, admonishing him to further exploits for the Christian cause:

> The Emperor would rather not go there:
> 'God!' said the King, 'my life is so full of suffering!'
> His eyes are brimming with tears, he tugs his white beard.
> Here ends the story that Turoldus tells.[16]

The *Chanson de Roland* is unanimously seen as the *chef-d'œuvre* of French heroic epic poetry. The action unfolds in a series of carefully elaborated scenes, in which the protagonists are precisely modelled by their words, gestures, and deeds. A number of scenes consist of 'parallel *laisses*', in which words and phrases are repeated and varied from one stanza to the next. Although typical traits characterize the Ruler, the Enemy, and the Hero, the various actors in this drama of treachery, bravery and vengeance are clearly presented as individuals. This is especially true of Roland and Oliver, the former a hotspur, impulsive in his feelings and their expression (as when he laughs scornfully when Ganelon drops the glove Charlemagne gives him) and always ready to do battle and risk his life. Oliver, on the other hand, is thoughtful and far-sighted; he tries to moderate his friend and avoid disaster by urging him to a more prudent behaviour. In the *Chanson de Roland* this contrast of character is summarized in the line: 'Rollant est proz e Oliver est sage' (Roland is worthy and Oliver is wise) (line 1093). Some of the scenes show great dramatic intensity, especially the scene when Roland finally blows his horn and his temples burst with the effort. As A. T. Hatto has stressed, this type of scene is found in the heroic poetry of many traditions: 'Epic poetry is apt to condense long-drawn tensions into brief scenes of dramatic power enhanced by visual magnificence, that is "epic moments"... That such moments do not need to be the result of fine writing is amply shown by the occurrence of similar passages, comparably situated, in oral epic.'[17]

Although the *Chanson de Roland* is not a historical account of Charlemagne's Spanish campaign, there is a historical event that must have inspired the legend: the Basque ambush of 15 August 778, also recorded by Einhard, from whose *Life of Charlemagne* I quoted at the beginning of this chapter. It is difficult to trace the development of the legend from the historical event to the full-blown epic, although there is at least some evidence for intermediary stages. Clearly an oral tradition lies behind the genesis of the *Chanson de Roland*. As in the case of *Beowulf* or the *Nibelungenlied* there is a voluminous literature on the controversial question of the extent to which the *Chanson de Roland* is 'oral': destined for oral performance, orally transmitted, or even orally composed. Extreme positions have been maintained and no proofs acceptable to all parties can be proffered; nevertheless there is an understanding among most scholars that the *Chanson de Roland*, like the *chanson de geste* in general, was destined for oral performance and was part of a minstrel's or jongleur's repertoire. By the same token, these oral epics have not only been written down by scribes but in a number of cases also composed by literate authors. Whether Turoldus of the last line of the *Chanson de Roland* was the poem's author, scribe or performer is a moot question. Whatever the role of an author in the composition of the *Chanson de Roland*, the result is a poem firmly grounded in the art of the jongleur. About one aspect of this art we have more information than in other epic traditions. Both on account of the commentary on the musical performance of the jongleur in a medieval treatise of the thirteenth century (by John de Groccheo), and with the help of various melodic scraps, we have an idea of how these narratives were sung: they were performed to fairly simple, repetitive melodies, and probably accompanied by the *vielle* (fiddle).[18]

The *Chanson de Roland* differs from *Beowulf* and the *Nibelungenlied* in its narrative stance. The narrating voice identifies with Charlemagne's men, called both Francs (Franks) and Franceis (French). They are 'our men', 'our warriors', fighting for 'our emperor' and for 'our cause'. The very first line of *Chanson* expresses this identification of narrator and listeners with the figures of 'our past': 'Carles li reis, nostre emprere magnes' (King Charles, our great emperor). The celebration of 'our Emperor' and his heroes is permeated with the spirit of a more contemporary age, the age of the crusades. This is encapsulated in a line like 'Paien unt tort e chrestïens unt dreit' (Pagans are in the wrong and Christians are in the right) (line 1015). The 'we' is here broadened to include not only Franks and French but the whole of Christendom, seen as engaged in a victorious battle against the Muslim world.

A similar crusading spirit characterizes also the *Cantar de Mio Cid* (or *Poema de Mio Cid*), here, however, adapted to the situation on the Hispanic Peninsula and focused on the personal fate of an outstanding figure of the Reconquista. The *Cantar* is the major Spanish medieval epic; the legend of Charlemagne and his Twelve Peers is represented in Spain only by later ballads, some fragmentary documents apart. The *Cantar de Mio Cid* is a poem of 3,730 lines, preserved in a fourteenth-century manuscript copy of a text written down in 1207. The epic is dedicated to the heroic deeds of the Cid (from Arabic *sayyid* 'lord'), a historical personage of the eleventh century, Rodrigo Díaz de Vivar (d. 1099). The framework for the epic's plot is provided by the Cid's unjust exile and his regaining the favour of Alfonso VI, King of Castile and Leon. Exiled from the king's court, the Cid and his faithful companions conquer a number of Moorish towns, most importantly Valencia, where the Cid sets up his rule. When he is finally pardoned by the king, he gives his two daughters in marriage to the Infantes (heirs) of Carilón on King Alfonso's suggestion, although the Infantes turn out to be cowards and blackguards. The height of their villainous behaviour is reached in the episode of the *Afrenta de Corpes*, the 'shaming of Corpes', when they strip their newly-wed wives to their shifts, beat them with spurs and straps and leave them lying half-dead in the oak woods of Corpes. The villains are, however, put to trial, defeated in a judicial combat by the Cid's supporters and punished. The epic ends with the restoration of the Cid's daughters' honour by their marriage to the Princes of Navarra and Aragón.

The *Cantar* is the youngest of all the epics here reviewed, and yet it exhibits many features of an archaic and vigorous tradition of heroic poetry. It is concerned with questions of honour and revenge, with the relationship between king and vassal and with the code of honour of a warrior society. Like the *chanson de geste* it is composed in *laisse*-type strophes, with assonance instead of rhyme; it is highly formulaic, with fixed epithets such as 'que en buen ora cinxo espada' (who girded his sword in a happy hour) or 'que en buen ora nasco' (who was born in a happy hour) for the Cid.[19] We find exclamations of the narrating voice, for instance: '¡Dios, cómo se alabavan!' (My God, how they rejoiced!) (line 580), and the narrator's comments on the aural reception of the epic: 'como odredes contar' (as you are about to hear) (line 684). While scholars of an 'individualist' persuasion hypothesize the composition of the epic in a literate and literary milieu, the main exponent of the 'neo-traditionalist school', Ramón Menéndez Pidal, has asserted, with good arguments, the oral background to the *Cantar*. Like other 'oral-derived' epics such as *Beowulf* and the *Chanson de Roland* it offers us a unique and precious view of medieval heroic poetry that has its roots undoubtedly in a pre-literate world of oral poetry.

NOTES

1 Einhard and Notker the Stammerer, *Two Lives of Charlemagne*, trans. L. Thorpe (Harmondsworth: Penguin, 1969), 82.

2 *Beowulf and its Analogues*, trans. G. N. Garmonsway and J. Simpson, including *Archaeology and Beowulf* by H. Ellis Davidson (London: Dent, 1980), 242.

3 Quotations are from W. Braune and E. A. Ebbinghaus, eds., *Althochdeutsches Lesebuch*, 17th edn (Tübingen: Niemeyer, 1994), 84–5, my translations.

4 Mircea Eliade, 'Littérature Orale', in *Histoire des Littératures. I. Littératures Anciennes, Orientales et Orales*, ed. Raymond Queneau (Paris: Gallimard, 1955), 3–26, this quotation p. 19 (my translation).

5 A. Heusler, *Die altgermanische Dichtung*, 2nd edn (Potsdam: Athenaion, 1943), 154.

6 My translation. For the original text, see *Klaeber's Beowulf and the Fight at Finnsburg*, ed. R. D. Fulk, R. E. Bjork, and J. D. Niles, with a foreword by H. Damico, 4th edn (Toronto: University of Toronto Press, 2008).

7 W. P. Ker, *The Dark Ages* (Edinburgh: Blackwood, 1904), 253.

8 J. R. R. Tolkien, '*Beowulf*, the Monsters and the Critics', in *An Anthology of Beowulf Criticism*, ed. L. E. Nicholson (Notre Dame, IN: University of Notre Dame Press, 1963), 51–103, 68.

9 H. M. Chadwick, *The Heroic Age* (Cambridge: Cambridge University Press, 1912), 324.

10 F. C. Robinson, 'Two Aspects of Variation', in *Old English Poetry: Essays on Style*, ed. Daniel G. Calder (Berkeley: University of California Press, 1979), 127–45, 129.

11 Quotations from G. P. Krapp, ed., *The Junius Manuscript*, Anglo-Saxon Poetic Records 1 (New York: Columbia University Press, 1931) (*Exodus*); *The Vercelli Book*, Anglo-Saxon Poetic Records 2 (New York: Columbia University Press, 1932) (*Andreas*).

12 Milman Parry, *The Making of Homeric Verse*, new edn (Oxford: Oxford University Press, 1987); Albert B. Lord, *The Singer of Tales*, 2nd edn, ed. S. Mitchell and G. Nagy (Cambridge, MA: Harvard University Press, 2000).

13 'If scholarship tells us anything, it is that this poem's semiosis is unlimited. Commentary could be extended indefinitely'; J. W. Earl, *Thinking about 'Beowulf'* (Stanford: Stanford University Press, 1994), 11.

14 Kenneth Sisam, *The Structure of Beowulf* (Oxford: Clarendon Press, 1965).

15 G. J. Brault, ed., *The Song of Roland: An Analytical Edition*, 2 vols. (University Park, PA: Pennsylvania State University Press, 1978), lines 1049–58.

16 *Ibid.*, lines 3999–4002.

17 A. T. Hatto, gen. ed., *Traditions of Heroic and Epic Poetry. I. The Traditions* (London: The Modern Humanities Research Association, 1980), 4.

18 See F. Gennrich, *Der musikalische Vortrag der altfranzösischen Chansons de geste* (Halle: Niemeyer, 1923) and J. Chailley, 'Autour de la chanson de geste', *Acta Musicologica* 27 (1955), 1–12.

19 Quotations are from *The Poem of the Cid*, ed. I. Michael, trans. R. Hamilton and J. Perry (Harmondsworth: Penguin, 1984).

5

JOHN FRECCERO

Dante and the epic of transcendence

In a famous essay of 1920 entitled *The Theory of the Novel*, Georg Lukács drew a sharp distinction between ancient epic and the modern novel.[1] The genres both sought to represent concrete reality, he maintained, but their perceptions of it were very different. The world of the epic was experienced as homogeneous, a totality of which the hero was part, while in the novel, the world was experienced as fragmentary and, with respect to subjectivity, radically 'other'. The 'blissful' world of Homeric epic was integrated and closed, bounded by the starry heaven, within which gods and humans felt equally at home, even as they struggled among themselves. The heroes of the epic lived through harrowing external adventures, but their inward security was such that their essence could never be seriously threatened. In the eternal world of the epic, the hero 'was the luminous centre', the passive, immobile point around which reality moved.

In contrast, the novel – the predominant genre of modernity – recounts an interior adventure in which the solitary hero is alienated from a world that is no longer hospitable. He yearns for integration, but finds it perpetually out of the reach of his desire. The gods have grown silent and the 'world of action loses contact with that of the self, leaving man empty and powerless, unable to grasp the real meaning of his deeds'. The hero of the novel is alone; an unbridgeable gap separates him from all others in a universe vastly expanded and no longer intelligible. The novel represents the 'epic of a world from which God has departed'.

Lukács's discussion of the contrast between the 'Hellenic' epic and the 'Western' novel unfolds brilliantly, if daringly, at the highest degree of generalization, with few textual citations and no historical detail. When he speaks of epic, he usually means Homer. Rome is largely ignored, except for Virgil, who is mentioned only once, in passing, and then with a touch of condescension, for having 'conjured up a reality that has vanished forever'. To Lukács, Christianity seems directed to a utopian dream to substitute the disappearance of the ancient *polis*, presumably with the City of God. As for the novel, his primary concern, the earliest work that fits his definition of the genre is *Don Quixote*.

In this synoptic view of the two millennia and more that separate Hellenism from Cervantes, it was impossible to avoid Dante, but the poet's towering genius made it equally impossible to categorize his work as either epic or novel. Lukács concluded, therefore, that it should be thought of as the historical transition between the genres, a singular tour de force, which, for the first time in Western literature, represented real personality:

> In Dante there is still the perfect immanent distancelessness and completeness of the true epic, but his figures are already individuals, consciously and energetically placing themselves in opposition to a reality that is becoming closed to them, individuals who, through this opposition, become real personalities.

It would follow from this observation (although he does not say so) that 'real personality' in the poem is to be found only where there is the clash between the individual and reality, which is to say, only in Hell. In this chapter it will be assumed that the sharp distinction between epic and novel has some validity, but we shall ask how, specifically, Dante transformed a few key epic themes into autobiography. We shall see that Augustine, who described his inner life as a spiritual odyssey, was Dante's predecessor in that endeavour and provided the poet with a model for recounting his own spiritual struggle.

Dante's poem (composed between 1308 and 1321, the year of his death) differs from classical epic in one very obvious way: it is narrated in the first person. In place of the detached third-person narrative that had described and admired the epic heroes as it were from the outside, Dante's poem looks from within. From the opening lines the poem is spoken in the voice of the poet himself: a figure whom he presents to us as a weary soul, arrived at mid-life, who embarks on the great spiritual journey that will take him through the three stages of salvation that he depicts (following the highly structured vision of medieval Catholicism) as three distinct locales: Hell, Purgatory, and Heaven. Through the three books or canticas of the poem (each subdivided into thirty-three cantos, with the *Inferno* having an extra 'prologue' canto, bringing the total to 100), Dante describes his slow, painful, but ultimately ecstatic progress towards salvation. For the first two canticas, the *Inferno* and *Purgatorio*, he is accompanied and guided by the spirit of Virgil; for the last, the *Paradiso*, by Beatrice, the ideal Lady of Neoplatonic and stilnovistic tradition, to whom the pagan and secular Roman poet courteously resigns his charge as a spirit more worthy to guide Dante to the heights of spiritual contemplation.

To speak of the epic in Dante thus inevitably recalls Virgil (to others if not to Lukács), and especially the revisionist Ulysses of the *Inferno*, about whom every 'Dantista' has had something to say. Ulysses is not only a character in Hell but an icon in the poem: unlike all other sinners, he has an 'afterlife' in both the *Purgatorio* and the *Paradiso*. He is the only major speaker in Hell not a contemporary, or near contemporary of the poet. He is clearly a surrogate, perhaps for Guido Cavalcanti (Dante's friend and fellow-poet), or for Dante himself, before he wrote the *Comedy*. The ancient hero is the archetype of the philosopher who believes in the sufficiency of human knowledge to reach secular happiness. In terms of the journey, Aeneas mediates between the pilgrim and the ancient mariner, as Virgil mediates between Dante and Homer. Our consideration of both Ulysses and Virgil can be very brief, because they have been so thoroughly studied, and by some very well. David Thompson has written about Dante and the epic, with particular emphasis on Virgil, and Winthrop Wetherbee has extensively examined the influence of Roman epic in the *Comedy*.[2]

In this chapter I will be primarily concerned with the prologue of the poem, where Odysseus is a submerged presence, ignored by most critics. I will also discuss not only the transformation of the epic into the novel, which is the essence of Dante's fictional account of Ulysses, but what Lukács calls the 'retransformation' of the 'novelistic' *Inferno* into the new epic of transcendence.[3] I will try to answer the unspoken historical question raised by Lukács's book concerning the provenance of Dante's representation of subjectivity, so foreign to the epic and essential in the novel. Augustine, Dante's exemplary forerunner, was something of a novelist himself. In fact, Phillip Cary has referred to him as the 'inventor' (in the Latin sense of 'discoverer') of the inner self.[4]

The novelistic quality of the *Inferno* seems indisputable. Hell is an autonomous region, totally separate from deity, where there is no court, but only a monstrous, Kafkaesque bureaucrat, mechanically and implacably meting out sentences to the sinners. Most readers have found the damned to be more memorable than the blessed. In their epic integration, the blessed, like happy families, are all alike, while the souls in Hell are alone together. They are irreducibly individual, even when they are paired, as Francesca and Paolo, Ulysses and Diomede or, horribly, Ugolino and Ruggieri. It is this individuality and 'loneliness' that Lukács takes for 'real personality'.

As in Lukács's reading of the novel, irony dominates in the *Inferno*, both verbal, in the exchanges with the pilgrim, and situational: we have only the testimony of the sinners about the mitigating circumstances surrounding their downfall, but their protestations are silently undermined by infernal reality. It is as if their relative moral culpability were transformed metaphorically into physical weight and the depth of their immersion into the abyss infallibly determined by 'specific gravity'. This fiction, derived from

Augustine's metaphor of the 'pondus amoris', implies that one *is* what one loves and that sin, stripped of its allure and disguise, is therefore its own punishment.[5] In this immanent justice, God bears no responsibility for the sinners' torment, other than for having created Hell, as He created heaven and earth. This reality is clearly novelistic, the antithesis of the 'blissful' world of the epic.

What is missing from this description of the *Inferno* is the prologue scene, which establishes the autobiographical dimension of the *Comedy*, thereby distinguishing it from both the epic and the novel, although it contains elements of both genres. It has no 'real personalities', nor any of the 'mimetic' quality for which Dante is famous, yet it is the only account we are given of the hero's alienation and aloneness when he sets out, lost in an interior landscape. It thus serves as the point of departure for this discussion.

Had the pilgrim begun his journey at the gates of Hell and ended it in utter defeat, the *Inferno* by itself might have qualified as the first novel, albeit with a relatively passive protagonist. The journey begins with a prologue, which theorists of Dante's 'realism' usually skip over when they read the *Inferno*, finding its allegorism to be vague and even tiresome. Yet the *Comedy* is primarily autobiography and the prologue is all we are told in the *Inferno* of his spiritual crisis. It is a prelude, a schematic map of a spiritual state, setting forth themes to which, from time to time, the poem will retrospectively refer – notably, the three beasts, of which only a child turning the pages of Dante's nineteenth-century illustrator, Gustave Doré, would ever be afraid. We should no more expect realism in those first two cantos than we would in an interior monologue or penitential meditation. The first explorer of this terrain, the 'inner self', was Augustine, whom Lukács does not mention. Nevertheless, the subsequent development of the novel of interiority seems inconceivable without his example.

As for the ending of the *Inferno*, it is a new beginning, both in theme and in literary genre. In modern narrative, one might expect the defeat or even death of an alienated hero, but Dante survives this destructive first part of his journey to begin an ascent from a cave at the centre of the universe. The descent into Hell is necessary simply to reach the cave, which for Plato, in the myth of the *Republic*, was the point of departure. Virgil and the pilgrim crawl down Satan's thigh through Cocytus, the lake of ice, turn upside-down, and climb to the other side of the 'mirror' of Hell. There, all dimensions are reversed: down is up, left is right, and Satan, the Prince of this world, is buried upside-down with respect to heaven. Perhaps Lewis Carroll was remembering this grotesque passage through the lake of ice when he led Alice into another world, beyond the looking glass.

The end of the *Inferno* is a rebirth and the beginning of a rehabilitation, as well as a return to the light that seemed unreachable in the prologue. The pilgrim is back where he started, this time in sharp focus, with a guide and no impediments. From the standpoint of the geometric imagination, it is literally a return. He has emerged from the vertex of the infernal cone to find himself at the circular base of a similar cone of immense volume, the mount of Purgatory, high enough so that its apex is beyond meteorological change.

In Canto XXXIV, 124 we are told that the material of the mountain was formed ('forse' (perhaps) says Dante, anticipating incredulity) when the earth was displaced by Satan's fall into the southern hemisphere.[6] Part of it rose up in the northern hemisphere to form the dry land, which previously had been covered with water (earth being heavier than water, in its 'natural' state) and part rose up in the southern hemisphere to form the mountain. Geometrically speaking, again, it is as if the mountain were extracted from the mould of Hell, leaving behind its negative impression in the rock. The path of the ascent of the mountain, the outside of the cone, spirals to the right, while the infernal descent spirals left, but, since the travellers turned upside down at the centre, their path is in the same absolute direction. Purgatory is Hell, turned inside out.

The bizarre myth of the similar shape of Hell and Purgatory is a physical representation of the theological doctrine of 'Justification'.[7] The word describes the action whereby a sinner is redeemed, or reborn. It is a continuous action, but it is logically two-fold: the destruction of a previous form (the sinful self, we might say) and the generation of a new self. Existentially, destruction and regeneration take place simultaneously – in life there can be no zero point. In the poem, however, Dante presents us with an 'anatomy' of regeneration, a 'living dissection', in which degrees of degradation in the realm of destruction correspond to degrees of elevation in the realm of generation. The zero point of the universe is a spiritual abstraction, the half-life of the soul, permitting Dante to say, 'Io non mori' e non rimasi vivo' (I did not die and was not still living) (*Inf.*, XXXIV. 25). The juxtaposition of the two otherworldly realms serves equally well as a spatial illustration of what Lukács refers to as the 're-transformation' of novelistic pessimism. An allegory of hope replaces infernal irony, its negative inversion, and is in turn replaced by ecstatic vision in an epic of transcendence.

To return to the question of infernal 'subjectivity', its origin is doubtless to be found in the ultimate moral negation, which is sin, as it is represented in Scripture. The inexplicable gap in Lukács's discussion of 'realism' is his exclusion of the Bible from consideration, a blind spot subsequently illuminated by Erich Auerbach, his contemporary, who used the Old Testament to contrast with Homeric realism in order to educe his own theory of 'mimesis'.[8] Conscience and consciousness (the Romance languages have a single word for both terms) seem to create the interior distance separating the sinners in Hell from each other and from reality. Their isolation and solipsism is evident in virtually all of the dialogues of the damned, an estrangement first suffered by Cain and made explicit by Satan's words: 'Which way I fly is Hell; myself am Hell' (*Paradise Lost*, 4.75).

The themes of alienation and exile have mythic roots in Genesis and claim historicity in Exodus, the epic of liberation. St Paul, the Roman citizen, for whom the theme of political liberation must have seemed somewhat remote, established a figural interpretation of the Exodus of more immediate and personal relevance. He reads it as a moral trope, applying it to himself and to his audience: 'All these things were done as a figure for us' (I Corinthians 10). The desert of Exodus thus became part of Paul's own experience and was thereafter universally accepted as the moral (or tropological) meaning of the desert in Christian exegesis. Augustine alluded to the desert of his inner life, referring to it with a Plotinian phrase: the 'region of unlikeness'. For Dante, Exodus became the dominant figure of the *Purgatorio*, the middle ground between infernal Egypt and the Heavenly Jerusalem.[9] But the first allusion in the poem occurs in the prologue, with the pilgrim hobbling across a 'piaggia diserta' (desert strand) (1.29), halfway between the sun and the dark wood. These interior landscapes are bleak, but unlike King Lear's heath, they can, with difficulty, be traversed.

The journey of the Jews through the desert has its counterpart in the sea voyage of Odysseus. The medium and the vehicle could not be more different, of course, but the goal is the same: to return home. The circular path of Odysseus's journey, *nostos*, seemed to later Neoplatonists an admirable emblem for the souls' fall from the heavens and their return. Such allegorizations transformed Homer into a theologian, whose subsequent history in Western literature has been traced by Robert Lamberton.[10] A realistic verse from the *Iliad* will serve to illustrate how persistent such allegorizations became, no matter how wildly incongruous they may appear to us. In Agamemnon's ironic exhortation to his men, calculated to have the opposite effect from its ostensible meaning, he urges them to give up the siege of Troy and return to their ships: 'Let us flee then to the beloved fatherland' (*Iliad*, 2.140). Plotinus, the most influential of 'homeric theologians', wrenched the verse from its context, associated it with the *Odyssey*, and claimed to read into it the soul's return to the One:

> We shall put out to sea as Odysseus did . . . 'Let us flee then to the beloved fatherland'. . . Our Fatherland is that whence we came, and the Father is there. What then is our journey, our flight? Not by feet is it to be accomplished; for

feet carry one from here to there all over the earth. Nor should you procure a chariot or ship; you should leave all such things behind and not look, but close your eyes and awaken another sort of vision instead – a sort of vision which everyone possesses but few use.[11]

As Paul 'interiorized' the epic of the Jews, Plotinus 'interiorized' the epic of the Greeks. In a sermon, St Ambrose echoed this passage, exhorting the faithful to flee with their minds, 'fugiamus animo', or with their 'interior feet', as did Augustine, in the *City of God*: 'Where is that Plotinus, when he says, "Let us flee therefore, to that dearest homeland . . ." What is the ship or the flight? It is to make ourselves like God' (9.17).[12] Homer's Agamemnon turns out to be the ultimate source of the verse in the first canto of the *Inferno* describing the panic of the errant pilgrim:

> E come quei che con lena affannata,
>   uscito fuor del pelago a la riva
>   si volge a l'acqua perigliosa e guata,
> così *l'animo* mio, ch'ancor *fuggiva*,
>   si volse a retro a rimirar lo passo
>   che non lasciò già mai persona viva.
> Poi che'èi posato un poco il corpo lasso,
>   ripresi via per la piaggia diserta,
>   sì che 'l piè fermo sempre era 'l più basso.   (*Inf.*, I.22–30)

(And as he who with labouring breath has escaped from the deep to the shore turns to look back on the dangerous waters, so *my mind* which was still *fleeing* turned back to gaze upon the pass that never left anyone alive. After I had rested my tired body a little, I again took up my way across the desert strand, so that the firm foot was always the lower.)

I have cited these three *terzine* in order to provide the context for the key phrase, 'fugiamus animo' (in Ambrose's version). The telltale word 'animo' indicates that this is a flight of the mind, in the philosophical tradition of Plotinus, rather than of 'anima', in the usual theological sense. The choice of the word is also a premonition of the subsequent failure; we shall see that a purely philosophical effort, on one's own, is not enough for a Christian, in spite of Plotinus's assurance that one needs no guide (*Enneads*, I, 6, 9). More than that, however, each of the *terzine* alludes to a motif drawn from the tradition of 'homeric theology': a near-drowning, a mental flight, and a hobbling across a desert. We shall see that the obscure lines that seemed tiresome to some critics constitute a network of intertextuality transforming three epic images into a drama of interiority.

Augustine explored his own interior landscape, the 'caves' and 'mansions' of memory, in which he found himself to be utterly alone. He compares his wandering in the desert with the story of the Prodigal Son (Luke 15.11–35) as well as echoes of Plotinus:

> One does not go far away from you or return to you by walking or by any movement through space. The younger son in your Gospel did not look for horses or carriages or ships; he did not fly on any visible wing, nor did he travel along the way by moving his legs when he went to live in a far country and prodigally dissipated what you, his gentle father, had given him on setting out . . . To live there in lustful passion is to live in darkness and to be far from your face. (*Confessions*, 1.18, 28)

James J. O'Donnell has remarked on the way Neoplatonic themes are here synthesized with the parable of the Prodigal Son. In this text, the key phrase, 'in regionem longinquam' (in a far country) echoes the Plotinian, but ultimately Platonic 'in regionem dissimilitudinis'.[13]

Augustine alludes to Plotinus again at the moment of his conversion in the garden:

> To reach that destination [the covenant with God] one does not use ships or chariots or feet. It was not even necessary to go the distance I had come from the house . . . It was necessary to have the will to go . . . provided only that the will was strong and unqualified, not the twisting and turning first this way, then that, of a half-crippled will [*semi-saucium*] struggling with one part rising up and the other falling down. (*Confessions*, 8.19)

Attentive readers of the prologue will recognize the lower 'firm foot' of the pilgrim in this description of the half-crippled will. These 'vehicles' of the interior journey correspond to the fictive or metaphoric 'vehicles' of the pilgrim's progress: the feet, then ship, then flight to God.

I have said that the *Purgatorio* announces the transformation of the novelistic dead-end of the *Inferno* into a new epic beginning. This may have seemed a generalization, but it is in fact exactly what the poet intended to convey. Not only does the *cantica* begin with a classical navigational metaphor but it invokes Calliope, the muse of epic poetry, so that 'dead poetry may rise again':

> Per correr miglior acque alza le vele
> omai la navicella del mio ingegno,
> che lascia dietro a sé mar sì crudele;
> e canterò di quel secondo regno
> dove l'umano spirito si purga
> e di salire al ciel diventa degno.
> Ma qui la morta poesì resurga,
> o sante Muse, poi che vostro sono;
> e qui Calïopè alquanto surga,
> seguitando il mio canto . . . (*Purg.*, 1.1–10)

(To course over better waters the little bark of my genius now hoists her sails, leaving behind her a sea so cruel; and I will sing of that second realm where the human spirit is purged and becomes fit to ascend to Heaven. But here let dead poetry rise again, O holy Muses, since I am yours; and here let Calliope rise somewhat, accompanying my song . . .)

Further evidence of the 're-transformation' of the novelistic dead-end into an epic of redemption, if needed, can be gleaned from examining the difference between the opening of the *Inferno* and the epic openings of the *Purgatorio* and the *Paradiso*.

Nautical imagery was commonly used in Latin literature as a metaphor for the writing of poetry. The composition of an epic might be compared to a seagoing voyage, while a lyric poem was more apt to be a fragile bark. In the numerous examples studied by E. R. Curtius, sails are unfurled in invocations and, after innumerable vicissitudes, lowered at journey's end.[14] There is always the threat of shipwreck but, in spite of reefs and storms, the outcome of such a voyage can never be in serious doubt, since the existence of the poem is proof of the success of the undertaking. No matter how arduous the journey, every poet's ship must come in, bearing its more or less golden fleece.

This is very different from the nautical imagery that served in antiquity to describe intellectual or spiritual adventure. The quest for truth was thought to be much more problematic than the search for rhetorical effect. In the biography of a philosopher, shipwreck, real or allegorical, was not merely a threat to the outcome of the undertaking, but rather the obligatory point of departure for a journey to wisdom and true happiness. The philosopher was described as a castaway, a lonely survivor of the wreckage of the unexamined life. In his book entitled *Shipwreck with Spectator*, Hans Blumenberg cites Lucretius, to whose work the title alludes, as well as many other ancients.[15] He concludes that 'shipwreck, as seen by a survivor, is the figure of an initial philosophical experience'. In the modern world, as well, some philosophers have thought of drowning, real or allegorical, as occasioning a review of one's life in retrospect, a hypothesis sustainable, obviously, only from the report of survivors.[16] We shall see that one of the initial similes of the poem suggests that the near drowning is a prelude for staging memories of Dante's life and times.

Like all great poets, Dante leaves no *topos* untouched, so that a simple enumeration of its occurrences in his works, such as Curtius provides, offers no hint of the complexity of his navigational imagery. The complexity derives from the fact that the famous exordia of the *Purgatorio* and of the final ascent in Canto II of the *Paradiso* erase the distinction between conventional figures for the writing of poetry and the literal fiction of the journey. At the opening of the *Purgatorio*, when he claims that the bark of his genius will now course over better waters and leave behind so cruel a sea, the theme and its vehicle seem inseparable. The *poeta theologus* uses the navigational vehicle to describe the progress of both his poem and his spiritual journey. His narrative creates a sequential illusion out of the logical distinction between the journey and its record, as though the experience preceded the writing of the story. In 'real time', they are one.

In the second book of the *Convivio*, Dante's earlier philosophical work, which he abandoned one third of the way through its projected length, he introduced a nautical image that was much admired by Curtius: '. . . lo tempo chiama e domanda la mia nave uscir di porto; per che, dirizzato l'artimone della ragione all'òra del mio desiderio, entro in pelago con isperanza di dolce cammino e di salutevole porto . . .' (. . . conditions bid and command my ship to leave port. So, having set the sail [*artimone*] of reason to catch the breeze of my desire, I put out to sea [*pelago*] with hopes of a pleasant journey and of a safe and honorable arrival . . .) (II.1). With erudite condescension, Curtius congratulates Dante on the use of the unfamiliar technical term 'artimone', a Mediterranean type of foresail, not realizing, any more than did the poet, the ominous implications of the word. In Acts 27.40, it is precisely the 'artimone' that drives Paul's ship to disaster off the island of Malta: 'levato artemone secundum aurae flatum tendebant ad littus'. The *Convivio* met a similar fate. It was never finished, but foundered instead in the *pelago*, on which it had set forth with such optimism, and Dante was forced to abandon ship. When he began *The Divine Comedy*, it was as a castaway, 'uscito fuor dal pelago alla riva' (emerging from the deep to the shore).

The journey of *The Divine Comedy* may be said to begin, metaphorically, with the wreck of the *Convivio*. The prologue of the *Inferno* has its initial nautical metaphor, as do the *Purgatorio* and the *Paradiso*, but, as we have seen in the three *terzine* quoted above, it is a metaphor of narrow escape from a near-drowning. The imagery has no descriptive function in the prologue scene, but rather serves to identify this moment as a philosophical conversion in an ancient tradition. Dante's shipwrecked mariner may be traced back to the *Odyssey*. In particular, the figure of a castaway gasping for breath recalls the episode from the fifth book of the *Odyssey*, when Odysseus swims from the wreckage of his raft to the Phaeacian shore and his encounter with Nausicaa:

> Swollen from hand to foot he was, and seawater
> Gushed from his mouth and nostrils. There he lay,
> Scarce drawing breath, unstirring, deathly spent.
> In time, as air came back into his lungs
> And warmth around his heart, he loosed the veil [of Ino] . . .[17]

Homer may have inserted the physical details simply to heighten the realism of the episode (because they were *there*, as Auerbach says of Odysseus's scar!), but allegorists read into those details significances never dreamt of by the poet. Felix Buffière studied the influence of Homeric myth on Greek thought and noted that Democritus, for example, read into Odysseus's gasping breath the presence of pneuma, the principle of the soul itself.[18] Dante's reference to the 'lena affanata' is derived, by however circuitous a route, from the Homeric detail.

More important for our purposes is a passage from the *Phaedo*, where there are several allusions to the *Odyssey*. The subject is the immanent death of Socrates and the efforts of his friends to understand what happens after death. Simmias thinks it would be best to discover for oneself or, if this is impossible, one should 'take the best and most irrefutable of human theories and let this be the raft upon which he sails through life – not without risk, as I admit, if he cannot find some word of God which will surely and safely carry him'.[19] This possible allusion to the raft of Odysseus – according to an acute hypothesis of Giovanni Reale[20] – suggested to Augustine the wood of the cross:

> It is as if one were able from afar to see the homeland, but were separated from it by the sea. He sees where he must go, but lacks the means of getting there . . . So [the Lord] has prepared for him the wood [*lignum*] enabling him to cross the sea. In fact, no one can cross the sea of this world unless he is carried by the cross of Christ [*nemo enim potest transire mare hujus saeculi, nisi cruce Christi portatus*].[21]

I do not know of a better gloss for the verse of *Inferno*, I.26–7: 'lo passo / che non lasciò già mai persona viva' (the pass that no man ever left alive).

To return to the shipwreck and survival of Odysseus, it was widely allegorized in antiquity as a philosophical adventure. In the *Life of Plotinus*, which Augustine knew, Porphyry relates the supposed praise of Plotinus by the Delphic oracle in a passage filled with reminiscences of the fifth book of the *Odyssey*, especially the lines that describe Odysseus swimming swiftly:

> Spirit! Once just a man, but now nearing the diviner lot of a spirit, as the bond of human necessity has been loosed for you, and strong in heart, you swam swiftly from the roaring surge of the body to that coast where the stream flows strong, far apart from the crowd of the wicked, there to set your steps firm in the easy path of the pure soul . . . you were struggling to escape from the bitter wave of this blood-drinking life, from its sickening whirlpools, in the midst of its billows and sudden surges.[22]

This oracle of Apollo may be taken as the paradigm for the ancient turning to the light. This form of philosophical salvation is an illumination, 'a shaft of light', guidance out of the 'crooked ways' to the 'direct path' to immortality. Apollo promises Plotinus the company of Plato and Pythagoras and kinship with the most blessed, as well as the judges of the underworld. The presence of Rhadamanthus identifies this place as Elysium, where Homer placed him. In this drama, Plotinus is transported directly from near drowning to immortal love. In the *Convivio*, in the full flush of philosophical enthusiasm, Dante imagined Heaven as a 'celestial Athens' much like this, where the ancient sages (including Epicureans!) would gather together to philosophize about God. He changed his mind in the *Comedy* and relegated them instead to a lugubrious Limbo, artificially illuminated, surrounded by the sighs of the unbaptized. Virgil, who is in their number, says: 'sanza speme vivemo in disio' (without hope, we live in desire) (*Inf.*, IV.42).

When William Butler Yeats rendered Porphyry's words about the oracle praising Plotinus, he intimated that it is not so easy to rinse away the bitter salt of the sea:

> Behold that great Plotinus swim,
> Buffeted by such seas;
> Bland Rhadamanthus beckons him,
> But the Golden Race looks dim,
> Salt blood blocks his eyes.
>
> Scattered on the level grass
> Or winding through the grove
> Plato there and Minos pass,
> There stately Pythagoras
> And all the choir of Love.[23]

The eyes of the philosopher are blood-shot, but it is his biographer who is sanguine. One is not so easily purged of the passions as to be acceptable to the clear-eyed judge. Yeats's arch critique is not very different from Augustine's, who insisted that tears of contrition were necessary for any such conversion. That is exactly what 'Purgatory' is for.

One has only to contrast Plotinus's landscape of light with Dante's prologue scene to understand the difference between a philosophical conversion of the mind and spiritual conversion with the grace of God. As Augustine says at the end of Book 7 of the *Confessions*, 'It is one thing from a wooded mountain-top [*de silvestre cacumine*] to see the homeland of peace and not to find the way to it, but vainly to attempt the journey along an impassible route, when one is beset . . . by the lion and the dragon, and quite another thing to hold to the way that leads there, defended by the protection of the heavenly emperor' (21, 27).

Book 7 of the *Confessions* recounts Augustine's discovery of the 'books of the Platonists' and his subsequent astonishment reading their 'theology' to find their doctrine of the word similar in every respect to the Logos of the Gospel of John, save only the most crucial: 'but that the word was made flesh and dwelt among us I did not read'. His vain attempts to reach the Plotinian light led him to acknowledge that only through Christ would he reach salvation and 'learn to discern the difference between presumption and confession, between those who see what the goal is but not how to get there and those who see the way which leads to the home of bliss'. He ends his meditation with a quotation from Matthew 11.25: 'you have concealed these things from the wise and prudent and have revealed them to babes'. The next Book, 8, is his account of his conversion under the fig tree in the garden of Milan.

The extraordinary parallelism between his spiritual experience and Dante's, at roughly the same age, even with comparable erotic distractions, would be exact, if it had been Neoplatonists rather than Aristotelians who led Dante to the overweening confidence in philosophy he seemed to share with Guido Cavalcanti, his 'first friend'. But by far the most striking similarity in the spiritual adventures of Augustine and Dante is that both chose to describe the crisis of the proud philosopher in terms of the Homeric allegory of Ulysses, although, as even the most casual reader of the poem knows, Dante's Ulysses dies in a shipwreck.

The return was the point of Homer's story, qualifying the *Odyssey* for the allegorization it was to receive for centuries. Dante's insistence on his revision of the story is too pointed to allow us to attribute it to his ignorance of Homer's text. The first canto of the *Purgatorio* claims: 'Venimmo poi in sul lito diserto, / che mai non vide navicar sue acque/omo, che di tornar sia poscia esperto' (Then we came on to the desert shore, that never saw any man navigate its waters who afterwards had experience of return) (*Purg.*, 1.130–2). If there were any doubt about who such a man might be, it would be dispelled by the next sentence, when Virgil girds Dante with the rush of humility, 'sì com' altrui piacque' (as pleased another) (1.133). This is the same phrase that ends the canto of Ulysses. His ship is swallowed by the sea 'com' altrui piacque' (*Inf.*, XXVI.141). The contrast between the drowning of the proud philosopher and the humility of the penitent could not be clearer.

In the prologue of an early work on happiness, *De beata vita*, Augustine recapitulated the major events of his spiritual struggle, not in the realistic terms of the *Confessions*, but in the guise of a transparent and somewhat tedious allegorical navigation towards the port of philosophy, in a tempestuous sea.[24] There is no mention of Ulysses, but he does speak of turning his ship to avert the Sirens. There is little doubt that Odysseus was his model. Jean Pepin has written an exhaustive study of 'The Platonic and Christian Ulysses', illustrating the great popularity of the figure in Augustine's day.[25]

Robert J. O'Connell expressed his doubts that Augustine could have known all the Greek texts amassed by Pepin, but nevertheless concluded from innumerable examples that Augustine's 'odyssey' was based on Homer's: 'The Odyssey image of conversion manifests all the main features one would expect of it. We, meaning our souls, find ourselves on the stormy sea of this world, wandering away from our homeland, confronting dangers of shipwreck from mists, sinking stars, and tempests; we have forgotten the homeland we left, and yet, we guard a certain vague nostalgia for it which prompts us to "look back" when we are given signals "reminding" us of it'.[26] There is good reason to believe that the odyssey of Dante's Ulysses was based on Augustine's.

Augustine's 'sinking stars' might have suggested to Dante 'Tutte le stelle già de l'altro polo / vedea la notte, e 'l nostro tanto basso, / che non surgëa fuor del marin suolo' (The night now saw the other pole and all its stars and ours so low that it did not rise from the ocean floor) (*Inf.*, XXVI.127–9) and Augustine's 'totis velis, omnibus remis' might have inspired 'de' remi facemmo ali al folle volo' (of our oars we made wings for the mad flight) (*Inf.*, 125), although the words also recall Daedalus's 'remigium alarum' (the rowing movement of his wings) in *Aeneid* 6.19. These are admittedly generic features of a stormy crossing. One feature is so strange, however, that it must have inspired Ulysses's sight of a 'montagna, bruna / per la distanza, e parvemi alta tanto / quanto veduta non avëa alcuna' (a mountain dark in the distance. . .[that] seemed the highest I had even seen) (*Inf.*, XXVI 133–5). Augustine provides us with both the mountain and its meaning:

> All who sail toward the land of happiness must be very careful to avoid at all cost that highest of mountains that rises up before the port, leaving a little room for those who would enter . . . what else would reason tell us that this mountain represents, to be feared by all who approach or enter, except proud vainglory? A mountain that is so hollow and empty, although apparently solid, that it will crack under those triumphant ones who tread on it, causing them to sink into the darkness below, depriving them of that beautiful homeland that they had just begun to discern.

The contrast between the slope of the mountain and its infernal belly inevitably remind us of the equally oneiric juxtaposition of the cones of Purgatory and Hell, Dante's version of 'mountain gloom, mountain glory'. In the *Tractatus in Joannem*, Augustine sums up the horror of the mariner's mountain: 'If a mountain is not illuminated by the sun it remains in darkness; remember this, lest, mistaking the mountain for the light, you suffer shipwreck instead of finding help.'[27]

The clearest recall of the *beata vita* in the *Comedy* occurs in the longest and most moving exordium in the poem, in canto II of the *Paradiso*, studied by Curtius, who was unaware of the Augustinian subtext. In his treatise, Augustine began by distinguishing three types of mariners, the timid, the adventurous, and the foolhardy. So in the last *cantica*, Dante addresses those 'in piccioletta barca' (little barques), whom he tells to turn back, then those who have already had a taste of the bread of angels, whom he invites to follow in his wake. He identifies himself as the Jason of poetry, 'L'acqua ch'io prendo già mai non si corse' (the water which I take was never coursed before) (*Par.*, II.7).

The journey through the *Paradiso* is a celestial navigation, with Beatrice as Dante's guide. When she appears to him in Eden, to scold him, he describes her with the most startling simile in his catalogue of her praises: 'Quasi ammiraglio che in poppa e in prora / viene a veder la gente che ministra / per li altri legni' (Like an admiral who goes to stern and bow to see the men that are serving on the other ships) (*Purg.*, XXX.58–60). She will lead him on his voyage through the celestial spheres. As the first mariner of the highest seas, returning with the golden fleece of the poem we read, he is the anti-type of Ulysses.

In his address to the reader, Dante compares himself to the captain of the Argonauts: 'Que' glorïoso che passaro al Colco / non s'ammiraron come voi farete, / quando Iasón vider fatto bifolco' (those glorious ones who crossed the sea to Colchis, when they saw Jason turned ploughman, were not as amazed as you will be) (*Par.*, II.16–18). Ovid tells the tale of Jason taming the bulls, but in this context, the word 'solco' (14) means 'wake', as well as 'furrow'. It is Dante's metaphor for the writing of poetry and following in his wake means reading it.

Much later in the *cantica*, as he circles within the constellation of the Gemini, there are two similes of Olympian detachment. The first is his truly epic glance down at the earth, which he calls 'L'aiuola che ci fa tanto feroci' (the little threshing floor that makes us so ferocious) (*Par.*, XXII.151), with all its hills and streams. The second is intensely private, edgy, and a touch triumphalist, when he looks down at the blank page of the ocean, marked only by an allusion to his own text: the 'varco / folle d'Ulisse' (the mad wake of Ulysses) (*Par.*, XXVII.82–3). With those two glances, he removes himself from the upheaval of his times and, perhaps, from the philosophical arrogance that he once shared with his first friend.

Finally, at the end of the poem, Dante finds himself unable to recall his vision and compares his forgetfulness to the oblivion of history since the voyage of the Argonauts: 'Un punto solo m'è maggior letargo / che venti-cinque secoli a la 'mpresa / che fé Nettuno *ammirar* l'ombra d'Argo' (One point is greater forgetfulness for me than have been the twenty–five centuries since Neptune wondered at the shadow of the Argo) (*Par.*,

XXXIII.94–6).[28] Neptune's amazement is also ours, greater than that of the Argonauts (*s'ammirarono*), as we follow in Dante's wake. For us, the shadow of the Argo is the poem. At the outset of the *Paradiso*, Dante prayed to Apollo to enable him to make manifest the shadow of Heaven in his memory (*Par.*, 1.23). The poem is that manifestation, a shadow of a shadow. Our distance from the experience, twice removed, gives us the perspective of Neptune, who sees the navigation as an overhead flight. The shadow of the Argo is a momentary eclipse of the light, the negative evidence of an otherwise omnipresent, and therefore imperceptible, deity. It is a metaphor for the *via negativa* of mystic theology. What makes it coherent is the ambiguity of the single word 'punto': the point in space, which is the vision of God, and the point in time, which is the *now* of the poem.

We recall that Ulysses referred to his navigation as a flight ('il folle volo'), but it ended, like that of Icarus, in disaster. Ulysses's words, 'de' remi facemmo ali', echo the 'remigium alarum' of Daedalus, but it is Dante who was the 'fabulous artificer'.

NOTES

1 Georg Lukács, *The Theory of the Novel* (Cambridge, MA: MIT Press, 1971), 29–39. The principal pages dedicated to Dante, paraphrased or cited here, are to be found on 68–70 and 80–3.

2 See David Thompson, *Dante's Epic Journeys* (Baltimore: Johns Hopkins University Press, 1974); and Winthrop Wetherbee, *The Ancient Flame: Dante and the Poets* (Notre Dame, IN: University of Notre Dame Press, 2008).

3 On this see also John Freccero, 'Dante's Ulysses: From Epic to Novel', in *Dante: The Poetics of Conversion*, ed. Rachel Jacoff (Cambridge, MA: Harvard University Press, 1986), 136–51.

4 Phillip Cary, *Augustine's Invention of the Inner Self: The Legacy of a Christian Platonist* (Oxford: Clarendon Press, 2000).

5 *Confessions*, 13.8: 'My weight is my love', in Augustine, *Confessions*, text and commentary by James J. O'Donnell, 3 vols. (Oxford: Clarendon Press, 1992), vol., III.

6 All quotations and translations from *The Divine Comedy* are taken from the text edited by Charles S. Singleton, 3 vols. (Princeton: Princeton University Press, 1970–5).

7 On this see also Charles S. Singleton, *Journey to Beatrice* (Cambridge, MA: Harvard University Press, 1958), ch. 3.

8 Erich Auerbach, *Dante, Poet of the Secular World*, trans. Ralph Mannheim (Chicago: University of Chicago Press, 1961).

9 Charles S. Singleton, 'In Exitu Israel de Aegypto', in *Dante: A Collection of Critical Essays*, ed. John Freccero (Englewood Cliffs, NJ: Prentice Hall, 1965), 102–21.

10 Robert Lamberton, *Homer the Theologian: Neoplatonist Allegorical Reading and the Growth of the Epic Tradition* (Berkeley: University of California Press, 1986).

11 *Enneads*, I, 6, 8, in *Plotinus*, ed. and trans. A. H. Armstrong, 6 vols. (Cambridge, MA: Harvard University Press, 1978). Subsequent quotations are cited from this edition.

12 Ambrose of Milan, *Liber de Isaac et anima*, VIII.79 (*Patrologia Latina*, 14.559).

13 *Confessions*, ed. O'Donnell, vol. II, 95–8.

14 E. R. Curtius, *European Literature and the Latin Middle Ages* (New York: Routledge and Kegan Paul, 1953).

15 Hans Blumenberg, *Shipwreck with Spectator: Paradigm of a Metaphor for Existence*, trans. Steven Rendall (Cambridge, MA: MIT Press, 1996), 10.

16 See George Poulet, 'Bergson et le thème de la vision panoramique des mourants', *Revue de theologie et philosophie* 3:10:1 (1960): 23–41.

17 *The Odyssey*, trans. Robert Fitzgerald (New York: Vintage Books, 1990), 5.540–4, p. 94.

18 Felix Buffière, *Les mythes d'Homère et la pensée greque* (Paris: Belles Lettres, 1956), 454–5.

19 Plato, *Phaedo*, 85B–88B, trans. R. Hackforth (New York: Liberal Arts Press, 1955), 97.

20 Giovanni Reale, *Agostino: Amore assoluto e 'terza navigazione'* (Milan: Bompiani, 2000). The volume contains the text and translation of the commentary *In epistolam Ioannis ad Parthos* and of *In Ioannis evangelium tractatus*, *Tractatus* II.

21 *In Ioannis evangelium* II, 2, 2; Reale, *Agostino*, 495.

22 Porphyry, *Life of Plotinus*, section 22, in *Plotinus*, ed. and trans. Armstrong, vol. I, 67.

23 'The Delphic Oracle Upon Plotinus', written in August 1931, in *The Collected Poems of W. B. Yeats* (London: Wordsworth Editions, 2000), 230.

24 These remarks summarize a previous work of mine (see Freccero, *Poetics of Conversion*, 15ff.). Giorgio Padoan was the first critic to underscore the importance of the *de beata vita* for Dante's portrayal of Ulysses: 'Ulisse "Fandi Fictor" e le vie della Sapienza', *Studi danteschi* 37 (1960): 21–61.

25 Jean Pepin, 'The Platonic and Christian Ulysses', in *Odysseus/Ulysses*, ed. Harold Bloom (New York: Chelsea House Publishers, 1991).

26 Robert J. O'Connell, *Soundings in St. Augustine's Imagination* (New York: Fordham University Press, 1992), 176–7.

27 *In Ioannis evangelium* II, 2, 5; Reale, *Agostino*, 503.

28 For a survey of 'distinguished scholarly' discussions of the simile, see 'Letargo' (*Par.*, XXXIII.94), by H. D. Austin and Leo Spitzer in *Modern Language Notes* 52 (1937): 469–75; and Peter Dronke, 'Boethius, Alanus and Dante', *Romanische Forschungen* 78 (1966): 119–25. For a more literary interpretation, see Georges Poulet in *Le Point de départ* (Paris: Editions de Rocher, 1964) and *Les Metamorphoses du cercle*, trans. Carley Dawson and Elliott Coleman (Baltimore: Johns Hopkins University Press, 1966).

6

GIUSEPPE MAZZOTTA

Italian Renaissance epic

In recent years the sources and conceptual foundations of the epic produced during the Italian Renaissance have been documented in great detail. We have been confirmed in the knowledge that this literary genre developed and was decisively shaped by the relatively small but cohesive city of Ferrara, and that it was promoted by its rulers, the dukes of the House of Este.[1]

The three major practitioners of the genre, Matteo Maria Boiardo (1441–94), Ludovico Ariosto (1474–1533), and to a lesser extent Torquato Tasso (1544–95), lived in that court and knew intimately the twists and turns of the Este genealogical history. They wrote their epics – respectively the *Orlando Innamorato*, the *Orlando Furioso*, and the *Gerusalemme Liberata* – in that courtly context and were immersed in its mythology and rituals. By living in close contact with the intellectual-political events of the court, they were bound to take part, as they did, in its lively cultural activities and innovations. These ranged from the theatre to humanistic theories of education, to steady speculations over ethical systems that more often than not slid into monotonous restatements of the nature of virtue and values, to elaborate artistic productions, such as the 'Sala dei Mesi' by Francesco del Cossa (1436–78) commissioned by Borso d'Este for the Schifanoia Palace.

These activities signal the Estes' efforts to make their city emerge from the grips of its provincialism. Both the role of the university and the presence of these intellectuals in Ferrara cannot be treated as random episodes in the court's cultural life. What holds together the diverse viewpoints and disciplines of these figures and defines the dukes' attempt to establish their principality as a cultural-political force is the pursuit of a coherent project that amounts to a comprehensive ideology widely known under the name of humanism. Rooted in the principles of classical education (the cultivation of history, rhetoric, and moral philosophy), humanism was meant to provide for the aristocratic ethos of the courtiers a new foundation for the traditional classical confidence in the dignity and powers of man.

Boiardo, Ariosto, and Tasso were nourished by these ideals and responded to them. They must have known, for instance, that Leonello d'Este, his half-brother Borso, and his successor Ercole I were tutored by the humanists in residence in the art of good government and in the theories of political order. They also knew, however, that for all its dazzling quality, life at court was accompanied quite early on by the dark presentiment of the court's inevitable decline and imminent dissolution. But within the frame of roughly one century Ferrara's 'three crowns' (as scholars call them in counter-symmetry to Florence's three crowns – Dante, Petrarch, and Boccaccio) turned the Este court into a magnificent scenario within which they would entertain the court, sing the encomium of the Este family and the glamour of its genealogical claims, and concur, although not uniformly, in the policies to preserve the court's fictions of order. But barely beneath the surface of the refined courtly entertainment, they would re-think history's great events – comical and tragic – and would narrate the dissolution of confidence in the solidity of their privileged social micro-cosm. All of them wondered, sceptically, whether Ferrara really mattered in the exciting although dangerously chaotic pageant of world-history.

To circumscribe the rich phenomenon of Renaissance epic exclusively within the ambitious but actually modest confines of Ferrara and its cultural traditions would be both inaccurate and something of a *hubris* akin to the megalomaniac fantasies of its founding myths. For all its value, the claim of autonomy – political and cultural – of the city-states flies in the face of reality. In 1483, almost contemporaneously with Boiardo, although unknown to him, Luigi Pulci, a gifted, eccentric hanger-on in the Medici household, a friend – as much as the humanist scholar and poet, Politian was – of Lorenzo and a protégé of Lorenzo's mother, Lucrezia Tornabuoni, published a brilliant mock-epic, *Morgante*.[2] Written in *ottava rima*, the stanza that since Boccaccio's *Teseida* had become the standard narrative unit of the genre, *Morgante* was conceived in the shadow of Dante's *Divine Comedy* and Leonardo Bruni's *History of Florence*. For all its Florentine focus, however, Pulci's work mixes local political chronicles with the larger perturbations of Western history. The point of departure for Pulci, as it is for Boiardo and Ariosto, is the world-shaping medieval event: the Muslim siege of Saragossa in 778 and the tragic defeat of Roland, Charlemagne's paladin at the pass of Roncevaux, on account of his *hubris*.

By conflating two separate but related interests – Florentine politics at the twilight of the conspiracies wrecking the city (such as the Pazzi conspiracy which, in 1478, sought to topple Medici rule) and the representation of European–Muslim antagonism – Pulci asks whether fifteenth-century Medicean Florence was simply a stitch in the web of a much larger world history.

He is mindful that in Florence's political mythology, Charlemagne, the Holy Roman Emperor, was credited with restoring the city's sovereignty. In the *Rolandino*, a poem that links Charlemagne to the vicissitudes of Italian history, the emperor liberates Rome from Moorish occupation. But all the major poets of Renaissance epic (including Tasso, who focuses on the first crusade, led by Godefroide de Bouillon in 1099 against the Moors) identify in the failure of the Christian army – as told in the *Chanson de Roland* – the tragic paradigm of history as a feared and apparently recurring confrontation with Moorish culture, beliefs, values, and dreams of mastery. The phantom of that *ur*-experience haunts their imagination and history and they were not alone in keeping alive its memory. The most cursory reading of texts of the so-called sixteenth-century *commedia erudita*, from Machiavelli's *Mandragola* to Cecchi's *L'Assiuolo*, all written in the aftermath of the fall of Constantinople (1453), shows the dissemination, popularity, and endless fascination exerted by the recollection of this seemingly immutable plot of history.

How Boiardo, Ariosto, and Tasso respond to this primal myth of Christianity's weakness, re-interpret it and use it as the look-out point on the morass of their own culture and the violence of a broken Europe will be discussed later in this chapter. One thing is clear: aware of the violence rampant in their midst, these poets share one central perspective: none of them is deluded by the current rhetoric of scientific discoveries, novelties, and all too real energy of their own culture. They do not escape the present, but they turn to the past and proceed by rewriting their predecessors' works. Ariosto's *Orlando Furioso* picks up the tangled thematic threads of Boiardo's *Orlando Innamorato*. Tasso's *Gerusalemme Liberata* formally starts at exactly the point where Ariosto ended his epic. The poets turn to the past because they know that memory is the real route to the future. As they move within the horizon of the ghost story of Roland's death, they keep it alive and try to transcend it by forging new perspectives and new values.

The existence of a consciously constructed Renaissance epic tradition is chiefly shown by the deployment not only of a common thematic nucleus but also of a technical device known as *entrelacement*: the systematic interweaving of episodes and multiple plot lines, such as love quests, battles, and a variety of characters. It is signalled, above all, by the hybrid form that epic takes on in the Renaissance. We generally tend to view the construction of the epic tradition – as much as the epics' systematic pattern of retrieving and rewriting past texts and the presence of erasures and self-erasures – as a merely philological problem. And as we do so we neglect the epistemo-logical implications of a genre: that epic and romance, as much as tragedy or the Petrarchan lyric, represent specific ways of knowing the world. In this sense, the tradition of the Italian epic and the process of its constitution in time and space provide a partial revelation of the formal complexity of the worlds Boiardo, Ariosto, and Tasso evoke.

Their poems cannot be termed simply 'epics'. We designate them epic romances: a sort of mixed or hybrid genre that develops from the countless vulgarizations and adaptations of the *Chanson de Roland* in Franco-Italian and Franco-Venetian cycles. The original 'Matter of France' (which centred on the Carolingian cycle of the *chansons de geste*) was grafted on to the so-called 'Matter of Britain' (which encompassed the legend of Arthur and the romances of the knights of the Round Table – Lancelot, Tristan, Yvain, and so on). Romances represent the absolute, adventurous world of love as an illusory labyrinth at the edge of history. Seen through the prism of its magic fantasies, romance constitutes the illusory utopian alibi to the absolute demands of epics' political imperatives. The steady tension between them was loosened by the further absorption of the 'Matter of Rome', into whose orbit fell classical myths linked with Roman history and drawn from tales of Troy (such as the *Roman de Troie* by Benoît de St Maure, Guido delle Colonne's *Historia destructionis Troiae*, the *Roman d'Eneas*, Petrarch's *Africa*, and Boccaccio's *Teseida*). The thematic triad of love, war, and politics appear as domains implicating each other and yet at odds with one another.

Whether or not the *Orlando Innamorato*, the *Orlando Furioso*, and the *Gerusalemme Liberata* could be called epics or just romances was hotly debated in Renaissance critical and literary theories. The battleground here was Aristotle's *Poetics* – recently 're-discovered' by humanist scholars (the Greek text was being copied, studied, and circulated in Italy from the 1470s) and further disseminated by Giorgio Valla's Latin translation, published in 1498 – and the argument ranged over issues of subject matter, suitable style, diction, and plot structure. Two men from Ferrara – Giraldi Cinzio (1504–73), himself the author of an epic poem, *Ercole*, and Giambattista Pigna (1530–75), who wrote a history of the Este family – not to mention Tasso in his *Discourses on the Heroic Poem*, presented their own arguments for competing interpretations of the epic model.[3] Cinzio agrees with Aristotle's view of the kinship between tragedy and epic in that both forms must inspire pity and fear. Pigna, on the other hand, argues for the difficulties of separating the two genres of epic and romance into discrete spheres and admits to the inevitability of their contamination. Tasso, finally, objects to Boiardo's and Ariosto's romance structure. He acknowledges Aristotle's theory about the epic edging towards tragedy, and, in addressing the relationship between poetry and history, he recommends that fiction be founded on history and on religious truths.

The numerous debates on the *Poetics* in the sixteenth century, briefly alluded to here, show that it would be a grievous error to reduce the phenomenon of Renaissance epic to a matter of rhetorical technicalities or sources and, as a consequence, to lose sight of the philosophical and theological questions it raises: either in the mode of Lucretius's a-theology or – quite explicitly in the case of Tasso – with the interrogation of the place human beings occupy within a divine economy. That this theological dimension is generally bracketed off is shown by the fact that the rich bibliography on the epic rarely mentions that the works of Pulci, Boiardo, Ariosto, and Tasso were written within a time frame marked by two major theological events and two decisive historical-religious events.

These events were, respectively, the Council of Ferrara–Florence (1437–9) and the Council of Trent (1545–63), and the fall of Constantinople (1453) and the Battle of Lepanto (October 1571). I do not mean to imply that these events determined the content of the Renaissance epics, even less that they were their source. At most, these historical occurrences constitute the epics' imaginary context, and they help to bring out the deeper metaphysical myth enfolding all epics and intriguing all poets, from Homer to Virgil, to Lucretius and Dante: the ethical imperatives of heroes in the face of the absolute demands of an either familiar, and yet mysterious, or an inexistent divinity. Boiardo, Ariosto, and Tasso certainly deploy, although not in a uniform way, some of the techniques of the classical epic: the *deus ex machina* which, in the form of an angel, descends from heaven, the depiction of hell, the heroes' duties to the emperor and to God. And they eschew the most insidious illusions about their culture's myths of history. These ancient epic traits displayed in the modern poetic prolongations trace the ground for some of their fundamental theological questions.

The Council of Ferrara–Florence (which extended what had actually started in Basel in 1436) was designed to resolve the doctrinal disagreements dividing the Western and the Orthodox churches and to heal the schism of 1107. It managed to draw together Greek scholars (including Plethon and Bessarion) and humanists, thinkers, and artists such as Lorenzo Valla, Nicholas of Cusa, and Leon Battista Alberti. The open wounds in the body of Christendom (disputes over the Trinity, papal authority, and Purgatory) were cauterized for a brief time, but the provisional doctrinal harmony that the Council achieved scarcely concealed Greek anxieties over the Turkish threat and the eventual seizure of Constantinople. However, there can be no doubt that the drama played out in Ferrara and Florence ended up releasing powerful intellectual energies.

Valla would go on to use his humanist scholarship to expose the moral scandal of the Donation of Constantine, and to consider the theological language of the Nicene Creed, the issue of Epicurean ethics (the place pleasure occupies in the Christian frame of reference), and the nature of religious vows, which he understands as acts of the will. Above all, he questions seemingly settled theories about the freedom of the will – a thesis over which Luther and Erasmus would notoriously wrangle about a century later.[4] Nicholas of Cusa travelled to Constantinople immediately after the early phase of the Council in Basel. During the terrifying time that followed the city's fall, he wrote two tracts focusing, respectively, on diversity of religion and the deeper purposes of the Koran. *De pace fidei* (*On the Peace of Faith*) unfolds as a dialogue between Western and Eastern Christians, Arab, Turkish, and Persian Muslims, and a Jew, who together ponder the possible unification of all conflicting religious principles and systems (the Trinity, the resurrection from the dead, etc.). The *Cribatio Alkorani* (*Scrutiny of the Koran*) looks like a response to the drawing apart of Christians and Muslims in the wake of their collision in Constantinople. It examines the nature of Gabriel's apparition to Mohammed, the meaning of Paradise as a garden of sensual delights, and the question of idolatry, and it calls for the overcoming of the tragic religious divisions between Muslims and Christians.

It has become a platitude to say that the tentative celebration of unity at the Council of Ferrara–Florence soon dissolved. The Council of Trent recognized that the illusions of the earlier Council became rubble as Luther's Reform divided Europe. At Trent the theologians sought to define, among other things, the nature of the sacraments and sacrifice, the efficacy of relics, and the role of tradition and history.[5] The re-statement of these doctrines marked the triumph of the Dominican theological strain (Aquinas's *Summa* was symbolically placed on the altar of the Council): the sidelining if not the defeat of the contemplative Benedictine order signalled the emergence of a desirable heroic faith that would revitalize what was left of the drained morale of Latin Christianity. Above all, the Council canonized a new aesthetic paradigm, a baroque style that would vindicate the value of images and make allowances for the architectural conception of churches as theatres, and that would promote the new polyphonic music of Palestrina, composed of separate melodies and contrapuntal voices and sounds bound into one sovereign harmony.

It would be impossible to register here the force of the impact that the decisions of the Council, as well as the reflections of Luther, Erasmus, Ignatius of Loyola, Bellarmine, and Filippo Neri, exerted on the epics of Tasso and, for that matter, on Marino's *Adone* in the seventeenth century. It may not even be possible to isolate one event, say the Battle of Lepanto, which acquired the status of an icon in the history of painting of the time and was celebrated by Titian, Tintoretto, and Veronese. There is no doubt, however, that Cusa's and Valla's ideas about the Trinity as the distinctive scandal against which stumble the aspirations to unity between Muslims and Christians, as well as between the Orthodox and the Western churches, nourish the aesthetics of one epic: the *Morgante*. Pulci's decision to start each canto of his poem with a reference to the doctrine of the Trinity is a nod in the direction of these two thinkers. By the same token, the Epicureanism of his voracious giants reflects, on the one hand, his satirical dismissal of Marsilio Ficino's Neoplatonic dietary prescriptions (vegetarianism, for example), and, on the other hand, Pulci's indebtedness to Valla's new ethics of pleasure.[6] The allusions go a long way in dramatizing the playful theology, indeed the 'divine' comedy, lying at the heart of Pulci's work. But it is time now to turn to the specific insights that Boiardo, Ariosto, and Tasso convey in their masterpieces.[7]

Matteo Maria Boiardo: poet of foundations

Matteo Maria Boiardo, the Count of Scandiano, was a courtier in Ercole d'Este's retinue in Ferrara and served him for several years as the military governor of Modena and Reggio Emilia.[8] His *Orlando Innamorato* (1495) stems directly from the glamorous world of the court and from the shared ceremonies by which the court reflects upon itself, its myths and its values: rituals of courtly love, dramatic and poetic performances, narratives of its origins, beliefs in its own superior aristocratic ethos of enlightenment, and, underneath the fantasies of power, the court's unavoidable anxieties about its future. In this socially coherent and enclosed world, Boiardo also plays the role that minstrels had in the fabled medieval courts of Provence and thus he prolongs their magic legends: he 'sings' the story of Orlando's love-passion, which the title of his poem announces. He also promises that around this romantic topic he will weave a fiction full of wonders, heroes, and monsters for the delight of the courtiers and the duke Ercole d'Este, to whom the poem is dedicated (*OI*, I.i.1).

Whether or not Boiardo's recitation forges connections between the beguiling fairy tales of romance and the courtiers' ethical values of human excellence and power, and whether or not he intends to enlighten them (and us) with respect to the inner darkness lurking behind their golden world, are questions he will raise and answer throughout the poem. But a hint of the genuine, complex concerns Boiardo will ponder throughout the *Orlando Innamorato* is provided by his turning to a seemingly innocuous, even witty, 'philological' detail: the origin of the story he is about to tell and his relationship to that origin. He will entertain, he says, the ladies and knights of the court by filling in the gaps in the 'true history' compiled by Turpin, archbishop of Rheims and friend of Charlemagne. The historian Turpin had repressed the apparently non-historical theme of Roland/Orlando's defeat in love in the conviction that his demeaning passion would dim the lustre of his heroism on the battlefield. Boiardo wants to amend the original imperfect record and highlight Orlando's all-absorbing distractions of eros (as if he were Troilo in Boccaccio's *Filostrato*). This authorial confrontation empha-sizes Boiardo's relative autonomy from his source; it suggests the presence of flaws in even the most authoritative documents of origins and that these gaps are productive of his own work. Finally, Boiardo projects the internal-ized world of romance as the portal to and, indeed, as the root of history. Right from the start, then, we face the two major challenges standing in the way of Boiardo's writing. The first challenge concerns his own poetic persona and voice. In denying the completeness of past historical accounts he takes on the perspective of one who has inherited that tradition, stands within the horizon of its historical time and rejects any acquiescence to its official rhetoric. In addition to offering a modern alternative to bishop Turpin's authority, however, he chooses to make explicit what Turpin had concealed. From this standpoint, Boiardo dons the mask of a historian (as Lucan, say, was thought to be a historian) who is bound to the past but who wills to remain free from the partiality and manipulations of Turpin's enterprise. The exercise of this imaginative freedom allows the poet to dwell, however briefly, on the distinctive trait of his historical epoch, and in particular on its cult of renewal or 'rebirth': the quintessentially Renaissance understanding of history as a movement forward into the future that alters the past but can never escape it.

The second challenge sheds light on the first. In passing from Turpin to Boiardo, paradoxically, we witness the movement from the official 'truth' of history to the deeper, naked truth of a poetry that claims to give a truer picture of, and humanizes the one-dimensional representation of, the hero. In effect, the theme of Orlando's love-passion casts the poem as a cross between two species of writings: Carolingian historical epic (so that epic comes through as the rhetoric of history or a historiography) and Arthurian romance adventures (as history's unacknowledged or secret matrix). The poet's shift to the love disorder in Orlando's mind cannot guarantee a comprehensive understanding of history. It merely allows Boiardo to raise the central question of his text: what is history? Is it reducible to politics and political power, or should we think of power in radically different ways that go beyond predictable theories of the will? In asking these questions Boiardo manages to unveil the court's obsessions with large chronologies, trans-historical lines of legitimate dynastic succession, historical foundations, and origins. As a matter of fact, the conceptual point of departure of the *Orlando Innamorato* lies in genealogy as the chart of reconstruction of the Este family tree. Genealogy presumes continuity and possible intelligibility of the structure of history. It identifies a point of origin leading to and justifying the present. Around this concern Boiardo draws what he thinks of as the essential questions of the epic.

The proem gives way to Turpin's own narrative. On the feast-day of Pentecost – a detail recalling Chrétien de Troyes's technique of unfolding his romances (*Yvain*, for example) against the background of the great events of the Christian calendar (Easter, Ascension, Pentecost, and so forth) – Charlemagne has proclaimed a tournament. It will be held in Paris, and he invites Christian paladins and Saracen knights to participate. Suddenly Angelica appears, and just as suddenly Orlando and other knights fall desperately in love with her. Lured by the sorcery and enigma of her beauty, Orlando travels all over the face of the earth, and his love quest leads him to encounter giants, monsters, and other temptations. The intrusion into the public space of Angelica and the spectacle of the passion she arouses, which disrupts the order of the tournament, induce Boiardo to what amounts to a self-reflexive justification of his narrative.

The text contrasts the feast of Pentecost and the play-image of the tournament (*OI*, 1.i.8). Pentecost commemorates the gift of language to the first apostles and it marks the point of origin for the constitution of the Church. Its historical origin occurs as a language event. Retrospectively, both Turpin's and Boiardo's historical-poetic accounts turn into parables of foundation. The descent of the Pentecostal Word promises the spiritual, prophetic unity of all believers. The tournament, on the other hand, trumps the myth of spiritual unity. As a playful ceremony, it marks time-off from the dangers of war and it stages a subtler drama: it focuses on the one goal all knights share, namely the need to overcome each other and establish a different rank ordering. In this way, the tournament confirms both the anxieties triggered by the war and the sense of the love pursuits. They both aim at enshrining a new hierarchy and at introducing the principle of absolute, if precarious, difference among warriors and suitors. For all the heterogeneity in the perspectives of epic and romance, Boiardo intimates their essential convergence and complementariness.

Accordingly, as a way of deciding whether ethical values can contain the chaos of the heart or are fragile constructions swept away by its impulses, the *Orlando Innamorato* displays the vast, contradictory phenomenology of love through a labyrinth of betrayals, cunning seductions, obsessive passions, masculine and feminine explosions of lust and revenge. Boiardo, who takes a bird's-eye view of all forms of desire, gathers all available perspectives on love. The poem is punctuated with hymns and invocations to love. The hymn to Venus (*OI*, II.xii.1–13) fuses together the contradictory cosmological views on the goddess held by Virgil and Lucretius and casts Venus as the divinity capable of subduing Mars and restoring peace. In the wake of Andreas Capellanus's *Art of Courtly Love*, the poem also expounds the nature of love as a power that educates the lovers and banishes avarice from them (*OI*, II.xv.52 ff.). It ends with the idyllic and playful scene of Fiordespina's lesbian attraction to Bradamante (*OI*, III.ix.1–25).

But Boiardo's insight into the sovereignty of love cannot be reduced to the narrow scope of sexuality. In so far as it appears as desire, it does impel Orlando to his great adventures (such as saving Origille or entering the Orgagna's garden). His love for Angelica sunders him from the Christian army and puts him on a quest leading him to encounter giants, Homeric Cyclops, and other monsters, until, like Odysseus spellbound by Circe, he is trapped by the sorceress Dragontina. She gives him a magic love potion by which he will forget both Angelica and Charlemagne. At the same time, the emir Gradasso travels to Paris from his kingdom in the Far East to get hold of the horse Bayard and the sword Durindan. And desire as appetite for power underlies the acquisitiveness of emperors, such as Alexander, Agramante, and even Rodomonte with his ambitious plans to be crowned King of France (*OI*, II.i.16). Above all, although inimical to war, the love-passion provides the raw energy for characters' actions, and yet, paradoxically, it induces strife and steadily shifts the lovers' perspectives on themselves and their worlds.

The routes of love are endless, its reach limitless. Its very power of transgression casts the romance genre as an all-encompassing absolute form. The quality of absoluteness is best explained by the experiences of the heroes, who are irresistibly drawn within an enchanted world (the domain of the sorcerer Malagigi's magic book). From this standpoint, even the epic, with its public and historical focus, is contained by the romance, part of its ever-widening circle. Because the seductive temptations of romance disrupt the world of epic, as much as the demands of epic tear the heroes away from the absorptions of romance, epic itself fails for Boiardo to appear as a totality. The relation between the two genres, which comes through as the relation between politics and psychology, city and eros, history and love, is dramatized in Book II, where Boiardo, wishing to retrieve the genealogy of the Este family (with a nod to Vespasiano Strozzi's reconstruction of the Este dynasty), introduces his hero, Ruggiero, as the founder of his patrons' house.

Genealogy, as a science of biological origins designed to discover a meaningful pattern underneath the chaos of history, turns into a fable of haphazard adventures deliberately straining all believability. Boiardo's starting point is once again Turpin's history, where he finds the legend of Alexander. The emperor founded the city of Alexandria out of love for Elidonia, who bore him three children, and from them descended Agolante, Troiano, and Agramante, the line responsible for invading Christian Europe. On the walls of Agramante's palace, a cycle of frescoes tells the story of his ancestor Alexander. Clearly, present-day enemies were once blood brothers. The dynastic narrative continues later in Book III.v.18–31, where Ruggiero traces his own origins to the fall of Troy and to Astyanax, son of Hector and Andromache, who does not really die during the Trojan war (as the *Iliad* had implied) but survives in a tomb, reaches Sicily, and marries the queen of Messina. The origins of Ruggiero and the Este family are thus established. Bradamante, for her part, tells her own genealogy from the Chiaramonte family tree (*OI*, III.v.39–40). The love between Ruggiero and Bradamante imposes order on the chaotic play of forces and, as much as Agramante's art, draws their claims within the illusory boundaries of romance.

Boiardo's sense of the tangle of erotic and social threads is best exemplified by one of Ranaldo's experiences. Like Orlando, Ranaldo (a slightly imperfect anagram of Orlando and his quasi double) starts out on his quest for Angelica and finds himself in the Arden Wood, in the middle of which runs a river, and, next to it, stands a fountain built by Merlin's magic art (*OI*, I.iii.33). We approach, literally, both the source of romantic impulses and the literary tradition of romance. Merlin's fount was meant to induce forgetfulness into Tristan's passion for Iseult. Ranaldo drinks from it and forgets Angelica. Angelica drinks from the Stream of Love and, on seeing Ranaldo asleep, falls in love with him (I.iii.91). Valla's and Pico's arguments about the freedom of the will lose all consistency. More poignantly, the imaginative contiguity between water and love (fully forged by Petrarch) suggests the fluidity of desire, its lability. However clear the water of the fountain appears, desire lacks all transparency. It is troubled and muddled: it robs Angelica of her powers of reflection while the freedom from it gives Ranaldo a false sense of moral superiority.

He will soon be captured as he crosses a bridge across a river that takes him to the Castle Cruel where a monster, who eats human flesh and demands human sacrifices, lives terrorizing the townspeople. The two figures of the bridge and the river punctuate the unfolding of the *Orlando Innamorato*. If the river marks the natural boundaries between two separate banks (or between the living and the dead, as does the Styx), the artifice of the bridge joins them. Ranaldo comes to this passageway and he will plunge into the depths of horror, recalling Dante's representation of the hellish afterlife with its condensation of treachery, violence, and human bestiality. Chained and threatened with death, Ranaldo learns from a friar the origin of the monster. In a world of refined courtly manners, Grifone hosts the knight Marchino, who falls desperately in love with Grifone's wife, Stella (I.viii.31). Marchino's love is a madness pushing him to kill Grifone, and the murder unleashes a series of crimes that at first appear as the characters' assertion of their freedom in the face of injustices done to them. In a jealous rage Marchino's wife, like Medea and Procne, kills their children and serves them to her husband on a plate. Driven by a common passion for revenge, both Stella and Marchino's wife plot to kill Marchino, who actually kills them. The story takes now a horrifying monstrous turn. Marchino repeatedly rapes the corpse of Stella in her tomb. The monster that Ranaldo will kill stemmed from Marchino's defilement of the grave and from the seed he deposited in her decomposed womb.

Ranaldo and Marchino, through whom Boiardo tells two different versions of origins, stand for two complementary epic narratives. The epic *topos* of the hero's descent to the world of the dead recalls the classical crossing of the boundaries dividing life and death by Ulysses, Aeneas, Dante, and Politian's Orpheus. Marchino's necrophilia, which literalizes the romantic bond between love and death and provokes revulsion, stages his refusal to accept Stella's death and, beyond that, a rancour against death itself. In his journey into the domain of the dead (which at the same time is the dark realm of sexuality), he erases all boundaries and, like Orpheus, seeks to abolish the finiteness of his human condition. He falls prey to the all too common desire to abolish history. Ranaldo, on the other hand, witnesses the evil threatening the city and kills the monster in a moral-political effort to purify the community. But his heroic action turns into a curse: it causes a rebellion from the townspeople, as if it is evil and the sacrificial victims the monster demands for his meal – and not love – that hold together the ethics of that community. A symmetry governs the two perverted narratives of birth and redemption and makes them converge: Marchino's blindness to the boundaries of time and space complements Ranaldo's dream of redemption, and both expose their obsessive pursuit of omnipotence.

Through their two experiences, Boiardo acknowledges the fertility of death, its immortal origin from which, like a root below the ground, life springs. The branches of family pedigrees may well re-enact this grim fantasy. At any rate, as he reveals that the dead are at the mercy of the living and as he depicts death as the ultimate essence swallowing up all that lives, Boiardo is haunted by the awareness of human longing for infinity and by the experience of desire's transgression of all measure – *mensura* – a word that, as Nicholas of Cusa has it, derives from *mens*, mind. Boiardo calls for an ethics of finitude, limitations, and self-limitations. He does not lose sight of the fact that human imagination is fired up by all that is destructive and measureless. Monsters, giants, Cyclops, and heroic fables punctuate the fanciful world of romance epics. They dominate historical action and engage the polished world of the court.

What usually strikes readers as a chance occurrence in history forced the poet to truncate his narrative. The memorable last stanza of the poem cuts short the idyllic interlude of Bradamante and Fiordespina and drives Boiardo's point home:

> Mentre ch'io canto, o Iddio redentore,
> Vedo la Italia tutta a fiamma e a foco
> Per questi Galli, che con gran valore
> Vengon per disertar non so che loco;
> Però vi lascio in questo vano amore
> De Fiordespina ardente a poco a poco;
> Un'altra fiata, se mi fia concesso,
> Racontarovi il tutto per espresso.   (III.ix.26)

(But while I sing, o my redeemer, I see all Italy on fire, because these French – so valiant! – come to lay waste who knows what land. So I will leave this hopeless love of simmering Fiordespina. Some other time, if God permits, I'll tell you all there is to this.)

History, in the guise of Charles VIII's French invasion of Italy in 1494, has intruded, and it replaces Turpin's book of the myths of French history. Boiardo surrenders his song, 'io canto', to history's realities. The circle is closed as the ending looks deceptively like a willed contrivance echoing the opening. In reality, it is an interruption, a provisional break. But Boiardo knows better. The apostrophe/prayer to God, calling for an impossible redemption from the outside – the intervention of a *deus ex machina* that this time won't work – desperately laments the political tragedy of Italy, the lack of 'virtue' in the land, the sacrilege of the invasion – the invaders' 'valour' makes a desert and most likely they will call it peace. The prayer projects history as the place of Fiordespina where history's hidden chaos all of sudden explodes, like an earthquake, and leaves behind it scars and craters of troublesome thistles.

Ludovico Ariosto: poet of freedom

In his *Discourses on the Heroic Poem*, Torquato Tasso comments critically that the *Orlando Furioso* (1516, 1521, 1532) was the continuation and completion of Boiardo's *Orlando Innamorato*.[9] In propounding this view he clearly has in mind the plot and formal connections between the two romance epics: the same heroes and heroines – Orlando, Angelica, Ruggiero, Bradamante, Rinaldo, Rodomonte – who keep wandering from place to place and whose movements account for the multiple plots of the two texts; the same techniques and metrical structures (such as *entrelacement* and octaves); the same dynastic purposes for the Este Duke; and the common dependence on the same narrator, Turpin.

No doubt Tasso is right in claiming that Ariosto's poem presupposes an uninterrupted continuity between himself and his Ferrarese precursor. One could add that he re-worked the thematic profusion of Boiardo's imagination so diligently that one cannot but infer that he wanted to bring the tradition of romance epics to a close. Yet the affinities between the two poems cannot obscure the sharp differences between them. There are differences of substance, and they constitute the remarkable originality of the *Orlando Furioso* that no accounting of sources can explain away. Ariosto had an extraordinary awareness of the problematic nature of his culture, whose dominant myths his poem reconstructs in all their complexity and which he submits to critical analysis. What for Ariosto overwhelms the culture of the Renaissance are its very virtues, the inherent self-contradictions of its values.

The madness of Orlando provides important evidence for Ariosto's radical critique of Neoplatonic love theories (Ficino, Equicola, and so on) and of Pico's exaggerated view of the role of rationality in his illustration of 'man's dignity' and ceaseless striving for absolute freedom against the objective limitations of the order of necessity. Although Ariosto does not simply reject these optimistic formulations, he nevertheless knew that they pointed in one potentially destructive and self-destructive direction. Consistently, he relates these Neoplatonic vindications of the privileged role human beings play in the scheme of things to Alberti's theory of perspective, which he advanced in his treatise *On Painting*, and its new aesthetics of the supreme value of individual, contingent perceptions and viewpoints. And Ariosto grasps the link binding the propositions of Alberti and Pico to Machiavelli's interpretation of politics as the theatre of excess and tragic energy in the prince's will to power.

For all his tenacious preoccupations with the weakness underlying Renaissance culture's claims and megalomania – epitomized by the glories of its humanism – these intellectual innovations share the same principle and the same creative impulse Ariosto identifies as a fundamental passion that turns out as the shaping force of his poetic vision. The name of this virtue is liberty. In Pico's *Oration on the Dignity of Man*, as hinted above, of all God's creation man is acknowledged as the 'most precious and the most free', and his freedom entails nothing less than the mind's openness to the greatest variety of possible experiences whereby a human being can rise up to the level of an angel or descend to the depths of a demon. One immediate corollary of such a dramatic conception draws the inference that freedom makes man like God. The notion justly took its place in the most disparate philosophical debates of the late fifteenth century and in the religious circles of the Reformation. The idea's impact was strengthened by Lorenzo Valla's major argument in defence of man's free will that brought him face to face with a jarring contradiction. To save his theory of man's free will, Valla had to posit a split between God's knowledge and God's will and argue that God does not necessarily will what he knows.

Valla's theological perspective on freedom needed intellectual clarification, and it came from predictable quarters. Almost a century had to elapse before two decisive conflicting interpretations of his paradoxical formulation emerged. Erasmus, a thinker who lived by reason and died by reason, infused his defence of free will with an ethical meaning: the authority of tradition and Biblical exegesis (which he wanted to uphold) taught him that this power of human discernment – the ability to choose either good or evil – rests on God's rational order, accessible to reason, and it precludes the view of God's unfettered arbitrariness over human events. The limitations of Erasmus's argument, which lie in his facile optimism, were readily apparent to Luther, who, in positing the bondage of the will – in his conviction that the will on its own can do nothing, for it wills and unwills against itself – comes through as, in the most literal sense, an *enthusiast* ('God is in him').

From the standpoint of his ecstatic Christian experience, Luther casts Erasmus's rationalism as Pelagian and concludes that Erasmus is a thinker for whom the power of the human will consists in willing but not in loving. By contrast, the true source of liberty, Luther argues, is irrational, numinous faith: faith cannot be bridled; it releases man from all obligations, shatters the ordinary criteria of life, places him beyond all ethics and all fear of civil disturbances. Plainly, in the tragic (because absolute), mad universe of faith that Luther inhabits (and that Erasmus had understood in *In Praise of Folly* in intellectual terms), faith is identified with liberty, and both introduce into the drama of history the principle of ugly dissonance and negation of the 'world'.

These two divergent conceptions of liberty and faith figure prominently throughout the *Orlando Furioso* and characterize Ariosto's desire to look beyond the illusory phenomena of the empirical world and the surface values of the culture of his time. A central instance of this concern with liberty is crystallized by Ariosto's own poetics, by the will to rewrite the literary tradition. From this perspective, Tasso was essentially on the right track in pointing out how much Ariosto's epic owes to Boiardo's. Indeed,

Ariosto stages his dependence on Boiardo, but also on Turpin, whom they both acknowledge as the common matrix of their fables, on Dante, Virgil, Statius, and others. The staging of Ariosto's authorial dependence (a rubric that encompasses his sense of 'imitation', fictionality, and originality) can only be explained as the acknowledgment of an impossible absolute autonomy from pre-existing models. And yet, the lack of control over the sources of his material does not entail a total surrender to the authority of his models. Clearly, their existence curtails his freedom: but just as Boiardo claims his artistic autonomy in constructing his own values and in opening up the romantic dimensions of experience unavailable to Turpin, so, too, does Ariosto with his recovery of the mythic roots of the epic. The aesthetic game he plays in his *Orlando Furioso* – his laughing at the world – is coextensive with his notion of the freedom of the imagination that can be free by paradoxically moving within a set of constraints.

Building on the foundation of art as a metaphor that draws together freedom and constraints, Ariosto represents the main adventures of his characters as a ceaseless fluctuation between freedom and bondage – a bondage to love, fate, or duty. The vicissitudes of Ruggiero and Bradamante make apparent the patterns of reversal of freedom and captivity in the poet's moral imagination. The two characters epitomize the dynastic, preordained strain of the *Orlando Furioso* as well as the observance of an ethics of self-restraint and religious conversion, all of which culminates in the ceremony of marriage. The motif of their freedom and captivity is thematized throughout the poem. At the start Pinabello tells Rinaldo he has seen Ruggiero imprisoned by Atlante in his enchanted castle. Bradamante pursues Pinabello and finds herself captive in a grotto, where the sorcerer Merlin predicts her fated marriage to Ruggiero. Eventually, Bradamante will free Ruggiero, who is kidnapped by the hippogryph (a cross between a horse and a griffin) and is ensnared by the witch Alcina. Orlando, for his part, will free Olimpia and, later, Isabella of Galicia, who was a prisoner of Gabrina. Astolfo, on the contrary, is trapped by Alcina, indeed is transformed into a myrtle, but with his magic book he frees the knights who are held prisoners of Atlante, and, riding the hippogryph all the way to the moon to retrieve Orlando's wits, he finally disengages himself from the gravity of the earth and enters the pure realm of the imagination.

Freedom's seduction counters the subtle fascination exerted by the state of bondage. Freedom is figured in the relentless vagrancy of both Christian and Muslim knights all over the continents of the earth, in the anarchic movement of desire across the labyrinthine architecture of the mind, and in the excitement of chance encounters. Bondage does not exclude other expressions of the quest for freedom. Rinaldo, for instance, is finally freed from the monster of jealousy. On the other hand, Orlando, unloved by Angelica, discovers that he wants to escape his destiny and will do so at a price: he sinks into the nightmare of his madness. He escapes into madness, where he is totally free from constraints: there the possible becomes real and all limits can be transgressed. He shuts himself in the prison of his mind and locks its door until Astolfo frees him.

Luther's radical experience of faith is haunted by the consciousness of its impossible synthesis with reason. In his visionary identification of faith as liberty he sets no limits to the scope of either. Ariosto does not repudiate Luther's claim, but he muddies the water. He confronts the Augustinian monk's insight into the knot of liberty and faith, pushes it one step further, and ends up completely reversing the direction of his thought. In effect, Ariosto taunts Luther by replacing his scenario: against Luther, he presents a character, Rodomonte, for whom freedom becomes pure will to total self-assertion and the source not of faith but of atheism. One does not have to look far in the hall of mirrors of the *Orlando Furioso* for Rodomonte's look-alikes. I have mentioned above Orlando's madness as freedom and Astolfo's freedom as playfulness. Rodomonte, however, is their champion. He has no laws other than the perpetually shifting, unpredictable rules he chooses. In his desire to rule he makes himself the source of all values and all destruction. Through him Ariosto probes the phenomenology of freedom and atheism.

We first meet Rodomonte at the siege of Paris (*OF*, xiv), where, fanatical and fierce, he leads the attack against the walls of the city. To convey his relentless anger, Ariosto traces Rodomonte's genealogy back to Nimrod, the builder of the Tower of Babel, who tried to overturn God's rule (*OF*, xiv.118). His genealogical destiny hints at a sort of predestination, but in reality Rodomonte has internalized his ancestor's excesses and has made him his model: like Statius's Capaneus, he recognizes only the law of force, submits to none, and when in danger he curses God (xiv.8). In this residue of classical gigantomachy, just as the battle provides the occasion for self-fulfilment, his blasphemy asserts his freedom: his dream to set Paris on fire and later to lay Rome to waste has petrified him in the project to impose his will on the whole of Christianity and outdo the achievements of the warriors in his own Muslim camp.

Rodomonte's first defeat occurs when the woman he loves, Doralice, chooses Mandricardo. She inflicts on Rodomonte a wound that no other knight could. The humiliation he experiences could set him free, but it imprisons him for ever. He distrusts all women and perpetuates his misogynistic belief (for trust and belief are subtly kept both distinct and correlated by Ariosto) when he hears from an innkeeper the story of the queen's guilty passion for a monstrous court dwarf/jester. Abandoned by Doralice, however, Rodomonte stands on the threshold of another possible freedom. He could break loose from the past when he falls in love with Isabella, who, having lost her beloved Zerbino and out of fidelity to him, wants to leave the 'world' and enter a cloister. Rodomonte, who openly professes atheism ('in Dio non credea / d'ogni legge nimico e d'ogni fede' (an unbeliever, he was hostile to every law, to every faith), XXVIII.99.7–8), laughs at her claims of fidelity. A perfect counterpoint holds their destinies together: faithful to Zerbino, Isabella is willing to die; faithful to his scepticism, Rodomonte tests her claims and ends up beheading her.

After killing Isabella and thinking he has been deceived by all, Rodomonte teeters on the edge of the abyss. Alone, unassimilable, completely 'outside' and dispossessed, he transforms himself into an enemy to all. At the siege of Paris he was not afraid of falling into the precipice. At the end of the poem, when he turns up, uninvited, at the wedding of Ruggiero and Bradamante, he is ready to throw himself over the edge. He challenges Ruggiero to a duel, for Ruggiero is to him his distorted mirror image: a treacherous convert to Christianity, who agrees to marry Bradamante, and so inaugurate the new history and the new Este dynasty. In his blind rage Rodomonte wants to destroy Ruggiero, which is to say that he wills his own destruction. Enclosed and hardened in his absolute distrust, he has dug a chasm into which he will fall. Like Virgil's Turnus (*Aeneid*, XII.950–3), Rodomonte, struck by Ruggiero's dagger, plunges to the gloom of Acheron.

Through Rodomonte's tragedy of freedom, Ariosto unveils Luther's tragic understanding of faith, which is nonetheless capable of shattering Erasmus's rational, limited understanding. Of the two contenders, Rodomonte against Ruggiero, Luther against Erasmus, Ariosto grasps the sublime, absolute quality of the radical theologian and the self-annihilating hero. And he even implies that Rodomonte, in his denial of God so that he may be free, ends up paradoxically looking like a grotesque inversion of God just as his freedom annuls all responsibility. From the viewpoint of the consequences of the claim of freedom, we understand Ariosto's retrenchment into authorial modesty by his acknowledgment of the debts incurred from Turpin, Boiardo, Dante, and their common tradition. He recognizes his dependence on previous voices and texts, which is to say that freedom cannot be regarded as a tragic dissolution of bonds.

The tragic end, finally, entails a new ethics for the modern Renaissance culture (adumbrated at the festive opening of the last canto of the *Orlando Furioso*, XLVI) with the enumeration of the rich and famous of the time. Ariosto's ethics is defined by his sharing Dante's, Valla's, and Cusanus's revulsion at the temporal power ratified by the Donation of Constantine

(*OF*, XLVI.84); he inveighs against Christian wars (XVII.83), and he attacks Pope Leo X's political schemes. But a far-reaching ethical argument is found in the aphorism appended after the last stanza of the poem: 'Pro Bono Malum'. The sense of the phrase was anticipated in *OF*, XLV.4: 'che 'l ben va dietro al male, e 'l male al bene ... follow hard upon each other). The context of the line sums up the Boethian and Dantesque image of the wheel of blindfolded Fortune, who, as she plays with the world, reverses the good into the bad, comedy into tragedy, and wealth into poverty. Whatever justice Fortune dispenses to jousting mortals, whatever transcendent order there may be in the cosmos, we don't get to know the causes. The image of Fortune stresses, however, the inseparability of freedom from dependency, and, as such, the author's self-limitation is contained within the sublime powers of his own character Rodomonte as much as, say, Erasmus is contained within Luther's absolute claims.

Torquato Tasso: poet of the sacred

That Tasso conceived his *Gerusalemme Liberata* (1581) as the turning point in the history of the epic is made clear at the start: the poem begins at the opposite point from where *Orlando Furioso* ends.[10] The death of Rodomonte recalls Turnus's death at the end of the *Aeneid* and seals the poem. The first line of Tasso's opening stanza picks up Virgil's opening line:

> Canto l'arme pietose e 'l capitano
> che 'l gran sepolcro liberò di Cristo:
> Molto egli oprò con 'l senno e con la mano,
> molto soffrí nel glorioso acquisto:
> e in van l'Inferno vi s'oppose, e in vano
> s'armò d'Asia e di Libia il popol misto;
> Il Ciel gli diè favore, e sotto a i santi
> segni ridusse i suoi compagni erranti.   (*GL*, I.1)

(I sing the reverent armies and the captain who liberated Christ's great sepulchre. Much he wrought with his wit and his hand; much he suffered in the glorious conquest. In vain did Hell oppose him, and vainly the combined peoples of Asia and Lybia took up arms. Heaven granted him favour and brought back under the holy standards his wandering companions.)

Tasso's acknowledgement of the *Aeneid* is two-faced. Conscious of the novelty of his work, he casts it using the Virgilian epic as a model for the representation of a heroic action altogether different from Ariosto's implications about the aporias of justice. For Tasso the new Aeneas is a pilgrim-crusader, Goffredo, who in 1099 led the First Crusade to Jerusalem to free the Holy Sepulchre – which is an *empty* tomb but is called 'great' to describe both the magnitude of the event and the hero's moral grandeur.

By turning to a historical event and a historical figure of heroic proportions, Tasso gives the first sign of his renewal of the epic genre. We are no longer lodged in the imaginary world of Arthurian romantic myths and Carolingian dramas. Nor is the *Gerusalemme Liberata* another dynastic poem: Alfonso II of the Ferrarese Este family is mentioned only to be politely asked to model himself on Goffredo, the leader capable of recalling his errant companions to the path of their moral purposes. In his *Discourses on the Heroic Poem* (1594) Tasso identifies history as the genuine argument of the epic and even stresses the divergence between poetry and history. Unlike Lucan, whom he calls a historian and not a poet, Tasso views poetry as more than history. History is the ground of existence, but poetry unveils its secret workings (monstrous violence, disquieting loves, endless impostures) and mystery. His focus on Goffredo and the Crusade makes his epic 'modern' because he now can tackle the crises inaugurated by contemporary religious passions in a way that the 'one' epic of Boiardo and Ariosto does not.

Even formally, Tasso's choice of one action is also meant to mark the fresh start of his enterprise. By deploying multiple plots, both the *Orlando Innamorato* and the *Orlando Furioso* affirm the overlapping of life's fluid experiences. At odds with them, the *Gerusalemme Liberata* can honour the diversity of events and yet subdue the proliferation of plots within the one overarching Aristotelian principle of the unities of action (the Crusade), place (the desert and the city of Jerusalem), and historical time. The formal unity of the poem, finally, is imparted by Tasso's own voice, singular yet capable of the subtlest modulations. Like Virgil, the poet can hold together the strains of the narrative and, like Ariosto (and, arguably, Dante), he wrestles at the edge of a possible shipwreck over the sea of his labours.

The risky wandering of the poet over history's occurrences unavoidably broaches the matter of fiction. The age-old debate over truth and lies in poetry makes Tasso turn to the anti-Virgilian epic writer, Lucretius. After the invocation to the unnamed Muse, Tasso asks forgiveness for interweaving history with fables:

> Così a l'egro fanciul porgiamo aspersi
> di soavi licor gli orli del vaso
> succhi amari ingannato intanto ei beve,
> e da l'inganno suo vita riceve.   (*GL*, 1.3, lines 5–8)

(So we present the feverish child the rim of the glass sprinkled over with sweet liquids; he drinks deceived the bitter medicine and from his deception receives life.)

We are no doubt meant to hear an echo of a well-known passage from *De rerum natura* (I, lines 936–42), in which Lucretius writes of the need to conceal the bitterness of his Epicurean doctrine by sweetening with honey the rim of the cup from which Memmius will drink the philosophical remedies to his sick beliefs in the gods and to the terrors that religion arouses.

In effect, Lucretius's poem, centred on 'Aeneadum genetrix' (I, line I), tells a subversive story both about Venus and Mars, the two gods of Rome's origins, and about the Virgilian myth of Rome. From Lucretius's standpoint, there is no room for the sacred in Rome's political ideology because the sacred has altogether vanished from the fabric of the world thanks to the Epicurean account of the origins of the universe. It follows that the desecrated picture of the world Lucretius disseminates is so harsh that it needs a palliative. Thus, the poet's predicament in mixing together philosophical truths and poetic fictions issues into the assertion of the therapeutic value of poetry: readers, such as the noble Memmius whom Lucretius wishes to educate, are like sick children the poet can heal. At the same time, he implies that the sweetness of poetic metaphor, which is a deception, is preferable to the bitter truths of Epicurean philosophy.

The allusion to Lucretius's thought and rhetoric forces us to look into the heart of Tasso's theological universe. In spite of the declared *pietas* and heroic faith of Goffredo, is Tasso insinuating – as Lucretius does with Epicurean philosophy – that poetry is preferable to theology? Is he brooding, like Lucretius, about unbelief, about the inevitable death of the world, and the nature of the void? These questions are not gratuitous. We recall Tasso's anxieties over the religious orthodoxy of his poem. We can reasonably infer that he really knew, above and beyond the romantic aura of his persecution complex, whether and how his poetry had crossed the line in transacting the problematic relation between history and fiction, and between theology and poetry. It may well be that Tasso's claims of poetic novelty are a symptom of his new tentative resolutions of the deeper substantial contradictions rampant in his times.

On the face of it, it is Book II of his *Discourses on the Heroic Poem* that enables us to read Tasso's epic in a new light. Reflecting on historical truth as the suitable starting point for the heroic poet, Tasso touches on the poets who deceive the reader by offering semblances of truth, and on the fables of Boiardo and Ariosto, and he discusses at length the Neoplatonic Premise in Iacopo Mazzoni's *Defense of Dante's Poetry*. Mazzoni makes 'phantastic imagination' the hinge of poetry. Tasso disagrees. He wants to invest poetry with the dignity and value claimed by other serious intellectual achievements and so he argues that it belongs to the circle of dialectics, logic, and theology. 'Indeed', he writes, 'poets and theologians were the same, not only according to Aristotle for the ancients – Linus, Orpheus, Musaeus – but for Boccaccio in his *Life of Dante*.' Tasso's definition of the poet as a 'divine theologian', understood as one who forms images and wills them into existence, rests on the authority of the Pseudo-Dionysius's letters and *Mystical Theology*.[11] He will even follow the latter's distinction between intellectual and affective mystical theology: unlike Aquinas, who assigns poetry to the lowest rank of the arts, Dionysius thinks that the mind is awakened by the contemplation of images.

We cannot be surprised by Tasso's knowing discussion of Dionysius. The latter's texts, translated by Ambrogio Traversari on the instigation of Nicholas of Cusa and published in Florence in 1516, found devoted readers in Valla, Ficino, and Pico, although Luther and the Reformers dismissed him outright. The *Mystical Theology*, a summary of Dionysius's reflections on divine darkness and hidden silence, on God beyond all being and all knowledge, finds in the ascent of Moses, as told in Exodus, the image of supreme consciousness – the mind plunging into the darkness of unknowing.

Like Ariosto before him, Tasso has the intellectual power to raise difficult questions. His *Gerusalemme Liberata*, a title that fuses together a vision of peace and freedom, confronts the wide spectrum of religious beliefs, idolatry, iconoclasm, sacrifices, and scepticism. He explores these spiritual manifestations and shows how each character of the poem is imprisoned in his/her own standpoint. How can he break out of the impasse of contradictory strains, exemplified by the war between Christians and Muslims, and how can they cohere and be unified? The *Mystical Theology*, which recalls the eremitic traditions of the Desert Fathers of the third and fourth centuries, provides a model for his poetic and theological thought. This is not to say, of course, that Tasso is a mystic. Rather, he found in Dionysius's mysticism a theological rationale for the paradox that the visible world is the image of the invisible world and that the divine remains nonetheless concealed in transcendent obscurity. He found in the mystical tradition the justification of the baroque panoply of ceremonies, rituals, images, and symbols appropriate for the things of God. In short, the concerns of the Tridentine Council, which canonizes the theatre of belief by making the image the locus of the sacred, are bent into unexpected and yet logical directions.

The *Gerusalemme Liberata* dramatizes the Christian faith of Goffredo at the start. He believes in his mission and his authority is rooted in his faith. By virtue of his 'fortitudo et sapientia', the two traditional attributes of the epic hero (line 3), Goffredo is the 'capitano', a word from the Latin *caput* suggesting a mystical-political body he eventually will lead to the 'Sepolcro' (*GL*, xx.144, line 8). This quintessentially baroque image of the mystery of faith – it stands simultaneously as a sign of Christ's triumph over death and, in its very emptiness, as a cipher of the Lucretian void and, as such, as a stumbling block to unbelievers – brings to light the sense of the sacred in Goffredo's hierarchical universe. He models himself in his role as leader on Moses in the desert of Exodus (*GL*, XIII.71). Like Moses, he is guided by God and by his angels. But the source of the sacred is found in the consecration of his whole life to the vow – a word that Valla interprets as the sacrifice of the will and that Dante links to 'vuoto' (void) (*Paradiso*, III.57) – he had taken.

Canto II of the poem quickly establishes a contrast, which is to say it draws a boundary line around Goffredo. The action moves to the Muslim camp, which lies under the rule of a 'tyrant' (II.1), a term that suggests the sovereignty of limitless and unlawful power. The hellishness of the camp is epitomized by the magician Ismeno, a Christian convert to the Muslim religion, who confronts and seeks to dismantle Goffredo's piety with his will to methodical sacrilege and blasphemy. Ismeno duplicates Rodomonte, in a way, and reverses Goffredo's values: he conjures up the dead from their tombs, manipulates images and simulacra, enchants the forest, and instigates the plan to abduct a sacred image from a Christian church. By the power of magic make-believe, whereby he controls the forces governing the natural world, reality becomes the projection of his will. His practice of profanation casts the sacred as the mere work of human hands. In contrast to Ismeno's iconoclasm, the Christian lovers Olindo and Sofronia invest the image of the Virgin with the power of reality and are willing to sacrifice their lives for it. One metaphor, however, illuminates the oppositions, play of semblances, and differences among these characters: the desert – the Biblical space of transition between bondage and freedom – figures as the locus of exile beset with temptations and choices, the middle ground where the prophetic and the idolatrous both converge and pull apart.

Tasso does not restrict himself to the representation of rival-complementary views of religious beliefs (even if Ismeno believes he can dispense with Christian revelation). Because, like Valla before him, he understands the danger in the reduction of faith to the abstract norms of reason, Tasso makes love and women – Clorinda, Armida, and Erminia – the point of refraction of all the questions triggered by religious faith. Love, as both the agent and the object of desire, removes faith from the sphere of intellectual abstractions and makes it part of concrete, existential experience. Faith as love can and will ignite scepticism, and the scepticism ranges from not knowing a woman's concealed identity or subterfuges, to uncertainty about being loved, to fear of losing one's self-possession or even the woman one loves. It also induces and trumps self-knowledge. More importantly, Tasso's three heroines, around whom many other women from past literatures revolve (Medea, the Siren, Penelope, Phaedra, Beatrice, Laura, and Angelica) appear as self-contradictory: strange, deceptive, but in the process of changing. In a way, they embody the principle of diversity: they recognize it and make it part of who they will become.

The tragic fate of Clorinda encompasses these issues about faith and love, and it puts us at the outer reaches of Tasso's radical thinking. The most haunting images surrounding her are Tancredi's love and pursuit of her tracks, her wound at the hand of Tancredi, her intercession for Sofronia and Olindo, her fearlessness as a warrior, her confession of faith when she is killed by Tancredi, and her words of forgiveness for him. From these scenes Clorinda emerges as the figure of utter dislocation: she is an alien to her family, she does not know her roots and religion, and she dies in the arms of her lover. Her dislocation – the sense of being somewhere else from where one should be or other than one wants to be – is the source of her religious consciousness. But it is in the final scene when Tancredi kills her that the tragic erupts in their lives. Overwhelmed by guilt and grief, he refuses to see that there may be any justice in her death (*GL*, XII.77). Clorinda, by contrast, forgives Tancredi and asks for his forgiveness: 'Amico, hai vinto: io ti perdon . . . perdona' (Friend you have won; I grant you pardon . . . you grant pardon), XII.66). The word of forgiveness she speaks – 'perdon' enfolds a 'dono' [a gift], and the pardon makes it that he can live after she dies.

All of a sudden, her tragedy is bound together with and opens up to a religious perspective that rescues her death from being a futile occurrence. Later in the poem, after visiting her tomb, Tancredi crosses the threshold of the profane, the 'profana soglia' (XIII.37) of the enchanted forest. The place of Ismeno's profanation turns into one of revelation, for one is the truth of the other. In a clearing, which has the form of an amphitheatre, Tancredi hears Clorinda's voice stopping him from committing further violence. The awesome image is exposed as a magical deception contrived by Ismeno. Disenchanted, Tancredi realizes that the sacred cannot be located, as if it were an object, in the magic animation of nature. As the phantasm of Clorinda returns to his broken mind, it makes his memory the theatre of his consecration to her and cures the sorrow and amorous languor afflicting him.

The tenuous proximity of and complicity between the sacred and the array of simulacra that parody and negate the sacred – empty tombs, ceremonies, imagination, dreams, and memory – hinge on and are made possible by two complementary metaphorical patterns that Tasso deploys as the pivot of his poem: the theatre and the desert. How do the two metaphors shed light on each other? The language of the theatre running throughout the text – spectacles, processions, rituals, amphitheatres – highlights Tasso's reduction of the world to a phenomenal and optical representation, whereby, as happens in baroque aesthetics, reality is contained within the boundaries of illusory and empty signs. Nonetheless, unlike Lucretius, Tasso invests the emptiness of signs with a vital ambiguity. Theologically, the 'emptiness' of Christ's tomb, for instance, announces through the muteness of the monument the silence at the heart of a transcendent faith. More to the point, emptiness, which the Greeks called *kenosis*, is an ancient theological concept. In Philippians 2:6–7 the link between visible signs and emptiness is forged as we read of Jesus who 'emptied himself...being born in the likeness of man'. In the tradition of negative mystical theology (as in Nicholas of Cusa), Christ's suffering signals the self-emptying of his divinity. The negativity of the sign turns religious faith – which concerns itself with invisible realities and mute ciphers – into a question of perspective.

Tasso's metaphor of the theatre, which implies a scenario of multiple, illusory and shifting perspectives, places us in the desert, the site of quests and questions, where all questers – Goffredo, Ismeno, Clorinda, Tancredi, Rinaldo, and Armida – are caught in a circle of mutual resemblances, temptations, errant experiences, mirages, enchantments and disenchantments, iconoclasm, and sacrifices which, for all their differences, can be perceived only as images of a common longing for what lies beyond images. Through these metaphors Tasso presents a radical theological vision transcending the partialities of single and rigid viewpoints. He grafts on to the theology of the Council of Trent the spirituality of the desert.

Tasso re-invented the epic by retrieving its most profound self-justification, which makes the epic exceed tragic texts and merely political fantasies: the encounter between women and men and the divinity as the very spirit of the age. Thanks to his vision, the future of the epic genre changed. In his wake, Marino and Milton wrote two radically divergent epics. One centres on the languor of the passive hero overwhelmed by the weight of Venus's love, and the other is a cosmological poem of theological rebellion.

NOTES

1 See Werner Gundersheimer, *Ferrara: The Style of Renaissance Despotism* (Princeton: Princeton University Press, 1973). On the humanistic culture of Ferrara, see Riccardo Bruscagli, *Stagioni della civiltà estense* (Pisa: Nistri Lischi, 1983), esp. 15–32.

2 Giuseppe Mazzotta, 'Modern and Ancient Italy in *Don Quixote*', *Poetica: Zeitschrift für Sprach-und Literaturwissenschaft* 38 (2006): 91–106.

3 Torquato Tasso, *Discourses on the Heroic Poem*, trans. Mariella Cavalchini and Irene Samuel (Oxford: Clarendon Press, 1973); G. B. Giraldi Cinzio, *Discorso intorno al comporre romanzi*, in *Scritti critici*, ed. C. Guerrieri Crocetti (Milan: Marzorati, 1973); G.B. Pigna, *I romanzi ... divisi in tre libri, nei quail della*

poesia e della vita dell'Ariosto con nuovo modo si tratta (Venice: Vincenzo Valgrisi, 1554). More generally, see the works by Jane E. Everson and Michael Murrin listed in the Guide to further reading.

4 Lorenzo Valla, 'Dialogue on Free Will', in *The Renaissance Philosophy of Man*, ed. Ernst Cassirer, P. O. Kristeller, and J. H. Randall, Jr. (Chicago: University of Chicago Press, 1956), 155–82; see also Erasmus and Luther's *Discourse on Free Will*, trans. Ernst F. Winter (New York: Ungar, 1961).

5 See Hubert Jedin, *A History of the Council of Trent*, trans. Dom Ernest Graf, O.S.B., 2 vols. (Edinburgh: Thomas Nelson and Sons, 1957). See also Thomas F. Mayer, *Reginald Poole: Prince and Prophet* (Cambridge: Cambridge University Press, 2000).

6 See Ficino's quasi-health manual, *De vita libri tres* (written between 1480 and 1489), which recommends such dietary prescriptions as based on Neoplatonic principles.

7 Citations are taken from Matteo Maria Boiardo, *Orlando Innamorato* (hereafter *OI*), ed. R. Bruscagli (Turin: Einaudi, 1995). The translation is taken from *Orlando Innamorato*, trans. Charles S. Ross (Berkeley: University of California Press, 1989); Ludovico Ariosto, *Orlando Furioso secondo l'edizione del 1532 con le varianti delle edizioni del 1516 e del 1521* (hereafter *OF*), ed. Santorre Debenedetti and Cesare Segre (Bologna: Commissione per i testi di lingua, 1960); the translated text is *Orlando Furioso*, trans. Guido Waldman (Oxford: Oxford University Press, 1974); and Torquato Tasso, *Gerusalemme Liberata* (hereafter *GL*), ed. Anna Maria Carini, Biblioteca di classici italiani (Milan: Feltrinelli, 1961); the English translation is *Jerusalem Delivered*, trans. and ed. Ralph Nash (Detroit: Wayne State University Press, 1987).

8 The bibliography on Boiardo is not extensive. In addition to the works by Peter V. Marinelli and Jo Ann Cavallo listed in the Guide to further reading, see Antonio Franceschetti. *L'Orlando innamorato e le sue componenti tematiche e strutturali* (Florence: Leo Olschki, 1975).

9 On Ariosto the most useful bibliographical items are Eugenio Donato, 'Per selve e boscherecci labirinti: Desire and Narrative Structure in Ariosto's *Orlando Furioso*', *Barroco* 4 (1972): 17–34; David Quint, 'Astolfo's Voyage to the Moon', *Yale Italian Studies* 1 (1977): 398–408. In addition to the works by Albert Ascoli and David Quint listed in the Guide to further reading, see also Sergio Zatti, *Il Furioso tra epos e romanzo* (Lucca: Pacini, 1990).

10 In addition to the books by C. P. Brand and Sergio Zatti listed in the Guide to further reading, see Guido Baldassarri, '*Inferno*' e '*Cielo*': *Tipologia e Funzione del 'meraviglioso' nella Liberata* (Rome: Bulzoni, 1977); Francesco Erspamer, 'Il pensiero debole di Torquato Tasso', in *La Menzogna*, ed. F. Cardini (Florence: Ponte alle Grazie, 1989), 120–36; Paul Larivaille, 'Le Tasse critique de l'Arioste', in *Les commentaires et la naissance de la critique littéraire (France-Italie XIV–XVI siècles)* (Paris: Aux Amateurs de livres, 1990), 245–54; and Walter Stephens, 'Metaphor, Sacrament, and the Problem of Allegory in *Gerusalemme Liberata*', *I Tatti Studies* 4 (1991): 217–47.

11 Tasso, *Discourses on the Heroic Poem*, trans. Cavalchini and Samuel, 33 and 32. Pseudo-Dionysius is the name given to an anonymous mystic and philosopher of the fifth and early sixth centuries whose works were erroneously ascribed to an earlier figure, Dionysius the Areopagite, whose conversion to Christianity is described in Acts 17.34.

7

GEORGE MONTEIRO

Camões's *Os Lusíadas*: the first modern epic

Of the great Western poets, Luis Vaz de Camões (*c.* 1524–80) remains the least known outside his native land, and, of the premier Western epics, his *Os Lusíadas* (1572) has the unenviable distinction of continuing to be poetry's best-kept secret. Yet a century and a half after the Portuguese poet's death Voltaire named him the 'Portuguese Virgil', and the nineteenth century, valuing the history and biography embodied in the poem, called him the 'Portuguese Plutarch'.

Camões has always had the respect of poets and critics. His poetic eminence was noted by poets such as Torquato Tasso, Góngora, and Goethe, and the dramatist Lope de Vega. In the twentieth century Erich Auerbach called the *Lusíadas* 'the most beautiful epic of the Iberian Peninsula'. It is 'the great epic of the ocean', he adds, 'which sings of Vasco da Gama's voyage around Africa and the Portuguese colonization of the Indies'.[1] The *Lusíadas* is universally taken as Portugal's national epic, celebrating the voyages of discovery that, in the fifteenth and sixteenth centuries, made that country a great maritime and imperial power. The 'Lusíadas' of the title are the sons or people of Lusus (the legendary founder of the province the Romans had named Lusitania), that is to say, the Portuguese. Much like Virgil, Camões celebrates the heroic deeds of his people in their foundation of a great empire, but where Virgil, in celebrating the Roman Empire, had looked back to its foundation many hundreds of years previously in the story of Aeneas, Camões describes the business of empire-building, a thing of the recent past, historically a moment of national greatness already in decline even as the poem itself was being written, published, and read. Including it among the four chief examples of the literary epic, the others being the *Aeneid*, *Gerusalemme Liberata*, and *Paradise Lost*, the great classicist and scholar of epic C. M. Bowra singled out the *Lusíadas* as 'the first epic poem which in its grandeur and its universality speaks for the modern world'.[2]

In the twentieth century, however, Camões's poem came in for critical attention of a different, less approving sort. In *The Descent from Heaven* (1963), Thomas Greene assesses the matter this way:

> The history represented in his poem [the *Lusíadas*] is authentic; he introduces few people who did not once exist, and he pronounces the exotic names of African and Indian places with the assurance of a man who has seen them. This sturdy spine of *wahrheit* amid the surrounding *dichtung* makes of the poem an historical artifact which is subject to the abrupt reverses of history, and thus *Os Lusíadas* today seems almost swamped by the twentieth century. Of the two great forces which animate it, imperialism and nationalism, the first is largely discredited in our time, and the second is beginning to be suspect.[3]

While one would not argue that the critical reader must grant Camões his subject both uncritically and without reservations, a disinterested reader of the poem cannot fail to acknowledge that the poem is remarkable for both its time and ours – full of striking incidents marked by poetic language and imagery of high order.

'The natural and usual setting for an epic is a time commonly thought of as marked by greatness of achievement: "there were giants in those days". Such was the period of discovery and exploration which began in the late fifteenth century, and the great Port[uguese] epic of the next century, the *Lusiads*, celebrates its achievements.'[4] If there is a caveat, this entry continues, it is that 'the immediate past rarely serves as matter for an epic'. Camões's closeness to the 'immediate past', in fact, becomes clear when it is noted that Gama, who would become the central historical figure of the *Lusíadas*, died just around the time that Camões was born. In Gama the poet took a figure whose historical significance, given the nature of his troubled and troublesome career, not to mention his questionable character, was still far from settled, creating, single-handedly, the legendary figure that to this day is enshrined in Portuguese history. As Gama's recent biographer puts it, 'Camões transforms Gama's voyage in tone and content, from the mundane to the divine'.[5]

The *Lusíadas* was almost immediately recognized as a great work by Torquato Tasso, whose own epic, *Gerusalemme Liberata*, appeared in print a decade after the *Lusíadas*. His acknowledgement of Camões's achievement was broadcast in a sonnet that begins as a tribute to Vasco da Gama (*c.* 1460–1524) and ends with a paean to Camões, the poet whose genius gave the Portuguese adventurer the 'splendour' of his name. The poet addresses Gama:

> Great as thou art, and peerless in renown,
> Yet thou to Camoens ow'st thy noblest fame;
> Further than thou didst sail, his deathless song
> Shall bear the dazzling splendour of thy name . . .[6]

Three centuries later, in the novel *White-Jacket*, Herman Melville introduced in the fictional Jack Chase, 'an ardent admirer' of the *Lusíadas* who would sing out verses ('in the original') from the epic by his 'Commodore' Camões.

The first modern epic extolled discovery, religious conversion, trade, and empire. Published in Lisbon eight years before its author's death, the *Lusíadas* is the magnum opus of the soldier, sailor, poet, and playwright who was Camões. Now praised just as highly, if not more so, for his lyric poetry, including his many sonnets in the tradition that began with Petrarch, Camões first achieved international fame as a great poet through his achievement in the epic genre. Spanish translations appeared in Castile in the year of Camões's death. 'Cervantes spoke of "the most excellent Camões", Lope de Vega called him "divine". Calderón, Tirso de Molina, and Herrera appreciated his work, Gracián referred to him as "immortal" ', writes Aubrey Bell, 'and Montesquieu, in a passage of *L'Esprit des Lois*, declared that Camões' epic "fait sentir quelque chose des charmes de l'*Odyssée* et de la magnificence de l'*Énéide*" '.[7] In Portugal, of course, the *Lusíadas* became almost immediately the centrepiece of Portuguese culture, inspiring numerous imitations.

Tradition has it that Camões worked on his great poem for twenty years while he was in exile from Portugal, and legend has it that he very nearly lost his manuscript in a shipwreck in the Mecon river delta, from which he managed to swim to shore, one arm held aloft with a copy of his work, thus saving his manuscript (and himself) from a watery grave. But the facts of his life are no less dramatic. As a student (probably at Coimbra) Camões became known for his poetry, a reputation that he seems to have carried with him to court. As a professional soldier, he served a stint in Africa, losing an eye in Portugal's victory at Ceuta. Upon his return to Lisbon, he fell out of favour at home and was sent into exile in the Far East, namely India and Macau, where he filled several private and governmental offices. Finally determined to return home, he suffered through a set of long, precarious, and often interrupted voyages, including being stuck penniless on the island of Mozambique, before arriving in Lisbon in 1570 or thereabouts. He did not return empty-handed, although his triumph had to await the publication of his poem, an event that should have provided him with adequate financial support to see him through his last years. He dedicated his poem to the young king, Sebastian, and was granted a small pension. But to Camões's personal misfortune, the enthusiastically pious king went off to Africa, where he was (presumably) killed in battle (his body was never found). The pension, meagre though it was, was stopped and, as tradition has it, the impoverished Camões died in an almshouse.

In choosing to write an epic that might be accepted as his nation's grand poem – something that others, especially the poet Antonio Ferreira, had been urging upon Portugal's poets – Camões had, of course, models outside Portuguese literature. The conventions of the epic were already well established in Homer's *Odyssey* and *Iliad* but especially in Virgil's *Aeneid*. Camões took what he found useful, followed some conventions faithfully, adapted others, and in almost every way renovated what was long established. He organized his poem into ten cantos, employed *ottava rima* (eight-line stanzas in iambic pentameter and rhyming abababcc), and, like Homer and Virgil, introduced a hero whose function is to narrate the events of his country's glorious past rather than always his own adventures. In settling on Gama, Camões is able to avail himself of the journey away from and return to home that was employed in the earlier epics, most notably the *Odyssey*. In doing so, he forgoes the theme of the founding of the city – Virgil's theme – that would have seemed to be an attractive choice, as legend has it that it was Ulysses who founded the city of Lisbon (from its old Greek name, Olissipo). Thus Camões celebrates not Virgil's 'arms and the man I sing' (*arma virumque cano*) but the whole of Portugal's people:

> *Armes, and the Men* above the vulgar File,
> Who from the *Western Lusitanian* shore
> Past ev'n beyond the *Trapobanian*-Isle,
> Through *Seas* which never *Ship* had sayld before;
> Who (brave in *action*, patient in long *Toyle*,
> Beyond what strength of *humane* nature bore)
> 'Mongst *Nations*, under *other Stars*, acquir'd
> A *modern Scepter* which to *Heaven* aspir'd.   (Canto I, stanza I)[8]

Echoing many before him, the twentieth-century Southern African poet Roy Campbell pointed to the fact that Camões, man of action as well as poet, drew upon his own experiences of dangerous and sometimes electrifying sea-travel, along with the drudgeries and braveries of warfare – a poet who, in the words of Jorge de Sena, 'had left his life in pieces scattered about the world' – when he imagined what Gama and his men had undergone.[9] In lines written on the slopes of Mount Kilimanjaro in the 1940s, Campbell expresses what he characterizes as the 'real comradeship' of one who 'alone, of all the lyric race' 'can look a common soldier in the face':

> Through fire and shipwreck, pestilence and loss,
> Led by the *ignis fatuus* of duty
> To a dog's death – yet of his sorrows king –
> He shouldered high his voluntary cross,
> Wrestled his hardships into forms of beauty,
> And taught his gorgon destinies to sing.[10]

'If Tasso knew history and geography from the printed page', writes Thomas Greene, 'Camoens knew them to the marrow of his ravaged body.'[11] Indeed, so convincing have some readers found Camões's accounts of encounters and incidents, not knowing that Camões was born some decades after Gama had made his famous journeys, that they have placed Camões aboard one of Gama's ships. That mistake was made by Voltaire, no less.

In choosing Gama as his hero, Camões rejected other possibilities, among them, notably, the soldier-administrator Alfonso de Albuquerque or Prince Henry the Navigator. The prince, however, was no sailor himself, being only too willing, as he was, to send out others to fulfil his dream to discover and his fantasy to conquer. To what extent Gama was Camões's own *beau ideal* of the successful adventurer – in sharp contrast with the poet's own record of small successes and large failures during his years of exile in the Far East – is matter for speculation that I will leave for others. Similarly, with his decision to retell the legend of Inez de Castro's murder, exhumation, and posthumous coronation as Portugal's queen, one can only wonder how this signature event in the way Portugal still wishes to talk about its virtue actually fulfilled some need in Camões's view of his own sentimental life. One thing is certain, however. In hitting upon the happy notion of having Gama, acting as if he were his king's ambassador, retell the history of his country to the king of Melinde, Camões successfully, through choice and emphasis, gave shape to Portugal's historic past. It became the country's narrative about itself, a mythology built, basically, on a substratum of bare facts. Audaciously, by way of 'prophecy', Camões even includes accounts of historical events that, in the biographical Gama's real time, had not yet happened.

Having chosen to practise his art in the genre of the epic, Camões was willing to adhere to the conventions of the epic whenever possible. His greatest challenge in this regard was whether to introduce the Olympian gods into his poem about 'modern' and Christian Portugal. He pared their number down almost exclusively to Jupiter, Venus, and Bacchus (supposed father or companion of Lusus) and gave them vital roles in determining the fate of Gama and his men. In later centuries critics would object to Camões's inclusion of pagan gods in this poem devoted to the history and virtues of a Christian people. Other readers objected (prudishly to the modern or neo-pagan mind) to Camões's introduction, in Canto IX, of the episode of the 'Isle of Love', in which Gama and his sailors are rewarded by Venus with an erotic interlude with beautifully willing maidens. Venus, the voice of myth, speaks to Gama's human flesh:

> There with every kind of food and drink,
> With fragrant wines, and sweet roses,
> In palaces of marvellous crystal,
> On lovely couches, themselves more lovely,

> In short, with countless special delights,
> The amorous nymphs should await them,
> Wounded by love, prepared to be tender
> To those who desire them, and surrender.   (Canto IX, stanza 41)[12]

A large body of scholarship has grown up around this part of the poem, with the possibility that the episode reveals something about Camões's own needs and desires being the most interesting for today's readers.

But this was not the case for all of them. For the 'Isle of Love' section can be read in feminist terms, setting aside as irrelevant the fact that Camões was employing a *topos* that was well worn by the time he used it. Such a reading foregrounds the episode as a clear instance of the prurient exploitation of women as mere implements of erotica and sex, not just by Gama and his men alone but by the poet himself and his approving readers. One particularly noteworthy criticism of Camões's 'Isle of Love' episode – especially its implications for the way Portuguese history, while sentimentalizing the 'Inez de Castro' episode of his royal history, has tended to view 'other' women – is the poem 'Brazil, January 1, 1502', by the American poet Elizabeth Bishop, long a resident of Brazil. Relocating Camões's 'Isle of Love' in time as well as place, to sixteenth-century Rio de Janeiro and resituating it historically to the moment when the Portuguese outsiders first encountered the native women of the Terra de Santa Cruz (as the Portuguese first called the land they had 'discovered'), Bishop stresses the notion of pursuit and rape, rather than the fantasy of innocent eroticism, describing the pursuers as 'Christians, hard as nails, / tiny as nails, and glinting, / in creaking armor'.[13] It will be recalled that the vision of the fabled 'Island of Love' and what happens there are the rewards Venus bestows on the successful Portuguese mariners. In an episode of free and boundless sex, Gama's sailors mate with nymphs in a luxuriously pastoral setting:

> Chase we these *Goddesses*; it shall be seen
> If they be *Real* or *Fantastical*.
> This said (more swift than *Bucks* o're *Pastures* green)
> Through the rough *Brakes* and Woods darted they *All*.
> The *Nymphs* went flying the thick boughs between,
> Yet not so *Swift* as *Artificial*;
> Shreeking and laughing softly in the close,
> They let the *Greyhounds* gain upon the *Does*.   (Canto IX, stanza 70)[14]

In Bishop's poem things are different. The Portuguese mariners 'came and found it all, / not unfamiliar', their old dreams of *luxuria* recreated as if, anachronistically, they had read Camões's account of Gama's sailors sporting on the 'Island of Love'. But history does not mesh readily with imagination, not even romance incorporated into a historical episode. Surely not the history imagined in 'Brazil, January 1, 1502', which records the actions of lascivious sailors,

> each out to catch an Indian for himself –
> those maddening little women who kept calling,
> calling to each other (or had the birds waked up?)
> and retreating, always retreating, behind it.

If they are *always* retreating in the fixed sylvan scene – here Bishop echoes Keats's 'Ode on a Grecian Urn' – one must assume that beyond the time-frame of Bishop's poem, rapes would have taken place. What the poem does not allow for (recall that 'always') is that the Indian nymphs acquiesced in the way Camões's 'Does' (being 'not so Swift as Artificial') had allowed the pursuing 'Greyhounds' to gain on them. The Indian women in Bishop's poem – if not in history or in the fantasy of Camões's 'Isle of Love' – remain forever unravished like the nymphs on the frieze of the urn celebrated in Keats's poem. Bishop is not unaware, of course, that in rehistoricizing Camões's idealized version of the 'Isle of Love' – a 'powerful and original version of a most popular theme from ancient and contemporary poetry, that is the *locus amoenus*, the bower of love, the abode of bliss, which in one form or another has an ancestry, in pastoral and narrative, stretching back to Homer' – she subverts something essential to the historical narrative regarding Portugal's national poem.[15] If, as Bowra concludes, 'the pleasures which Camões gives to his sailors are, if literal, unsuitable for heroes and improper for men', Bishop gives us the historical reason why that is so.[16]

Just about the time Bishop's poem was published, the pre-eminent Camonian, Jorge de Sena, who, like Bishop, was then living in Brazil, noted that over time much had 'aged' in the *Lusíadas*.[17] The major way in which the *Lusíadas* had already 'aged' was that at least one school of literary and cultural criticism now deprecated what was once celebrated in the poem: its rather straightforward account of an historical Portugal that was unapologetically an imperial state. There are many routes by which to trace this career from celebration to deprecation of the *Lusíadas*. My way of looking at the matter involves the poem's reputation in the British Isles and English-speaking countries, where translations began as early as 1655, with *The Lusiad, or, Portugals Historicall Poem: Written in the Portingall Language by Luis de Camoens; and now newly put into English by Richard Fanshaw Esq.* 'Now newly put into English' meant something like 'for the first time in the English language', since Fanshawe's spirited version was not only the first translation done outside the Iberian Peninsula but the first one done into English – one fully in consonance with a British people in enjoying a country created through the unleashed energies and worldly ambitions of the age of Elizabeth.[18]

With William Julius Mickle's translation in 1776, 121 years after Fanshawe's, however, the *Lusíadas* 'became' a British poem, one offered to an imperial power in the midst of what seemed to be unlimited overseas growth. While Mickle's translation has often been criticized for its alterations of Camões's text – excisions and interpolations of considerable amounts of material, varying the meaning of the poem in substantial ways, and the poet Longfellow describes it, rather harshly, as 'rather a paraphrase than a translation' – it nevertheless, in its numerous editions (it is still in print), continued to reign as the edition of the *Lusíadas* best known to English-language readers with little or no Portuguese.[19] It was from Mickle's version that Melville got his Camões, for instance, and that Longfellow quoted in his anthology *Poets and Poetry of Europe*, in which he included the episodes of the posthumous crowning of Inez de Castro and the appearance of Adamastor, the monstrous 'Spirit of the Cape'. In fact, even as he offered his own competing translation of Camões's poem in the 1880s, Richard Burton admitted that Mickle's 'poem with all its faults of stilted, turgid smoothness, of "flimsy, pompous chime", has maintained up to the present the hold which it took upon the last century; and has become a pseudo-classic in English literature' – a questionable status, surely, but one that his own mock-Elizabethan version failed to achieve.[20]

Trumping all or any of its perceived faults, however, was the fact that Mickle presented his version as *the* epic of trade and commerce. No Englishman had written such a poem, and Mickle, himself a poet, domesticated it for imperial Britain by 'Englishing' it to his own liking. He complemented this work by discussing the *Lusíadas* in an introductory essay. It was hardly a disinterested performance, for Mickle had ties to the East India Company, whose interests (along with his own) the poem would serve in its disguise as propaganda for the continued unfolding of Britain's commercial empire. At the start, Mickle announces his theme and reveals his purpose: 'If a concatenation of events centred in one great action, events which gave birth to the present commercial system of the world; if these be of the first importance in the civil history of mankind, the Lusiad, of all other poems, challenges the attention of the philosopher, the politician, and the gentlemen.'[21] Distinguishing it from Milton's *Paradise Lost*, 'the Epic Poem of Religion', he describes the *Lusíadas* as 'a poem founded on such an important period of history', as especially important for the Britain of his day, for it offers evidence to counter the arguments of those 'who lament that either India was ever discovered, and who assert that the increase of trade is big with the real misery of mankind, and that commerce is only the parent of degeneracy, and the nurse of every vice'.[22] On the contrary, argues Mickle rather baldly, commerce and trade have introduced to native and barbarous populations the advantages of Europe's superior civilization. In short, Camões's poem, on 'the grandest subject it is (of profane history) which the world has ever beheld', is celebrated:

> A voyage esteemed too great for man to dare; the adventures of this voyage, through unknown oceans, deemed unnavigable; the Eastern World happily discovered, and for ever indissolubly joined and given to the Western; the grand Portuguese empire in the East founded; the humanization of mankind, and universal commerce the consequence! What are the adventures of an old fabulous hero's arrival in Britain, what are Greece and Latium in arms for a woman, compared to this? Troy is in ashes, and even the Roman empire is no more. But the effects of the voyage, adventures, and bravery of the hero of the Lusiad, will be felt and beheld, and perhaps increase in importance, while the world shall remain.[23]

In stressing that the *Lusíadas* (like Gama's voyage) was about 'universal commerce', Mickle was well aware that he was in defiance of Camões's intentions. As David Quint has written,

> Propaganda for the discoveries ran up against a time-honored aristocratic disdain for mercantile activities . . . If profit was a matter in which a gentleman was not supposed to take any interest, the Portuguese aristocracy could view its participation in the imperial enterprise primarily in terms of its traditional role as a military caste, in terms of personal honor, patriotism, and religious zeal. These are the terms of the *Lusíadas*, and indeed they are the traditional terms of epic, a genre historically linked to aristocratic values . . . Exchanging gain for glory, Camões provided a version of the Portuguese ventures in the East that plays down their commercial character, a version that was both consonant with epic norms of behavior and congenial to the self-image of a noble reader.[24]

Immediately recognized as one of Camões's most memorable achievements, the figured avatar of the 'Spirit of the Cape', Adamastor, may not be, as Mickle rather rashly called it, 'the grandest fiction in human composition', but it has had its many admirers and imitators down through the centuries.[25] 'There is nothing in his [Camões's] models to equal the terrifying grandeur of the apparition of the Spirit of the Cape of Good Hope, as the Giant Adamastor, or the prophetic truth of his allocution to the Portuguese Argonauts of Vasco da Gama as they round the Cape of Storms for the first time', writes Campbell.[26] A. Bartlett Giamatti comments: 'For Camoens, the sea was all those forces presented by the giant figure of Adamastor (Canto v) and Portugal's glory consisted in braving them. It is the passionate sense of individual and collective heroism, and the feeling that the sea is the proper scene for that heroism, that hold this poem together.'[27] Yet it seems to me to be something of an exaggeration, though it is still worth noting, in the words of a recent commentator, that 'more than any other episode of the *Lusíadas*, it [the Adamastor episode] has given the poem its place in world literature, a place to which Camões and even his hero da Gama self-consciously lay claim'.[28]

Here is Mickle's rendering of Camões's description of Adamastor, the fierce 'Spirit of the Cape,' just before the monster offers his prophecies:

> I spoke, when rising through the darken'd air,
> Appall'd we saw an hideous Phantom glare;
> High and enormous o'er the flood he tower'd,
> And thwart our way with sullen aspect lour'd:
> An earthly paleness, o'er his cheeks was spread,
> Erect uprose his hairs of wither'd red;
> Writhing to speak, his sable lips disclose,
> Sharp and disjoin'd, his gnashing teeth's blue rows;
> His haggard beard flow'd quivering on the wind,
> Revenge and horror in his mien combined;
> His clouded front, by withering lightnings scarred,
> The inward anguish of his soul declared.
> His red eyes glowing from their dusky caves
> Shot livid fires: far echoing o'er the waves
> His voice resounded, as the cavern'd shore
> With hollow groan repeats the tempest's roar.
> Cold gliding horrors thrill'd each hero's breast,
> Our bristling hair and tottering knees confess'd
> Wild dread; the while with visage ghastly wan,
> His black lips trembling, thus the fiend began . . .   (Canto v, stanzas 39–40)[29]

While Mickle omits some of Camões's original description, notably a comparison with the Colossus of Rhodes, he expands enthusiastically on the horrifying aspects of the monster's appearance, and since most of Camões's English-language readers after 1776 read his poem, not in the original Portuguese but in Mickle's translation, it is Mickle's Adamastor that has lodged itself in the minds of readers and writers alike.

Until recently, it seemed satisfactory to gloss Camões's monster simply as the symbol of 'both a natural phenomenon and the dangers of the voyage'; or to explain that 'the horror which the vision of Adamastor arouses is based on a natural fear of going too far and has a real relation to experience. The grisly and revolting phantom is an apt symbol of the horrors which may well appal those who break into waters where no men have sailed before'.[30] This no longer seems adequate, however, for there have been important changes of late in how Adamastor is viewed by Camões's readers, particularly his English-language readers in Southern Africa. Beginning with Campbell's 1926 poem, 'Rounding the Cape', praise for Camões's creation has been invaded by a consciousness of its tragic significance in past and present African history:

> Farewell, terrific shade! though I go free
> Still of the powers of darkness art thou Lord:
> I watch the phantom sinking in the sea
> Of all that I have hated or adored.
>
> The prow glides smoothly on through seas quiescent:
> But where the last point sinks into the deep,
> The land lies dark beneath the rising crescent,
> And Night, the Negro, murmurs in his sleep.[31]

For Campbell, the natural dangers posed by dangerous seas and storms are tied in with the dangers posed by Africa itself – the Dark Continent. Later writers in Southern Africa have taken the hint, finding in Camões's Adamastor the symbolic key to the unpleasant truth about the dire and destructive history Africa had been made to share with Europe. The grand symbol of danger and potential destruction – by which the conquerors justified their civilizing missions – was to be recognized for what it really was: an imposition of Eurocentric meaning on African history. Describing the *Lusíadas* as 'the national epic of the Lusitanian bogeymen', Stephen Gray speaks for many when he argues:

> It is imperative to examine it by a reverse-angle shot, as it were; we look at Camoens from the vantage point of the cruel, dark and vengeful interior that he and his hero viewed as unfit for human habitation. . .The figure of Adamastor is at the root of all the subsequent white semiology invented to cope with the African experience: he is menacing and inimical, and seen across a barrier; he belongs to an older but defeated culture, and is likely to sink the new European enlightenment if allowed within its purlieu; although his size is gigantic, his responses are essentially childish and they obey paternalistic directives; he is capable of love, but only carnally, so that if he advances too presumptuously he is to be humiliated and rendered impotent. . .His Titanic force, tantamount to a block mountain's, his rumbling and earth-shaking, is not only the pent power of a vast and frighteningly unknown continent, populated by serpents and burning stones, but a symbol of the awe with which Africa was regarded in early experiences of the untamed.[32]

In short, the 'myth' of Adamastor – in the revisionary work of writers such as David Wright, Douglas Livingstone, and André Brink – 'expresses the white man's anxieties about Africa', not the intrinsic reality of Africa itself.

It is but a short step from Gray's re-casting of the figure of Adamastor as a symbol for Europe's African 'anxieties' to saying that 'the giant Adamastor is a blown-up figure of the African natives and of the price that will be exacted by their resistance to Portuguese mastery and conquest'. If 'Adamastor's name means "the untamed one", and he suggests the nature of the Africans who turned out to be less domesticated than they first appeared', as such a post-colonial reading would have it, 'Camões' monster, born of the initial encounter of Portuguese imperialism and its native subjects, is the first in the line of specters haunting Europe'.[33]

By way of conclusion, however, I would point to Jorge Luis Borges's celebratory sonnet. Borges takes the familiar trope of the sea commander who has successfully completed his long voyage, replacing, in effect, Gama by Camões and Gama's ship by Camões's poem. Echoing Tasso's four-centuries-old poem, Borges restates the triumphant notion that the great poetry of the *Lusíadas* has withstood the mutabilities of human history:

> Displaying neither pity nor anger, time
> wears through the swords of the brave. O
> Captain, beaten down and saddened, nostalgia
> brought you back to your dying homeland to die
> – the very flower of Portugal's manhood having
> perished in the mystic desert, and the harsh
> Spaniard, formerly subservient, now menacing
> vulnerable coasts. What I would want to know is
> – when you were crossing that last river, did you,
> in your humility, know that what had been lost –
> the East and West, the sword and the standard –
> had been made permanent, free from the mutability
> of all that's human, in your poem,
> in Lusitania's *Aeneid*.[34]

NOTES

1 Erich Auerbach, *Introduction to Romance Languages and Literature* (New York: Capricorn Books, 1961), 185.

2 C. M. Bowra, *From Virgil to Milton* (London: Macmillan, 1945), 86.

3 Thomas Greene, *The Descent from Heaven: A Study in Epic Continuity* (New Haven: Yale University Press, 1963), 219–20.

4 *Dictionary of World Literary Terms*, ed. Joseph T. Shipley (Boston: The Writer, 1970), 101.

5 Sanjay Subrahmanyam, *The Career and Legend of Vasco da Gama* (Cambridge: Cambridge University Press, 1997), 155.

6 Quoted in William Julius Mickle, 'Dissertation on the Lusiad', in *The Lusiad; or The Discovery of India: An Epic Poem*, trans. Mickle (London: W. Suttaby, B. Crosby and Co., and Scatcherd & Letterman, 1809), xcvii.

7 Aubrey F. G. Bell, *Luis de Camões* (Oxford: Oxford University Press, 1923), 81–2.

8 *The Lusiad by Luis de Camoens[,] translated by Richard Fanshawe*, ed. Jeremiah D. M. Ford (Cambridge, MA: Harvard University Press, 1940), 29. For the original text, see Frank Pierce, ed., *Os Lusíadas* (Oxford: Clarendon Press, 1973), 1.

9 Jorge de Sena, 'Em Creta, com o Minotauro', in *Peregrinatio ad loca infecta* (Lisbon: Portugália, 1969), 112.

10 'Luis de Camões', in Roy Campbell, *Collected Works, I, Poetry*, ed. Peter Alexander, Michael Chapman, and Marcia Leveson (Craighall: Ad. Donker, 1985), 351.

11 Greene, *Descent from Heaven*, 219.

12 Luis Vaz de Camões, *The Lusiads*, trans. Landeg White (Oxford: Oxford University Press, 1997), 185.

13 Elizabeth Bishop, 'Brazil, January 1, 1502', in *Questions of Travel* (New York: Farrar, Straus and Giroux, 1966), 5–7.

14 Ford, *Lusiad*, 261. For the original text, see Pierce, *Os Lusíadas*, 215.

15 Pierce, *Os Lusíadas*, xxxi.

16 Bowra, *From Virgil to Milton*, 130. For further analysis of Bishop's 'corrective' poem, see George Monteiro, *The Presence of Camões: Influences on the Literature of England, America, and Southern Africa* (Lexington: University Press of Kentucky, 1996), 104–5.

17 Jorge de Sena, 'Camões: the Lyrical Poet,' in *Camões[,] Some Poems Translated from the Portuguese by Jonathan Griffin[,] essays on Camões by Jorge de Sena and Helder Macedo* (London: Menard Press, 1976), 14.

18 Fanshawe's translation in 1655 was followed by those of William Julius Mickle (1776), Thomas Moore Musgrave (1826), Edward Quillinan (five cantos) (1853), Sir Thomas Livingston Mitchell (1854), J. J. Aubertin (1878), Robert Ffrench Duff (1880), Richard Francis Burton (1880), James Edwin Hewitt (1883), Leonard Bacon (1950), William C. Atkinson (1952), and Landeg White (1997).

19 *The Letters of Henry Wadsworth Longfellow, Volume VI, 1875–1882*, ed. Andrew Hilen (Cambridge, MA: Harvard University Press, 1982), 302–3.

20 Quoted in Ford, *Lusiad*, xxix.

21 Mickle, 'Introduction,' *Lusiad*, i.

22 *Ibid.*, i.

23 *Ibid.*, xciii.

24 David Quint, *Epic and Empire: Politics and Generic Form from Virgil to Milton* (Princeton, NJ: Princeton University Press, 1993), 257.

25 Mickle, 'Dissertation', *Lusiad*, xciv.

26 Roy Campbell, 'The Poetry of Luiz de Camões', *London Magazine*, 4:8 (1957), 30.

27 A. Bartlett Giamatti, *The Earthly Paradise and the Renaissance Epic* (Princeton, NJ: Princeton University Press, 1966), 211.

28 Quint, *Epic and Empire*, 114.

29 Mickle, *Lusiad*, pp.120–1. For the original text, see Pierce, *Os Lusíadas*, 118.

30 Pierce, *Os Lusíadas*, 118 note; Bowra, *From Virgil to Milton*, 126.

31 Roy Campbell, 'Rounding the Cape', in *Adamastor* (London: Faber and Faber, 1930), 38.
32 Stephen Gray, *Southern African Literature: An Introduction* (New York: Barnes and Noble, 1979), 17, 27–8.
33 Quint, *Epic and Empire*, 116, 125.
34 Jorge Luis Borges, 'A Luis de Camoens', in *Obra Poética, 1923–1977* (Buenos Aires/Madrid: Emecé Editores/Alianza Editorial, 1977), 147, my translation.

8

CATHERINE BATES

The Faerie Queene: Britain's national monument

In Book II, canto x of *The Faerie Queene*, Prince Arthur and Sir Guyon – heroes of the poem and Book respectively – settle down to a lengthy sojourn in one of the chambers of Alma's castle. Unusually for *The Faerie Queene*, however (and, indeed, for the epic tradition more generally), this indulgence is not coded as negative, as the kind of regressive, erotic deviance that typically holds the hero back or delays the successful achievement of his quest. On the contrary, although the two knights are said to be 'burning both with feruent fire' (II.ix.60), the activity that engages them is presented as a wholly legitimate pleasure – the 'naturall desire of countreys state' (II.x.77) – and as a necessary preparation for, if not condition of, their future success.[1] As they immerse themselves in reading the history of their native lands – Arthur, in a book called *Briton moniments*, Guyon, in a volume entitled *Antiquitie of Faerie lond* – they learn the dynastic trajectory of their two nations, a trajectory that in both cases culminates in the present moment if not directly in themselves (Arthur's text tells the story of Britain from the Bronze Age up to the reign of his own father, Uther Pendragon; Guyon's, the story of the Faerie dynasty up to 'the fairest *Tanaquill*', II.x.76, that is, the Faerie Queene whom he serves and whose image he bears on his shield).

The fact that Spenser waxes self-consciously epic at this point – invoking the help of the Muses, of Apollo, and of the '*Mœonian* [Homeric] quill' (II.x.3) in order to accomplish the 'labour huge' (II.x.2) he is about to undertake – suggests that he views these chronicle histories as forming an integral part of the epic tradition, and that here, as there, a knowledge of the past is crucial in establishing both the identity of the hero and the latter's sense of purpose, the larger *telos* to which his mission is directed. In writing his country's first national epic – one designed, much as Virgil's had been, to celebrate the ruling family and existing regime – Spenser situates the Elizabethan present at the near end of a foundational history that stretches back into the distant past, as far back, indeed, as Troy. Moreover, as canto x proceeds and the chronicle histories lengthily unfold, we find that we are reading what Arthur and

Guyon read, looking over their shoulders, as it were, and following the same texts from page to page, as their reading matter temporarily converges with ours. The equivalence is highly suggestive for, in effect, it positions *us* as heroes: if heroes can be engrossed in an act of reading, by the same token the act of reading can be taken as a heroic task, and not least the act of reading *The Faerie Queene* itself. Indeed, that Spenser is presenting his knights' reading as a metonym for our own is suggested by the fact that the 'immortall scrine' (II.ix.56) in which Eumnestes keeps these precious volumes in Alma's chamber of memory echoes the 'euerlasting scryne' (I.Pro.2) of similar histories on which Spenser claims to draw for the poem as a whole, leading critics to view this episode as a particularly self-conscious moment in which the poem 'comments on its own mode of being', and provides, in Arthur and Guyon's sudden onset of bibliomania, an 'allegory of epic endeavour itself'.[2]

I emphasize the point because, at similarly self-referential moments in classical epic, representations of the poem-within-the-poem invariably take on either a visual or a verbal but never a literary form. When the Troy story appears as an aesthetic object within the larger frame of the Homeric poems, for example, it is either as an *ekphrasis* (Helen, for instance, weaves a great red robe into which she works images of the Achaians and the Trojans in the *Iliad* Book 3) or as a straightforward depiction of the *epos* – the Greek word for story or poem – as an act of oral recitation (as when Achilles sings of men's fame in the *Iliad* Book 9; or when the court of Ithaca listens to Phemios's song of the Achaians' bitter homecoming in the *Odyssey* Book 1; or Odysseus, to Demodokos's tales of Troy in Book 8; or the Phaiakaians, in turn, to Odysseus's account of his own protracted *nostos* in Book 11). In the *Aeneid*, the larger story in which Aeneas plays his part similarly appears either as something verbal – such as the future fate of Rome that Jupiter dictates to Venus in Book 1 (*fatum*, from *fārī*, to speak, is literally 'that which is spoken'); the narrative that Aeneas himself delivers to the spellbound court at Carthage in Books 2 and 3; and the verbal commentary that Anchises adds to the underworld pageant of future heroes in Book 6 – or as something visual: the great shield of Aeneas in Book 8, for example, or (in an episode to which Arthur and Guyon's reading of history books has been seen directly to allude) the murals depicting the history of Troy that decorate Dido's temple to Juno and which Aeneas and his companion Achatës pore over in Book 1. Notwithstanding the status of the *Aeneid* as a 'secondary' or literary epic, Virgil remains true to the pre-literate Bronze Age society that was depicted in the Homeric poems and in which his own story is set. Although characters in the *Aeneid* read any number of different things – signs, portents, unusual animal behaviours, freak weather events, images, visions, dreams – not one of them ever sits down to read a book.

The Faerie Queene, of course, is indebted to classical epic at every level. It draws on the same set of stock characters, geographical settings, set-piece scenes, and stylistic conventions. It reproduces specific episodes that appear in Homer and Virgil (such as descents into the underworld, I.v.31–44, II. vii.21–66; encounters with Ate, IV.i.19; or with bleeding trees, I.ii.30–44). It makes explicit parallels between its characters and theirs (interestingly, these are often female – Una, for example, is compared with Odysseus, I.iii.21; Belphoebe with Dido, II.iii.31; and Britomart with Penelope, v.vii.39 – a consequence, perhaps, of the fact that, unlike previous epic poets, Spenser is heroizing a queen). It quotes directly from their texts (as in the Homeric formula of the 'rosy-fingred Morning', I.ii.7, for example, or the potted *Aeneid* to which Britomart listens in Malbecco's house and which is peppered with quotations from Virgil's poem, III.ix.41, 43, 53). Indeed, the opening stanzas of *The Faerie Queene* quote the first lines of the *Aeneid* as it appeared in Renaissance editions: as bold a statement as any that Spenser had ambitions to be (as his contemporaries clearly saw him) the new 'Virgil of England'. Nonetheless, the extent to which *The Faerie Queene* presents and perceives itself as, above all else, a *literary* text – something that is, by definition, written down, and distributed specifically in *book* form – is what marks perhaps its most distinctive difference from the classical tradition that precedes it.

It is true that Arthur and Guyon also view purely visual representations in Alma's castle – in the chamber of reason that precedes that of memory, for example, the walls 'were painted faire with memorable gestes...and with picturals / Of Magistrates' (II.ix.53) – but it is not here that they dwell and not on these that Spenser models his poem. Rather, they choose to sequester themselves in Eumnestes's crammed and musty library, among his 'rolles', 'old records', 'books', 'long parchment scrolles', and 'antique Registers' (II.ix.57, 59), much as Spenser identifies his own literary project with that of Clio – the Muse of history whom he invokes more often than any other – drawing a parallel between his poem and her 'great volume of Eternitie' (III.iii.4) or her 'rolles, layd vp in heauen aboue, / And records of antiquitie' (IV.xi.10). In classical epic, history is not written down but preserved in the minds of old men who serve as repositories for the collective cultural memory. Indeed, for Plato's Socrates, the art of writing positively endangers memory and threatens to enfeeble the powers of mental recall.[3] Spenser, however, has no such reservations and instead conjures up (with some relish, it has to be said) the paper-filled world that would have been all too familiar to him as a Tudor bureaucrat and civil servant. For him, memory is a great archive in which his characters read books very like his own, emphasizing, as one critic puts it, that here 'the nation assumes its shape by reading, not by remembering'.[4] Spenser's understanding of the strictly *scribal* nature of history, moreover, is underscored by the very special sense in which he uses the word 'moniment', for what this term signifies is not a building or structure so much as a distinctive mark, trace, imprint, engraving, or inscription. Belphoebe's face, for example, is said to be an 'iuorie...table' engraved by Love, making it a 'soueraine moniment of mortall vowes' (II.iii.24, 25); coins are normally stamped with the monarch's head or royal insignia, so those that are not are said to be 'withouten moniment' (II.vii.5); a knight's shield bears as 'old moniments' the marks or 'signes' (II.xii.80) of his former triumphs, although these can be scratched out or erased. When Arthur reads a book called *Briton moniments*, therefore, it represents a history of history, a monument to other 'moniments' – of empire, of victory, of success – that find themselves inscribed on the cityscapes and countryside of Britain: it is the written record of a history that has already left its record on the land. As Elizabeth Bellamy suggests, Arthur's reading of such a volume thus 'constitutes a distinctly textual moment' indeed.[5]

This basic perception of epic as a distinctly literary genre is something *The Faerie Queene* shares with the other great epics of the sixteenth century (especially the poems of Ariosto and Tasso, on which Spenser drew, of course, no less heavily than on Homer and Virgil), for, whatever the undeniable continuities of the epic tradition as a whole, the invention of the printing press in the late fifteenth century constituted perhaps the greatest change – rupture, even – in the genre's millennia-long history. In the classical poems, epic had been represented as a visual or a verbal phenomenon because, in either form, it was immediately accessible to a group: as an *ekphrasis* or oral recitation, the epic story could be apprehended by any number of people, so long as they had eyes to see or ears to hear. The reception of epic was clearly understood to be a communal activity: a collective, even ritual experience in which a given people, tribe, nation, or race could confirm and celebrate their cultural identity together. In a post-Gutenberg world, however, epic shifts from something that is seen and heard to something that is read, and as such its reception moves decisively from a public to a private event. Henceforth, epic would be understood as a text to be analysed, absorbed, and enjoyed – much as it is by Arthur and Guyon – in an armchair and in solitude. This radical change had class implications, as well. Formerly, epic had been a shared exercise in which the group not only celebrated the founding fathers but also demonstrated a continued allegiance to their values: that is, to the same social hierarchy with its military aristocracy or ruling elite. In future, however, this semi-sacred and essentially conservative function would come under threat. With the invention of printing, epic entered the world of mechanical reproduction and, from a group experience, it became a product to be bought and sold on the open market, an object to be consumed by a new and bourgeois book-buying class. This, the most transformative of epic's many re-definitions over time, finds its logical conclusion, perhaps, in the moment when Don Quixote finds in circulation multiple printed copies of the story he is in, except that his own, august view of the adventures on which he is engaged finds itself strangely at odds with the tales of madness and folly that the population avidly devours. Cervantes's parody (which is also, pointedly, in prose) shows how far the epic had come – from the reverential expression of shared values to a popular commodity that debunks those same values and whose very entertainment value is what boosts its sales. The new form that *Don Quixote* (1614) here anticipates – the novel – signals, arguably, the end of epic as we know it.

Epic had not yet come to this pass when Spenser was writing, however. On the contrary, he specifically harnesses his epic poem to the two great movements that had embraced print technology as a force for good in the Renaissance: humanism and the Reformation. *The Faerie Queene* is powered, on the one hand, by the humanist emphasis on education and the development of reading skills and textual scholarship as a means of arriving at truth, and, on the other, by Protestant Bible-reading practices that aimed at nothing less. The whole poem is geared to the 'right' reading that would direct the reader to this desired end. When characters saw or listened to heroic tales in the classical epics, the experience was shown to produce in them certain key responses: typically, pleasure, pathos, or wonder. Each of these is evident in *The Faerie Queene* (Britomart is pierced with 'deepe compassiowne' at hearing the story of Troy, III.ix.39, for example; Arthur responds with both 'secret pleasure' and 'wonder' to *Briton moniments*, II.x.68), but to these Spenser adds something new that has no parallel in the classical texts: the sense that responding to epic also involves *labour*, the sheer difficulty of working through a text that is designed from the outset to be read. 'Abrod in armes, *at home in studious kind* / Who seekes with painfull toile, shall honor soonest find', instructs Belphoebe (II.iii.40, my italics), driving home the point that sitting down and reading a book is just as worthy an enterprise as the more muscular activities traditionally associated with epic and, indeed, no less heroic.

The labour involved in reading *The Faerie Queene* is manifest on every page, not least in the poem's presentation of itself as a 'continued Allegory, or darke conceit' that demands of its readers the constant exercise of interpretative intelligence and hermeneutic vigilance. Indeed, as Spenser goes on to explain to his first and, perhaps, model reader, Sir Walter Ralegh – 'for your better light in reading therof' – the poem's use of allegory to signify one thing by means of another needs to be grasped from the beginning.[6] *The Faerie Queene* is not a book to be read aloud from the chimney corner, as it were, but to be studied intently with a pen in hand, ready to jot down apt marginalia (like Gabriel Harvey, another of Spenser's earliest readers). Only an eye trained to the page, for example, will be able to pick up on the puns and double meanings that Spenser's specialized orthography allows for ('woeman', 'foeminine', 'abhominable', 'Geaunt', 'Slowth', and so forth). This was a writer, after all, whose first publication, *The Shepheardes Calender* (1579), had self-consciously cultivated the physical properties of the printed book in order to present itself as a distinctly literary production. The accompanying notes and commentaries were designed to make it look like a school-text or literary classic, and editorial glosses were provided to explain 'wordes and matter' that the reader might otherwise 'passe in the speedy course of reading'.[7] From the beginning, that is, Spenser was addressing his works to an audience trained in the arts of reading, and whose ability to decipher, decrypt, read between the lines, relate to different languages, and refer to different texts he could safely assume.

The Faerie Queene is not weighed down with a scholarly apparatus as the *Calender* is but it requires of its readers a textual awareness no less painstaking and diligent. It is for this reason that the very portal through which we enter Spenser's epic is a lesson in nothing less than right reading. The first encounter that the poem stages – within a matter of fifteen stanzas or so – is not with any generic monster or adversary but, very specifically, with an incarnation of misprision or wrong-reading: the serpent Errour. The Redcrosse Knight's initial failure to read the warning signs correctly is what leads him directly to Errour's den, and, although he defeats her after a heroic struggle, the perils of misreading are still very much alive. As he proceeds through Book I, Redcrosse is constantly required to interpret situations – a disguise, a building, a false premise, a dream – and, just as routinely, he reads them wrong. Had he had his wits about him, the implication seems to be, had he honed his interpretative skills, he would have been better able to avoid the disastrous mistakes that cost him so dearly. For, while none of these situations are literary texts in themselves, they might just as well have been. Indeed, throughout Book I, error repeatedly appears associated with written forms: the 'bookes and papers' that clog Errour's loathsome vomit, for example (I.i.20), do not disappear at her death but uncannily re-surface in the deceptive 'booke' that hangs from Archimago's hermit disguise (I.i.29); in the 'Magick bookes' and 'balefull bookes' with which he conjures evil spirits and false spells (I.i.36; ii.2); in the 'Portesse' or breviary that Idleness, one of the Seven Deadly Sins, carries,

'That much was worne, but therein little red' (1.iv.19); in the 'eternall booke of fate' with its 'accurst hand-writing' that Despair waves in Redcrosse's face, almost inducing him to commit suicide (1.ix.42); or in the 'sad lines', 'byting words', and 'letters vaine' with which, even as late as the end of canto xii, Duessa and Archimago are still trying to suborn Una and Redcrosse (1.xii.26, 29, 34). It is by such textual means, Book 1 seems to insist, that evil is most capable of insinuating itself and most likely, therefore, to lead the good knight astray. Against the ever-present dangers of wrong reading it is necessary to range a series of weapons powerful enough to mount a counter-attack, and among these are such exemplary alternatives as the New Testament that Redcrosse gives Arthur, 'writ with golden letters rich and braue' (1.ix.19) or the 'sacred Booke' with which Fidelia instructs the latter in the House of Holiness (1.x.19).

The greatest weapon of all, however, is knowing how to read correctly in the first place, and here we might add *The Faerie Queene* itself to these 'good' books that aim to redirect the reader towards the path of righteousness. For it is not just the Redcrosse Knight who learns – the hard way – to get better at interpreting the signs around him. Encountering the same situations and being confronted with the same decisions, we are subject to the same tests and trials ourselves. Redcrosse might pass out of the wood of Error and proceed 'forward on his way' (1.i.28) but he is no more out of the woods than we are, as we remain for the duration of the poem amid the dense thicket of Spenser's text, obliged to find our way through an increasingly complex narrative texture with its multiple levels of meaning and its tangled *entrelacement* of ever proliferating plots. Errour might be dead by the poem's twenty-fourth stanza but, as Patricia Parker writes, she leaves her trace 'in the serpentine progress of the poem itself, the *vestigia* the reader must follow in order to thread the labyrinth'.[8] And the maze is to be negotiated at every level: from the smallest units of individual letters, words, and names, through the complex and astonishingly dense internal structures of the Spenserian stanza (rhymed ababbcbcc), to overarching themes, allusions, repetitions, and numerological patterns that structure the epic as a whole. In the struggle that follows, as we work our way through this difficult poem, we find ourselves embroiled and implicated in its twists and turns, forced to engage in the tortuous business of making sense, of weighing up the options, and of learning to discriminate between appearance and reality. As often as not we find ourselves – like the Redcrosse Knight – confused, tripped up, or proven wrong, but we are also – like him – educated in the process. For it is here that we experience our own epic labours and triumphs at first hand: here that we learn to hone our reading skills, to develop our powers of judgement, and to flex our intellectual muscle in the ongoing battle of trying to get things right, or at the very least trying not to get them wrong.

Indeed, Spenser is putting into practice here a tenet basic to Renaissance poetics: the idea that – since it exercises the same qualities of prudence, discernment, intelligence, and caution – to read well is, essentially, to live well. 'Of all the activities of human reason', Tasso wrote in his *Discourses on the Heroic Poem* (1594), 'none is harder, none more praiseworthy than intellectual choice.' Since choosing is proper to man – and 'choosing well is most proper to the prudent man' – what better field could there be for exercising that prudence than poetry, the material of which is more uncertain, variable, and inconstant than anything else? 'Supremely prudent he must therefore be', Tasso goes on, 'who would not go wrong in choosing where there is so much variability and uncertainty in the things involved. And the material [of poetry] is like a dark forest, murky and without a ray of light. Hence, if art does not illuminate it, one might wander without guide and perhaps choose the worse instead of the better.'[9] By planting just such a forest at the beginning of *The Faerie Queene* – and by obliging us to enter his poem through it – Spenser effectively casts the reader as a hero knight and implies that the struggles and combats to follow will be fought, for the most part, on the page.

Bookishness, therefore, is perhaps the most distinctive feature of *The Faerie Queene*. Indeed, Spenser's presentation of the epic form as, before anything else, a *text* – designed to be appreciated by a highly literate and preferably scholarly readership – constitutes his single greatest contribution to the genre, and for that reason, I suggest, it should be the lens through which his treatment of other epic themes is focussed. Even such large-scale issues as the perennial tension between the epic poet's 'public' and 'private' voice or between optimistic and pessimistic assessments of the epic task in hand are mediated, typically, via literary means. When Spenser wants to validate his epic project, for example, he turns naturally to etymology. One of the first things that Arthur learns when he opens *Briton moniments* is that 'Britain' derives from Brutus – the ancient forebear and great grandson of Aeneas (himself the great grandson of the founder of Troy). Spenser would have found this ancient legend in Geoffrey of Monmouth's *Historia regum Britanniae*, among other places (it re-surfaces later in Book III when Britomart and Paridell discuss how 'The *Troian Brute*' came to Britain and there founded London, also known as '*Troynouant*', III.ix.46, 45), and it allows him to locate the name of his nation and people in the distant heroic past. Virgil does exactly the same thing, of course, when he suggests in Book I of the *Aeneid* that Julius Caesar, Augustus's great-uncle and adoptive father, derived his name from that of Aeneas's son, Iulus, and that the latter derived his, in turn, from Ilus, the legendary founder of Ilium or Troy. The etymological link is clearly part of Virgil's overt strategy to authorize the ruling family by tracing its (implicitly unbroken) connection with the ancient heroic past. When Spenser promises that *Briton moniments* will reveal to Queen Elizabeth 'Thy name...thy realme and race' (II.x.4), he is engaging in a project quite as justificatory, not only indulging the Tudors' conceit of an Arthurian heritage but also extending that ancestry further still, from Arthur back to Brutus and the Trojans. Spenser is consciously deploying the classic epic device of the *translatio imperii* here. But he also brings something new to it and, in so doing, goes considerably further than Virgil. For what he adds is a humanist belief in etymology, the confidence – based on the work of humanist writers and biblical scholars of the Renaissance – that through philology and historical linguistics, through the study of what words meant in context and how they changed and evolved over time, it would be possible to trace their original meanings and so to establish the truth once and for all. Moreover, since, as R. Howard Bloch puts it, 'language seems to function in a family way', the art (or science) of etymology follows the same principles as genealogy – adopting the same model of linear teleology, the same structure of vertical descent – so that, just as a noble family or ruling house might trace its heritage back through the generations to a founding ancestor, so a word might be traced back through the vagaries of usage and dialect to an original and God-given meaning.[10] In both cases the aim was the same: legitimization. The true meaning of a word could be verified and validated by going back to its origins just as a family could be legitimated, indeed, authorized to rule.

This humanist understanding of language extends the scope of etymology considerably. From the relatively local use to which it had been put in Virgil, etymology becomes in *The Faerie Queene* a global phenomenon, an over-arching rationale that governs the entire poem. Names can be traced back not only to illustrious forebears but further still to their original meanings, to the truth itself. In allegory – a mode that personifies its key terms – the question is particularly moot, for it is from the names such characters are given (Orgoglio, Pyrocles, Malbecco, and so on) that the reader is to divine what they mean. Not for Spenser the nominalism of a Juliet: a rose by any other name might smell as sweet, but for him it would be called 'rose' for a reason. Towards the end of Book IV, Spenser indulges in an etymological *tour de force* when, in describing the wedding of the Thames and Medway, he fulfils a long-standing intention to give all the English rivers 'their righte names', and proceeds to show how they have the names they have because these reflect their true natures. Thus, the 'stately' Severn is so called because *severane* is an archaic form of 'sovereign', the 'storming' Humber because it comes from the Greek word for storm (ὄμβρος), the Wylibourne because of its winding passage, the Mole because it passes underground, the Trent because it harbours thirty (French, *trente*) kinds of fish, and so forth (IV.xi.30, 32, 35). This procession of rivers, moreover, is introduced with the same heroic flourish as *Briton moniments*, for this is one of the points in the poem at which Spenser invokes the help of the Muse, Clio – 'To whom those rolles, layd vp in heauen aboue, / And records of antiquitie appeare' (IV.xi.10) – as if the business of tracing the etymologies of the rivers were as monumental a task as tracing the origins of Arthur's Britons. The river names, too, are 'moniments of passed times' (IV.xi.17). For that matter, it is not only names to which this etymological treatment can be applied. Insofar as every lexical element has a 'genealogy', etymology can be extended to all words. Every word, potentially, is a 'moniment' that can be patiently excavated in order to recover the true sense that may have become obscured through the passage of time. Indeed, it is this belief that licenses Spenser's ubiquitous wordplay. 'How brutish is it', Arthur exclaims, looking up from *Briton moniments*, 'not to vnderstand, / How much to her [Britain] we owe' (II.x.69) – how brutish, that is, not to know you are British.

In the preface to *The Shepheardes Calender*, EK – the text's supposed 'editor' and compiler of its learned commentaries and glosses – had praised Spenser for restoring 'as to theyr rightfull heritage such good and naturall English words, as have ben long time out of use and almost cleare disherited'.[11] The terms of such praise evidently invoke the image of language as a family or clan whose legitimacy is to be affirmed – its inheritance preserved, its birthright restored – by establishing a proper genealogy for each of its members or terms. One of the things Spenser sought to do by such means – both in the *Calender* and in *The Faerie Queene* – was to make the case for English: to claim it as a noble language on a par with the classical tongues and as worthy a medium for the writing of epic poetry as they (clearly something Virgil did not need to do). But Spenser is also doing something more: he is validating his epic project. He is not only demonstrating that, by writing a great national epic in the vernacular, English culture can hope to compete with that of the classics. He is also exploiting all the resources that historical linguistics, comparative philology, multi-lingual puns, etymology, and word-play made available to him (all of them to be picked up on by his ideally attentive reader) in order, yes, to celebrate the ruling family and to glorify the nation, its people and language, but in addition and beyond all that, to go back to the beginning of things, to return to the original meaning of words, and by that means to arrive at the truth.

So much for the positive. All the while, however, a more doubtful, ambivalent, even negative shadow broods over *The Faerie Queene* for, like all great epics, Spenser's poem is shot through with contradictions and counter-currents, and, this being Spenser, the latter are expressed in characteristically literary terms. The last word that Arthur reads in *Briton moniments*, for example, is 'Succeding'. The pun is intended since, in genealogical epic, success depends upon succession. When Arthur arrives at this point in the narrative, 'There abruptly it did end' (II.x.68) because the next person to succeed Uther Pendragon is Arthur himself, except that Arthur does not know this yet. As he explained to Una back in Book I, the identity of his father and the lineage from which he derives 'from me are hidden yit' (I.ix.3). The determination to find his own identity – his own place in the genealogical line – is precisely what motivates, indeed constitutes, Arthur's epic quest: both looking backwards to discover the father, family, nation, and race from which he descends, and looking forwards to continue that lineage by marrying and fathering children, thereby continuing the line down to future generations. In Book II, however, Arthur is yet to achieve either goal, and indeed he fails to do so in the course of *The Faerie Queene* as we have it. He remains ignorant of his father and he does not find the Faerie Queene, the figure (as, again, he confides to Una) he has dreamed of and whom he is determined to make his bride. Both these goals remain postponed, indefinitely deferred beyond the bounds of Spenser's poem.

We might ask, then, to what extent *The Faerie Queene* can be said, as an epic, to 'succeed'? And this uncertainty – a doubt that suddenly halts our confidence in the sense of epic progression much as it suddenly arrests Arthur's reading – is not a momentary blip but a deep and pervasive misgiving. In Book III, canto iii, Britomart hears from Merlin a prophecy about the people and race that are to succeed her: a vision that effectively 'book-ends' *Briton moniments* in the sense that, if the earlier catalogue traces the line of the Britons from Brutus back to Arthur, this later one (also written in Clio's 'great volume of Eternitie', III.iii.4) continues the line from Arthur – via his half-brother, Sir Artegall, whom Britomart is destined to wed – down to Queen Elizabeth. As a teleological narrative geared to the glorification of the ruling family and current regime, Merlin's prophecy is typical of dynastic epic (and alludes to the pageant of future Roman heroes that Anchises reveals to Aeneas in the *Aeneid* Book 6). But, like *Briton moniments*, this narrative too is denied closure. It also breaks off abruptly – 'But yet the end is not...' (III.iii.50) – as epic triumphalism once again is threatened and put on hold. Merlin tells Britomart that 'enrooted deepe must be that Tree' from which will come the 'fruitfull Ofspring, [that] shall from thee descend' (III.iii.22, 23); and in the following canto Spenser reiterates the point to Queen Elizabeth, that the 'stock, from which the branches sprong' would eventually culminate in herself, 'Whose lignage from this

Lady I deriue along' (III.iv.3). This image of the family tree is the very stuff of genealogical epic. But what happens if that tree is cut off, truncated, if it fails to 'succeed'? Virgil had faced a similar dilemma when Anchises's great roll call ends with the tragic death of Marcus Claudius Marcellus, Augustus's nephew and possible heir; and it was all too real a prospect for Spenser in the 1590s when the childless and unmarried Elizabeth was still refusing to nominate a successor. The uncertainty that threatened the stability of the nation could also jeopardize the epic project itself, yet history showed such an eventuality to be only too possible, even likely. Back in *Briton moniments*, Arthur reads that, seven hundred years after Brutus's founding of the nation, 'The noble braunch from th'antique stocke was torne'; factions and internecine strife followed, with the result 'That in the end was left no moniment / Of *Brutus*, nor of Britons glory auncient' (II.x.36).

If Arthur's book, like Merlin's vision, relates a genealogy, it is a story not of continuity and 'success' but of rupture and dislocation. The brutal realities of history are capable of overturning epic triumphalism in an instant. However illustrious an ancient forebear may have been, it is evidently possible that he might leave 'no moniment' after all – nothing but a name, tragic testament to all that has been lost, sacrificed to the sheer messiness and contingency of history. And the same melancholy pessimism attaches to verbal 'genealogies', as well – the confidence that etymology would be able to track down the primary meaning of words and reveal the truth behind them is overshadowed by similar doubt. Seen from the other end, etymology shows only how easily words can be corrupted or bastardized, how far they can fall from their original pristine meanings to obscurity and error through the distortions and accretions of time. The gloom is particularly noticeable in the later Books of *The Faerie Queene*, and especially in Book VI, which opens with a jettisoning of etymology with what can only, in the context, be described as a sour irony: 'Of Court it seemes, men Courtesie doe call' (VI.i.1). In fact, courtesy is shown to be anywhere but, as Sir Calidore, the hero of Book VI, spends most of his time away from the court and secluded instead in pastoral retreat, Spenser's caustic satire expressing itself, this time, via the *dis*connect between a word and its etymon. Book VI is full of misreadings – of words taken out of context, of false rumours spread – the chief agent of these being the Blatant Beast, 'A wicked Monster, that his tongue doth whet / Gainst all, both good and bad, both most and least, / And poures his poysnous gall forth to infest / The noblest wights with notable defame' (VI.vi.12). This is the monster that Calidore is charged with destroying, but Book VI ends with the Beast still at large, fomenting misinformation and peddling lies, and not even the poet himself is immune: 'Ne spareth he the gentle Poets rime' (VI.xii.40).

Pessimism thus counters optimism, cynicism some of the more idealizing aspects of the epic drive. In his complaint poem, *The Teares of the Muses* (1591), Spenser opens with the lament of Clio. Her task, she tells us, is to commemorate great deeds, 'all noble feates ... To register', but the present time is so fallen – its values so corrupt, its people so selfish and vain – that she can find 'nothing worthie to be writ, or told'. As a result, she declares flatly, there will be no epic poem to memorialize the present age – 'nor moniments of time' – because she can find nothing worthy to heroize: 'I nothing noble have to sing'. That is her last word on the subject, as she falls to weeping and is followed in turn by each of her equally lachrymose sisters. This is the shadow that threatens to fracture the 'moniment', to subvert, destabilize, even to negate the epic project itself. But perhaps this clash between success and failure – this unresolved ambivalence between epic and history, between idealism and reality – is, when all is said and done, the most abiding quality of epic poetry, the one characteristic that is shared by texts otherwise so remote from one another in culture, language, and history, and what therefore makes *The Faerie Queene*, for all its unique qualities, an exemplar of the genre.

NOTES

1 Edmund Spenser, *The Faerie Queene*, ed. Hiroshi Yamashita, Toshiyuki Suzuki, and A. C. Hamilton, rev. edn (London: Longman, 2007). *The Faerie Queene* was first published in 1590 (Books I–III only) and again in 1596 (Books I–VI).

2 James Nohrnberg, *The Analogy of The Faerie Queene* (Princeton: Princeton University Press, 1976), xiii; Elizabeth J. Bellamy, *Translations of Power: Narcissism and the Unconscious in Epic History* (Ithaca: Cornell University Press, 1992), 222.

3 Plato, *Phaedrus* 274c–275b.

4 Elizabeth Mazzola, 'Apocryphal Texts and Epic Amnesia: The Ends of History in *The Faerie Queene*', *Soundings* 78 (1995): 131–42, 138.

5 Bellamy, *Translations of Power*, 222.

6 Quotations from *A Letter of the Authors*, prefaced to the 1590 version of the poem, ed. Yamashita, Suzuki, and Hamilton, 714.

7 *The Yale Edition of the Shorter Poems of Edmund Spenser*, ed. William A. Oram *et al.* (New Haven: Yale University Press, 1989), 19.

8 Patricia Parker, *Inescapable Romance: Studies in the Poetics of a Mode* (Princeton: Princeton University Press, 1979), 69.

9 Torquato Tasso, *Discourses on the Heroic Poem*, trans. Mariella Cavalchini and Irene Samuel (Oxford: Clarendon Press, 1973), 21.

10 R. Howard Bloch, *Etymologies and Genealogies: A Literary Anthropology of the French Middle Ages* (Chicago: University of Chicago Press, 1983), 41.

11 *Yale Edition of the Shorter Poems*, 16.

9

DAVID LOEWENSTEIN

The seventeenth-century
Protestant English epic

During the seventeenth century, the Protestant English epic found its most daring and original expression in Milton's two major epics, *Paradise Lost* (1667, 1674) and *Paradise Regained* (1671). In this chapter I examine the generic, political, and religious distinctiveness of the Protestant English epic, especially as it culminated in Milton's epic poems published during the Restoration. This was a period of enormous political and religious hostility and uncertainty for Dissenters like Milton, 'fall'n on evil days' and anxious that his might be 'an age too late' to raise the 'name' of epic to new heights (*PL* 7.25, 9.44–5).[1] In discussing Milton's *Paradise Lost* and *Paradise Regained* and the striking ways in which Milton as visionary poet revises and subverts the epic tradition, I will concentrate on what makes them especially distinctive radical Protestant epics. Although Milton's spiritual epics, with their expansive and highly nuanced handling of biblical materials, remain at the centre of this discussion, Lucy Hutchinson's *Order and Disorder*, another notable biblical epic by a Dissenter committed to republican causes and initially published anonymously in 1679, deserves special attention as well: the first English Protestant epic by a female author, it is only now beginning to receive critical assessment.

Paradise Lost as visionary epic

In *Paradise Lost* Milton, the radical Protestant poet, combined epic form, sacred themes, and prophecy to create a daring and highly original poem retelling the most universal of biblical subjects: the Fall of humankind. Milton's epic poem rivals its classical and Renaissance precursors, as well as the Bible itself. Its vast narrative of more than 10,500 lines re-imagines the story of the Fall of humankind and the titanic struggle between the forces of Satan and God with great freshness and psychological subtlety. Its scope, befitting an ambitious epic poem, is cosmic – Heaven, Hell, and Earth – as well as intensely domestic: the story of our first parents, Adam and Eve, and their tragic disobedience and its long-range consequences in human history.

Milton's epic on the Fall of humankind was most likely composed between 1658 and 1663, a transitional and politically uncertain period in Milton's life in which he was concluding his career as a controversial pamphleteer and then living and writing as a religious Dissenter during the Stuart Restoration, which he had fiercely opposed. Milton had used his immense talents as a controversial writer to oppose the Stuart monarchy (he had defended the traumatic execution of King Charles I in 1649), and he opposed any kind of formal religion, ceremonial worship, and the idea of a national church – whether that be the pre-revolutionary Church of England, with its emphasis on a ceremonialist church led by Archbishop William Laud (d. 1645), or a Presbyterian dominated church. The Restoration of 1660 returned not only the king but the Church of England, and with this came a great wave of militant Anglicanism, strict censorship, and religious persecution. By the time Milton wrote *Paradise Lost*, he was a blind man in his fifties (having gone totally blind by February 1652), he was disappointed with church and national reformation, and yet he aspired to write a new kind of epic poem focusing on sacred truths and attempting, after the collapse of the English Revolution, to 'assert Eternal Providence, / And justify the ways of God to men' (1.25–6). Milton did not publish the first edition of the poem until 1667; nor did the radical Protestant epic poet, alienated in the midst of a hostile Restoration world, have any kind of traditional, powerful patron or patroness – only his 'Celestial Patroness, who deigns / Her nightly visitation unimplor'd' (9.21–2). The unadorned 1667 quarto edition contained no front matter, no dedicatory or commendatory poems, and no epistles from the author or publisher: Milton was avoiding the apparatus of courtly publication. *Paradise Lost* was first published in ten books, a structure resembling Lucan's republican epic, *Pharsalia*, about the tragic defeat of the Roman republic. It was reissued in 1668 and 1669 with the addition of the prose Arguments and a defiant note on verse explaining why the poem does not rhyme and conform to Restoration cultural expectations. It was then published in 1674 in twelve books, a modified design more closely following Virgil's epic, although Milton's visionary epic revises Virgil's imperial associations. Abraham Cowley had attempted in the 1650s to compose a biblical epic on the early career and troubles of David, a poem also 'designed into *Twelve Bookes . . .* after the *Pattern* of our Master *Virgil*', but, unlike Milton, he never followed through on his ambitious plans and managed to publish only four books.[2]

In *Paradise Lost* Milton composed and self-consciously revised what was by far the most ambitious, expansive, and encyclopaedic of all literary genres.

Renaissance poets and critics regarded the epic or 'the Heroical' poem as the highest form of literature – 'the best and most accomplished kind of poetry', as the English Protestant poet Sir Philip Sidney put it in his *Defence of Poetry* (published in 1595). Moreover, for Sidney the epic also celebrated the achievements of warrior-princes and the leaders of nations ('let Aeneas be worn in the tablet of your memory, how he governeth himself in the ruin of his country').[3] Milton is acutely self-conscious about writing in this ambitious, comprehensive literary form and yet attempting to do something remarkably fresh with it. 'What if it were a Composition Intirely New', one of Milton's early biographers, Jonathan Richardson, acutely observed regarding the audaciousness and originality of *Paradise Lost* as epic, 'and not reducible under any Known Denomination?'.[4] Already by the age of Virgil (70–19 BC) the epic as genre had been well established with such features as beginning in 'the midst of things' (as Milton's Argument to Book 1 puts it), the invocation of a muse, the emphasis on aristocratic and martial themes, the legendary heroes and exploits, the epic journey, the use of long similes and epic catalogues, and the intermixing of the deeds of gods and men. In Milton, however, we constantly discern a tension between convention and originality. Milton incorporates these epic features into his poem as he challenges and revises many of the themes and conventions of classical epic, including its emphasis on the heroic and martial pursuit of glory. To be sure, there is warfare in *Paradise Lost* – especially the cataclysmic war in Heaven narrated in Book 6 – in which the rebel angels (who fight like Homeric warriors, while also employing gunpowder technology) reach a stalemate with God's loyal angels. But warfare is also revised into apocalyptic struggle and triumph: only the Son of God, expressing divine wrath on his spectacular and sublime apocalyptic 'Chariot of Paternal Deity' (6.750), itself a revision of the epic chariot of war, manages to overcome God's enemies, hurling them down to Hell. Moreover, Milton diverges strikingly from both classical and Renaissance models of epic achievement – Virgil, Spenser, and the sixteenth-century Portuguese poet Luis de Camões, and others – by choosing not to write his epic on a more traditional national and imperialistic theme, and instead giving his long narrative poem more universal subject matter and much greater interior emphasis. The character in *Paradise Lost* who embodies the old-style martial virtues and heroic ideology of the epic tradition – as he manifests the rage and impulse for revenge of Homer's Achilles and the skill and cunning of Odysseus – is Satan in his unwavering pursuit of personal glory and imperial ambitions.

The sacred subject matter of Milton's inspired poem is 'Not less but more Heroic' (9.14) than that of his classical precursors whose heroic values his poem continually challenges, subverts, and transcends. Milton's focus is startlingly new: he writes an epic about a great sacred theme and the sweep of his poem moves typologically from the Old Testament to the New, from the first Adam to the second (Christ, that 'one greater Man' [1.4] rather than Virgil's Augustus prefigured by Aeneas). *Paradise Lost* is a sublime, prophetic Protestant epic that moves, like the Bible itself, from the Creation (freshly narrated in Raphael's brief hexaemeral epic of Book 7 which relates that six-day event) to the end of time itself. With the help of his Heavenly Muse, Milton attempts to soar above the classical Mount Helicon ('th' *Aonian* Mount', 1.15), sacred to the Muses, all the way to the realm of God. As he promises to sing of 'Things unattempted yet in Prose or Rhyme' (1.16), Milton seeks to raise the name of epic to a new height, as he ironically echoes a similar claim to novelty made by Ariosto in 1516 in his great romance epic, *Orlando Furioso* ('Cosa non detta in prosa mai, ne in rima', Canto 1.2). Unlike Ariosto, whose poem combines chivalric and epic materials, the visionary Protestant poet soars beyond his classical and Christian epic precursors and even beyond the Mosaic text itself as his poem unfolds a vast mythic narrative about the origins of the Fall and elaborates upon the terse, cryptic details of Genesis.

Yet the drama of this poem's ambitious action is not only the entire cosmos, including Heaven and Hell, but the mind and heart of the Protestant individual. Milton's great Puritan epic takes a radical turn inward, not only by rejecting or revising the martial and imperial values of its pagan and Renaissance epic models, but by rejecting all external and human religious authorities, as the blind prophetic poet seeks, as he puts it in his great probing invocation to light and internal illumination, to 'see and tell / Of things invisible to mortal sight' (3.54–5). As *Paradise Lost* swerves away from the older heroic values of outward trials and warfare, it transforms the epic into a much more interior mode of spiritual trial and visionary poetry. As it does so, it revises the epic genre, giving it a much more interior Protestant character. The sublime Protestant epic of its age, *Paradise Lost* fully rivals and supersedes its classical and European precursors – a poem written by a blind, visionary poet inwardly illuminated by the light of God.

Paradise Lost and radical Protestant theology

Paradise Lost stands out as the most explicitly theological of Protestant epics in early modern Europe. Unlike Milton's major theological treatise, *De Doctrina Christiana*, which presents theological doctrines, including unorthodox ones, in a systematic way, the epic *dramatizes* major theological issues – including predestination, foreknowledge, free will, and providence – central to both the religious controversies that grew out of the Reformation and the religious ferment of the English Revolution. *Paradise Lost* is a daring poetic theodicy, as the poet attempts to 'justify the ways of God to men' (1.26) rather than attempting (as readers might expect) to justify the ways of men to God. Theology and theological debate are therefore central to Milton's poem in a way that they are not in any other Renaissance epic. In his major work of literary criticism, *Discourses on the Heroic Poem* (1594), the Italian critic and epic writer, Torquato Tasso, had suggested that a poet 'is not to show himself ambitious in theological questions', instead leaving such matters to schools of theologians.[5] Milton, however, clearly does not follow such advice: writing as both artist and theologian, his radical Protestant poem revitalizes controversial doctrinal themes, treating them in his biblical epic with unusual power and drama.

The council in Heaven in Book 3, an imaginative revision of the celestial council found in classical epics, enables Milton to present, as he puts it in his *Christian Doctrine*, 'that play-acting of the persons of the godhead'.[6] In *Paradise Lost* both Father and Son appear as dramatic characters as they address, in their dialogue, such central theological issues as divine justice, free will, sufficient grace, determinism, and providential foreknowledge. There is a tension at the very heart of Milton's theology, and one powerfully dramatized in his poem: this is a Protestant poet who attempts imaginatively to highlight the freedom of human agency, though without ever abandoning a belief in God's omnipotence. Milton's God can speak defensively as he righteously justifies his own ways to his Son (3.96–9). He can speak like an angry, irritable, and passionate parent concerned about his 'youngest Son' (3.151); while God intends to show mankind mercy (3.132–4, 202), from which none is excluded, he also feels compelled to show justice. The God of *Paradise Lost* is a deity of emotions – expressing wrath and indignation as well as 'pity' (3.405) – who struggles with his own decrees and with the poem's central theological issues. Consequently, the poem's reader is prompted to struggle with its theology.

Milton's belief in the exercise of free will in order to achieve salvation is a radical form of Arminianism and a rejection of the stark Calvinist determinism that prevailed in early seventeenth-century orthodox Protestant theology and that was common among Calvinist Puritans. Milton had read the Dutch theologian, Jacobus Arminius (d. 1609), who had posited a more Pelagian challenge to Calvinism by stressing that individuals were free to accept or reject the offer of God's grace needed for salvation – in contrast to Calvinism's intensely negative view of human agency and will.

Consequently, God may have foreknowledge in *Paradise Lost*, but he has in no sense predetermined the fall of humankind (see 3.112–19): man falls freely and possesses the means to resist temptation. Adam himself recognizes the importance of the gift of free will when he tells Eve, just before she goes off on her own in Book 9, that 'God left free the Will, for what obeys / Reason, is free' (351–2). Book 9, which brilliantly elaborates upon the elliptical details of the Book of Genesis, treats the temptation and tragic fall of Adam and Eve with enormous psychological delicacy, showing that our original parents possess the ability to choose and to use their reason (since 'Reason also is choice', 3.108) as they face the seductive rhetoric and arguments of the guileful Satan as serpent. The issue of human free will thus enable Milton's theodicy to exonerate God from responsibility for the Fall. God reiterates this point after the Fall, when he reminds the angels and the Son that 'no Decree of mine' was 'Concurring to necessitate his Fall, / Or touch with lightest moment of impulse / His free Will' (10.44–6). Moreover, unlike orthodox Calvinist writers, Milton imagines in his poem a dynamic prelapsarian world in which human beings 'by degrees of merit rais'd' may work their way up to Heaven (7.157–61) since they, as God observes, are 'Authors to themselves' in 'what they judge and what they choose' (3.122–3). The freedom of choice in determining one's spiritual destiny is central to Milton's poetics of temptation in *Paradise Lost*: by stressing that 'Man . . . shall find grace' (3.131) after falling (unlike the rebel angels), God further underscores the poem's radical Arminian theology, which sets *Paradise Lost* apart from the more orthodox Calvinist determinism of Milton's age. While Milton's God is all-powerful and all-seeing (unlike the poem's anti-Trinitarian Son who is neither co-equal nor co-eternal with the Father), he is not a God of arbitrary will, but, significantly, a God of 'permissive will' (3.685): God hinders 'not *Satan* to attempt the mind / Of Man' (10.8–9), thus allowing Satan and humans to exercise their freedom of unconstrained choice. Milton has given his radical Protestant poem a notable and daring theological dimension, which he develops dramatically and poetically in *Paradise Lost* rather than presenting as pure, untested doctrine.

The Fall as tragedy

Central to the vast narrative of *Paradise Lost* is the domestic human tragedy, as Milton attempts to retell freshly the original story of the Fall. This is one of the most distinctive dimensions of Milton's Protestant epic: his probing and nuanced expansion of the story of the Fall. From the terse, elliptical, cryptic account in Genesis, Milton brilliantly elaborates in Books 9 and 10 a tragic drama of separation, temptation, and falling, followed by the terrible psychological and emotional torment suffered by Adam and Eve. The modulation to tragedy in *Paradise Lost* signals a firm break in the poem's design as the poet changes his 'Notes to Tragic' (9.6), now that the philosophical, intellectual, and social discourse between man and angel are finished (the subject of Books 5–8). Milton treats the Fall with great pathos and feeling, although his poem repeatedly reminds us that there is no doubt that Adam and Eve were wrong – the sole and simple prohibition was 'easy' as Adam tells Eve (4.433) and as the poet himself suggests (7.47–8). The fruit itself – a thing neither good nor evil – was symbolic of their obedience freely observed. Yet the tragic fall of our primal mother and father does differ from the terrible and titanic fall of Satan: their disobedience and rebellion is not prompted by meditated revenge, wilful maliciousness or hatred. Unlike the rebel angels, their fall is not brought on 'by their own suggestion' as if they were 'self-tempted, self-deprav'd' (3.129–30).

In elaborating the domestic drama between Adam and Eve, *Paradise Lost* delicately registers emotional tensions that exist even in the unfallen state. In Book 9 Milton invents a marital debate which revolves at first around economic efficiency, but which also allows Milton to explore the complex emotional relations between Adam and Eve, as well as their vulnerabilities. The domestic drama enables the poet to explain why Eve was alone when the serpent tempted her (Genesis is ambiguous on this point). Moreover, the poet suggests Eve's attractiveness and vulnerability when he describes her in pastoral and elegiac terms at the moment that Satan discovers her alone (see 9.423–33).

Milton also elaborates upon the temptation by having the guileful Satan tempt Eve with the language of Renaissance love poetry (much different from the martial oratory which characterizes his impressive speeches in the poem's early books). Satan's extravagant language – such as when he addresses her with the daring oxymoron 'Goddess humane' (9.732) – is meant to provoke the vulnerable Eve (who tends towards vanity, while Adam tends towards uxoriousness) to aspire beyond her human condition. The most brilliant feature of Satan's temptation is his autobiographical narrative (9.571–612), the last autobiography in the poem (Eve has hers in Book 4 and Adam his in Book 8) and a highly imaginative addition to the biblical story. Satan essentially tells Eve a fictional story of self-creation – how he rose a notch in the chain of being by eating the alluring fruit. Milton dramatizes a complex process of temptation: Eve's reason continues to operate, but she is gradually taken in by Satan's skilful rhetoric and seductive language. The poet, however, takes only two lines to narrate the key action whose tragic consequences for human kind are so immense: 'So saying, her rash hand in evil hour / Forth reaching to the Fruit, she pluck'd, she eat' (9.780–1). Milton invests his story with considerable pathos as he presents the fallen Eve idolizing the fair tree (indeed, she is the first human to engage in an act of idolatry, 9.795–810), giving it her maternal care, showing a new concern for role-playing, and expressing a new sense of female inadequacy and a fear of displacement.

Unlike Eve, Milton's Adam is not deceived at all; yet in his fall, he reveals that he too is emotionally vulnerable. Milton's uxorious Adam cannot imagine life without Eve (9.896–916) and certainly never considers divorcing her. His emotional response is heroic and chivalric, but the marriage of our original mother and father is also being crucially redefined so that spiritual companionship is lost; the union of their fallen marriage now entails 'one Guilt, one Crime' (971), when it had previously been defined as 'one Flesh, one Heart, one Soul' (8.499), Milton's striking expansion of the definition of marriage in Genesis 2:24 (where the man and wife are described as 'one flesh'), emphasizing the remarkable degree of intimacy between Adam and Eve. The postlapsarian lovemaking of Adam and Eve is perfunctory, and Milton, diverging again from the Bible, emphasizes their psychological nakedness and unrest (9.1054–63) by focusing on their faces rather than their genitals (9.1077–8). Book 9 ends tersely, and on a note of unresolved bitterness. Only after much painful struggle and inward torment do Adam and Eve make peace with each other in the fallen world. Crucially it is Eve who is the first repentant human being and who plays a major restorative role by leading Adam out of his terrible, mazelike psychological state. Her redeeming softness (see 10.865) triumphs over his fierce bitterness and misogynistic accusations and establishes a new kind of heroism in the fallen world, bringing the fruitless battle between our original mother and father to an end. The tragedy of the Fall, *Paradise Lost* suggests, will also have significant implications in postlapsarian history (see below) as Milton explores the long-range impact of Adam and Eve's disobedience on human religion and politics.

Paradise Lost: Protestant epic and religious politics

As a Protestant epic, *Paradise Lost* reveals much evidence of Milton's ongoing imaginative engagement with the religious politics of his age. To what extent, we might ask, did Milton's radical religious voice in *Paradise Lost* remain 'unchang'd / To hoarse or mute', especially given the cold political climate of the Restoration when the solitary, blind poet had 'fall'n on evil days' and 'evil tongues' (7.24–6)? To what degree do Milton's politics and religious convictions remain interconnected in his great spiritual poem? Milton presents *Paradise Lost* as an epic poem of restoration in the provocative sense that religious radicals and Dissenters would have understood it: the 'one greater Man' who will 'Restore us' (1.4–5), the poet prophesies, is not a Stuart king but the Messiah himself. In this section, I examine some of the ways the religious politics of *Paradise Lost* further define the poem as a distinctive and daring Protestant epic.

The multiple perspectives Milton provides on the fallen angels in Books 1 and 2 enable the epic poet to qualify the splendour and heroic posture of the devils and their forceful oratory in ways that reveal his polemicism with regard to religious politics. The impressive catalogue of fallen angels in Book 1 (lines 376–522), for example, highlights themes of idolatry and pagan practices (as well as themes of lust and violence) as it looks forward to the decline of the church narrated in Book 12. Milton's reference to 'gay Religions full of Pomp and Gold' (1.372), in the midst of this narrative of idolatry and idolatrous cults, evokes Roman Catholic as well as Laudian religious ceremonialism during Milton's age. In his controversial prose, Milton had blasted 'these gaudy glisterings' of ceremonial religion (encouraged by Laud in conflict with the English Reformed tradition) when 'altars indeed were a fair forwardnesse' and prelates 'were setting up the molten Calfe of their Masse again' (*CPW* 1:828, 771). Ironically, when the devils complain about the religious rituals of Heaven, including singing 'Forc't Halleluiahs' (see 2.241–4), they make themselves sound like victims of religious conformity and Laudian ritualized worship.

The tense encounter between Satan and Milton's fiery angel Abdiel (his name means 'servant of God') narrated in Books 5 and 6 likewise dramatizes the religious politics of the epic in distinctive ways. In the great rebellion in Heaven, Satan employs 'Ambiguous words' (5.703) to fuel his resistance and provoke the rebel angels, reminding us of Milton's depiction, in his anti-monarchical prose, of European monarchs who rebel against the King of Kings and derive their power from the Beast of Revelation as 'doutbfull and ambiguous in all thir doings' (*CPW* 3:598–9). However rousing it may sound, Satan's political language is slippery and equivocal (see 5.773–802), and Abdiel responds with fiery zeal and the scorn of the righteous, Miltonic prophet who dares to utter the 'odious Truth' in the midst of 'a World perverse' (11.704, 701). Abdiel characterizes Satan's inciting speech as 'argument blasphémous' (5.809), evoking the Beast of Revelation (13:5–6) who opens 'his mouth in blasphemy against God' and makes war with the saints (as God's loyal angels are called in the War in Heaven: 6.47, 767, 801, 882). Abdiel's response (see 5.809–48) reminds the poem's discerning readers of heaven's special political circumstances – God's kingship is unlike any other kind of kingship and certainly does not resemble an earthly monarchy. Abdiel thus attempts to restrain Satan's dangerous rhetoric and to counter his astonishing (if exhilarating) assertion that he and his legion are 'self-begot, self-rais'd' (5.860): Satan's primal sin is his desire to exist on his own and to create an identity for himself not created by God.

The affinity between Abdiel, scornfully rejected by Satan's camp, and the daring visionary Miltonic poet, 'with dangers compasst round, / And solitude' (7.27–8), is underscored by Milton's description of the fearless 'flaming Seraph' who is 'Encompass'd round with foes' (5.875–6). Like the poet whose radical voice remains 'unchang'd / To hoarse or mute' in the midst of the evil days of the Restoration, Abdiel will not 'swerve from truth, or change his constant mind / Though single' (5.902–3) and reviled with reproach. Like the solitary Jesus in *Paradise Regained*, who finds himself repeatedly harassed and tempted by Satan in the wilderness, the faithful seraph remains unmoved, unshaken, and unaltered. Moreover, there is much pointed irony when the rebel Satan himself reviles the faithful seraph as 'seditious' (6.152), an inflammatory epithet that evokes the religious and political controversies of the English Revolution and its aftermath. John Lilburne the Leveller complained in his *Just Defence* (1653) that it was common to be labelled 'factious and seditious, men of contentious and turbulent spirits . . . for no other cause, but for standing for the truth'; and the stern Conventicles Act of 1670 (as we will see in the next section), attempted to prevent any sectarian insurrection during the Restoration, warning against 'dangerous practices of seditious sectaries and other disloyal persons'.[7]

The language of religious controversy is likewise crucial to the poem's war in Heaven; referring to God's other loyal angels, Abdiel speaks ironically to his adversary on the battlefield, throwing the language of sectarianism back in the face of the rebel Satan:

> but thou seest
> All are not of thy Train; there be who Faith
> Prefer, and Piety to God, though then
> To thee not visible, when I alone
> Seem'd in thy World erroneous to dissent
> From all: my Sect thou seest, now learn too late
> How few sometimes may know, when thousands err. (6.142–8)

Abdiel's polemical words fuse the discourse of radical religion and nonconformity with tense political events of Milton's Heaven – a dramatic reminder that the political upheavals of the 1640s and 1650s, as well as the fierce backlash after 1660 against dissidents, had been fuelled by religious ferment and acute fears of radical sectarianism. In the poem's mythic Heaven, where rebellion leading to the 'horrid confusion' (6.668) of civil war is not generated by the faithful dissenter (i.e. Abdiel), Milton is prompting his readers to reconsider the relations between political rebellion, sectarianism, and civil confusion which orthodox Protestant authorities were keen to link in the previous decades of turmoil.

Milton's religious politics are especially evident in the poem's final books, often closely based upon the Bible and moving from the time of the expulsion to the time of Christ and beyond. Here, at the end of *Paradise Lost*, we can discern poignant tensions in the poet's responses to postlapsarian history. The tragedy of the Fall, Milton's epic shows, has disturbing consequences for human history and politics. The last two books, in which the archangel Michael presents dispiriting visions and narratives of human history characterized by human tribulation, often evoke the turbulent world of Milton's revolutionary England, as well as the religious tensions of the Restoration. The final books depict a handful of faithful individuals – for example, Enoch, Noah, Abraham, and Moses – who emerge in the midst of dark periods of lawless tyranny, warfare, and heavy religious persecution 'in a World perverse' (11.701). Milton's Enoch, mentioned as a figure of faith in Hebrews 11:5, finds himself as the lone 'Just Man' (11.681) rising up in a world of Homeric strife and destruction, as he utters 'odious Truth' (704), speaking (much like a Miltonic prophet) 'of Right and Wrong, / Of Justice, of Religion, Truth and Peace, / And Judgment from above' before being rescued by heaven 'to walk with God / High in Salvation' (11.666–8, 707–8). As the case of Enoch shows, these lone, vehement prophets in human history may not be successful in renovating their fallen or backsliding world afflicted by oppression and violence. Milton's Noah himself is a zealous preacher and just spokesperson, 'the only Son of light / In a dark Age', rising up in a sybaritic, ungodly period of 'luxury and riot' (recalling Milton's condemnation of Restoration culture in his late prose tracts) and vainly preaching 'against allurement' and 'custom' while 'fearless of reproach and scorn, / Or violence' (11. 715, 808–12). Nonetheless, as Adam struggles to interpret the history lessons presented to him (without having read any of Milton's antimonarchical tracts), his vehement response, especially to the aggressive tyranny of Nimrod, is instinctively republican (see 12.64–71) as he recognizes – much as John Locke would in his *Two Treatises of Government* (published in 1690) – that God's donation in Genesis 1:28 did not give Adam 'Monarchical Power over those of his own Species'.[8] It is notable that Milton, not the Bible, has dared to imagine our first father's response to such matters as absolute power and sovereignty, political servility, natural freedom, and republicanism.

The final books of the poem consequently address a sad consequence of the Fall in human history: earthly monarchy and tyranny, along with the loss of inward and outward liberty. Nevertheless, after the often sorrowful lessons of postlapsarian history, Adam can speak of a subversive weakness that would have had pointed resonance for the besieged godly of the 1660s: 'by things deem'd weak / Subverting worldly strong, and worldly wise / By simply meek' (12.567–9). *Paradise Lost*, moreover, offers at the end the consolation of the 'paradise within' (12.587), a replacement for the lost earthly Paradise (certainly 'happier far' than the wreckage of the fallen Eden Adam and Eve leave behind them) and a reminder that the only true church – like God's 'living Temples, built by Faith to stand' (12.527) – lies within the self. The 'paradise within' underscores how radically inward Milton has made the epic poem. Yet that internal impulse and Milton's tragic vision, as we have seen, did not mean that the radical godly poet withdrew from politics into faith when the English Revolution collapsed; Milton's responses to the Restoration were more varied and conflicted than that. Despite the universal appeal of *Paradise Lost*, as it imaginatively and freshly retells the story of the Fall of humankind and its sorrowful consequences, the poem's emphasis on the 'paradise within' the individual believer also speaks movingly to a generation of Dissenters whose unorthodox and polemical writings had challenged all forms of external and institutionalized religion as they sought – like Milton himself – guidance instead from the inner Spirit or light.

Paradise Regained: Milton's radical Protestant 'brief' epic

The other highly original biblical epic Milton published during the hostile years of the Restoration was *Paradise Regained* (published in 1671), an imaginative and politically provocative retelling of the multiple temptations (sensual, active, and intellectual) of Jesus by Satan in the desert and a sequel to *Paradise Lost*. *Paradise Regained* is Milton's 'brief' epic and he bases this four-book poem primarily upon the scriptural account in Luke 4:1–13 (although see also Matthew 4:1–11 and Mark 1:12–13), but he has also added other temptations (for example, the luxurious banquet temptation of Book 2) and made the epic into a poem deeply concerned with interior spirituality and with Jesus's discovery of his prophetic vocation. *Paradise Regained* is indebted to the Book of Job (Jesus is compared to the patient, 'righteous' Job at 1.147, 1.369, 1.425, 3.64, 3.67, 3.95), considered during the Renaissance a model of the biblical brief epic, but in undergoing his many trials – he is 'fully tried / Through all temptation' (1.4–5) – Milton's Jesus supersedes Job, showing greater patience and perseverance. This intensely inward poem about the triumphs of the second Adam over his guileful adversary, however, lacks much of the epic machinery of *Paradise Lost*.

Moreover, Milton's Jesus is no typical aristocratic epic hero: he is unknown, meditative, poor, and humble, and he prefers to use 'winning words' and 'make persuasion do the work of fear' (1.222–3) rather than employ military force to achieve political and religious liberty as Judaea suffers under the decadent tyranny of Tiberius and imperial Rome. He is hardly the traditional aristocratic epic hero who defines himself by mighty deeds of martial prowess and external heroism and who has seen or experienced the glorious empires, kingdoms, and spectacular courts of the world. This is an inward-looking epic about the quiet heroism of spiritual warfare fought by a solitary, obscure, and introspective Jesus. Yet the Protestant epic poet presents Jesus's 'deeds' as paradoxically 'Above Heroic, though in secret done' (1.14–15): in his spiritual and verbal combat with Satan he exemplifies yet once more how mighty weakness can overcome 'Satanic strength' (1.161), a theme that would have especially resonated among oppressed religious Dissenters during the Restoration.

To be sure, *Paradise Regained* is full of plenty of traditional epic themes, but they are subverted or drastically revised in the course of the poem. Satan wants to test Jesus with 'manlier objects' and temptations (2.225) and urges the contemplative Jesus (insisting his 'years are ripe, and over-ripe', 3.31) to assert himself much more actively and aggressively – to pursue earthly glory, fame, and power, as well as military prowess and heroism. Satan compares the slow-moving, inexperienced Jesus with Alexander, 'young Scipio', 'young Pompey', and 'great' Julius Caesar, classical military heroes inflamed with the thirst for glory (3.32–9). Yet the inward-looking Jesus denounces martial heroism, conquest, and Homeric violence (3.71–92), undermining the traditional epic emphasis on achieving glory by means of warfare and a 'great duel' (1.174). This is not to say, as some critics have suggested,[9] that *Paradise Regained* altogether eschews militant means to subdue the ungodly when they are stiff-necked and persist in their idolatry: 'the stubborn only to subdue' (1.226), Jesus observes to himself in his first meditation on his vocation, reminding us that the brief epic was published in 1671 along with Milton's dramatic biblical poem, *Samson Agonistes*, a work that concludes with Samson's spectacular and terrifying destruction of the Philistine temple of Dagon with its 'Idolatrous Rites' (*SA*, line 1378). Yet when Satan displays for Jesus in Books 3 and 4 great empires and military powers – including Assyria, the mighty Parthians, and the spectacle of glorious Rome itself – Jesus remains unmoved and firm in his resistance to the appeal of imperial ambitions and conquest.

The poem's emphasis on spiritual inwardness – on Milton's Jesus who descends 'into himself' (2.111) as he contemplates his vocation – is striking, hardly fitting the traditional epic with its emphasis on the achievement of the highest external deeds and actions. Led by the 'Spirit' or 'some strong motion' into the wilderness (1.8, 189, 290), and in the process of discovering his ministry as the promised Messiah, Jesus walks alone and is highly contemplative, studious, precocious, and retiring. Even his mother Mary is an internalized presence whose words concerning his vocation as Messiah resound in the mind of her son (see 1.227–58). Milton's Jesus resembles much more a hero of faith following the guidance of the Spirit than he resembles any kind of traditional epic hero or national deliverer. On the threshold of his ministry, he has prepared himself in solitude and engages in 'holy Mediations' (1.195). This sense of interiority accords with the notion of the Spirit of truth dwelling in 'pious Hearts, an inward Oracle' (1.463), a theme that would have resonated with the inward spiritualism of radical Puritans in Milton's England. Likewise, Jesus's observation that 'he who receives / Light from above, from the fountain of light / No other doctrine needs' (4.288–90) also gives the poem a radical Puritan emphasis by stressing the Spirit's inner illumination – even above the letter of Scripture itself.

Nonetheless, the inward-looking Jesus finds himself presented with ostentatious visual displays, great spectacles of power, and numerous alluring temptations that appeal to the senses. The extravagant banqueting temptation is one of Milton's most spectacular additions to the Bible. It is described in richly sensuous and exotic details, and as a lavish temptation to appetite it far exceeds Satan's temptation of Adam and Eve, as Satan displays for Jesus

> A Table richly spread, in regal mode,
> With dishes pil'd, and meats of noblest sort
> And savor, Beasts of chase, or Fowl of game,
> In pastry built, or from the spit, or boil'd,
> Grisamber steam'd; all fish from Sea or Shore,
> Freshet, or purling Brook, of shell or fin,
> And exquisitest name, for which was drain'd
> Pontus and Lucrine Bay, and Afric coast.
> Alas how simple, to these Cates compar'd,
> Was that crude Apple that diverted Eve! (2.340–9)

Satan's banquet is a decadent aristocratic feast – *haute cuisine* – and the series of conjunctions 'or' underscores the myriad nature of desire as well as the multiple enticing choices Jesus is presented with. Yet the Son of God, despite feeling hunger, is unmoved by this sensuous regal feast, resisting the temptation to which the first Adam and Eve succumbed. The fact that the banquet is presented 'in regal mode', thereby anticipating the temptations to wealth and regal power later in the poem, gives the temptation a sharper, more polemical edge in this Restoration Puritan poem. Milton himself expressed disdain for the display of the 'vanitie and ostentation' of decadent 'regal splendor' (*CPW* 7:429), as he put it in *The Readie and Easie Way*, his polemical jeremiad published on the eve of the Restoration, warning the backsliding English of their monarchical leanings and the seductive dangers of choosing 'a captain back for *Egypt*' (*CPW* 7:463). The temporal world in *Paradise Regained* is often presented by Satan as an alluring spectacle, and yet temptations to all forms of regal or aristocratic life and power ('To gain a Scepter', Jesus sharply comments, is 'oftest better miss't' [2.486]) will not move the Son of God.

Despite all his rhetorical assaults, subtleties, and guilefulness, Satan finds himself increasingly perplexed and frustrated when he cannot get Jesus to submit to his power and finds himself baffled when he cannot unfold the meaning of the Son of God's identity (see 4.501–20). Temptations to riches, martial glory and fame, revolutionary military action (Satan urges Jesus to follow the example of Judas Maccabeus), imperial power, earthly monarchies, and Greek learning and arts – among the most impressive temptations presented by his adversary – will not alter the Son of God's resolve. In this sense, the inward-looking Jesus as 'perfect Man, by merit call'd' (1.166) Son of God is a model for the Restoration godly tried by all worldly temptations – all Satan's 'solicitations' (1.152) including temptations to power and kingdoms – and yet able to resist and remain unmoved. Sometimes Jesus responds to Satan's verbal assaults with patience, sometimes with disdain and vehemence. Moreover, under a state of siege, he himself sounds like one of the Restoration godly who must endure constant harassment, abuse, and suffering by hostile authorities as he is 'tried in humble state, and things adverse, / By tribulations, injuries, insults, / Contempts, and scorns, and snares, and violence', while 'suffering, abstaining, quietly expecting / Without distrust or doubt' (3.189–93). In this sense, Milton's portrait of Jesus in *Paradise Regained* would have conveyed a kind of model of a faithful Dissenter constantly exercised and undergoing 'many a hard assay' (1.264) in the 'wilderness' of the Restoration world, a place of perpetual trial and temptation.

As Jesus is tried 'though all temptation' (1.5), his disciples, having fallen on 'evil days' (*PL* 7.25) and living in a time of fear, express anguish, doubt, perplexity, and an urgent yearning for deliverance from kingly oppression:

> God of *Israel*,
> Send thy Messiah forth, the time is come;
> Behold the Kings of the Earth how they oppress
> Thy chosen, to what height their power unjust
> They have exalted, and behind them cast
> All fear of thee; arise and vindicate
> Thy Glory, free thy people from their yoke! (2.42–8)

Such lines would have been especially resonant during the Restoration – conveying a yearning for God's Messiah to liberate the dissenting and suffering godly. Moreover, The Conventicle Act of 1670, issued the year before Milton published *Paradise Regained*, banned groups of people meeting for religious worship outside the Church of England services, urged would-be informants to spy on and expose nonconformists, and was a particularly harsh penal law against Dissenters (its penalties included heavy fines) intended to provide 'more speedy remedie against the growing and dangerous practices of seditious sectaries and other disloyal groups, who under pretence of tender consciences. . . contrive insurrections'.[10] Milton's fellow poet and friend, Andrew Marvell, considered the Act 'the Quintessence of Arbitrary Malice', while Milton's Quaker student, Thomas Ellwood (who claimed he prompted Milton to write *Paradise Regained*), characterized the law against Dissenters as 'unjust, unequal, unreasonable, and unrighteous'.[11] Milton's Protestant epic, in which the introspective hero rejects all worldly temptations and invokes the authority of the 'light from above', is indeed provocative in such a religious and political context.

In this contentious religious poem, where the duelling and combat are verbal more than martial, Milton's inward-looking Jesus is increasingly fervent in his responses to that 'persuasive Rhetoric' that 'won so much on Eve' (4.4–5). Basing his prophetic authority on 'Sion's songs' (4.347), Jesus also seems fervent in his rejection of Greek arts, learning, and eloquent oratory when they are presented so attractively to him by Satan in Book 4. Yet there is no need to conclude that Milton is altogether rejecting the classical culture, learning, and models he so deeply admired. *Paradise Regained*, after all, was published in the same volume as *Samson Agonistes*, a dramatic and psychologically powerful retelling of the Samson story based upon Greek tragedy. The more likely explanation is that Milton's Jesus, in responding to Satan's temptation to learning, is responding polemically: characterized by verbal duelling (rather than conventional epic duelling), *Paradise Regained* is a poem full of contentious exchanges, charges, and counter-charges, and in his controversial prose, we may recall, Milton admired 'the high and vehement speeches of our Saviour' (*CPW* 2:668). Milton especially admired the polemical, sharp-tongued, fervent Jesus who took on the rigid Pharisees, countering one extreme with another: 'And as the offence was in one extreme, so the rebuke, to bring more efficaciously to a rectitude. . . stands not in the middle way of duty, but in the other extreme' (*CPW* 2:668; cf. 2:282). Nonetheless, in preferring the songs of Zion to the arts of Greece, and in preferring the 'majestic unaffected style' (4.359) of the Hebrew prophets to classical oratory, Milton's Jesus highlights the radical

Protestant character of *Paradise Regained*. By the end of the poem, after the violent temptation on the pinnacle (where Jesus stands in his 'uneasy station', 4.584, and reveals that he is both man and God), Jesus proves victorious over Satan, a victory with eschatological implications, foreshadowing the Last Judgment. *Paradise Regained* has dramatized how the second Adam, manifesting perfect obedience in the midst of the wilderness of the world, 'hast aveng'd / Supplanted Adam', 'regain'd lost Paradise', and overcome the 'Infernal Serpent' (4.606–8, 618). There is more spiritual warfare yet to come, but the poem's apocalyptic vision of Christ's spreading kingdom dashing 'to pieces . . . / All Monarchies . . . throughout the world' (4.149–50) and the prophecy of Satan being 'trod down / Under his feet' (4.620–1; cf. Romans 16:20 and 1 Corinthians 15:25) would have sounded especially resonant to radical Protestants struggling during the Restoration and wondering, as Jesus himself wonders in wilderness: 'Where will this end?' (2.245).

Order and Disorder: Lucy Hutchinson's Protestant epic and female authorship

Colonel John Hutchinson was one such godly republican whose voice, like Milton's, remained 'unchanged' during the Restoration.[12] His highly accomplished wife, Lucy Hutchinson (1620–81), is especially well known as the author of *Memoirs of the Life of Colonel Hutchinson*, a vivid account of the life and actions of her staunch republican and Puritan husband, before and during the English Civil Wars and Interregnum, as well as during his harsh captivity in the early years of the Restoration (he died in prison in 1664). The *Memoirs* examine the operation of divine providence in her life and in the tumultuous and volatile political and military career of her husband, a leading Civil War officer in Nottingham. Like Milton, the Hutchinsons belonged to no one religious sect, although they were sympathetic to sectarians during the English Revolution and to the adverse plight of Dissenters during the Restoration. Unlike Milton, however, Colonel Hutchinson was strongly Calvinist in his religious convictions and view of providence, as was his wife. Her religious convictions, including her view of the depravity and frailty of human nature, as well as her keen sense of the ephemeral nature of earthly happiness, need to be kept in mind when considering one of her other major accomplishments: *Order and Disorder: Or, The World Made and Undone*, an ambitious though unfinished biblical and hexaemeral epic consisting of twenty cantos. Besides translating Lucretius and composing a number of devotional works, Hutchinson was author of the first epic by an English woman.

Hutchinson's poem, based closely on Genesis and its accounts of Creation, the Fall, and its consequences, naturally bears comparison with *Paradise Lost*, although there is no firm evidence that Hutchinson, who may have composed parts of her epic as early as 1660–4 (its first five cantos were printed in 1679), was closely familiar with Milton's biblical epic (despite some verbal parallels). Andrew Marvell, one of the most astute early readers of Milton's Protestant epic, worried that the audacious Milton might ruin 'the sacred Truths' by turning them into 'Fable and old Song'; likewise, Lucy Hutchinson 'tremble[s] to think of turning Scripture into a romance'.[13] Like Milton, she stresses that 'a great part of the Scripture was originally written in verse; and we are commanded to exercise our spiritual mirth in psalms and hymns and spiritual songs' (p. 5), and this also helps justify her decision to write a biblical epic. Like Milton, Hutchinson also felt that it was more urgent than ever to write about 'the mighty and glorious truths of God' during the hostile political and religious climate of the Restoration, 'this atheistical age' (p. 5) in which a dissolute English nation had grown (as Milton put it) 'more excessively vitious then heretofore'.[14] Her epic is thus a creative, visionary, and polemical work of opposition and dissent; and, as David Norbrook has shown, it remains a crucial expression of her republicanism.[15] Yet that republicanism, including her strong anti-court and anti-monarchical sentiments, is expressed in biblical epic: another reminder that republicanism during seventeenth-century England was sometimes (though not always) closely interconnected with godly religion.

Theologically, however, *Order and Disorder* is more conservative than *Paradise Lost*: unlike Milton, Hutchinson emphasizes the orthodox Trinity ('All coeternal, all coequal, are', 1.96) and she views the godly and the reprobates from the Calvinist theological perspective of double predestination (see 18.82–100). She also handles the biblical narrative in a more conventional way and retells Genesis chronologically using heroic couplets, unlike Milton who, in attempting to raise the name of epic, more brazenly spurns the contemporary Restoration vogue for the 'bondage of Riming'.[16] Hutchinson begins with the creation of the universe and humankind and then moves on to narrate the Fall and its tragic consequences in human history; by contrast, Milton begins *in medias res*, in Hell itself, with the restless Satan and the fallen angels continuing to challenge the power of Heaven, refusing to repent, and planning revenge against God and humankind. Hutchinson does not attempt to imagine the cataclysmic war that results from the great rebellion in Heaven by Satan and the rebel angels ('Of their rebellion and their overthrow / We will not dare t'invent', 4.44–5), as Milton does in Books 5 and 6 of *Paradise Lost*. Her treatment of paradisal marriage, however, conveys acute insights into human nature and needs that recall Milton's epic: she stresses the importance of 'conversation' in marriage and imagines a relationship in which 'both soul and sense partici-pate' (3.304), much like Milton who, as we saw, expands upon the 'one flesh' of Genesis 2:24 to depict a more intimate marriage between our original mother and father. Milton, however, has Adam (not God) articulate his powerful need for human fellowship, 'collateral love, and dearest amity', thereby elaborating greatly upon Genesis 2:18 (see *PL* 8.379ff.), whereas Hutchinson comments: 'Whether he begged a mate it is not known' (3.312). Hutchinson conveys the theatricalism and subtle rhetoric of Satan disguised as a serpent tempting Eve, although, once again, Milton treats these aspects more expansively, in addition to inventing an autobiography for Satan. Overall, Milton is imaginatively more adventurous as he elaborates upon and interprets Scripture.

Yet Hutchinson's re-telling of Genesis conveys with considerable psycho-logical power the immediate consequences of the Fall, including the acute sense of shame and guilt of Adam and Eve expressed (as in Milton) in 'their sad face' (4.244). Hutchinson also movingly laments the tragic conse-quences of the Fall for womankind, including the difficulties, pains, and cares that attend pregnancy, childbirth, and motherhood (5.127–80). Moreover, Hutchinson devotes an even larger portion of her epic (cantos 6 to 20) than Milton does to the long-term tribulations, violence, and tragic conflicts suffered by 'th'unhappy race of sinful man' (7.94), a history Milton condenses into Books 11 and 12 of *Paradise Lost* (although his chrono-logical range is greater). Like Milton, Hutchinson explores the notion that Hell becomes internalized and a state of mental anguish (6.306; cf. *PL* 4.75), so that she presents Cain, the first murderer, lashed by a guilty conscience and Macbeth-like torments as he is 'persecuted in his dreams' and tortured by 'a thousand terrors' (6.280, 283). Throughout her poetic account of the turbulent, dissolute history of humankind after the Fall, Hutchinson explores the relation between God's past and present mercies and humankind's 'pollutions' (8.394) and iniquity.

Some stories in Genesis are vividly retold by Hutchinson: the drunken Noah, the story of Ham and his cursed descendants, the story of Babel and the Lord's derision at human arrogance, the spectacular destruction of Sodom with its stately palaces and temples, become occasions for her to meditate obliquely yet sharply and ominously upon the calamities of the Restoration and its prodigal culture and upon the mighty nature of divine justice, power, and vengeance.[17] Hutchinson's narratives of other episodes and characters from Genesis – for example, her detailed representations of Sarah, Rebecca, and Rachel – enable her to reflect on ideals of godly female modesty, piety, patience, and eloquence in relation to the behaviour of ungodly courtly women in the Restoration: 'Great ones lived not like slothful drones as now' (12.237). In *Order and Disorder* Hutchinson's gender may not result in extensive self-conscious reflections about a woman daring to write in an unusually ambitious genre like epic. Nonetheless, the combination of her gender and her composition of a biblical epic enable the godly republican Hutchinson, writing in the hostile world of Restoration England, to reflect acutely and extensively on the struggles and roles of women in marriage, motherhood, politics, and religion.

NOTES

1 Citations from Milton's poetry are from *John Milton: Complete Poems and Major Prose*, ed. Merritt Y. Hughes (New York: Odyssey Press, 1957).

2 Abraham Cowley, 'The Preface', in *Poems* (London, 1656), sig.b^v.

3 Sir Philip Sidney, *A Defence of Poetry*, ed. J.A. Van Dorsten (Oxford: Oxford University Press, 1966), 47.

4 *The Early Lives of Milton*, ed. Helen Darbishire (London: Constable, 1932), 316.

5 *Discourses on the Heroic Poem*, trans. Mariella Cavalchini and Irene Samuel (Oxford: Clarendon Press, 1973), 51.

6 *Complete Prose Works of John Milton*, gen. ed. Don M. Wolfe (New Haven: Yale University Press, 1953–82), 6:213, hereafter *CPW*.

7 William Haller and Godfrey Davies, eds., *The Leveller Tracts, 1647–1653* (New York: Columbia University Press, 1944), 452; J. P. Kenyon, ed., *The Stuart Constitution: Documents and Commentary*, 2nd edn (Cambridge: Cambridge University Press, 1986), 356.

8 John Locke, *Two Treatises of Government*, ed. Peter Laslett (Cambridge: Cambridge University Press, 1988; rpt. 1994), 1.4.28 (161); see also 141–71.

9 See, for example, Michael Wilding, *Dragon's Teeth: Literature in the English Revolution* (Oxford: Clarendon Press, 1987), 255, who stresses the contrast between Samson ('the old-fashioned, active, military hero') and Jesus ('the new hero' who 'abjures force and saves mankind').

10 Kenyon, *The Stuart Constitution*, 356.

11 *The Poems and Letters of Andrew Marvell*, ed. H. M. Margoliouth, 3rd edn, 2 vols. (Oxford: Clarendon Press, 1971), vol. II, 314; Thomas Ellwood, *The History of the Life of Thomas Ellwood*, ed. C. G. Crump (London: Methuen, 1900), 169–70. For Ellwood and *Paradise Regained*, see Ellwood's *Life*, 145.

12 Lucy Hutchinson uses this precise word in *Memoirs of the Life of Colonel Hutchinson*, ed. N.H. Keeble (London: J. M. Dent, 1995), 289, 312.

13 *Order and Disorder*, ed. David Norbrook (Oxford: Blackwell, 2001), 5 (The Preface); quotations from Hutchinson's poem are cited from this edition. Marvell's 'On *Paradise Lost*', added in the second edition of Milton's epic, appears in *Complete Poems and Major Prose*, 209–10.

14 I refer to Milton's *Of True Religion* (1673), where he complains of the Restoration as a time of 'bold and open Atheism every where abounding' in the nation 'grown more excessively vitious' (*CPW* 8:438).

15 David Norbrook, 'John Milton, Lucy Hutchinson, and the Republican Biblical Epic', in *Milton and the Grounds of Contention*, ed. Mark R. Kelley, Michael Lieb, and John T. Shawcross (Duquesne: Duquesne University Press, 2003), 37–63.

16 See Milton's note on the verse, *Complete Poems*, 210.

17 See, for example, *Order and Disorder* 13.185ff, where the dreadful portents and divine judgments against Sodom, including pestilence and fire, very likely evoke the Great Plague (1665) and the Fire of London (1666).

IO

CLAUDE RAWSON

Mock-heroic and
English poetry

Sometime during the Restoration, the status of epic as the highest poetic genre went into a decline from which it has never recovered. As T. S. Eliot said, 'since Milton, we have had no great epic poem'.[1] Great poems with epic aspirations or pretensions have continued to be written: Wordsworth's *Prelude*, Byron's *Don Juan*, Keats's *Hyperion* poems, Eliot's *Waste Land*, Pound's *Cantos*, and of course (though in prose) Joyce's *Ulysses*. The great example in our time is Walcott's *Omeros*. None of these, however, belongs straightforwardly to the genre of the *Iliad*, the *Aeneid*, or *Paradise Lost*, in the sense of being a long poem, in elevated language, on a high theme of tribal glory, or national origins, or scriptural myth, containing narratives of battle, and usually a high valuation of martial prowess. Many of them remained unfinished, or (like the *Waste Land* and perhaps the *Cantos*) mimic the unfinished state in being organized in 'fragments'.

All these works bear some relation to the epic tradition, allusive and often ironic, but each proceeds from a sense that the primary or traditional form is no longer available to good poets. Some (*Don Juan*, the *Waste Land*, *Ulysses*) sustain a pointed ironic relationship, and use epic reminders and mock-heroic procedures to exploit continuities and disjunctions between past and present, or the collision of grandiloquent perspectives with a lowered reality. In this regard, they were descendants of what one might call the first mock-heroic moment, when, perhaps for the only time in history, some of the best poets devoted some of their strongest energies to a hybrid genre that parodied the epic but did not satirize it. Their style, though seemingly designed to deflate, was protective of the older epics, and, by retaining and even absorbing some of the primary majesties it was travestying, actually aspired in its way to emulating them, achieving through parody the status of what Dryden called 'Heroique Poetry it self'.[2] The aspiration of mock-heroic was thus for the very thing it purported to travesty, which could only be attempted through a mocking imitation. The subsequent history of the form is a continuous effort to come to terms with, and even to overcome, the constraints imposed by this contradiction.

At stake for the first mock-heroic writers (Boileau, Dryden, Garth, and Pope, in verse, Swift and Fielding in prose) was the preservation or recovery of a high style for which the epic had once been an obviously hospitable medium. Dryden and Pope both contemplated epics of their own, which were abandoned, and the spectacle of completed epics by Blackmore suggested that the resource of forcing a new epic through the barrier of cultural inhibition was not seriously available. A second alternative, heroic tragedy, intermittently practised by Dryden, cannot have seemed much more satisfactory. Dryden sometimes professed to think a heroic play was the dramatic counterpart to an epic, but was also somewhat uneasy about it, as an inferior popular surrogate, safe from the risks of epic emulation. With its accentuated rant and often extravagant stage effects, it also teetered on the edge of the ridiculous, its excesses unwittingly becoming a kind of visual or theatrical equivalent of irony.

An alternative impulse to displace epic action to a high discursive mode is evident in Pope's plans for his unwritten epic on the British Brutus, which was to consist of disquisitions on various subjects rather than scenes of combat, and also in Pope's parallel ambition to write a long philosophic poem, which survives only in a few separately published sections. The smaller-scale *Essay on Man*, a discursive Lucretian poem with Miltonic evocations, including an ambition to 'vindicate the Ways of God to Man' while relieving the poet from the obligations of a heroic action, was, like Wordsworth's *Prelude*, a kind of prologue to an unfinished work. The *Prelude* itself is the product of comparable Miltonizing aspirations, with the discursiveness turned inwards. Wordsworth's philosophic poem was never completed, just as Pope never completed his own philosophical opus magnum, as though a shrinking from grand inclusive summations went hand in hand, in the modern sensibility, with a shrinking from the grandeurs of epic.

Two other paths suggested themselves to Dryden and Pope in particular. The first was translation, where epics could be produced by proxy, with reduced risk of self-exposure (it is no coincidence that Dryden and Pope between them produced major translations of Virgil and Homer). The second – devised mainly by the French poet Boileau, but perhaps brought to perfection in English poems, culminating in Pope's *Dunciad* – was to project epic aspiration through a filter of irony. The heyday of serious mock-heroic was the period between 1674, when the final twelve-book version of *Paradise Lost* and the first edition of Boileau's *Lutrin* were published, and 1743, the year of the *Dunciad in Four Books* and Fielding's novel, *Jonathan Wild*.

These works have in common a residual belief in the epic as the highest genre, an acute sense of its unavailability to the poet, and (in Pope's but not Fielding's case) the ambition to recapture it through loyalist parody. Their objective is not to undermine a revered form, but to affirm its worth by exposing the modern realities that fail to rise to its standard. Their relation to epic originals, though continuously coloured by irony, is a matter of structural resemblance and specific allusion. They variously differ from Wordsworth, Byron or Keats, or Eliot or Pound, not only in the thoroughness of their evocation of Homeric, Virgilian and Miltonic originals, but in the systematic irony which accompanies and defines the whole enterprise. At no other time before or since has a significant number of leading writers turned parodic exercises into poems of great power and distinction, making of mock-heroic a dominant idiom of the age. This early expression of the mock-heroic impulse was the product of an active and conflicted cultural disaffection with the epic. The demise of military epic threatened to deprive poetry of certain cherished opportunities for an elevated style. It seemed that this could only be recovered by irony, and the subsequent history of the form has been characterized by efforts to discard the irony, while retaining its protective function.

When Milton wrote *Paradise Lost*, he may not have known that he was producing the last great classical epic by a European poet of distinction. He seemed to advocate an imminent demise for the genre, while retaining an immense investment in it. The poem everywhere exhibits its emulative admiration of Homeric and Virgilian antecedents, in its use of language, exploitation of formulae, deployment of speeches, and choice of incidents. These even included a battlefield episode, where none was necessarily to be expected in the story, and in defiance of Milton's declared disapproval of poems in which war, as throughout the main stream of epic tradition, was 'the onely Argument Heroic deem'd' (9.28–9).[3]

Milton's attitude was based on a common assumption that Christian values were superior to those of pagan antiquity, and that, for all the syncretic reliance on classical models, the Holy Spirit was a surer guide to high poetic performance than any Muse, enabling the poet to achieve 'Things unattempted yet in Prose or Rhime' (1.16). The most ardent admirers of classical antiquity during the Renaissance were naturally conditioned to some version of this view of Christianity, though not all shared the fervour and baldness of Milton's assertion of it. Disaffection with heroic militarism was, among other things, a specialized manifestation of this sense of superior allegiance. Thus Milton affirmed that his theme was 'not less but more Heroic' (9.14) than those of both classical and chivalric epics, though Christianity in fact had not noticeably inhibited the martial ardour either of the chivalric poems or of the Christian epics of succeeding centuries. The anti-war sentiment expressed by Milton, which would be taken for granted today as normal to thinking persons, not necessarily pacifists, was increasingly taking root in his time, but it had not always been widespread. In the sixteenth century, when a martial education was still thought desirable for young gentlemen, and clergymen preached the virtue of war and extolled military prowess from the pulpit, denunciations of warfare had been relatively uncommon. Erasmus's condemnation of militarism and war had been a minority view in his time. This is not to say a dislike of militarism, or an acute sense of the cruelty of war, were the exclusive preserve of Christians, and signs of them may even be detected in some of the earliest military epics.

Changing attitudes to war played a part in the gradual extinction of the idea that heroic poems were the greatest work that the soul of man was able to perform, a definition repeated by rote as late as Dryden's translation of Virgil (1697). An increasing bourgeois readership, the dilution of aristocratic aspirations and classical values, were further predisposing features of a culture increasingly inhospitable to epic. The emergence of mock-heroic in the narrow sense is one of the poetic consequences, as is the 'rise' of the novel with its familiar trade-mark of 'realism'.

The mock-heroic moment is the product of a state of mind that could no longer write epic straight but would not leave it alone. It depended on a continuous tension between surviving loyalties to the epic and the impossibility of writing it. Milton's resolution of this dilemma was to write an epic that included within itself a critique of epic militarism. He even inserted a major battle, complete with triumphalisms of victory. But he also made sure that no one was killed, since all the participants were angels and thus 'incapable of mortal injurie / Imperishable' (6.434–5), so that there is no slaughter in human terms. He did not balk at giving Satan a spectacular wound, and his armies an even more spectacular rout, and he enlarged rather than diminished the play of deadly violence by adding the carnage of gunpowder and artillery, presented literally as the invention of the devil. Gunpowder was often considered inimical to epic. It minimized hand to hand combat. Its long-range hostilities emphasized randomness and the cowardice of distance, as against individual bravery. It was subversive of social rank, an essential precondition of older heroic codes, because a low-born marksman could kill a prince, anonymously. And (not unimportant) it reduced the scope of warrior speech-making, a complaint made in respect of both literary texts and real-life military behaviour, in contexts as widely separated as Pope's notes to Homer and the samurai culture of early modern Japan. Milton's point, however, was not that gunpowder was un-epic, but that it intensified the Satanic depravity of warfare, always remembering he made sure nobody died.

Paradise Lost, thus uncoupled from the discredit of martial celebration, became an immediate progenitor of mock-heroic, not only because it shows its villains in comic discomfitures and postures of un-heroic abasement not far removed from slapstick (creeping, crawling, squatting like a toad), or because of the peculiar chemistry by which, through his blasphemous enormities, Satan sometimes becomes a figure of ridicule, but because the formula of the battle without killing became an essential pattern of the mock-heroic canon from Boileau's *Lutrin* (1674) to Pope's *Dunciad* (1728–43).

Boileau's poem, announcing its 'burlesque nouveau' in the very year of publication of the final version of *Paradise Lost*, relates in mock-Virgilian strains a church squabble over the placing of a pulpit. Like Swift's *Battle of the Books* (1704), it allegorizes the quarrel of the Ancients and Moderns, and its first version in four cantos ended without a battle. *Le Lutrin* reappeared in 1683 in a six-canto version that does include a battle, in which the missiles hurled by the warring clerics are nothing more deadly than books.

That this may be seen as a comic shadow of Milton's assurance that his combatants cannot die is perhaps as fortuitous as the fact that Boileau's poem first appeared in the year of the final version of Milton's, though both coincidences have an iconic force. Boileau is unlikely to have read *Paradise Lost*. His own epic inhibition came not from the martial ethos but from a claim that, like Horace, he was not suited to the task, combined with a withering contempt for modern practitioners of the genre. Nor did Boileau shrink from celebrating the military belligerence of Louis XIV, or from gloating over the crushing of an enemy city in his *Ode on the Taking of Namur* (1693).[4] But in creating the mock-epic, a genre subsequently to be adopted in its most distinguished forms by English more than by French poets, he instinctively seized on a feature which, as in Milton, enabled 'epic' battles to elude the taint of a martial subject matter.

The English followers of Boileau, who did know their Milton, developed a poetic device whose most brilliant and wittiest realization was Pope's *Rape of the Lock* (1714), and which was brought to a new level of poetic consummation in the *Dunciad* (1728–43). The merging of Milton and Boileau was paradoxical. Milton's warranty of non-deadliness, like his disavowal of military epic, was designed to shield the poet himself from the discredit he is conferring on epic even as he is writing it. The effect of Boileau's little fiction, on the other hand, is to protect the epic itself, not the poet, from the discredit of epic carnage, despite the fact that Boileau himself felt no queasiness on the subject. The aspiration of mock-heroic is to reinstate rather than reject the heroic.

English writers assimilated the Miltonic inhibition, including explicit certifications of non-deadliness (these were even introduced in English translations of *Le Lutrin*, though they are not found in the original). But they followed Boileau's model of an 'epic' fiction in which a high style is applied to battles which allegorized learned and professional disputes or sexual imbroglios and have nothing to do with slaughter and destruction. In the medical scuffle in Garth's *Dispensary* (1699), pill-bottles and phials are used as missiles in the manner of the books in *Le Lutrin*. Garth's poem did, as it happens, contain a ranting sequence of 'Homeric' upheaval, in which, briefly and unusually, '*Blood, Brains, and Limbs the highest Walls distain, / And all around lay squallid Heaps of Slain*' (4.190–1).[5] This turns out, however, to be an enraptured recitation by the real-life poet Sir Richard Blackmore of scraps from his own epic poems, inserted verbatim into Garth's narrative. Although offered up for discredit and ridicule, the episode shows no hint of hostility to similar features in the Homeric original. It becomes a parable of the fatuity of writing such stuff nowadays, with the moral that it takes a bad poet like Blackmore to try, recalling Boileau's contempt for untalented authors of French modern epics.

This pudeur about scenes of battle, in works that are after all comic imitations of poems about battles, acquires an escalating momentum in subsequent mock-heroic works. Swift's *Battle of the Books* (1704) playfully rehearses graphic descriptions of 'Homerican' carnage but warns us at the outset

> to beware of applying to Persons what is here meant, only of Books in the most literal Sense. So, when *Virgil* is mentioned, we are not to understand the Person of a famous Poet, call'd by that Name, but only certain Sheets of Paper, bound up in Leather, containing in Print, the Works of the said Poet, and so of the rest. ('The Bookseller to the Reader')[6]

This reminder is reactivated in scenes of seemingly brutal carnage, repeatedly neutralized by leaps of bookish fantasy. For example, the ancient poet Pindar severs the modern Cowley in two with his sword, leaving him 'to be trod in pieces by the Horses Feet', an atrocity ritually followed by a disclosure that the victim, in an amusing literary allegory, is a volume of Cowley's *Works*, not the person; that Venus quickly repairs the binding; and that the pages or 'leaves' experience a genial Ovidian transformation. Unlike Milton's effort to cover his own poem against the epic taint, the practice of Swift, Garth and Pope is protective of the parodied form, and sanitizes the objects of parody in a way that was no part of Milton's design. In Swift's *Battle*, indeed, epic parody is diluted or deflected by competing objects of parodic attention, since the *Battle* is also a mock-edition, and a pretended newspaper report (*A Full and True Account of the Battel Fought Last Friday. . .*).

Swift differs from the mainstream in not seeking in mock-heroic a pathway to the 'lofty style', an idiom he 'declined'. The *Battle* is written in the flattened medium of prose rather than the inflated accents of heroic verse. His friend Pope, on the other hand, followed more closely in the line of Boileau, Dryden, and Garth. In the *Rape of the Lock* (1714), he offered a sustained and exquisite mock-inflation in the high accents of the English heroic line: 'What dire Offense from am'rous Causes springs' (1.1).[7] There is a continuous thread of Miltonic evocation. When, like Swift's Cowley, the sylph is cut in two getting between the 'Sheers' to protect the heroine's lock of hair, this mutilation, like Satan's wound, or those of the Homeric gods, is instantly healed, since 'Airy Substance soon unites again' (3.152). At the poem's climax, in Canto 5, there is a battle of the sexes in which no one dies except in the punning sexual sense, and where notice of immunity is again given in advance in language that specifically recalls Milton's 'incapable of mortal injurie':

> No common Weapons in their Hands are found,
> Like Gods they fight, nor dread a mortal Wound.   (5.43–4)

The battlefield heroics in this sexual confrontation are cunningly merged with commonplaces of love poetry, ladies killing with their eyes, lovers dying from a frown (or bawdily 'reviving' at a smile). Pope's poem puts under friendly but critical scrutiny the elegant fragility of his society's mating rituals. While the 'heroic' style is partly set up for deflation, it generates a grandly orchestrated commotion, conferring a busy amplitude on insignificance itself.

It is in the *Dunciad* (1728–43) that the eschewal of deadliness is taken to the extreme. No blood is spilt, because there is no battle. The *Dunciad* is a massive repository of every epic commonplace, from formulaic phrasings to heroic games, an underworld visit, a Virgilian East–West journey, and an urban re-enactment of Milton's Hell. But it lacks a battle, the main action of most epics, which even Milton felt the need to include, though his Biblical source did not invite this. The poem is so unsanguinary that virtually its only word evoking gore is 'bloodless', in an aldermanic phantasmagoria of 'bloodless swords and maces' (1.87).[8]

Boileau's *Lutrin* thus helped to advance the formula that enabled the English mock-heroic writers to purge their epic reminders from the discredit of war. His even more considerable contribution – perhaps also an intuitive rather than clearly formulated objective – was to introduce a style in which epic grandeurs could be recovered through a protective membrane of parody. It is in a discussion of *Le Lutrin*, in the 'Discourse concerning

Satire', that, some twenty years later (1693), Dryden formulated his important account of mock-heroic as:

> the most Beautiful, and most Noble kind of Satire. Here is the Majesty of the Heroique, finely mix'd with the Venom of the other; and raising the Delight which otherwise wou'd be flat and vulgar, by the Sublimity of the Expression . . . as in Heroique Poetry it self; of which this Satire is undoubtedly a Species.
>
> (p. 84)

These remarks codify a practice Dryden had already explored some eighteen years earlier, when he may have begun *Mac Flecknoe*, the inaugural example in English of the new genre, around 1675, the year after *Le Lutrin* was published. Unlike Boileau's poem and its major English descendants, *Mac Flecknoe* is not based on a traditional epic story. But it plays an important role in the evolution of the genre, because of the particular chemistry of its application of Virgilian and Miltonic style to low matter, and also because it contributed to Pope's *Dunciad* the idea of a literary culture assaulted by an immense noxious 'Dulness'. Dryden may or may not have been aware of Boileau's example at the time. He is reported to have persuaded himself that it was he himself who had written 'the first piece of ridicule written in heroics', a phrase which does not take account of Boileau or Tassoni, an omission handsomely rectified in the 'Discourse' of 1693.[9]

The resemblance of *Mac Flecknoe* to *Le Lutrin* was superficial, but the phrase 'ridicule . . . in heroics' hardly does justice to Dryden's achievement. *Mac Flecknoe* went further in applying the future remarks of the 'Discourse' than anything suggested by Boileau's theory, or his practice. There is nothing in Boileau like:

> All humane things are subject to decay,
> And, when Fate summons, Monarchs must obey,

an opening couplet of such deceptive weight that the parodic derision could naturally be mistaken for genuine eloquence at first reading.[10] It is, in the first instance, a joke with a straight face. But during the instant that a reader doesn't realize this, it acquires a heroic bravura which shadows forth the aspiration of mock-heroic to transcend its parodic element, and which maintains a lingering quizzical presence throughout the poem.

This is evident in Dryden's parodic use of other English epics, as when Milton's Satan is worked into the portrait of the poem's villain, the poet Thomas Shadwell: 'High on a Throne of his own Labours rear'd' (107), where the Satanic majesty already carries, in its Miltonic original (*PL*, 2.1), a primary weight of negative enormity, later also exploited in Pope's *Dunciad* (2.1). Another extended passage, describing London's Barbican district and its brothels – 'Where their vast Courts the Mother-Strumpets keep' (72) – is drawn from a description of hell in Abraham Cowley's uncompleted epic *Davideis* (1656): 'Where their vast *Court* the *Mother-waters* keep, / And undisturb'd by *Moons* in silence sleep' (1.79–80). Dryden retains much of Cowley's imposing infernal atmospherics, while conferring a jeering magnificence on its low subject, which is in some ways the flipside of Dryden's direct celebrations of monumental London in *Annus Mirabilis* (1667). Another line, 'Amidst this Monument of vanisht minds' (82) is quoted from Sir William Davenant's also uncompleted epic *Gondibert* (1651), where 'vanisht minds' originally referred to deceased writers, not empty heads (II.v.36).

Dryden's parody preserves a species of perverse splendour whether his epic original is programmed for disapproval (Milton and Cowley) or not (Davenant). This effect, only partially exorcised by an ambiguously disapproving adjective or noun, also occurs in the line 'Thoughtless as Monarch Oakes, that shade the plain' (27), where 'thoughtless', applied to an otherwise handsome landscape, is capable of suggesting a serene freedom from thought, not necessarily the satirical connotation of vacuousness. The equivocal elevations of *Mac Flecknoe*, where mocking lines themselves acquire an eloquent beauty, create an elusive effect in which the textbook formula of mock-heroic, of past grandeurs invoked in opposition to a lowered modern reality, is teasingly destabilized. A risk, which is sometimes also a potential richness, exists that the irony, which is an ambivalent instrument for filtering homage, might overspill into loyalist territory. While Dryden, like Pope in the *Dunciad*, is speaking of modern London, the survival of monumental grandeurs in undiminished but polluted form hints at a story different from the textbook version of mock-heroic, which would suggest that there are no grandeurs left in a fallen time, a distinctly recessive intimation in these poets, which was to be powerfully developed in the allusive style of Eliot's *Waste Land*.

Dryden's 'Discourse Concerning Satire' is not confined to mock-heroic in the strict sense. His idea that satire might become a species of heroic poetry in its own right may seem counterintuitive. It runs against the implication that satire, which deals with low and unedifying matter, is antithetical to epic, and also against the tendency of satirists, from Horace to Pope, to pronounce themselves unfitted both for epic and panegyric (a particularly insistent theme in Boileau). In his *Odes*, Horace extended the principle to lyric poetry, proclaiming for example the unfitness of the lyric to sing of wars and victories, though in fact the *Odes* and *Epodes* sometimes contradict this self-denying rule. Juvenal's repeated rants against epic poets similarly convey the idea that the times are not fit for epics, that only bad poets will attempt them, and that satire is the only response to a depraved culture. Juvenal's outbursts against epic poets themselves may imply that it takes very bad poets to write epics in an age that is not fit for them, an anticipation of the English Augustan phenomenon.

But Roman satire has its own built-in relationship to epic, and satirists often adopt postures of heroic militancy. Horace described his satire as a sword (*Satires*, II.i.39–40), a claim repeated by later poets, including Pope and Ezra Pound ('Verse is a sword', cited in chapter 12 of this volume). Of all Roman satirists, it is Juvenal who most indulges in luxuries of majestic denunciation, finding a personal substitute for the epic elevation which he felt his subject matter denied him. For all his jeering at the feeble epic writers of his day, Juvenal uses a good deal of epic allusion, with a heroic image of the satirist himself, epitomized by Lucilius charging on horseback and wielding a sword (*Satires*, 1.19–20, 165–6). Dryden, whose 'Discourse' is prefixed to his translations of Juvenal and Persius, said of both poets, 'Let not them be accounted no Poets, who choose to mount, and shew their Horsemanship' (78). This horsemanship has remained an enduring icon of the poet as hero, which Yeats perhaps saw in his friend Robert Gregory ('Soldier, scholar, horseman, he'). In his sense of a lowered modern time, Yeats spoke of 'that high horse riderless, Though mounted in that saddle Homer rode', which he sought to recover through nostalgia rather than irony.[11] The image is consistent with Dryden's ideas of a potentially re-sublimated mock-heroic.

Dryden's project of mock-heroic aggrandisement rested largely on the use of high language for low subjects, as in Boileau's *Lutrin*, instead of the other way round. The technique had of course existed since antiquity, and is found in the pseudo-Homeric *Battle of the Frogs and Mice*, and the pseudo-Virgilian *Culex* ('gnat'). An even more significant predecessor was Tassoni's *Secchia rapita* (1622), whose subtitle *Poema eroicomico* seems to have been one of the main precursors of the term 'mock-heroic'. The *Secchia rapita*, which tells the story of a battle between two cities caused by the stolen bucket of the title, was acknowledged by both Boileau and Dryden. Pope took from it not only the idea of a 'mighty Contest' arising from the theft or 'rape' of a 'trivial Thing', but also a hint for the title of his *Rape of the Lock*. But the *Secchia rapita* is a curious hybrid, its high style blended with coarse knockabout and demotic rant, and containing a raw element of deadly fighting, almost invariably excluded in Augustan mock-epics. Tassoni's manner is thus very different from the distinctive elevated style, applied to comic unsanguinary subject matter and urbanely tempered by irony, which Boileau developed as the product of a seemingly simple technical decision.

When Boileau seized on his stylistic technicality as a 'new' burlesque, he was helping to introduce a heightened level of poetic ambition into the genre, transcending mere parody or loyal joke, and making of it, for two or three generations, an unprecedentedly cherished mode of expression, to which the finest poets of the age devoted some of their best imaginative efforts.

Boileau never matched Dryden's vigorous style of grandeur or the spirited coarseness with which he could speak of bad poems as 'Martyrs of Pies, and Reliques of the Bum' (101). *Mac Flecknoe* is especially remarkable for the boldness and energy with which Dryden pursued a powerfully high style in the teeth of scatological indecencies and other low matter, some of it evoking farce, which seem almost to have been planted by him to provoke the defiance. In this sense too, Dryden went beyond Boileau, who would have deplored the practice, achieving in his own way a freedom from the constraints of 'correctness' that French writers from Voltaire to Baudelaire and Jarry professed to envy and sometimes despise in the English. His poetic practice, like his theoretical formulations, thus went further than Boileau in directions Boileau may be said to have charted.

Moreover, Boileau cannot compete with Dryden's 'Discourse' in providing the explicit 'theoretical' rationale for his experiment, speaking rather casually of having come up with or thought up the idea of a 'new burlesque' in the French language ('dont je me suis avisé en notre langue'). Boileau was concerned to distinguish his poem from a recently fashionable burlesque, the *Virgile travesti* of Paul Scarron (1648–53), where 'Dido and Aeneas spoke like fishwives and porters', and to promote a new style, in which 'a clockmaker and his wife speak like Dido and Aeneas'.[12] The significance of this seemingly minor technical distinction, which Dryden understood with special clarity, was that it offered a form of parody that did not necessarily damage the dignity of its originals, and to which the term 'mock-heroic' became increasingly attached. The older genre, which showed high persons traduced in low language, went on being referred to as burlesque.

The opposite workings of the two styles may be observed in two parodies, both appropriated from the French, of the famous opening of Virgil's *Aeneid* ('Arma virumque cano'), which Dryden translates as:

> Arms, and the Man I sing, who, forc'd by Fate,
> And haughty *Juno*'s unrelenting Hate,
> Expell'd and exil'd, left the *Trojan* Shoar:
> Long Labours, both by Sea and Land he bore,
> And in the doubtful War, before he won
> The *Latian* Realm, and built the destin'd Town.

In the old burlesque of Scarron, adapted into English by Charles Cotton in 1664, this becomes

> I *Sing the man*, (read it who list,
> A *Trojan*, true, as ever pist)
> Who from *Troy* Town, by wind & weather
> To *Italy*, (and God knows whither)
> Was packt, and wrackt, and lost, and tost,
> And bounc'd from Pillar unto Post.[13]

Cotton's lively and amusing lines closely follow the opening of the *Aeneid* in the style Boileau was rejecting. They deflate rather than emulate the high style of the original, and offer no opportunity for residual majesties to survive. This may be contrasted with Boileau's own opening of *Le Lutrin* ('Je chante les combats'), as translated by John Ozell (1708):

> *Arms* and the *Priest* I sing, whose Martial Soul
> No Toil cou'd terrify, no Fear controul.[14]

This wears its ridicule on its sleeve, but it is tempered (even more strongly in the original than in the translation) by a manifest responsiveness to the grand notes of the Virgilian prototype. One eighteenth-century critic claimed that *Le Lutrin* was more truly epic than *La Henriade*, Voltaire's serious attempt at a national epic.[15]

The early versions of Pope's *Dunciad* (1728, 1729) also imitate Dryden's Virgil:

> Books and the Man I sing, the first who brings
> The Smithfield Muses to the Ear of Kings. (1.1–2)[16]

This is not the *Dunciad* at full maturity, but one would have to have a tin ear to think that its difference from Cotton's *Scarronides* is a mere technicality. Each style has its excellence, and both are ironic rewritings of a heroic original. Pope's raw material is 'low', like Cotton's, matter for the 'Smithfield Muses', but the sweep and elevation of Pope's language and metre, and the wittily ambiguous vibrancies of the Virgilian echo, suggest a perspective far removed from the swarming daily energies of Grub Street, though these are, in their way, given their due in the *Dunciad* too. The idea of 'Smithfield Muses' being brought to 'the Ear of Kings' has an allure of large-scale disturbance of cultural proprieties that is part of the poem's scenario of catastrophic disarray. At the same time, the opening couplet has a relaxed sweep, and a mastery of its material, that suggest confidence in the poetic containment of unruly forces. The potential for bombast in the Virgilian allusion is held in exact check, its grandeurs modulated through an idiom of conversational confidence and urbane triumphalism.

The *Dunciad in Four Books* of 1743 has an even more resonant sense of catastrophe, and a corresponding drop in the feeling of urbane certainty. Its opening lines show significant variations from the earlier version:

The Mighty Mother, and her Son who brings
The Smithfield Muses to the ear of Kings,
I sing. Say you, her instruments the Great!
Call'd to this work by Dulness, Jove, and Fate;
You by whose care, in vain decry'd and curst,
Still Dunce the second reigns like Dunce the first;
Say how the Goddess bade Britannia sleep,
And pour'd her Spirit o'er the land and deep. (*1743*, 1.1–8)

The switch in the first line from the mock-Virgilian flourish of 'Books and the Man I sing' to a menacing 'Mighty Mother' brings a suggestion of archetypal forces, soft and sinister, poised to engulf the nation. The closing couplet (lines 7–8) is not in *1728* or *1729*, and its evocation of terminal torpor marks an extension of Pope's mastery of mock-heroic idiom that reaches far beyond the initial parodic joke. This is most fully realized in the Miltonic orchestration of the *Dunciad*'s finale, where all thought of satiric diminution disappears, and where an enormity of catastrophic decline is commensurate, in an inverted way, with the magnitude of epic counterparts. The full weight of Miltonic resonance is invoked not in order to confer pomp on 'trivial Things', but to express the undiminished enormity of its evil subject. The apocalyptic vision of the culture being smothered under the weight of Universal Dulness speaks of the Creation going into reverse and of a return to primeval Chaos. The *Dunciad*'s London, viewed in this light, is a mundane replica of Milton's Chaos and Hell, in the grotesque and massive amplitude of its degradation.

The *Dunciad* marks a *ne plus ultra* in the conversion of heroic mockery into a negative or inverted sublime. In the progress towards making satire into a species of 'Heroique Poetry it self', there was a further step the *Dunciad* could not take, though it may have pointed the way. The poem's atmosphere of Miltonic disaster reaches beyond the parodic joke which brought it into being, but which Pope had no means of jettisoning, since it remains the precondition for his use of an epic mode, and the carrier of his weighty vision of catastrophe. The achievement of an elevated style in a satire that partly deals with heroic themes, but is neither epic nor ironically dependent on the epic relationship, belongs to Johnson's *Vanity of Human Wishes* (1749). Johnson's poem, an imitation of Juvenal's Tenth Satire, includes reflections on the vanity of war and military success which, for example, superficially resemble a critique of clamorous panegyrics of conquest, of the kind addressed to Louis XIV by Boileau, even in *Le Lutrin*, as well as by those enemies of Boileau whom he mocked for doing the same thing. But Johnson instead presents heroic ambitions and disasters in a style of solemn uncastigating meditation on the failure of human schemes, broadly following the contours of the Juvenalian original, a satire bristling with angry sarcasms, which Johnson invariably converts into ironies of compassionate circumstance rather than guilty behaviour.

The poem's memorable account of Charles XII of Sweden, a much denigrated figure in contemporary satire, often portrayed as a conquering thug, displays a dignified sense of Charles's impressiveness as a steely and tireless conqueror, and, without conferring approval, a subdued sympathy for him in his decline, his 'miseries in distant lands' (line 212), and especially his stark and solitary fall:

> His fall was destin'd to a barren strand,
> A petty fortress, and a dubious hand;
> He left the name, at which the world grew pale,
> To point a moral, or adorn a tale.   (lines 219–22)

In transcending the satirical joke of his vitriolic Latin original, the poem's grave and sombre eloquence achieves what Pope had not been able to do in the *Dunciad*. The demand for an ironic distance from loyal epic imitation created constraints for Pope from which Johnson, recounting heroic events but not formally in dialogue with a heroic genre, was free, as though a high style unencumbered by irony might have been impossible if Johnson's original had been an epic.

An opposite way of portraying Charles XII, accentuating rather than eschewing satirical derision while retaining ancient loyalties in a nuanced way, occurs in Fielding's mock-heroic novel *Jonathan Wild*, published the same year as the final *Dunciad* (1743), in which the king is subjected to considerable opprobrium, and the heroic, instead of providing an elevated antithesis to a lowered modern reality, turns into a tarnished analogue. In this fiction of low life, which equates heroes with gangsters and politicians, high language is harshly accommodated to sleazy realities in a way that is no longer informed by the primary aspirations to eloquence that were protective of ancient grandeurs. The 'heroic' past is partially tarred with modern degradation in a manner which, while retaining close ties with Augustan satire, looks forward to Eliot, Joyce, and Brecht.

The non-derisive mode in which Johnson rewrites Juvenal, while broadly following his original, might be described as a species of un-parodying, an upward reformulation which is an important but little-regarded phenomenon, especially likely to appear in literary environments where parody is a natural feature of primary literary expression. This couplet from the *Dunciad*

> In cold December fragrant chaplets blow,
> And heavy harvests nod beneath the snow,   (1.77–8)

shows a latent re-sublimation of its own mocking mimicry. It derides poets who get their genres and images wrong, but also reaches beyond the mimicry to acquire a surreal lyrical quality of its own. Pope is known to have had a particular fondness, beyond their satiric appeal, for some of his more memorable satirical lines.

Un-parodying has assumed many guises in the general upheaval of literary forms since the late seventeenth century, and plays a particularly striking role among the mutations of mock-heroic, sometimes in the hands of later writers. Thus Dryden's portrait of Zimri in *Absalom and Achitophel* (1681),

> A man so various, that he seem'd to be,
> Not one, but all Mankinds Epitome.   (lines 546–7)

exposes a latter-day degradation of the idea of the Renaissance complete man, which may be said to have been 'unparodied' in Yeats's 'In Memory of Major Robert Gregory'. Yeats praises Gregory as 'Soldier, scholar, horseman, he, / As 'twere all life's epitome', thus reinstating a version of Dryden's fallen ideal, with accretions of fervour, a process whose wit lies in taking out the sting rather than putting it in. This dialogue between present and past, or Yeats and Dryden, resembles Eliot's complex mock-heroic transactions in the *Waste Land*, which look back to Pope's or to Shakespeare's way of looking back to their own precursors. There is a sense in which mock-heroic parody, in its more ambitious forms (*Mac Flecknoe*, the *Dunciad*), is always striving to un-parody itself.

The *Dunciad* did for mock-heroic what *Paradise Lost* did for the epic. It is the masterwork that stopped serious emulation. By 1743, it is arguable that the high estimation of epic, which survived in the culture for several generations after poets stopped writing epic poems, ceased to be a live and vital element. There was bound to come a time when mock-heroic would run out of steam, as conflicted loyalties to epic gradually settled into indifference, and epic could no longer serve as a basis for irony. The animating power which epic could still provide for mock-heroic at the time of the *Dunciad* was giving way to a lowered status, in which non-heroic narratives, especially novels, were challenging the sense of the epic's natural primacy.

If the epic ceases to matter, the ground for serious mock-heroic disappears. In the aftermath of Pope, mock-heroic often becomes a matter of secondary parroting, as the titles, from *The Rape of the Smock* (1717) to *The Lousiad* (1785–95), by Giles Jacob and 'Peter Pindar' respectively, suggest. In *The Kite* (1722), an early political pastiche of the *Rape of the Lock*, the heroine embroiders flowers named after famous military leaders, one of whom is Louis XIV, recently deceased, who is now 'More Powerful on Her Apron, than his Throne'.[17] The location that gallantly outshines regal glory seems a throwback to the cross on Belinda's white breast, which Jews might kiss and infidels adore, an enfeebled garrulous recycling of Pope's sharply focused quip. The recourse to irony – which had once opened up the possibility of a return to heroic accents – becomes dissipated in a coyly smutty jokerie.

The slightness of the *Kite* and the coarse triviality of the *Lousiad* show that irony no longer facilitated the aggrandisement of insignificant things (a clerical squabble, a lock of hair) to a plane of higher concern, but sank to the level of its declared subject (a kite, or royal louse). Another project for keeping the mock-heroic alive was to minimize or remove the irony altogether, on the apparent assumption that a form of primary heroic seriousness could be recaptured simply by jettisoning the filter of derision that had enabled the epic voice to survive in the first place. The two principal carriers of this impulse were the *Scribleriad* (1751), by Richard Owen Cambridge, and the *Triumphs of Temper* (1781), by William Hayley, both of whom thought they had found a method that improved on the example of Pope.

The author of the *Scribleriad* starts from the traditional notion that 'A Mock-Heroic poem should, in as many respects as possible, imitate the True Heroic', interpreting it in the strictly literal sense that 'It should, throughout, be serious, because the originals are serious'. From this perspective, 'the *Lutrin, Dispensary, Rape of the Lock*, and *Dunciad*' do not 'come up to the true idea of a Mock-Heroic poem', because they use heroic imitation as a vehicle for satire, destroying the illusion of a heroic fiction by the intrusions of satirical content which make 'Churchmen, Physicians, Beaus and Belles, or Booksellers . . . talk the language of . . . the Heroes of Antiquity'.[18] Cambridge's ideal is 'that grave irony which *Cervantes* only has inviolably preserv'd', because Don Quixote's extravagant rhetoric is a donnée of the character, formed by his reading of fictions, as that of the *Scribleriad*'s hero is formed by the crazed erudition of the original Martinus Scriblerus. The pull of Richardsonian 'realism' seems evident in the way Cambridge identifies the straight-faced joke with the fictional illusion.

Hayley's *Triumphs of Temper* pays tribute to the *Scribleriad*. Hayley is, however, a particular admirer of the *Rape of the Lock*. He favours Italian models, citing Tassoni in the original, and proposes to unite 'the sportive wildness of Ariosto, and the more serious sublime painting of Dante' (an unusual ambition at this date), with 'the enchanting elegance, the refined imagination, and the moral graces of Pope'. Hayley's main ambition is to render his poem 'more interesting to the heart', a formulation which, like the *Scribleriad*'s, moves towards the Richardsonian novel, but by the route of 'sensibility' rather than of a purified technique, a surprising but symptomatic variation of the *Dunciad*'s striving to move beyond its own satiric joke.[19]

The opening of the poem sets the tone:

> The Mind's soft Guardian, who, tho' yet unsung,
> Inspires with harmony the female tongue,
> And gives, improving every tender grace,
> The smile of angels to a mortal face;
> Her powers I sing; and scenes of mental strife,
> Which form the maiden for th' accomplish'd wife;
> Where the sweet victor sees, with sparkling eyes,
> Love her reward, and Happiness her prize. (1.1–8)

It is possible that Blake remembered the phrase 'mental strife' when he spoke, in the lyric 'Jerusalem', written in the period 1800–4, of never ceasing from 'mental fight'.[20] Hayley was his patron and collaborator (Blake composed six plates for *Triumphs of Temper* in 1803), but Hayley's phrase, which occurs more than once, has no more to do with Blake's embattled spiritual energies than it has with epic battles. In his world of sensibilitous 'fair sexing,' where victors are 'sweet' and victory occurs without battle, 'strife' means 'striving', that is, 'effort' rather than 'conflict', and refers to the moral efforts of the maiden growing up to be 'th' accomplish'd wife'. For a poem whose professed stylistic framework includes Tassoni and Pope, it is remarkably free either of heroic evocations or of mockery. The Drydenian project has taken a form purged of both heroism and satire. The idea that it was possible to re-enter the heroic by the indirect route of irony has been attenuated to a point where the epic presence has become shadowy and without meaning. The *Scribleriad* and Hayley's *Triumphs of Temper*, which attempt mock-heroic with minimal mockery, are a remarkable demonstration of the fact that even in a context of resolute humourlessness, the option of returning to an unmediated form of heroic expression did not appear to suggest itself. The pathway was not a return to epic idiom but an un-parodying of parodies of that idiom. Byron called Hayley's poem 'For ever feeble and for ever tame'.[21]

The two most important poems of the Romantic period that draw on the mock-heroic tradition are Shelley's *Peter Bell the Third* (1819) and Byron's *Don Juan* (1819–24, together with the *Vision of Judgment*, 1822). They do so by deflation, not inflation. Shelley's poem is self-consciously offered as a mini-*Dunciad*, its grandiloquence studiously flattened. The poem is stripped of all Miltonic or Dunciadic aggrandisement, while not at all disguising its witty reminders of Milton or Pope. Its 'Hell is a city much like London – / A populous and a smoky city' (lines 147–8), evoking *Paradise Lost* (9.445–6) in a low key, is the antithesis of the *Dunciad*'s use of Milton.[22] The vast enveloping Dulness of Pope's poem is demoted to vacuous society chatter

('Peter was dull – he was at first / Dull – O, so dull – so very dull!', lines 703–4). Byron's *Don Juan* has a similarly hard-edged casualness. It offers a flip simulacrum of heroic forms ('My poem's epic and is meant to be / Divided in twelve books'), replacing the heroic montage of the *Dunciad* with throwaway pretensions of epic integrity ('So that my name of Epic's no misnomer', 1.200) which no one is expected to take seriously, and which must be balanced by the declaration that *Don Juan* was intended as 'a poetical T Shandy'.[23] There is no temptation in either poet to use mock-heroic in order to retrieve a high style.

Shelley and Byron retained the ease with which the contemporaries of Pope could take the epic for granted. Both had an unforced reverence for Homer, and both were able to be light-heartedly dismissive about heroic inflation or the length of epic poems. In some ways, doubtless personal rather than cultural, their Homeric loyalties were sustained with a naturalness greater even than Pope's. They show none of Pope's flustered embarrassment at Homeric cruelty, his urge to sanitize it in translation or eliminate it in mock-heroic by replacing warfare with unsanguinary capers. They, as well as Pope, would have understood the tenor of Blake's nearly contemporaneous comment in 'On Homer's Poetry' (*c.* 1820) that it was 'the Classics! & not Goths nor Monks, that Desolate Europe with Wars'.[24] But they freely allowed this perspective to figure in their mock-heroic writings, as Pope would not. Homer is freely invoked, for example, in the carnage of *Don Juan*'s war cantos, without any attempt to conceal the essential resemblance between Homeric epic and the realities of war, but also without disowning the *Iliad*:

> Oh, thou eternal Homer! I have now
>   To paint a siege, wherein more men were slain,
> With deadlier engines and a speedier blow,
>   Than in thy Greek gazette of that campaign;
> And yet, like all men else, I must allow,
>   To vie with thee would be about as vain
> As for a brook to cope with Ocean's flood;
> But still we moderns equal you in blood.   (*Don Juan*, 7.80)

Byron is unembarrassed about the stinging moral equivalence, as well as unreserved in his praise. One remarkable feature is that, by comparison with Pope, the two perspectives are united in the same poem. Another is that while the passage recycles the conventional Scriblerian scorn of Grub Street journalists, this takes the form of a good-natured remark about Homer himself, and does not diminish him, even as the *Iliad* is equated with the lists of war dead in an official newspaper. The joke, which assimilates 'eternal Homer' to the journalistic hacks rather than separating him from them in Swift's or Pope's manner, is maintained, not, as in Pope, through a mimicry of high epic style, but in the teeth of a cheeky eschewal of it. The mock-heroic has become unmoored from any heroic elevation, as though claims of heroes to heroic style had themselves become unworthy or not worth making.

Byron and Shelley rejected the epic manner, not because they repudiated elevation but because they looked for it elsewhere. When they do attempt heroic elevation, it is in a voice of defiant rebellion, derived from Milton's Satan, but differing from him in being presented with heroic endorsement, a species of the Romantic sublime not closely resembling classical epic. The satirical mode of *Peter Bell the Third* or *Don Juan* does not spill over into *Prometheus Unbound* or *Lara*, or carry any mock-grandeurs from Shelley's or Byron's 'serious' poems, any more than from the older epics they are in dialogue with. Although these satirical poems look back wittily to Popeian mock-heroic, they have jettisoned Pope's heroic accents much as the *Scribleriad* and the *Triumphs of Temper* had jettisoned mockery. The Augustan practice of holding satire and sublimity in orchestrated coexistence is no longer attempted, and does not fully reappear in a major poem until Eliot's *Waste Land* (and then in a modified form, in which the primary objectives are no longer satiric, and the allusive background more Shakespearean than Homeric or Miltonic).

The epic idiom that conferred weight on a sub-heroic satirical theme had become inadequate to the purpose. It was either misapplied to times incapable of accommodating a language of high mockery, or else rejected as no longer able to provide the requisite weight for such mockery in the first place. The Romantic sublime of rebellious Byronic heroes was too fragile and self-regarding to nourish a high parodic style. If *Don Juan* is not mock-Homeric or mock-Miltonic, like the *Dunciad*, nor is it a mocking inversion of Byron's own high styles, no more a mock-*Corsair*, or even a mock-*Childe Harold*, than a mock-*Iliad*. It is closer to the novelistic mode of ironic self-exploration of *Tristram Shandy*, episodic, fragmented and unfinished, like Pound's *Cantos*. Ezra Pound, who disliked Byron, nevertheless acknowledged *Don Juan* as a model.

Both *Don Juan* and the *Cantos*, like *Tristram Shandy*, belong to a type that Swift satirized as typically modern in *A Tale of a Tub* (1704), in advance of any fully-fledged example. Sterne perceived Swift's work as an advance parody of himself, and proceeded in *Tristram Shandy* (1759–67) to un-parody it, creating in the process a formal prototype of uncompleted self-exploration whose character is continuous and additive, points to no conclusive moment, and in practice is often stopped only by the author's death. There is no question, in such a model, of the traditional great action, only a focus on the narrator's or protagonist's 'life and opinions', a subject which epic protocols discouraged, and whose self-directed ironies would not be naturally suited to a heroic idiom. In this, as in other ways, these works differ from epics like Pope's unfinished or aborted attempts, whose design did not foresee non-completion, though both kinds of incompleteness are reflections, in their way, of a resistance or loss of nerve that has accompanied the epic ambitions of poets since Milton.

Epic aspiration, often in a Miltonic guise, persists in English poetry, even when prevailing conventions, or individual preferences, shrink from grandiloquence, affirm the worth of humble subjects, or prescribe a 'neutral tone'. This is evident in Wordsworth's adoption of an idiom of Miltonizing elevation in a long autobiographical poem. Epic purposes do not include introspective self-exploration by the poet, and the result is a great poem in what is perhaps a new kind. Even so, as we have seen, the *Prelude*, like Pope's planned epics, and also like both versions of Keats's *Hyperion*, was never 'finished', as though the epic impulse continued to lack stamina in whatever form: a phenomenon not unconnected with the use of the fragment as a form of expression in Eliot's *Waste Land*, an accredited heir to the mock-heroic tradition of Pope's *Rape of the Lock* and *Dunciad*.

Matthew Arnold's alternative attempt to revive the classical epic in the middle of the nineteenth century comes over with a nostalgic air of academic reconstruction. Arnold had little feeling for Dryden and Pope, whom he found lacking in high seriousness, and whose natural blending of satire and elevation could not easily be accommodated in his conception of epic dignity. There seem to be no important works in a serious mock-heroic mode, however modified, between Byron and 1922, the year of both *Ulysses* and the *Waste Land*, just as there were no genuinely successful un-mocking epics, except those which, like Wordsworth's *Prelude*, were so different as to be largely outside the scope of this discussion.

By the end of the eighteenth century the idea of the lyric as the standard for great poetry, what Walter Pater called 'the highest and most complete form of poetry', and the idea that the short poem of great intensity constituted a truer poetry than long narrative poems, were becoming established, a supplanting of the epic's status which has, in its way, survived to the present, although poets have continued, in one way or another, to profess epic ambitions.[25] The conviction, entertained by Coleridge and baldly promoted by Poe, that the long poem was 'a flat contradiction in terms', gave the short lyric the enhanced dignity it still enjoys today.[26] The authors of the *Waste Land* and the *Cantos*, the two great modern poems that (however ambivalently) exhibit serious epic ambitions, displayed a continued anxiety over the issue of length (not unlike Poe's feverish arithmetic about the exact number of lines in 'The Raven'), but organized their poems in 'fragments' or short sections, with moments of lyric intensity, the forms most disliked by Arnold. These poems show that lyricism has penetrated the ironic or self-conscious adoption of high styles whose nature partly derives from mock-heroic. It has entered satirical verse in Eliot's 'Preludes' and 'Morning at the Window', and in many poems by W. H. Auden and Louis MacNeice, who adapted short lyric forms to satirical matter, as the disavowal of long poems and of high styles also reduced the scope for traditional satire on the Augustan model.

In the 1930s Yeats thought modern poetry was entering a dry Popeian phase, dislodging the Victorians and 'developing a poetry of statement as against the old metaphor'. He saw T. S. Eliot as the leading figure in the development.[27] Yeats 'loathed' Pope, with whose aspirations for 'the great manner' he nevertheless had much in common.[28] His analysis, and his notorious treatment of Eliot in the *Oxford Book of Modern Verse*, were eccentric, but Eliot's centrality in a tradition that derives from Pope had indeed shaped modern poetry, and has more to do with Yeats's aspiration to restore that 'high horse riderless' than he perceived, because of an ironic distancing Yeats alone, among the great English poets, could not accept.

The *Waste Land* is in any event the heir of the mock-heroic tradition of Dryden and Pope, which Arnold deplored, as he deplored a poetry of lyric intensities and 'fragments'. Eliot was notably responsive to Dryden's rendering of London's polluted grandeurs in *Mac Flecknoe*. While writing the *Waste Land*, Eliot dealt admiringly, in an essay on Dryden, with the Barbican 'Brothel-houses' and 'Mother-Strumpets', as an example of how 'Dryden continually enhances: he makes his object great, in a way contrary to expectation. . .the total effect is due to the transformation of the ridiculous into poetry'.[29] It is what Dryden said, more baldly, of Boileau's *Lutrin*: 'His Subject is Trivial, but his Verse is Noble' ('Discourse', 83). Dryden helped, in such places, to shape a poetry of the city's degradation, with an equivocal elevation which, in some later writers, swerves from satire into a kind of lyricism of grandeur. Behind the urban infernos of the satirists lie the horrific *enchantements* of the 'fourmillante cité, cité pleine de rêves' (Swarming city, city full of dreams) ('Les sept vieillards'), with its prostitutes and beggars, of Baudelaire, whom Eliot quotes in the essay on Dryden as a poet of comparable magnificence, 'who could see profounder possibilities in wit' (p. 314).

Eliot spoke later of Baudelaire's 'use of images of the sordid life of a great metropolis' and his 'elevation of such imagery to the *first intensity* – presenting it as it is, and yet making it represent something much more than itself', an achievement beyond Dryden's reach but for which the urban hell of the satirists prepared the material.[30] The radiant grandeur in downbeat surroundings of Eliot's own Magnus Martyr, with its 'Inexplicable splendour of Ionian white and gold' (265), resembles neither Dryden nor Baudelaire except in developing their apprehension of polluted urban grandeurs. Eliot's majestic evocations of London's neoclassical churches both enhance and deplore their present scabrous settings, and suggest, against notional mock-heroic expectations, that the past is implicated in present degradations. A destabilized sense of the past–present relationship is perhaps not far below the surface of the Augustan masters themselves, in a secondary or recessive way. The extraordinary lyricization that enters the modern treatments is a transcendence of the satirical impulse that implies no diminution of the sense of a lowered present.

The procession of the living dead in 'The Burial of the Dead' may tell us something about Eliot's place in the evolution of mock-heroic.

> Under the brown fog of a winter dawn,
> A crowd flowed over London Bridge, so many,
> I had not thought death had undone so many. . . .
> Flowed up the hill and down King William Street,
> To where Saint Mary Woolnoth kept the hours
> With a dead sound on the final stroke of nine.[31]

Saint Mary Woolnoth is one of London's Augustan churches, like St Magnus Martyr, though without the latter's explosive lyric radiance, and casts a melancholy stateliness over the slow processional trudge of the silent rush hour crowd. Its ironic register is different from those of either Pope or Johnson. It has none of Pope's sting and something of Johnson's gravitas. A comparison of processional passages by all three poets is instructive. If we set the majestic idiocy of the *Dunciad*'s aldermanic processions beside the pageantry of Charles XII's one-time ascendancy, 'The festal blazes, the triumphal show, / The ravish'd standard, and the captive foe' (lines 175–6) in the *Vanity of Human Wishes* (also greatly admired by Eliot as 'quite perfect in form . . . Great poetry') we see how far both Johnson and Eliot are from Pope's jeering at the trappings of heroic pomp and processional majesty.[32] But while Johnson's lines are designed to 'point a moral', Eliot's main effect is to evoke an atmosphere, and to that extent, as well as in its personal note of painfulness, it, too, verges on the lyric.

Eliot's London crowd is a secular version of Dante's Inferno (III.55–7), as Pope's London is of Milton's Hell. The style of allusion has much in common, in a technical sense, with the dialogue of past and present, and the confrontations of high and low, which Pope's mock-heroic poems exploited with great virtuosity. Dante is often for Eliot the focus of an allusiveness for which mock-heroic is a classic model. But the extensive range of authors in the *Waste Land* differs from that of Pope's allusions, which are predominantly anchored in the unitary epic triad of Homer, Virgil, and Milton. The fact is not unconnected with the fragmented character of Eliot's poem, reflecting a world whose markers of stability are scattered and dispersed.

Pope's mock-heroic was one of the major inspirations of the *Waste Land*, and it is possible to see Eliot's poem as yet another extension of the mock-heroic perspective, stripped of satire. That important satirical impulses may be (and indeed were) perceived in Eliot's poem, without finally emerging as satire, reinforces rather than attenuates the sense of Eliot's place in the evolution of mock-heroic into a mode of poetic expression that is separated from, and transcends, the satirical element that brought it into being.

Eliot's poem grew partly out of a discarded pastiche of the *Rape of the Lock*, with which the *Waste Land* shares its theme of sexuality as a source of social disarray. Ezra Pound told Eliot to remove the passage, because he couldn't parody Pope if he couldn't write better verse than Pope.[33] The couplets were to have opened 'The Fire Sermon'. Their atmosphere of sexual seediness is more reminiscent of Swift than of Pope, though it is Pope's metre that Eliot is intermittently mimicking. Like the *Rape of the Lock*, the *Waste Land* is a poem about a fallen present, though it also looks back to a past whose poetic grandeurs are themselves polluted. Its allusive traffic between past and present is one which Pope perfected, though it has emancipated itself from the sarcastic sting of a parodic joke. Eliot's poem also shares the *Dunciad*'s theme of cultural catastrophe, and the *Dunciad* may be seen as, in some important ways, Pope's own *Waste Land*.[34]

The famous opening of 'A Game of Chess', beginning 'The Chair she sat in, like a burnished throne', recalls, among a characteristic multiplicity of other evocations, Belinda's toilette from the *Rape of the Lock*, but the principal focus of its allusion is of course Shakespeare's description of Cleopatra in her barge ('The barge she sat in, like a burnish'd throne', *Antony and Cleopatra*, II.ii.191).[35] The contrast between Eliot's devitalized and neurotic lady and the passionate sensuous magnificence of Cleopatra and her entourage goes beyond the classic confrontation of low present and high past. It is coloured in Shakespeare himself by Cleopatra's tarnished reputation. Shakespeare's play had a large presence in Eliot's imagination, and he was in particular a lifelong admirer of the lines from the Cydnus description, which he clearly viewed as possessing a primary as well as an adulterated grandeur, suggesting here and elsewhere that the seediness it is being compared with is not only the antithesis of the Shakespearean original but also inherent in it. There are many indications in Eliot (for example, in the allusion to Ovid's story of the rape of Philomel, which figures on the modern lady's mantle-piece) that the past was hardly an example of sexual wholesomeness, and Eliot himself is no celebrant of unbridled sexual prowess. The irony which is used in mock-heroic to expose a lowered present against a higher model, and was at least potentially capable of undermining the higher model itself, has a modified presence in Eliot, whose sceptical reservations about past and present are conveyed not through verbal irony or satirical thrusts, but through a downbeat atmosphere, the evocation of conflicting examples, and a note of lyricized distress.

Shakespeare's special place in the poem (as in Joyce's *Ulysses*, whose formal model is the *Odyssey*) is the mark of a major change in the status of both epic and mock-heroic. By the end of the nineteenth century it is Shakespeare, rather than the authors of Graeco-Roman antiquity, who provides the 'high' norm for nuanced mock-heroic comparisons of high and low, or past and present, replacing the epic triad that had served English poets of the time of Dryden and Pope. He seems in modern times, in Jarry, or Brecht, or Ionesco, to have become the common source for allusive evocations of 'heroic' styles and behaviour, replacing the classical epics without invariably sharing their endorsement of the heroic ethos. This evolution is due partly to Shakespeare's wider currency in cultures no longer steeped in the classical poets, and partly to the fact that his own work already embodies, in itself, an un-illusioned critique of the heroic which is less easily discernible in Homer or Virgil. But it was perhaps not until the *Waste Land* that serious Shakespearean allusion became naturalized as a high poetic form, comparable to Pope's use of the classical masters.

The decline of the military epic and the style that goes with it blocked a path to elevated style that poets have been trying to reopen ever since. A great deal of English poetry is characterized by the search for an alternative 'answerable style', which matches the old heroic while conceding its unsustainability. Irony became the enabling factor in the formal mock-heroics of the age of Dryden and Pope, and their intimate engagement with the epic provided a starting point for many later writers, from Shelley and Byron to T. S. Eliot. The interposition of irony has even penetrated some of the higher forms of lyricism. But if much of English poetry, from Dryden to Eliot, has been characterized by a need to secure the protection of irony, it has also shown a corresponding impulse to remove the guard. The *Dunciad*'s implicit striving to transcend or jettison the parodic joke was only the beginning of a long dialogue with the epic and the impossibility of writing it.

NOTES

1 T. S. Eliot, 'What is a Classic?' (1944), in *On Poetry and Poets* (London: Faber, 1957), 64.

2 Dryden, 'Discourse concerning Satire' (1693), in *Works of John Dryden. Volume IV: Poems 1693–1696*, ed. A. B. Chambers and William Frost (Berkeley: University of California Press, 1974), 83–4; subsequent references are to this edition.

3 John Milton, *Paradise Lost* (1667–74), in *The Riverside Milton*, ed. Roy Flannagan (Boston: Houghton Mifflin, 1998); subsequent references, abbreviated to *PL*, are to this edition.

4 Translated by Samuel Cobb, 1712, in *Works of Monsieur Boileau*, 2 vols., (1711–12), vol. II.

5 Sir Samuel Garth, *The Dispensary* (1699), in *Poems on Affairs of State: Augustan Satirical Verse, 1660–1704*, vol. VI, ed. Frank H. Ellis (New Haven: Yale University Press, 1970).

6 Swift, *A Tale of a Tub* (1704), ed. Marcus Walsh (Cambridge: Cambridge University Press, 2010), p. 141.

7 Alexander Pope, *The Rape of the Lock* (1714), ed. Geoffrey Tillotson, 3rd edn (London: Methuen, 1962).

8 Unless otherwise indicated, references are to the final four-book version of the *Dunciad* (1743), ed. Valerie Rumbold (London: Longman, 1999).

9 Joseph Spence, *Observations, Anecdotes, and Characters of Books and Men*, ed. James M. Osborn, 2 vols. (Oxford: Clarendon Press, 1966), vol. I, 274–5 (no. 664).

10 John Dryden, *Mac Flecknoe* (1682), lines 1–2, from the California Edition of the *Works of John Dryden*, vol. II, ed. H. T. Swedenberg, Jr. and Vinton A. Dearing (Berkeley: University of California Press, 1972).

11 Yeats, 'In Memory of Major Robert Gregory' (1918), 'Coole and Ballylee, 1931'.

12 Nicolas Boileau-Despreaux, *Le Lutrin* (1674–83), 'Au Lecteur', prefixed to the first edition of 1674.

13 Charles Cotton, *Scarronides, I: Le Virgile Travesty*, 1.1.1–6, in *Charles Cotton's Works 1663–1665*, ed. A. I. Dust (New York: Garland, 1992), 121.

14 John Ozell, *The Lutrin . . . Render'd into English Verse* (2nd edn, 1711), in *Works of Monsieur Boileau*, 1712, vol. I.

15 Charles Batteux, *Parallèle de la Henriade et du Lutrin* (Paris, 1746).

16 *The Dunciad (1728) & The Dunciad Variorum (1729)*, ed. Valerie Rumbold (London: Longman, 2007).

17 Phanuel Bacon, *The Kite* (Oxford, 1722), 2.

18 Richard Owen Cambridge, *The Scribleriad: An Heroic Poem* (1751), Preface, v–vi.

19 William Hayley, *The Triumphs of Temper* (1781), Preface, x, ix.

20 Blake, *Milton*, Pl. 1, line 33.

21 *English Bards and Scotch Reviewers* (1809), line 314, in George Gordon, Lord Byron, *Complete Poetical Works*, ed. Jerome J. McGann, 7 vols. (Oxford: Clarendon Press, 1980–93), vol. I, 238.

22 *Peter Bell the Third*, lines 147–8, in *Shelley's Poetry and Prose*, ed. Donald H. Reiman and Sharon B. Powers (New York: Norton, 1977).

23 Byron, *Don Juan* (1819–24), 1.200, in *Complete Poetical Works*, ed. McGann; final quotation from Byron to Douglas Kinnaird, 14 April 1823.

24 William Blake, 'On Homer's Poetry' (c. 1820), in *The Poetry and Prose of William Blake*, ed. D. V. Erdman and Harold Bloom (New York: Doubleday, 1970), 267.

25 Walter Pater, *Studies in the History of the Renaissance* (London, 1910), 137.

26 Edgar Allan Poe, 'The Poetic Principle' (1850), in *Essays and Reviews*, ed. G. R. Thomson (Cambridge: Cambridge University Press, 1984), 71.

27 Louise Morgan, Interview with W. B. Yeats, *Writers at Work*, 1931, *W. B. Yeats: Interviews and Recollections*, ed. E. H. Mikhail, 2 vols. (London: Macmillan, 1977), vol. II, 200.

28 R. F. Foster, *W. B. Yeats: A Life. II: The Arch-Poet 1915–1939* (Oxford: Clarendon Press, 2003), 419, 736 n. 83; *Oxford Book of Modern Verse 1892–1935*, ed. W. B. Yeats (Oxford: Oxford University Press, 1936), xxi–xxii.

29 T. S. Eliot, 'John Dryden' (1921), in *Selected Essays*, 3rd edn (London: Faber, 1952), 308.

30 T. S. Eliot, 'Baudelaire' (1930) in *Selected Essays*, 426.

31 T. S. Eliot, *The Waste Land* (1922), lines 61–8, in *Complete Poems and Plays* (London: Faber, 1969).

32 T. S. Eliot, 'Johnson as Critic and Poet' (1944), in *On Poetry and Poets*, 180.

33 T. S. Eliot, Introduction to *Ezra Pound, Selected Poems* (1928) (London: Faber, 1948), 18; *The Waste Land: A Facsimile and Transcript of the Original Drafts* (London: Faber, 1971), 22–3, 38–41, 127n.

34 See Claude Rawson, *Order from Confusion Sprung: Studies in Eighteenth-Century Literature from Swift to Cowper* (London: George Allen and Unwin, 1985), 201–21.

35 *The Riverside Shakespeare*, ed. G. Blakemore Evans et al. 2nd edn (Boston: Houghton Mifflin, 1997).

II

MICHAEL O'NEILL

Romantic re-appropriations of the epic

Epic and generic hybridity

Epic serves as a bright star towards whose seemingly steadfast light many Romantic poets aspire. And yet Romantic poetry thrives on transformations of genre, on a remodelling of past works in the interests of new, often hybridized forms, resulting in what, borrowing a phrase from Wordsworth's Preface to his poems of 1815, Stuart Curran refers to as the 'composite orders' favoured by Romantic poets.[1] A major ingredient in the new generic recipes produced by Romantic poets, epic is understood by Romantic practitioners and theorists to be a genre marked by its width, inclusiveness, openness – and also by its virtual unattainability in its purest form. In *A Defence of Poetry*, Shelley defines the epic poet as a poet 'the series of whose creations bore a defined and intelligible relation to the knowledge, and sentiment, and religion, and political condition of the age in which he lived, and of the ages which followed it: developing itself in correspondence with their development'.[2] If this complex formulation allows for epic to be regarded as a form that evolves historically, it also serves as an evaluative way of putting the case. To deserve the 'title of epic in its highest sense' (p. 692), Shelley, in effect, asserts, a poem must display an original, renewing creativity which, at this point at least, he ascribes to Homer and Dante, but finds wanting in – among other famous examples of epic – the *Aeneid* and *The Faerie Queene*.

Epic, then, is a genre that, on the one hand, is fluid and used with great practical resourcefulness by Romantic poets, and yet, on the other hand, is accorded an apartness, a special place by them. After mildly deploring the absence of '*lofty imaginings*' in Southey and his favouring of '*story & event*', and commenting that 'The *story* of Milton might be told in *two pages*', Coleridge speaks with amusing eloquence in April 1797 of the time required to write an epic, suggesting as he does so that the task was, for him, well-nigh impossible:

I should not think of devoting less than 20 years to an Epic Poem, Ten to collect materials and warm my mind with universal science. I would be a tolerable mathematician. I would thoroughly know Mechanics, Hydrostatics, Optics, and Astronomy, Botany, Metallurgy, Fossilism, Chemistry, Geology, Anatomy, Medicine – then the *mind of man* – then the *minds of men* – in all Travels, Voyages and Histories. So I would spend ten years – the next five to the composition of the poem – and the five last to the correction of it. So I would write haply not unhearing of that divine and rightly-whispering Voice, which speaks to mighty minds of predestinated Garlands, starry and unwithering.[3]

The letter, half-intentionally, sends up the very dedication it describes. But it establishes Coleridge's theoretical commitment to an Enlightenment belief in 'universal science' and a quasi-Miltonic trust in the inspiration of a 'Voice' kin to that of Urania's in *Paradise Lost*: 'thou / Visit'st my slumbers nightly' (7.28–9), writes Milton of his Muse as he pleads with her, 'still govern thou my song' (7.30).[4] The letter reveals the synthesis of ideals associated with epic in the mind of a gifted young poet in the 1790s, a poet who would go one better than Milton by turning Urania's 'nightly' visits into a 'rightly-whispering Voice': 'rightly-whispering' cheats the ear that expects 'nightly' and suggests a 'Voice' speaking in the accents of that 'benevolent determinism', in Seamus Perry's phrase, by which Coleridge was attracted during this period.[5] In the context of a poetic career whose 'Garlands' seemed to their owner to 'wither', the letter strikes a proleptically tragic note. 'To William Wordsworth', Coleridge's great but self-mutilating poem of admiration for Wordsworth's *The Prelude*, sees epic promise fulfilled in his friend's 'orphic song' (45) and, indeed, confirms a view of epic as an exclusive tradition: Wordsworth's poem enrols its author 'in the choir / Of ever-enduring men' (49–50), where 'enduring' suggests that such writers have successfully 'endured' what they imagine and that they will 'endure', last. By contrast, Coleridge deploys the Miltonic mode in a spirit of self-abnegation as he imagines 'triumphal wreathes / Strewed before' Wordsworth's 'advancing' (81–2).[6]

To note how Coleridge pursues (however indirectly) his epic ambitions sheds light on the pervasive way in which the impulse to re-appropriate epic shapes Romantic poetry. An attempt is launched in *The Destiny of Nations*, a poem begun in the middle of the 1790s as part of Coleridge's contribution to revising Southey's epic *Joan of Arc*, then reworked in 1815. In this mini-epic-cum-philosophical poem, an over-heated but daring product of the millennial 1790s, Coleridge invokes 'AUSPICIOUS REVERENCE' (1), offers his lines as themselves embodying that 'Freedom' he defines as 'the unfetter'd use / Of all the powers which God for use had given' (13–14), speculates boldly on the nature of Godhead as he rebukes materialist thinking that would untenant 'creation of its God' (35), and defends 'Wild phantasies' (115) as appropriate to 'Epic Song' (127) since they bear witness to a 'Power / That first unsensualizes the dark mind' (80–1). The verb 'unsensualizes' captures a process by which the mind learns to imagine before progressing to a more enlightened stage. It reminds us that the poem assumes a form typical of poems of the period, one in which, inspired by the French Revolution, the poet envisions, in M. H. Abrams's words, 'a dark past, a violent present, and an immediately impending future which will justify the history of suffering man by its culmination in an absolute good'.[7]

True to Romanticism's wilful, unexpected ways with genre, however, Coleridge comes closest to epic in his *The Rime of the Ancient Mariner*, a poem the story of which might be told in less than two pages and which, if one allows for the process of revision that resulted in the 1817 version, the first time the poem was published under Coleridge's name, took the best part of two decades to crystallize in final form. Its imagery ranges widely, drawing on the marine chemistry of phosphorescence, on hydrostatics ironically reconceived as fluid at rest when the mariner's ship is becalmed, on astronomy (the moon and the stars), and not least on 'the *mind of man*'. Coleridge's balladic masterpiece has lyric depths, as does *Paradise Lost*. An example in the later poem is the cry of loneliness wrung from the seemingly deserted mariner terrified at being an outcast in what Friedrich Schiller speaks of as an 'entgötterte Natur' (a godless or undeified Nature).[8] But as that parallel with Schiller suggests, the poem's experience takes on larger cultural significance. In its reprise of the voyage as an archetypal, existentialist journey of discovery, and in its descent into something close to hell and its intermittent glimpses of something not far off an earthly (or oceanic) paradise, *The Ancient Mariner* has living commerce with Homeric, Virgilian, and Dantean epic, in however estranged and elusive a form. Above all, it sets itself to address a major moral conundrum, the nature of evil and suffering. Milton sought to 'justify the ways of God to men' (*Paradise Lost*, 1.26); Coleridge, building on a project sketched in a notebook entry of 1796, 'The Origin of Evil, an Epic Poem', also seeks a justification of God's ways, concluding with a moral that reassures us that 'the dear God who loveth us, / He made and loveth all' (616–17; 1834 text).[9] We live, that is, in a potentially good and holy universe, and yet something goes mysteriously awry. If epic encapsulates a culture's deepest sense of its relations to past, present, and future, *The Ancient Mariner*, enacting fears and imaginings at the heart of the Romantic period, shows the epic form at work and being reworked.[10]

Epic, romance, and lyrical dream: Hayley, Shelley, and Southey

Any account of Romantic epic is bound to over-simplify, to ignore what now seem mere curios, the now forgotten and copious endeavours of the period (by women as well as by men), to operate with very different frames of awareness from those in place at the time, as is suggested by the fact that some of the major appropriations of epic (*The Prelude, The Fall of Hyperion*) were not published in their authors' lifetimes.[11] But the Romantic epic story begins with, or was at least given a kick-start by, William Hayley's *Essay on Epic Poetry* (1782). This work, written in emphatic, upbeat, exhortatory couplets, urged poets to be fired with ambition and write an epic poetry that extolled 'Freedom'. Such freedom, opposed to slavish adherence to generic laws, would repeat in artistic terms the spirit of liberty supposedly triumphant in the Glorious Revolution. Moreover, to quote Southey's anti-epic, derisive take on the matter, it supports the view (queryingly ascribed by Southey to Addison) that 'an Epic poem ought to be national'.[12] Hayley hoped that

> Our verse may prove this animating truth,
> That Poesy's sublime, neglected field
> May still new laurels to Ambition yield;
> Her Epic trumpet, in a modern hand,
> Still make the spirit glow, the heart expand.
> Be such our doctrine! our enlivening aim
> The Muse's honour, and our Country's fame![13]

Hayley's couplets may seem tepid today, but they inspired a generation of poets to seek 'new laurels' through epic 'Ambition'. At the same time, 'enlivening aim' suggests the drive to reanimate, breathe new life into, the ancient form of epic, and presages the reclamation and reworking of Miltonic epic, in particular, in the Romantic period. And although Southey may have mocked the notion that 'an Epic poem ought to be national', the notion still possessed, as we shall see, a potent hold over the imaginations of writers of epic in the period. Hayley's dislike of French neoclassical rules is also influential, and, indeed, Romantic poetry shows, in its approach to the epic, a readiness to take issue with any 'decisive laws'.

Essay on Epic Poetry reminds poets that 'Eastern riches are unrifled still' (5.274), a reminder that bears fruit in the work of Southey. Coleridge, his collaborator in poetry and marriage, commented on the times as 'a happy age ... for tossing off an *Epic* or two', and Southey himself spoke of the age as marked by 'epomania', a phenomenon he ascribed with some justification to the success of his *Joan of Arc*.[14] Southey added with comic immodesty that 'it is not every one who can shoot with the bow of Ulysses', and the whirligig of literary fortunes has ensured that he is among the principal targets for critical assaults on questions of epic merit and identity.[15] Many commentators subscribe to a distinction between Southey's genuine epics, *Joan of Arc* (1796) and *Madoc* (1805), themselves marked by their disdain for certain epical characteristics (the Preface to *Madoc* speaks of 'the degraded title of Epic'), and his romances, poems such as *Thalaba the Destroyer* (1801) and *The Curse of Kehama* (1810).[16] But Shelley's *Laon and Cythna* (1817), itself hard to categorize (its genre is glossed as that of 'a symbolic romance-epic'), is as indebted to the latter kind of Southeyan precursor text as the former.[17] Indeed, discussion of Shelley's Spenserian epic helps to clarify the nature of Southey's generic bequests to later Romantic poets.

Shelley's epic ambitions in the poem are unmistakable, even if, influenced by Southey as well as by Spenser, romantic narrative serves as their vehicle. The action in *Laon and Cythna* is resolutely human-centred, marking something of a departure from Southey's concern with fate and destiny, and has at its heart the banishment of 'God', a human-created obstacle to freedom and liberty, according to Cythna in her major speech in canto VIII (especially stanzas 5–9). Brian Wilkie has noted that, true to his assertion that the poem 'is narrative, not didactic' (Preface, p. 131), Shelley employs the epic convention of 'flash-back narrative' in and after canto I, and here renews our consciousness that we are hearing '*argument*, intellectual persuasion'.[18] It is not merely a question, on Shelley's part, of wishing to avoid the 'didactic', even when Cythna voices his own most cherished Godwinian views. Shelley addresses the question of the betterment of the human lot through the inspiring deeds and, especially, words of his two revolutionaries, bound by an incestuous love that unloosens the fetters of convention. Sexual freedom mirrors poetic daring, a daring at the heart of the poem's re-appropriation of epic. The poem locates heroism in the act of poetry, in the attempt, as Shelley puts it in his Dedication, to 'charm the minds of men to Truth's own sway' (10.87). So Laon asserts that his 'song / Peopled with thoughts the boundless universe' (11.30.928–9) and that Cythna 'felt the sway / Of my conceptions, gathering like a cloud / The very wind on which it rolls away' (11.31.937–9). The wording and rhythmic movement exemplify ways in which *Laon and Cythna* re-conceives of epic as a vehicle for the sharing of 'conceptions': in his Preface, Shelley sets himself the task of 'kindling within the bosoms of my readers a virtuous enthusiasm for ... doctrines of liberty and justice ... faith and hope in something good' (p. 130). His poem enacts the process of that 'kindling'. So, Cythna 'felt the sway' of Laon's 'conceptions', a responsiveness that is embodied in a figure of speech whose syntax is reluctant to distinguish between agent and acted-upon: since the cloud can be construed as 'gathering' 'The very wind on which it rolls away', Cythna gives shape and purpose to Laon even as he activates her feelings.

At the same time, the cloud imagery implies something potentially evanescent about the process, a darker intimation borne out by the tragic undercurrent of the poem. If it paints a '*beau ideal ... of the French Revolution*', much of its power derives from the fact that its idealizing acknowledges that it is unlikely to be realized.[19] The universe turns out to be 'boundless' in that it is both an arena permitting sublime 'conceptions' and a place resisting Laon's 'sway'. Only in the post-mortal 'Temple of the Spirit' (XI.41.4815), first mentioned in canto I as the place from where Laon's narrative is told and reached, as part of that narrative, in canto XII, is there a sense of human achievement, and its distance from the arena of political and historical struggle is eloquent; human potential can realize itself only, in this darkly Utopian epic, as a transcendent fiction. Shelley mingles epic not only with romance but with a characteristic note of tragic quest in some of the poem's finest passages, as in Cythna's speech towards the end of canto IX. Autumnal imagery later to be used in 'Ode to the West Wind' may recall Milton's comparison between the fallen angels and the leaves at Vallombrosa (*Paradise Lost*, 1.302–3) or Dante's lost souls in the *Inferno*, canto III.112–14, but it serves as an earnest of hope: if 'The blasts of autumn drive the wingèd seeds / Over the earth' (IX.21.3649–50), it serves to herald not only 'dreary winter' (IX.21.3651) but also 'Spring' (IX.21.3653), which sheds 'love on all that lives, and calm on lifeless things' (IX.21.3657), much as the epic poet seeks to do. At the same time, although 'Spring comes', 'we must pass, who made / The promise of its birth' (IX.25.3688–9), a passing which shares in a determined process not easily aligned with hope: 'All that we are or know', Cythna continues, 'is darkly driven / Towards one gulf' (IX.35.3779–80). Indeed, it is the very awareness of how 'darkly driven' we are that lends tension and a sombre colouring to Shelley's epic dream.

The poem uses epic with remarkable self-reflexiveness, a self-reflexiveness enhanced by its ability to play variations on Southey's themes and modes. Southey's relation with the epic tradition was distinctly and productively ambiguous. His finest long poems, *Thalaba* and *The Curse of Kehama*, mingle romance with epic in ways that bear out a readiness to experiment with generic mixing. In this respect, Southey is an exemplary Romantic poet. In arguing correctly for a connection between Spenser and Southey, Brian Wilkie wants to distinguish epic from Spenserian romance, but Spenser offers an approach to epic that mixes the didactic, the allegorical and the imagined. An example of how this approach influences Southey occurs in Book VI, in what Wilkie calls 'an episode describing the destruction of a bower of bliss'.[20] Here, after not much dallying on the hero's part (and only slightly more on the narrator's), the 'voluptuous vale' (VI.283) self-destructs when confronted by the hero's and heroine's unalterable will: 'Earth shook, Heaven thunder'd, and amid the yells / Of evil Spirits perished / The Paradise of Sin' (VII.262–4). The abruptness takes us close to the centre of the quasi-epic vision of *Thalaba*, one in which the hero occupies a virtual, fictive space and embodies the will to overcome all adversaries and obstacles, and, in doing so, performs the will of a higher power. Thalaba is both agent and instrument, and he exists in a poem that shows with the clarity of an X-ray how the Romantic period renews an interest in epic as the vessel of heroic endeavour. In Southey, as in other poets, this heroic endeavour often takes the form of wishing to rid the world of evil and is fundamentally Utopian.

Dreams of a renovated political or imaginative universe run like a crimson thread through the tapestry woven by Romantic dealings with epic. It is associated in Southey with one of his most influential generic modifications of epic, the intermittent lyricization of the form. There are moments of this kind in *Paradise Lost*, in a passage such as the address by Eve to Adam at 4.639 ('With thee conversing I forget all time'). Indeed, Keats sees such lyrical moments in Milton as, in effect, portending the struggle in his own work between high seriousness and 'poetical Luxury', writing that Milton 'devoted himself rather to the Ardours than the pleasures of Song, solacing himself at intervals with cups of old wine'.[21] But such lyrical 'pleasures' subsume themselves within 'Ardours', even as they play against them, in Romantic as in Milton's epic. Even if he does not vary his metrical scheme, Milton allows us to 'forget all time', as his figures perform their rhetorical dance to establish Eve's sense of complete 'converse' (meaning 'communion', *OED* 4) with Adam. The passage represents a still point in a turning and turbulent epic, the high point of an Edenic happiness about to be destroyed.

In *The Curse of Kehama*, the famous curse (II.143–69) irradiates its terrifying, Medusa-like power throughout the poem. A curse arrests time, enchants it, bends it to its directive will; a form that is picked up by Byron in *Manfred* (1816–17) and Shelley in *Prometheus Unbound* (1820), it serves as a compacted version of the central agon of the entire poem. Lyrics inserted in larger Romantic epic or quasi-epic forms serve less as escapist solace than as thematic guide and distillation: in *Prometheus Unbound*, for example – subtitled a 'lyrical drama', but manifestly intent on rivalling and outpacing Aeschylean drama and Miltonic and Dantean epic – lyric frequently takes the reader to new depths or heights of apprehension. 'Life of Life'

(II.v.48–71) crystallizes the work's intuition of transformation, suspending narrative description in favour of a privileged access to a visionary encounter. The lyric involves a dazzling series of redefinitions that induce a sense of joyously dizzy near-vertigo. A lilting metre and a nimble-footed syntax marry in an evocation of a presence that resists visualization, 'And all feel, yet see thee never, / As I feel now, lost forever!' (64–5). The poem's epic labour of conveying 'beautiful idealisms of moral excellence' (Preface, p. 232) into the reader's mind, heart, and imagination celebrates itself exultantly. The city that it founds is a community made up of 'the souls of whom thou lovest' (68), that is to say, all those who are inspired by the poem.

Indeed, the poem's reworking of Miltonic epic, apparent in the flurry of echoes from *Paradise Lost* with which it opens, participates in a 'composite order' that subsumes epic within itself. Generally, although with some misgivings, such echoes reclaim as admirable Satanic traits of pride and unalterable will that in *Paradise Lost* are critiqued: *Prometheus Unbound* internalizes Miltonic struggle. Whereas Satan fights an unwinnable battle against God, Prometheus wars with himself; there is a strong suggestion that the Furies, 'Crawling like agony' (1.491) within Prometheus, represent his own doubts and inward temptation to despair. But epic agon, however reshaped, passes into a Shelleyan poetry to which it is impossible to assign a clear generic identity, even as it bears out, in its own heterodox fashion, Wordsworth's 'opinion in respect to epic poetry' as relayed to Southey in 1815:

> Epic poetry, of the highest class, requires in the first place an action eminently influential, an action with a grand or sublime train of consequences; it next requires the intervention and guidance of beings superior to man, what the critics, I believe, call machinery; and lastly, I think with Dennis that no subject but a religious one can answer the demand of the soul in the highest class of this species of poetry.[22]

The main 'action' of *Prometheus Unbound* – the hero's expression of pity for his cruel, tormenting alter ego, Jupiter, and revocation of his former curse – occurs towards the end of the work's initial speech. This is the moment when in traditional epic the poet offers his poem's *initium*, setting out the poem's first action, and wonders about near-tragic trains of causality, as when Milton bids his Muse, 'say first what cause / Moved our grand parents in that happy state, / Favoured of heaven so highly, to fall off / From their creator, and transgress his will' (1.28–31). Shelley adapts the formula to a poem that is rewriting the epic rule-book: Prometheus (with Asia's help) will undertake an enquiry into causes, but only so as to release himself (and humankind) from one inexorable chain of events into an attempt to instigate another, one in which potential for good and the spread of happiness is fulfilled. As for 'machinery', the poem bears out Shelley's claim that it contains 'characters & mechanism of a kind yet unattempted', where, in the very act of claiming absolute newness, he alludes (the paradox is central to epic's fascination with originality as derivable only from tradition) to Milton's boast that his 'adventurous song' (1.13) 'pursues / Things unattempted yet in prose or rhyme' (1.15–16) (the latter, in turn, being a quotation from Ariosto).²³ The 'characters' include mythological figures given new, updated roles (Mercury is recast as the tyrant's sorrowful hench-man, Prometheus himself as the modern intellectual suffering agonies at the fate of institutional Christianity and political impasse after the seeming failure of the French Revolution). And a thronging choir of spirit voices, lyricizing desires and ideals, compose a 'mechanism' that tilts the poem in the direction of generic innovation.

Moreover, the poem's subject is 'religious' in that it addresses the relations between human beings and godship: both the false gods that belonged to the superseded 'dark and mighty faith' whose ruined memorials the Spirit of the Hour describes in the long speech that concludes Act III, and the new 'divinity in man', as Shelley will call it in *A Defence of Poetry*, that is celebrated in Act IV. That act's delight in the changed physical universe corresponds to jubilation that it can now define the human and the divine in terms of one another, as when the Earth evokes 'Man, one harmonious soul of many a soul, / Whose nature is its own divine control' (IV.400–1): there, the rhyme shows how the collective 'soul' of human kind bears witness to the 'divine' potential of the human by obeying its own self-sustaining, self-monitoring 'control'.

In Act IV, the lyrical drama evokes 'language' as 'a perpetual Orphic song, / Which rules with daedal harmony a throng / Of thoughts and forms, which else senseless and shapeless were' (IV.415–17), lines that capture the nature of Shelley's dealings not only with language but also with genre. Here, the lyrical drama may seem to have left behind Miltonic epic. Yet Shelley never completely ascends into an artistic heaven where genres (such as epic) and their histories are near-forgotten specks. When, at the work's close, Demogorgon addresses the dramatis personae, he offers 'spells' (IV.568) that will permit the re-conquest of tyranny, should it return; in so doing, he reminds the reader that the triumph enacted in the play is a virtual poetic one, that the rapturously inspired cosmic choruses of Act IV may be silenced, giving way to the inflections of epic struggle with which the play began. Georg Lukács argues that 'Any attempt at a properly utopian epic must fail because it is bound, subjectively or objectively, to transcend the empirical and spill over into the lyrical or dramatic; and such overlapping can never be fruitful for the epic.'²⁴ Shelley writes positively where Lukács reads negatively. In the lyrical drama of *Prometheus Unbound* epic gives way to the 'lyrical' and 'dramatic', even as Shelley never seals the compartments so tightly that generic 'spilling' is unlicensed, or regarded as an aesthetic flaw. Rather, true to his sense that the 'properly utopian' must ground itself in 'the empirical', he encourages dialogue, interplay, even the threat of reversibility. So, epic is a potently temporary absence from the play's close, a close that takes us back to the opening when Demogorgon enjoins future freedom fighters, 'Neither to change, nor falter, nor repent' (IV.575). The line alludes to Satan's assertion, 'yet not for those, / Nor what the potent victor in his rage / Can else inflict, do I repent or change' (*Paradise Lost*, 1.94–6). The allusion tells us that we may need, we always may need, to wheel back to a start which was itself a redirection of earlier energies. Shelley readapts for his hero and presents in a generally positive light Satanic traits of which Milton officially disapproved.

Revising Milton: prophecy and anxiety in Wordsworth and Blake

It is in relation to Milton that Romantic poets assert their twin sense of inheritance and renewal, appropriating for new purposes their formidable predecessor's poetic scope. As Thomas Vogler notes, Wordsworth and Blake often place in the foreground the 'problem of achieving a state of consciousness or mode of vision that would be a sustaining basis for the creation of an epic vision of man to succeed Milton's *Paradise Lost*'.[25] In his Preface to *The Excursion* (originally thought of as a 'Prospectus to "The Recluse"', the unfinished epic project that haunted the poet), Wordsworth alludes to Milton yet goes beyond him:

> 'fit audience find, though few!'
> So prayed, more gaining than he asked, the Bard,
> Holiest of Men – Urania, I shall need
> Thy guidance, or a greater Muse, if such
> Descend to earth or dwell in highest heaven!
> For I must tread on shadowy ground, must sink
> Deep – and, aloft ascending, breathe in worlds
> To which the heaven of heavens is but a veil.   (23–30)[26]

Milton bids Urania 'Descend from heaven' at the start of Book 7 of *Paradise Lost*, saying that 'Up led by thee / Into the heaven of heavens I have presumed' (12–13). Wordsworth will consciously go one step further than this, will 'breathe in worlds / To which the heaven of heavens is but a veil'. These and surrounding lines enact in their enjambments effects of depth, ascension, and exhalation with a quietly daring triumphalism; Milton's 'heaven of heavens' is only now a 'veil' through which Wordsworth sees, as if about to enter a new realm, that realm he will name a few lines later as 'the Mind of Man' (40). Martin Priestman notes that the lines suggest a 're-enactment of Satan's flight through Chaos towards Earth in Book II of *Paradise Lost*', and yet Wordsworth is even more dexterously sure-footed in untrodden and transgressive terrain than is Milton's rebel archangel.[27] Wordsworth asserts that his theme involves 'the spousal verse / Of this great consummation' (57–8), but this epic epithalamion is, arguably, less his true topic than 'the Mind of Man, / My haunt, and the main region of my Song' (40–1).

Wordsworth's sense of competing with and outdoing Milton is a tangled affair, since it coexists with a haunting feeling of failure. As mentioned, Wordsworth himself appeared to feel that he ought to write a more philosophical poem, the so-called and never-completed *Recluse*. But his failure to write this poem connects intimately with his success in writing *The Prelude*, the great autobiographical poem – or personal epic is perhaps the better description – that tells the story of the development of his own poetic vocation, the 'growth of a poet's mind'. Always intending this poem to stand as 'prelude' to or within the ambitious but unfinished *Recluse*, Wordsworth worked on it from 1798 until his death, producing a short two-book version in 1799, a thirteen-book version in 1805 (this was not published until 1926), and a fourteen-book version in 1850 (published shortly after his death). In both its 1805 and 1850 versions, the poem begins with a nod towards the end of *Paradise Lost*, only to underline the fact that, for the Romantic poet, the exploration of the self is matter equal in epic significance to Milton's attempt to 'justify the ways of God to men'. At the end of *Paradise Lost* Milton describes the departure of Adam and Eve from Eden in this way: 'The world was all before them, where to choose / Their place of rest, and providence their guide' (12.646–7). Wordsworth starts his epic of consciousness by exclaiming, 'The earth is all before me!' (1.15).[28] He alludes to Milton's 'The world was all before them', concerned, like the seventeenth-century poet, with futurity. Yet Milton's glimpse of the future is at once ironic and safeguarded against final shock: ironic, because the reader is a long way into the historical process whose origins are Milton's subject, and because the complex nature of human choice, with all its errant wrong-turnings (including, most recently, a throwing away of the liberties achieved through the Puritan Revolution), is only too evident; safeguarded, because Providence will, ultimately, win through and bring all things to their wisely appointed ends. Wordsworth may write in a spirit of optimism, yet this optimism is almost giddily self-generating since it depends, not on Providence, but on inspiration: 'should the guide I choose / Be nothing better than a wandering cloud, / I cannot miss my way' (1.17–19). He cannot miss his way because of his trust in his imaginative powers, a trust that assures him he will be guided to his goal by 'nothing better than a wandering cloud'. Such a trust is almost indistinguishable from a commitment to existential uncertainty and 'wandering' thought. Wordsworth's epic will seek to reveal the godlike power of the human imagination, a power as fugitive in its manifestations as the very 'cloud' used by the poet as a figure for his sources of inspiration.

Wordsworth's choice of epic theme mingles modesty with daring: he chooses his topic since it is 'a theme / Single and of determined bounds' (1.668–9), yet he speaks in the same book of 'a dim and undetermined sense / Of unknown modes of being' (1.419–20), memorably evoked by him in the aftermath of the boat-stealing episode. Indeed, in Book III, 'the might of souls' (178) is said to be 'in truth heroic argument / And genuine prowess' (182–3), a typically Romantic recasting of the military prowess lauded in conventional epic, and a reworking of Milton's own remodelled sense of epic significance (Milton himself is unwilling to write about 'Wars, hitherto the only argument / Heroic deemed', *Paradise Lost*, 9.28–9). Yet if Wordsworth's epic theme 'lies far hidden from the reach of words' (III.185), the heroic agents of his epic of consciousness are words as they struggle to communicate the barely communicable, and give us intuitive glimpses of infinite potential, 'something evermore about to be' (VI.542). The poem's subject and manner reworks epic *topoi*: the Miltonic theme of fall and redemption recurs as Wordsworth betrays his imaginative powers to destructive analysis in the metaphorical hell of post-Revolutionary disillusion in which he 'lost / All feeling of conviction' (X.897–8), lines that oblige the reader to tumble across the abyss of the line-ending into a loss, not just of 'conviction', but of 'All feeling of conviction'. The centrality of feeling to Wordsworth's epic enterprise is hard to over-emphasize. Throughout, 'feeling comes in aid / Of feeling' (XI.325–6); it is the spur and earnest of the very imaginative activity which is both the poem's substance and guarantee that it is, indeed, a modern epic. Wordsworth's 'heroic argument' is that he is meant to be a poet, and his recovery, in Book X of his 'true self' (915) represents an explicit confirmation of a destiny whose implicit evidence is *The Prelude* itself.

In 'The Reason of Church Government' Milton writes of his questioning whether drama modelled on the Greeks might be more 'doctrinal and exemplary to a nation'[29] than an epic such as Tasso's, but the implication is clear: that he seeks to offer a poem that would be of lasting value for enshrining uncomplacently and even chasteningly the nation's sense of itself at its worthiest. In their different ways, many of the major Romantic poems that have commerce with epic seek – in their own terms – to be 'doctrinal and exemplary to [the] nation'. Above all, they appropriate the power of epic to combat the claims of worldly power, and frequently endorse a stance critical of the status quo. The poet-prophet Los, in Blake's *Jerusalem* (1804–20), engages in a mental fight as he seeks to keep 'the Divine Vision in time of trouble' (30[44]: 15) and warns against the destruction of a mechanistic society caught up in the toils of the Industrial Revolution, militarism, political reaction, and scorn for art.[30] In tense poetry filled with often tormented images, Los adapts the Miltonic posture of stoic defiance to a near-paranoid, eloquent rage. Epic in Blake is the labour to recover, with an effort close to agony, the awareness that all negatives entomb a positive alternative that needs to be resurrected:

> Instead of Albions lovely mountains & the curtains of Jerusalem
> I see a Cave, a Rock, a Tree deadly and poisonous, unimaginative ...
>
> (43[38]: 59–60)

Objects here have fallen asunder, divorced from 'imaginative' vision. The epic poet's task is to heal the process of division, and the task involves Los's confrontation with his Spectre (symbol of his self-doubt), a figure who is at once the creative artist's deadliest enemy and most needed ally. Los stigmatizes his Spectre as 'my Pride & Self-righteousness' (8: 30), but in virtually the same breath he concedes that he needs this aspect of himself, commanding it to harness its energies to the work of inspiration. 'Take thou these Tongs: strike thou alternate with me: labour obedient' (8: 40), he asserts, in a line that is at once imperative and (by virtue of the repeated 'thou') entreaty. Traditionally the epic hero experiences a tussle of impulses: Aeneas is torn between duty and emotion in his dealings with Dido, and Virgil's poetry sympathizes so deeply with the nightmare-assailed queen that it is impossible not to feel that the hero errs in not erring from the path of heroic duty. Epic here becomes a form that reflects on the burden of expectations laid on the epic hero. Blake modernizes Virgil by placing his own struggle to the fore, even as he is always on the lookout for evidences of hope, raiding his store of hope-sustaining metaphors much as signs and auguries are consulted in classical epic – and often with a comparable underlying desperation. To say that 'There is a Grain of Sand in Lambeth that Satan cannot find' (41[37]: 15) is to concede the uphill nature of the battle fought by the epic poet, even as the particularity of place has its own power to confer a sense of resilient uplift. In a very real sense the poem is always operating *in medias res*, always looking for or seeking to shape such affirmations. Early on, in a moment that in its idiosyncratic way recalls Milton's authorial interventions, Blake talks about and enacts his assumption of an epic burden:

> Trembling I sit day and night, my friends are astonish'd at me.
> Yet they forgive my wanderings, I rest not from my great task!

To open the Eternal Worlds, to open the immortal Eyes
Of Man inwards into the Worlds of Thought: into Eternity
Ever expanding in the Bosom of God.   (5: 16–20)

Infinitives and participles imitate the prolonged, suspended nature of the poet's 'great task', its existence in a recurrent, ever-returned-to present. Blake's emphasis on vision illustrates the inwardness that marks Romantic epic, and is apparent in Wordsworth's *The Prelude*, with its emphasis on consciousness. This is not to see Romantic epic as ignoring or evading the claims of history. *Jerusalem*, like *The Prelude*, grapples with the spiritual crisis caused by the failure of revolutionary hope and seeks to address the nation, to insist that it confronts its true destiny. Blake reminds us that epic is as much of an ordeal for the readers as for the poet or hero. He even makes his poem 'a test for the Public that is being addressed' through continual provocations to thought that divide the readers into the 'SHEEP' and 'GOATS'.[31] He engraved these at a late stage on plate 3 (after erasing references to friendlier words such as 'love' and 'friendship'): the juxtaposition of text and image in a mode of coloured printing which means that 'English, the rough basement' (40[36]: 58) floats up to us through washes of visual suggestion; or the wall of words that confronts us in imageless pages, or the use of reversed writing.[32] Equally, *The Prelude* seeks to assert the greatness of the human spirit in the face of political disillusion: this assertion has been read as escapist, but unfairly so. The poet-prophet who emerges in Blake's and Wordsworth's long poems salvages, it is true, belief in the greatness of the mind from the wreckage of history; yet he does so in a spirit caught by Shelley when he writes of the poet that he is a 'prophet' in this sense: 'he not only beholds intensely the present as it is ... but he beholds the future in the present, and his thoughts are the germs of the flower and the fruit of latest time'.[33] The poet-prophet cannot foretell the future, but he can penetrate to the heart of forces at work in a culture. Witness to the power of Shelley's argument is supplied by the hold over subsequent poetry and thought of the Romantic project, collectively central to 'that great poem'[34] written by all poets: the ultimate epic, perhaps.

Irony and epic passion: Byron and Keats

Romantic epic's many appropriations also incorporate as their most surprising and brilliant example Byron's capacious and unfinished *Don Juan* (1819–24). 'Thou shalt believe in Milton, Dryden, Pope' (1.205.1633), urges Byron with wicked correctness, flying in the face of Romanticism's 'wrong poetical revolutionary system' as he couples the arch-exponent of epic with the great masters of mock-epic.[35] The poem undercuts epical pretensions at every turn: who but Byron could write, 'Hail, Muse! *et cetera*' (III.1.1), where the solemn invocations of countless poets crumble to ashes in the flame of his rakishly languid irony? And yet the poem has a sweep, a knowledge of men and women, an ambition and range that make its disregard for convention seem both meta-literary and at the service of a hunger for reality. Byron's poem stays in the memory as a bravura exposure of and defence against 'the Nothingness of life' (VII.6.548). 'A versified Aurora Borealis, / Which flashes o'er a waste and icy clime' (VII.2.11–12), it illuminates unsparingly much that is 'waste and icy' in contemporary society, even as its many-coloured spectrum include hues that are transcendental as well as tragic, tender as well as bleakly funny. His *ottava rima* is an affront to the Milton who chose blank verse and rejected the 'bondage of rhyming', but it also declares Byron's admiration for 'the tyrant-hater' praised in the furious and funny 'Dedication' (10.81) since it avoids any immodest competition. Byron's tones are unique and uniquely double, and he turns the anxiety of influence into a charter for generic novelty, composing a richly creative mix of idioms: his poem mocks epic pieties, but manages to create a vision that has an epic validity.

If difference from previous epic models turns out to serve Byron's advantage, Keats's practice in his two *Hyperion*s (1818–19, 1819), both left as unfinished fragments, reveals a remarkable process of experimentation with the epic. In the lines with which *Hyperion* begins, starting 'Deep in the shady sadness of a vale' (I.1), Keats displays fascination with Miltonic '*Stationing* or *statuary*', a power of presentation that bears witness to the way in which the older poet 'pursues his imagination to the utmost' and glossed as follows: 'He is not content with simple description, he must station' ('Marginalia', p. 344). It is as though Keats is trying, more literally than any other Romantic, to write an epic for the present day that challenges Milton on his own ground, as though it were possible to write a poem of epic 'objectivity'. Yet, alluding to Wordsworth's lines from his Preface to *The Excursion* quoted above, he wondered a few months before composing the poem whether 'Wordsworth has in truth epic passion, and martyrs himself to the human heart, the main region of his song' (p. 396). In the first *Hyperion*, with its sculptured masses, Latinate constructions, and emphasis on the objectification of feeling, caught here in Saturn's motionless posture of 'realmless' dejection (I.19), Keats avoids the Wordsworthian mode of representing 'the human heart, the main region of his song'. He would not have known *The Prelude*, but responded enthusiastically to Wordsworth's quasi-epic philosophical poem, *The Excursion*. Keats admired the account of the mythmaking activities of the 'lively Grecian'

(IV.714), in a passage that granted the creator of classical myth the ability to have access to intimations of 'Life continuous, Being unimpaired' (IV.751). Yet, on the evidence of strongly affecting echoes in the third and seventh stanzas of 'Ode to a Nightingale', he was especially responsive to the saddened note of the passage's close, in which Wordsworth describes what such a vision of 'Being' transcends, the awareness, for example, that 'Man grows old, and dwindles, and decays; / And countless generations of Mankind / Depart; and leave no vestige where they trod' (IV.760–2). The epic design of *The Excursion* permits continual recursions to downcast meditations on 'accident' (IV.755); and Keats evidently saw how Wordsworth's text, to its advantage, found ways of overcoming its own palpable design upon the reader.

In the *Hyperion*s there is a vivid undercurrent of awareness that a modern epic poet may wish to be 'like the fore-seeing God' to whom Keats compares Apollo 'and shape his actions like one' (p. 371), but that his wish may founder on the reality of the need to engage with 'epic passion' and martyr 'himself to the human heart'. The phrase 'epic passion' suggests both that the poet will discover his true theme when he addresses what in *The Fall of Hyperion* is called 'the miseries of the world' (1.148) and that he will bring to this theme the suffering caused by the very attempt to be an epic poet. The poem may, indeed, move us most when Keats seeks to find an answer to its epic ambitions in the posture of patient submission before inevitable engagement in complication evoked in the almost atemporal rhythms of the close of Book 1. Hyperion, hearing Coelus's voice, its 'region-whisper' (1.349), is depicted thus: he 'on the stars / Lifted his curved lids, and kept them wide / Until it ceas'd; and still he kept them wide: / And still they were the same bright, patient stars' (1.350–3). Momentarily the poem stills the turbulent storm of unrest that its own epic ambition evokes.

Anxiety, mingled with a near-defiant sense of the poet's fated individualism, suffuses the conclusion of the opening of *The Fall of Hyperion*: the lines, 'Whether the dream now purposed to rehearse / Be poet's or Fanatic's will be known / When this warm scribe my hand is in the grave' (1.16–18), reveal that dreams of a post-Miltonic, post-Wordsworthian escape from subjectivity have foundered on the rock of belatedness, but also been transformed into a new awareness of possibility. Able 'To see as a God sees' (1.304), the poet is like Dante's 'Glaucus, when he tasted of the herb / That made him peer among the ocean gods', as Cary's translation of *Paradiso* 1.68–9 has it.[36] Yet if *The Fall of Hyperion* chooses Dante as its guide as it takes us behind the scenes of a would-be epic poem, it is acutely conscious of its own chastened, purgatorial aloneness, the poet left, in his dealings with fallen majesty and the recriminations of Moneta, 'Without stay or prop / But my own weak mortality' (1.388–9). At this fine but desolate moment in the poem, those absent props include the structures of epic genre, and Keats reminds us that Romantic re-appropriations of epic may involve not only metamorphosis into something new, but also an undoing of the form until it contemplates its own dissolution.

NOTES

1 Stuart Curran, *Poetic Form and British Romanticism* (New York: Oxford University Press, 1986), 181.

2 *Percy Bysshe Shelley: The Major Works*, ed. Zachary Leader and Michael O'Neill (Oxford: Oxford University Press, 2003), 69.

3 *Collected Letters of Samuel Taylor Coleridge*, ed. E. L. Griggs, 6 vols. (Oxford: Clarendon Press, 1956–71) vol. I, 320, 320–21; hereafter *CL*.

4 *John Milton: A Critical Edition of the Major Works*, ed. Stephen Orgel and Jonathan Goldberg (Oxford: Oxford University Press, 1991). All subsequent references to Milton's works are cited from this edition.

5 Seamus Perry, *Coleridge and the Uses of Division* (Oxford: Clarendon Press, 1999), 282. The reading 'rightly-whispering' is in Griggs; Cottle's reading in *Reminiscences of Samuel Taylor Coleridge and Robert Southey* (New York: Wiley and Putnam, 1847), 77, is 'nightly-whispering', as it is in *Coleridge's Poetry and Prose*, ed. Nicholas Halmi, Paul Magnuson, and Raimonda Modiano (New York: Norton, 2004), 618.

6 Coleridge's poems are quoted from the 'Reading Text' in *Poetical Works*, ed. J. C. C. Mays, 3 vols. (Princeton: Princeton University Press, 2001).

7 M. H. Abrams, *Natural Supernaturalism: Tradition and Revolution in Romantic Literature* (New York: Norton, 1971), 332.

8 Friedrich Schiller, '*Die Götter Griechenlandes*' (The Gods of Greece) (1788).

9 See *Coleridge's Notebooks: A Selection*, ed. Seamus Perry (Oxford: Oxford University Press, 2002), 4.

10 See Karl Kroeber, '"The Rime of the Ancient Mariner" as Stylized Epic', *Transactions of the Wisconsin Society of Sciences, Arts, and Letters* 46 (1957): 179–89, and Michael O'Neill, 'Coleridge's Genres', in *The Oxford Handbook of Coleridge Studies*, ed. Frederick Burwick (Oxford: Oxford University Press, 2009).

11 See Curran, *Poetic Form and British Romanticism* for an account of 'the proliferation of epics in England' in the period. For information about women writers of epic (or approaches to or evasions of epic), see chapters 2–6 of Herbert F. Tucker's *Epic: Britain's Heroic Muse 1790–1910* (Oxford: Oxford University Press, 2008).

12 *New Letters of Robert Southey*, ed. Kenneth Curry, 2 vols. (New York: Columbia University Press, 1965), vol. I, 238.

13 1.42–8; the poem is quoted from the text available in the database, Literature Online.

14 *CL* I, 646; *The Life and Correspondence of the Late Robert Southey*, ed. Charles Cuthbert Southey, 6 vols. (London: Longman, 1850), vol. II, 121; hereafter *LC*.

15 *LC*, II, 121–2.

16 *Poems of Robert Southey*, ed. Maurice H. Fitzgerald (London: Oxford University Press, 1909), 460. For critical comment see, for example, Brian Wilkie, *Romantic Poets and Epic Tradition* (Madison: University of Wisconsin Press, 1965), 36–40.

17 See *Shelley's Poetry and Prose*, ed. Donald H. Reiman and Neil Fraistat, 2nd edn (New York: Norton, 2002), 101n.

18 Wilkie, *Romantic Poets and Epic Tradition*, 130, 131.

19 *The Letters of Percy Bysshe Shelley*, 2 vols. (Oxford: Clarendon Press, 1964), vol. i, 564, hereafter *LS*.

20 Wilkie, *Romantic Poets and Epic Tradition*, 40.

21 'Keats's Marginalia to *Paradise Lost*', quoted from *John Keats*, Oxford Authors, ed. Elizabeth Cook (Oxford: Oxford University Press, 1990), 336. All quotations from Keats's poetry are also from this edition, unless otherwise attributed.

22 *Letters of William Wordsworth: A New Selection*, ed. Alan G. Hill (Oxford: Oxford University Press, 1984), 185.

23 *LS*, ii, 294.

24 *The Theory of the Novel: A Historico-Philosophical Essay on the Forms of Great Epic Literature* (1915), trans. Anna Bostock (Cambridge, MA: MIT Press, 1971), 46.

25 Thomas A. Vogler, *Preludes to Vision: The Epic Venture in Blake, Wordsworth, Keats and Hart Crane* (Berkeley: University of California Press, 1971), 61.

26 Quoted from William Wordsworth, *The Excursion*, ed. Sally Bushell, James A. Butler, and Michael C. Jaye, with the assistance of David García (Ithaca: Cornell University Press, 2007).

27 Martin Priestman, *Romantic Atheism: Poetry and Freethought, 1780–1930* (Cambridge: Cambridge University Press, 1999), 183.

28 References are to the 1805 text in William Wordsworth, *The Prelude: The Four Texts (1798, 1799, 1805, 1850)*, ed. Jonathan Wordsworth (Harmondsworth: Penguin, 1995).

29 *John Milton: A Critical Edition*, ed. Orgel and Goldberg, 170.

30 William Blake, *Jerusalem: The Emanation of the Giant Albion*, ed. with introduction and notes by Morton D. Paley (London: William Blake Trust / Tate Gallery, 1991). Numbers in square brackets refer to alternative pagination in two of the six known copies of the text.

31 *Ibid.*, 133n.

32 *Ibid.*, 133n, 10–11.

33 Shelley, *Major Works*, ed. Leader and O'Neill, 677.

34 *Ibid.*, 687.

35 *Lord Byron: The Major Works*, ed. Jerome J. McGann (Oxford: Oxford University Press, 2000).

36 The allusion and quotation from Cary are from *The Poems of John Keats*, ed. Miriam Allott (London: Longman, 1970), 676n.

12

JOHN WHITTIER-FERGUSON

Ezra Pound, T. S. Eliot, and the modern epic

'A second time'

I take the epigraph of this chapter from a moment in the first of Ezra Pound's *Cantos* when Odysseus, having gone to Hades so that he may learn from the dead how he is to find his way home, is greeted by Tiresias, the Theban seer who will show him his future: 'A second time? why? man of ill star, / Facing the sunless dead and this joyless region?' (1/4).[1] Tiresias's question makes no literal sense (Odysseus has not been to Hades before) but springs instead from a set of textual errors, mistakes deriving from small but significant slips in transcription and translation, and it usefully focuses our attention on crucial characteristics of modern epics. Pound is not speaking or singing this beginning of his epic poem; like all modern epics, the *Cantos* is pre-eminently a textual production, fundamentally and ostentatiously a product of the library rather than the battlefield, the mead hall, or the court. 'A second time' is Pound's translation of a phrase he found in a Renaissance translation of the *Odyssey* by Andreas Divus, whose version confuses two similar Greek adjectives: Odysseus's identity shifts, over the course of time, from 'noble' to 'twice-born' or 'double', and Pound turns this epithet into the opening query from the dead seer. But Pound's phrase introduces an idea of more consequence and complexity than any mere characterological insight about Odysseus's birth. Seven lines later in the same canto, interrupting Pound's version of one of the most vividly realized scenes from Homer's *Odyssey* (Book 11), when Odysseus sees his mother, Anticlea, among the dead, Andreas Divus breaks into Pound's poem. The dead translator insists, as it were, that his book be acknowledged for the part it plays in this story:

> And then Anticlea came.
> Lie quiet Divus. I mean, that is Andreas Divus,
> In officina Wecheli, 1538, out of Homer.   (1/5)

Gathered among these shades, enabling their speech and the memory of their speech, is a host of authors, the unquiet Divus and Homer among them. Not sacrificial blood, but the printing house gives them voice, and the publication details recorded on a book's title page ('In officina Wecheli, 1538') matter as much as a hero's blazon or ancestry.

We must understand 'a second time' not simply as an error introduced in the historical transmission of this ancient episode from the *Odyssey* but, more broadly, as an acknowledgement that we live and read and write among the books that have come before us. It is a paradox to which we shall return along a variety of paths in this chapter: one of the hallmarks of modernism's epics is that they continually signal their belatedness, their status as 'second-time' productions, and one of their most recognizably modern features is that their authors write while looking over their shoulders at the shelved books, the textual archives that precede them. This backwards gaze becomes a central subject and shapes the form of the texts that are at the heart of my survey: T. S. Eliot's *The Waste Land* and Pound's *Cantos*. In his seminal essay on the historical position and contemporary practice of the modern poet, 'Tradition and the Individual Talent' (1919), Eliot captures the unavoidably recursive nature of modern writing: 'Someone said: "The dead writers are remote from us because we *know* so much more than they did". Precisely, and they are that which we know.'[2] Pound's famous injunction to 'make it new' can be put into practice only by measuring novelty against the innovations of predecessors; in the reflexive texts of the period, these acts of measuring become one of the signs of the epic enterprise. Like the epics that precede them in Western culture, these modern works aim to assemble, on the grandest possible scale, a model of the world that will both represent and explain the way things are, how they came to be, and the position of the human subject in the scheme of things, and yet the obstacles to this gigantic act of making in the modern era are so great that the attempt to make the model, and the record of others' attempts at such constructions, past and present, move to the centre of the epic enterprise. The paramount achievement recorded in the modern epic is not the justification of God's or gods' ways with us, or a hero's battles, or journey, or the foundation of a nation or an empire. It is an aesthetic act that may or may not have some social, cultural, political, or theological ramifications: the author's unlikely writing of the book we read.

The most revealing locus to introduce the challenges to and the forms of success in the modern epic is *The Prelude* (1805, 1850), Wordsworth's long, posthumously published preamble to what he planned to be his epic proper: '*The Recluse*, or Views on Nature, Man and Society'.[3] Begun in 1798–9, bearing a series of preliminary, private titles ('The Friend', 'Poem on the Growth and Revolutions of an Individual Mind', 'the poem on the growth of my own mind' [xxxvii]), revised throughout its author's life, titled by his sister at its publication three months after her brother's death, *The Prelude* arguably stands as the most important long poem of the nineteenth century and as the first modern epic. For our purposes, four characteristics of the poem are particularly significant. First, Wordsworth begins his poem with an extensive consideration of how, in a secular, sceptical era, one might compose an epic, considering in turn the almost insurmountable problems of audience, vocation, genre, subject, and scope. Second, he reluctantly but unavoidably turns from writing 'some work / Of glory' (1.78–9), 'some old / Romantic tale by Milton left unsung' (1.168–9), to autobiography – the one subject authentically at his command. Memory has always been a crucial faculty for the epic poet, whether it was used to recall the thousands of lines to be sung in a banquet hall or to write the story of a people, a nation, human history itself, but in the nineteenth and twentieth centuries, the use of memory becomes more idiosyncratic and more private, more personal: no less essential but more circumscribed. Third, the impasse with which the poem begins proves generative of a long poem that is epic in scope without claiming the genre of epic for itself: 'the story of my life', Wordsworth tells himself somewhat ruefully at the end of the first book of his poem, is 'a theme / Single and of determined bounds; and hence / I choose it rather at this time, than work / Of ampler or more varied argument' (1.640–3). He had begun his poem with a scene rich in revisionary echoes of the end of *Paradise Lost*, where pure possibility beckoned the poet 'From the vast city': 'The earth is all before me. With a heart / Joyous, nor scared at its own liberty, / I look about; and should the chosen guide / Be nothing better than a wandering cloud, / I cannot miss my way' (1.7, 14–18). Such freedom from guidance, however, such absence of a divine plan made manifest or a workable aesthetic form discoverable by the poet himself, quickly leads to an aimless wandering. In the momentary verses that come to him, he records his failure: 'the banded host / Of harmony dispersed in straggling sounds, / And lastly utter silence!' (1.97–9). The poem ends several hundred pages later, with a hopeful invocation of the still-unwritten epic that the poet and his friend, Samuel Taylor Coleridge, might together present to some future audience: 'we to them will speak / A lasting inspiration . . . / what we have loved, / Others will love; and we may teach them how' (XIV.444–7). Fourth, this posthumously published 'prelude', this record of a lifetime's preparation for the work to come – work that cannot be undertaken before amassing decades of experience – exhibits another characteristic of modern epics: these texts are in many ways deliberately provisional, open-ended, formally unfinished and distinguished throughout by the sense of possibility, of inclusion rather than perfected and completed design. A sentence from Virginia Woolf's diary captures one hopeful version of this aesthetic: 'What a discovery that would be – a system that did not shut out.'[4] Sometimes celebrated, but as often lamented by their authors, the centrifugal forms of the modern epic result in capacious works-in-progress (to borrow Joyce's designation for *Finnegans Wake* during the seventeen years of its composition), as unfinished in and by principle as the processes of memory itself, with its continual re-scripting of the past in the light of new experience.

Pieces of an epic: *The Waste Land*

In a wry quatrain summarizing recent poetic history, W. B. Yeats offers an image for what remains now that the grand forms of art are no longer possible:

> 'The Nineteenth Century and After'
>
> Though the great song return no more
> There's keen delight in what we have:
> The rattle of pebbles on the shore
> Under the receding wave.[5]

Even the theatrical, tragic-heroic humanism of Matthew Arnold pondering the shingles of Dover Beach is now dated, but there are local consolations to be found in the fragments left after the 'sea of faith', as Arnold figured it, has receded; after the modern reading audience has broken into even more constituencies than were comprised by nineteenth-century readerships; after the Great War has turned 'arms and the man' into a subject impossible to frame in heroic terms. 'Pebbles', or 'fragments' (to use Eliot's more well-known description of his great modernist poem, *The Waste Land*, 1922): both figures capture the most immediately evident characteristic of all long modern works of poetry or prose: all are assemblies of distinguishable and often separable parts.[6] Small wonder that unity of the whole – organic or mechanical, intrinsic or imposed from without – is a chief concern in the early reviews of the works I discuss in this chapter and becomes a central category of the 'New Criticism', the theory of literary analysis that has its roots in Anglo-American modernism: these are texts that come to us in pieces.

On the level of poetic form, Eliot's intentionally broken masterpiece displays more openly than *The Prelude* the radical understanding of subjectivity that lies behind both works. The Victorian aesthetician and man of letters, Walter Pater, presents this understanding in a famous formulation that is useful to us for its clarity. In his 'Conclusion' (1873) to a collection of essays titled *The Renaissance*, Pater describes humans not as lords and ladies holding dominion over themselves and the earth, but as an unstable collection of physical substances and forces, a 'combination of natural elements' in 'perpetual motion', elements whose chemical process 'extends beyond us: it rusts iron and ripens corn'. Correspondingly, 'the inward world of thought and feeling' is characterized by a 'whirlpool still more rapid', a 'flame more eager and devouring'.[7] Nothing, not events or objects, not impressions or thoughts, stands still long enough for us to believe wholeheartedly in a single narrative point of view, or a poetic 'speaker', or even a Cartesian, reflective 'I':

> It is with this movement, with the passage and dissolution of impressions, images, sensations, that analysis leaves off – that continual vanishing away, that strange, perpetual weaving and unweaving of ourselves.   (188)

Eliot, who in 1913–14 had drafted chapters of a dissertation for the philosophy department at Harvard on the scepticism of F. H. Bradley, the British idealist philosopher (see his note on Bradley in *The Waste Land*, 54, n. 412), follows the implications of this sceptical strain of thought in the form of his poem, as well as at a number of thematic points. Incorporating part of the 'fable of the meaning of the Thunder' from the *Upanishads* (54, n. 402), he places the Sanskrit word for 'sympathy' beside the most profound obstacle to the actual practice of sympathy – a powerful emblem of modern solipsism:

> *Dayadhvam*: I have heard the key
> Turn in the door once and turn once only
> We think of the key, each in his prison
> Thinking of the key, each confirms a prison.   (lines 412–15)

Those last two lines, repetitively pacing out our confinement along an extremely limited verbal track, brought up against the same final word each time, provide us with a formal representation of the cul-de-sac of the self. In his 'Conclusion', Pater had argued that our experience is 'ringed round for each one of us by that thick wall of personality through which no real voice has ever pierced on its way to us, or from us to that which we can only conjecture to be without' (187). Clearly, there is no space in these little rooms for that most expansive of poetic forms, the epic.

What Eliot gives us instead, in *The Waste Land*, is a poem that is less an epic than a gathering of parts that might belong in an epic, none of them developed for more than a handful of lines, many so burdened with irony that they demonstrate how poorly the ancient, heroic genres (the quest-romance, the epic, the spiritual life-narrative and parable) fit the twentieth century. A poem of 434 lines, divided into five parts (not cantos, not books), with no single narrative passage sustained over more than twenty or thirty lines cannot, even on the face of it, be called an epic, since one of the fundamental requirements of an epic is length and extended narrative. And yet, in a letter Pound wrote to Eliot in 1921, as the two were collaborating on revisions to Eliot's poem, Pound addresses Eliot's anxiety about its brevity: 'The thing now runs from "April . . ." to "shantih" without a break. That is 19 pages, and let us say the longest poem in the English langwidge. Don't try to bust all records by prolonging it three pages further.'[8] Pound awards it the 'longest poem' denomination using 'poem' in the same sense as Edgar Allen Poe in 'The Philosophy of Composition' – as a form of art that demands focus and whose 'brevity must be in direct ratio of the intensity of the intended effect'; 'one-half of the *Paradise Lost*', Poe irreverently declares, 'is essentially prose'.[9] For the purposes of a discussion of modern epic, one way to read the distilled poem that Eliot achieves with Pound's editorial assistance (which consisted largely of excision, particularly of narrative sections) is as an extended lyric that also comprises a gathering of epic parts, a concentrated though selective anatomy, with little of the connective tissue provided by narrative, of a genre that is not practicable in this era after the great songs have all been sung.

There are thematic elements, many of them emphasized in Eliot's 'Notes on "The Waste Land"', that evoke the related genres of quest-romance and epic: the summoning of the 'dead land' and the corpse returning to life; the sublime erotic-spiritual encounter between one of the poem's 'speakers' and the young 'hyacinth girl' or the gorgeously enthroned woman at the beginning of part 2; the meetings with fortune tellers and seers (Madame Sosostris and Tiresias); the ruined kingdom and blighted land in need of rejuvenation; the gruelling journey to the 'empty chapel' that may hold the promise of sacramental knowledge; the word of a god, uttered in non-human speech ('what the thunder said'). The much discussed 'Notes' to the poem serve, among other things, to add weight to the poem, emphasizing its mythic, its archetypal elements. They provide a scaffolding not only of literary quotations and allusions but of references drawn from the newly developing science of culture itself – anthropology – a modern discipline that promises to recover the deep structures of civilization. By citing, in his introductory note, 'Miss Jessie L. Weston's book on the Grail legend' and 'another work of anthropology . . . which has influenced our generation profoundly; I mean *The Golden Bough*' of Sir James George Frazer, Eliot expands the scope of a poem so personal, so challengingly idiosyncratic as to be considered, upon its publication and for many years afterwards, a paradigm of the almost insurmountable difficulties with which modernism confronts its readers (50).

It does not matter that scholars have demonstrated Weston and Frazer to be late additions rather than foundational texts for Eliot as he composed

The Waste Land. The same belatedness is to some extent true of the *Odyssey*'s application to Joyce's *Ulysses*; and Pound, never proposing a single 'key' to his *Cantos*, offers a range of structural analogues over the course of the work's composition, many of which similarly bind the poetry to the bedrock of culture. As Eliot uses Frazer, Pound singles out Leo Frobenius as a visionary anthropologist-guide to understanding human history and societies. Hilda Doolittle (H. D.) steeps her *Trilogy* (1944–6) in the ancient wisdom discoverable, in the middle of the twentieth century, by means of psychology, archaeology, comparative theology, and a range of mystical practices, urging us to 'search the old highways / for the true rune, the right-spell, recover old values' (2/511), practising a poetic submersion 'that yet connects us / with the drowned cities of pre-history' (33/603).[10] All of these ambitious works aspire to connect the personal with larger forces, deeper knowledge. In his notes Eliot shows us a way to move from 'I' to 'we', to push lyric towards epic, to read the poem, for all its brevity and in all its fragmentation, as 'epic' in at least one crucial sense of the term: like these other texts, it becomes a work addressing the originary myths of a people and a culture. *The Waste Land* takes us to the roots of our civilization, beyond mere first-person anguish and insight, towards the most powerful, most primitive symbols and narratives underlying the 'stony rubbish' of modernity and the isolated self. By means of his allusions, his notes, the richly evocative images and haunting narratives he briefly develops, Eliot generates interpretive impulses in his readers that lead us towards the grand themes and archetypal patterns of the epic. Sorting through these pebbles on the strand, we discover that they are thousands of years old, and that they were once part of much greater geological formations.

Still lifes and history: the *Cantos*

A few months after the publication of *The Waste Land*, in an important essay titled 'Ulysses, Order, and Myth' (1923), Eliot reviewed Joyce's novel, published eight months before the first appearance of Eliot's poem. Eliot praises the way *Ulysses* maintains 'a continuous parallel between contemporaneity and antiquity' and heralds Joyce's discovery of 'the mythic method'.[11] The novel, Eliot argues, 'is a form which will no longer serve'; *Ulysses* belongs in another category: 'if you will call it an epic', he adds, with characteristic equivocation, 'it will not matter' (482). The daily lives of modern men and women, the complexities of consciousness and the riot of circumstance besetting consciousness can be connected to archaic narratives and characters in ways that are not simply ironic but that show us pattern where we had seen only unmotivated stimulus and response. Joyce's 'method' provides the artist with

> a way of controlling, of ordering, of giving a shape and a significance to the immense panorama of futility and anarchy which is contemporary history . . . It is a method for which the horoscope is auspicious. Psychology . . . ethnology, and *The Golden Bough* have concurred to make possible what was impossible even a few years ago. Instead of narrative method, we may now use the mythical method. It is, I seriously believe, a step toward making the modern world possible for art. (483)

Clearly, Eliot also has his own work in mind (the references to Frazer and ethnology are telling) and, as we turn our attention to Pound and the *Cantos*, it is worth noting that Joyce, Eliot, and Pound are all working on extensive aesthetic forms – long poems, and an extraordinarily ambitious novel – art for the 'modern world', as Eliot puts it, at roughly the same time, and that their epic experiments influence one another. Eliot begins *The Waste Land* in late 1919, drafts it, with Pound's editorial help, over the next two and a half years, and first publishes it (without the notes), eight months after the publication of *Ulysses*, in October of 1922. Joyce is mailing drafts of *Ulysses* chapters to Pound and to Eliot, and the two poets are reading instalments of the novel in the *Little Review* from 1918 until its suppression for obscenity in 1920.

Pound writes his first three cantos in 1915 and publishes them in *Poetry* magazine in 1917. He publishes his fourth canto in 1919, then turns to his last major poem that is not part of the *Cantos*, 'Hugh Selwyn Mauberley' (published in 1920) – a two-part suite of eighteen poems that is best read as an extended assessment of the state of modern letters in general and, with particular point, Pound's own poetic career up to 1920. Between 1920 and 1922, Pound has trouble progressing with his long poem but, for a variety of reasons, including the examples set by Eliot and Joyce, he begins a newly intense and fruitful period of work on the *Cantos* again in 1922. He rearranges the order of his existing cantos. He writes in a newly elliptical style (honed, in part, as he edited Eliot's drafts of *The Waste Land*). He includes documentary materials from prose sources as well as quotations from poetry in a number of languages; he develops, in cantos VIII–XI, his presentation of the first and one of the most important of his poem's heroes – the Renaissance condottiere and patron of the arts, Sigismundo Pandolfo Malatesta. By 1925, he has completed what he titles *A Draft of XVI Cantos*. His subtitle to this deluxe, limited-edition publication, as open-ended as Wordsworth's working titles for his *Prelude*, tells us that these sixteen cantos are 'for the Beginning of a Poem / of some Length'.

'*Draft*' tells us that even these first sixty-five pages are likely to change before the long poem achieves its final form. The next year, in December of 1926, he publishes all of his shorter poetry in a collection titled *Personae*. From this point until 1966, six years before his death, when he adds his last 'Fragment' to his magnum opus, all of Pound's poetry will be part of his long poem: 116 cantos and assorted fragments; 824 pages in the most recent edition; released (not counting special editions) in nine published volumes, from the *Draft of XXX Cantos* in 1930 to *Drafts and Fragments of Cantos CX–CXVII* in 1969. There is no other work of such scope, such ambition, or such difficulty in twentieth-century poetry.

Pound himself, in letters and comments about his poem over the course of his life, measures the obstacles confronting readers of his work. In a long letter he wrote, in July of 1922, to Professor Felix Schelling, who had taught Pound English in his freshman year at the University of Pennsylvania (in 1901, when Pound was fifteen), he puts Eliot forward as the most important illustration of his generation's achievement: 'Eliot's *Waste Land* is I think the justification of the "moment", of our modern experiment, since 1900. It shd. be published this year' (*Letters*, 180). He is more provisional, and much more discursive, about his own poetic accomplishment to date:

> Perhaps as the poem goes on I shall be able to make various things clearer. Having the crust to attempt a poem in 100 or 120 cantos long after all mankind has been commanded never again to attempt a poem of any length, I have to stagger as I can.
>
> The first 11 cantos are preparation of the palette. I *have to* get down all the colours or elements I want for the poem. Some perhaps too enigmatically and abbreviatedly. I hope, heaven help me, to bring them into some sort of design and architecture later. (*Letters*, 180)

One could compose a sizable anthology of Pound's letters like this, from the nineteen-teens forward, that defend his project, confess its provisional nature, hold out hopes and promises of 'some sort of design' to be revealed in the future, and express, always, the urgency, the importance of this task and the energy with which Pound undertakes it. *The Waste Land* – formally complete, difficult but comprehensible, closer in the compression and the flow of its lines to lyric poetry than to any more extended verse form – may be marshalled in a 'movement's' defence. The *Cantos*, as Pound himself is already realizing, will be too large, too antagonistic towards the culture they diagnose, too much an unfinished work to be employed as an example or justification for the uninitiated. His poem amounts to something different: among many things, the *Cantos* are a lifetime's consideration of the means by which and the conditions under which an epic might be written.

And, with mounting insistence from the middle of the 1930s through the publication of the *Pisan Cantos* in 1948, they also attempt to intervene as directly as it is possible for poetry to intervene in the socio-political sphere in order to bring those conditions into being.

I have already singled out 'a second time' as a paradigmatically modernist interruption of the first canto – an interruption that calls our attention to the textual nature of Pound's strategy for beginning his poem, grafting his writing onto epic stock that comes 'out of Homer' (I/5). The phrase also evokes one of the most important characteristics of the *Cantos*. To an extent unequalled by any of his peers, Pound's writing is never far removed from an abiding desire to bring about the return of the dead and, in a related act of ghostly recall, to summon gods and spirits to become part of his poetry. His 1912 poem, 'The Return', in which he describes the gods' reappearance in the modern world, is by any measure one of his greatest short poems. Its success is due in large part to the intensity, the completeness with which Pound has imagined how such a reawakening and manifestation would occur. The opening cantos are filled with a host of such returns, such 'second times', such voicings and moments of possession, when the unseen and silent become visible and speak. In *Time and Western Man* (1927), Wyndham Lewis (his acerbic, difficult friend and sometime collaborator) analyses Pound's tendency to exhume pieces of the past, to serve as ventrilo-quist for the dead in his work:

> Life is not his true concern . . . His field is purely that of *the dead*. As the *nature mortist*, or painter essentially of still-life, deals for preference with life-that-is-still, that has not much life, so Ezra for preference consorts with the dead, whose life is preserved for us in books and pictures. He has never loved anything living as he has loved the dead.[12]

Like virtually everything Lewis wrote as a critic, this is both deeply unfair and terribly accurate. That Pound moved the *Nekyia* (the journey to the land of the dead) from what had been part of Canto III in 1915 to the opening of Canto I by the time he published the first collection in 1925 demonstrates the importance of this episode to his undertaking.

In its earlier form, from the 1915 *Three Cantos*, Pound introduced the episode as a set piece, an imperfect mimicry of Divus.[13] In the revised Canto I, we confront the unframed archaic narrative from the moment we begin the poem, and the justice of Lewis's comments about Pound's loving the past seems indisputable. Unlike first-time readers of *The Waste Land* or *Ulysses*, readers new to the *Cantos* must be immediately struck by how Pound's poem sounds ancient rather than modern: primitive in its alliterative verse (formally alluding to Old English tetrameter, though this is free verse that feels often as though it wants to be blank verse); dated in its diction, archaic in its phrases. We enter the *Cantos*, *in medias res*, 'And then'; we find Homeric formulae ('godly sea', 'trim-coifed goddess'); we are caught up in a story, an epic adventure:

> we went over sea till day's end.
> Sun to his slumber, shadows o'er all the ocean,
> Came we then to the bounds of deepest water . . .
> Swartest night stretched over wretched men there.
> The ocean flowing backward, came we then to the place
> Aforesaid by Circe. (1/3)

We start this long poem sailing backwards, as it were, with Pound speaking in a voice not his own but belonging to a long-dead man-become-legend: Odysseus, brought down to us via Homer, Dante, Divus, Chapman, and others. We voyage back on a journey already foretold, back into the Anglo-Saxon roots of English (to a time when night was 'swart' instead of 'black'), back into a genre little suited for the twentieth century. As Noel Stock, Pound's authorized biographer, reports, Pound explained to his mother, in 1909, why he could not write an epic:

> The conditions necessary for an epic, he told her, were (1) the beautiful tradition, (2) a unity in the outline of that tradition, as was to be found in the *Odyssey*, (3) a Hero, mythical or historical, and (4) a 'damn long time for the story to lose its garish detail and get encrusted with a bunch of beautiful lies'.[14]

The journey against the current of history – until the poet finds himself among the 'cadaverous dead' – thus becomes a necessary condition for this writing. 'Out of key with his time', Pound had written in his mock-epitaph for 'E. P.', the poet interred in the first poem of 'Hugh Selwyn Mauberley'. This misfit poet 'passed from men's memory' at the beginning of 'Mauberley', allowing a motley assortment of moderns to take over the suite of poems.[15] But we might discover him or his near kin returning here in the guise of Elpenor, the 'unwept, unburied' oarsman of Canto I, whose voice is the first quoted speech in the *Cantos*. Elpenor takes a paradoxical precedence over Tiresias, and Anticlea, and hosts of heroes. He comes out of sequence: dead but not yet buried, able to speak even though the blood sacrifice has not been made for him. His drunken, accidental death is unworthy of a hero, and yet his importunate claims to speech allow him (like 'E. P.' in 'Mauberley') to compose his own epitaph. He asks that Odysseus write on his tomb: '*A man of no fortune, and with a name to come*' (1/4). His short speech, eight lines breaking into the second page of the first canto, occupies a position analogous to the *Cantos* itself – an utterance unbidden, indeed unwarranted, presumptuous and unlikely, not conventionally epic-heroic but nevertheless successful in claiming our attention and in at least partly setting the terms under which it will be understood.

In the *Odyssey* it is simply 'a cairn' Elpenor requests be built, after Odysseus and his men have seen to the burning of his body and possessions, 'an unknown sailor's mark for men to come'.[16] Pound's version – the tomb inscribed 'With a name to come' – stands similarly as a placeholder, a tribute to the anonymous, numerous company of the dead. It is in many ways comparable to the contemporaneously erected London Cenotaph (literally 'empty tomb') commemorating the dead of the First World War, first built in wood for the Allied Victory Parade (1919) and then, more permanently, in Portland Stone the next year, inscribed only with the phrase 'The Glorious Dead', standing for all those whose limbs have 'been cast on the wide earth', as Pound phrases it (1/4). War is traditionally at the heart of the epic. It is an occasion for heroic contests, and the gods' spectacular interventions in human affairs. Nations are made and broken in war; humans achieve such glory that they become worthy of song. The First World War finds its way into *The Waste Land*, *Ulysses*, and the *Cantos* not as an event that generates narrative and heroism but as an enormously powerful force of negation, of anti-enlightenment that produces corpses and blighted landscapes, that deforms bodies and poetry and gives us another plausible explanation for why the dead populate these works so thickly.

Anglo-American literary modernism, in its period of greatest achievements, is framed by the First and Second World Wars. Although I have characterized these years as a time in which traditional epics cannot be composed, the doubled cataclysm of the world wars ironically makes modernism a period especially hospitable to the martial aspects of the epic, even if the forms the genre takes must be reinvented. Pound's *Cantos* demonstrate this ancient though renegotiated contract between wars and the epic form in a number of ways. In his 1934 essay, 'Date Line', Pound had offered a formulation he was to repeat often in the years to come: 'An epic is a poem including history.'[17] Although it does not lay out its history in extended narrative form, the *Cantos* is a long poem that not only 'includes' history but, with increasing energy in the 1930s and during the Second World War, courts the events of history on virtually every page, seeking to affect those events and welcoming evidence of commerce between the poem and the world wherever such evidence can be discovered. One extraordinary, notorious outcome of this courtship is the *Pisan Cantos* (1948), substantial portions of which Pound wrote when he was imprisoned in a United States Army detention centre in the summer of 1945, held as a traitor awaiting extradition and trial for his pro-fascist broadcasts on Radio Rome during the Second World War. The political controversy that ensues when the Library of Congress chooses him, in 1948, to be the first recipient of the newly created Bollingen Prize for Poetry for this volume of cantos is so fierce and so widespread that the United States congress votes to end all further government connections to the award. This is a poem that is ultimately, fittingly violated by history-in-the-making.

Pound's refusal to rest content with merely writing a long poem, his desire to change the world around him, is reflected in the epic hero, as Pound conceives of him: above all things a man who exercises his will, who brings things to pass. 'The whole of the Divina Commedia', he writes in *Jefferson and/or Mussolini*, 'is a study of the "directio voluntatis."' [18] The willed ideas themselves matter, of course, and with increasing single-mindedness, from 1930 (when the first XXX cantos are published) until the Second World War, Pound dedicates his poem to an enormous project of enumerating and offering examples of good governance in theory and practice, taken primarily from American and Chinese history, with ventures into Renaissance Italy and with some counter examples that he hopes will serve to make his lessons even more clear. In a neo-Romantic (particularly Shelleyan) assertion of poets' importance to society, their often unsung ability to influence affairs of state and of culture (revealing his longstanding frustration about the lack of direct social power accorded to poets in the modern age), Pound writes excitedly: 'You put one of these ideas somewhere, i.e. somewhere in a definite space and time, and something begins to happen' (*Jefferson/Mussolini*, 21). 'Verse is a sword', he had written in the middle of the 1930s to John Masefield, the poet laureate of England, urging him as a poet – one of 'those who have the word in our keeping' – to take up his 'responsibility in the face of crass ignorance and of crass falsifications'. [19] It is hardly surprising that Pound embraces fascism in Italy, given the simplicity of the syllogism by which he evaluates political systems:

A good government is one that operates according to the best that is known and thought.
And the best government is that which translates the best thought most speedily into action . . .
Mussolini has a more responsive instrument [i.e. 'government'] than any other I can think of, something does appear to get started with 'bewildering frequency'. . . the BOSS does something about it.   (*Jefferson/Mussolini*, 91)

Arguing from these reductive terms, it follows that the Second World War will be 'about' bringing coherence to an unruly world. For Pound, 'hysterical Hitlerian yawping' occurs largely because most people are too witless to understand the appeal of fascism on a purely intellectual level; 'the Duce', he predicts in the early 1930s, 'will stand not with despots and

the lovers of power but with the lovers of ORDER' (127, 128). Pound's anti-
Semitism similarly offers him a spurious clarity: a simple 'cause' for the
effects he laments around him. The First World War revealed the corruptions at the heart both of monarchies and of liberal democracies and
displayed the symbiosis between capitalist economies and war. Fascist Italy
is showing the world the way to rectify these related corruptions, and the
next war occurs because moneyed interests and entrenched governments
cannot abide the change fascism represents. And Pound's epic, he comes to
believe during the 1930s, has been preparing a place in its pantheon for
Mussolini and his fascist programme since before Mussolini's seizing of
power in his March on Rome in 1922. Pound has constructed a work of
art that has foretold, partly created, and now intersects miraculously with
events unfolding as the writer writes.

His first epic hero in the *Cantos* was engaged in the active life, like
Mussolini and, to a lesser extent, like Pound himself. In the early cantos
focused on Sigismundo Malatesta (VIII–XI), Pound offers us a portrait of a
warrior who is part artist – a man of action and discriminating taste who
knows what it means to work in the trenches:

> We have had to dig a new ditch.
> In three or four days
> I shall try to set up the bombards.   (VIII/30)

But Malatesta also makes time for labour that promotes beauty – his
acquisition, say, of art for the temple he has built as a memorial to his
mistress, who became his third wife, Isotta degli Atti:

> Whose men, Sigismundo's, came with more than an hundred
> two wheeled ox carts and deported, for the beautifying
> of the *tempio* where was Santa Maria in Trivio
> Where the same are now on the walls.   (IX/36)

He is a mercenary whose often violent ends justify his means, whose plunder
turns out to be an act of preservation. His unfinished but praiseworthy
temple, erected on the foundations of an earlier church that is not destroyed
but incorporated in the later construction, arises in the most unlikely
circumstances. It is built by a man beset by conspiracies, betrayed throughout
his violent, opportunistic life:

> He, Sigismundo, *templum aedificavit*
> In Romagna, teeming with cattle thieves,
>> with the game lost in mid-channel,
> And never quite lost till '50
>> and never quite lost till the end, in Romagna.   (VIII/32)

His is the first extensive portrait in this poem of an epic hero, which is also to say, in this long poem that is often more personal, more private, more subjective than it desires to be, that Malatesta is one of Pound's reference points and avatars (and that Malatesta's beautiful, incomplete, heterogeneous *tempio* is one of the many analogues for the *Cantos* themselves). Lewis called Pound not an individual but 'a little crowd'.[20] One way to understand the assembly of acclaimed artists, politicians, philosophers, soldiers, engineers, economists, anthropologists, and others who throng this poem is that they are different aspects, different expressions of energies and capacities that Pound hopes to cultivate in himself and to discover in the world for which he writes. Thomas Jefferson, John Adams, Confucius, the poet's grandfather Thaddeus Pound, the Chinese emperors Yeou (Yao) and Yong Tching, and many others – all 'speak' through quoted documents in the pages of the *Cantos*, and also, Pound insists, find themselves expressed in one of their most active recent versions, Benito Mussolini.

Pound's selective form of historiography allows him to move among epochs and across geopolitical boundaries finding individuals who rhyme in essentials of character and deed. (Thus the startling link proposed in his title to his polemic: *Jefferson and/or Mussolini*.) Pound's poem is built around the principle of echo and repetition. Before his Canto I, Odysseus goes down to the ship many, many times in Western literature. An Italian troubadour, Sordello, is resurrected by Robert Browning in a Victorian epic poem and then brought back once more by Pound in Canto II. The perfect Median capital of Ecbatan, 'city of patterned streets' (V/17), can be glimpsed again in Troy, in Ithaca, in Rome, in the city of Wagadu (the legendary city of the Soninke people of Africa), and (figuratively, potentially) in the *Cantos* themselves as they attain their intended order. The Chinese ideogram, as Pound understands it, is a linguistic instance of Pound's historical and poetic method: a rhyming collection of particular instances, synchronically and diachronically intersecting in a single image. The example he cites most often is the Chinese character for the colour 'red', which is a representational amalgam of signs for 'rose', 'cherry', 'iron rust', and 'flamingo'. The making of a single ideogram from these different things, he explains, 'is very much the kind of thing a biologist does (in a very much more complicated way) when he gets together a few hundred or thousand slides, and picks out what is necessary for his general statement. Something that fits the case, that applies in all of the cases.'[21] Those last two conditions – fit and widespread applicability – are principles Pound uses as he combs through texts, muses over histories, reads the day's newspapers. His ideogram for 'ruler', or for 'epic hero', is one that would continue to accrue to itself all pertinent instances, and the unity of an epic celebrating such a constructive, constructed figure will come if we can see the similarities between the poet's assembly of different but related slides:

> The heritage of Jefferson, Quincy Adams, old John Adams, Jackson, Van Buren is HERE, NOW *in the Italian peninsula* at the beginning of fascist second decennio, not in Massachusetts or Delaware.   (*Jefferson/Mussolini*, 12)

'A second time' comes, 'HERE, NOW', into its most important but not quite its final phase of meaning. Not simply a phrase derived from an error of translation, nor only a sign of textual borrowing, the idea of repetition as Pound comes to understand it becomes a mode of understanding and evaluating history and taking sides in the present day. Perception of patterns across time is an ability common and essential to great artists and statesmen. Pound's poetry and prose is increasingly driven to display these patterns. As one reads the three volumes of cantos published between *A Draft of XXX Cantos* and the *Pisan Cantos*, it is easy to lose one's place in the long stretches of history Pound surveys, so familiar do its repetitions become:

> ten thousand brave men, ten thousand
> > desperate sieges
> > like bells or a ghazel   (LVIII/318)

A *ghazila*, the *Companion to the Cantos* tells us, is 'a form of Persian love poetry in couplets rhyming on the same sound: *aa, ab, ca*, etc'.[22] Like the pealing of bells, the tightly rhymed poetic form is a perfect simile for human behaviour and the panorama of history when parsed by this poet. Mussolini rhymes with Jefferson, and both rhyme with Confucius. Malatesta rhymes with Odysseus, and both are part of an unfinished *ghazila* composed over thousands of years by Homer, Divus, Pound, and others to come.

A related, though comic-grotesque version of this trans-historic vision occurs also near the end of the first part of *The Waste Land*, 'The Burial of the Dead', in a tellingly ambivalent encounter between a speaker and an acquaintance on the street:

> There I saw one I knew, and stopped him, crying: 'Stetson!
> You who were with me in the ships at Mylae!
> That corpse you planted last year in your garden,
> Has it begun to sprout? Will it bloom this year?
> Or has the sudden frost disturbed its bed?' (lines 69–73)

Stetson and the speaker inhabit the present day (the preceding lines in this stanza have described a contemporary scene on the London city streets) and also seem to have shared a boat in the battle at Mylae between the Carthaginians and the Romans in the First Punic War, in 260 BC. That battle may, in turn, echo some un-referenced naval conflict in the recently concluded war. The question about the sprouting corpse is a question Pound and Eliot (and Joyce and H. D. and Yeats and Frazer and Weston and many other moderns) ask of history: do the dead return? Is history patterned enough that we would recognize a sprouting corpse for what it is: the past become present, the 'mythic method' embodied? Joyce makes the method work figuratively throughout *Ulysses*, but Eliot's reference to the dead body, juxtaposed with his evocation of Mylae, might make us hesitate to welcome his version of new growth – of something actually returned from the past.

Pound gives us, early in his *Cantos*, an even more terribly literal version of what 'the mythic method' might look like if taken to its logical extreme – referring not only to art and mythic figures but to men and women in actual, historical time. When he came to power in the mid-fourteenth century, King Pedro of Portugal, whose mistress-become-wife, Ignez da Castro, had been murdered by his father before his son's accession to the throne, insisted that Ignez be exhumed and that his court pay homage to her corpse: 'Ignez da Castro murdered, and a wall / Here stripped, here made to stand' (III/12). It is a consequential moment for Pound at the beginning of his long 'poem including history', since it captures a fear of what the modern epic might look like if the animation of the past is incomplete or unsuccessful, if the various returns of the gods and historical men and women are only partly realized. The poet, like the obsessed King Pedro, would then preside over a failed epic that is little more than a collection of corpses. Pound imagines the important scene in more macabre detail at the end of *A Draft of XXX Cantos*:

> After Ignez was murdered.
>
> Came the Lords in Lisboa
>   a day, and a day
> In homage. Seated there
>   dead eyes,
> Dead hair under the crown,
> The King still young there beside her. (XXX/148)

The white spaces that surround every phrase in those middle three lines – silences, pauses, the equal but different stillness of the dead body, the stunned Lords, the crazy King – show us Pound's mastery of poetic form.

The grim tableau helps us to understand the horror and the fury with which Pound responded to the news that, on 28 April 1945, the current hero of his developing epic had, along with his mistress Clara Petacci, been shot and then hung by the heels and beaten by a crowd of Italian anti-fascist partisans, furious at their leader's betrayal of the nation. The actual, vital centre of Pound's poem, its chief 'artifex' (*Jefferson/Mussolini*, 34), who had literally been founding a new nation – who had, in other words, been planning and building in the present moment the 'patterned streets' Pound had been calling for in poetry and prose at least since Canto V – was now as dead as the murdered Ignez. His corpse presides over the first of the *Pisan Cantos*, the fact of his double execution adding yet another twist to the phrase – 'a second time' – I have used for organizing much of this chapter:

> The enormous tragedy of the dream in the peasant's bent shoulders
> Manes! Manes was tanned and stuffed,
> Thus Ben and la Clara *a Milano*
>   by the heels at Milano
> That maggots shd/ eat the dead bullock
> DIGONOS, Δίγονος, but the twice crucified
>   where in history will you find it?   (LXXIV/425/445)

Dionysus had been 'born' twice (*digonos* is Greek for 'twice born') – taken in embryo from his mother Semele after her death, carried to term and his second birth in the thigh of Zeus. The frenzied practices of his worshippers make him a god fit to preside over the lynching of Mussolini. Manes (Mani), the third-century AD Persian prophet who founded the gnostic religion Manicheanism (a theology whose dualism perfectly suits Pound's poem and habits of thought), suffers indignities after death. His being flayed, stuffed, and put on display links him associatively with the exhumed Ignes and the hanging 'Ben and la Clara'. But in an irony that the opening question insists we understand, Pound, searching for a pattern on to which he can graft this recent historical horror, is left without a rhyme for double death. It is the way of nature that maggots should eat the dead bull; it also seems to be natural that the mob will turn on its leaders. This scene of the small devouring the great is so common historically as to be the rule rather than the exception. And, in fact, Pound's case that this death is *sui generis* is not really convincing, since history is filled with public figures enduring repeated insults and assaults at the time of their deaths (the crucifixion of Jesus is itself augmented by scourging beforehand and a centurion's spear in Christ's side when he hangs on the cross).

But Pound's 'twice crucified', like his earlier phrase 'a second time', is on one level not concerned with accuracy. It is an intensifier, a multiplying of force, a claim for significance. With the death of *Il Duce*, or 'The Boss', as Pound often called him, this epic-in-progress has lost its heart and its possibility for becoming something of more weight than a poem. It can no longer prepare the way for and help usher into being a new nation, a pattern for the modern world. The most painful word in this canto's first line, it could be argued, is 'dream', since it signals the first of many retreats that mark the

Pisan Cantos and the later volumes of Pound's poem. The inarticulate peasant, whose bent body Pound reads for us, is now condemned only, and not
even consciously, to dream of something better than the labour under which
he stoops. The rage in these opening lines comes from a poet who has been
driven by circumstances back from affairs of state (or from the illusion that he
was part of those affairs) into the limited confines of his dreams. He is left
with rhetoric rather than power, with brutal verbs: 'tanned and stuffed';
deliberately ugly phrases 'maggots shd / eat the dead bullock'; exclamations
and repetition: 'Manes! Manes' '*a Milano* . . . at Milano' – as though his
disbelief compels him to say the city's name twice, once in Italian and once in
English, just as it caused him to shout Manes's name and to claim unique
status for the death of his hero and his hero's beloved.

He turns then for consolation to an imagined audience – some Horatio
who will report the case aright to the one other witness who might understand and care, once again showing sincerity through repetition: 'yet say this
to the Possum: a bang, not a whimper, / with a bang not with a whimper'.
The comparative intimacy of the old nickname for Eliot introduces us to one
of the most important strands of the *Pisan Cantos* and of the cantos to
follow: memory, particularly memory of a time when Pound and modernism
were both young and vigorous, in London and Paris, in the nineteen-teens
and -twenties, becomes increasingly central to this poem. This fact ironically
testifies to a certain kind of defeat in Pound's epic project, since the goal of
his poem has been not merely to record 'the growth of a poet's mind' or to
quote from the poems of his literary compatriots. The nature of this allusion,
too, to the parodic, surreal conclusion of 'The Hollow Men' (1925), a poem
in which Eliot had anatomized the absurdity and paralysis of modern
men and women, hardly makes an unequivocal case for the dignified end
of the *era fascista*. One of Eliot's epigraphs for his poem, 'A penny for the
Old Guy', and the scarecrows that lean together in its first stanza may even
recall Manes and the corpses of Mussolini and Clara Petacci.

With the abrupt shift in the next lines, we come to another major poetic
register of the later cantos. From this point forward, Pound's lyrical-meditative
strain will become an increasingly necessary antidote to the frustrations of
history and contemporary politics. He will write more poetry about natural
processes, sometimes shifting into a mystical-allegorical realm; he will often
cultivate a Confucian balance, on a formal as well as a philosophical level.
All of these modes are on display as Pound moves from political fury and
wounded memory to temporary acceptance:

> To build the city of Dioce whose terraces are the colour of stars.
> The suave eyes, quiet, not scornful,
> > rain also is of the process. (LXXIV/425/445)

The city is not Rome, now, but Ecbatan, capital of Media under Deioces, almost as far in the past as the stars are from earth. The lovely eyes will appear again to Pound in moments of blessing – eyes of goddesses, manifestations of forgiveness and *eros*, emblems of reconciliation and generative power. 'The process', a phrase Pound holds to like a compass in this time of lost directions, derives from Confucius's *The Unwobbling Pivot*, which Pound was then translating, and refers to something like 'fate' or 'direction': 'the inborn nature' of all things.[23] The plea that ends canto LXXXIII, in its broken refrain and self-pitying exhaustion, sounds like a moment shared by Lear, Kent, and Edgar on the heath:

> Down, Derry-down /
> Oh let an old man rest. (LXXXIII/536/556)

Pound had ardently hoped that his ideas about government would be underwritten by Mussolini's regime; now his own precarious condition ironically provides his poem with a ballast of reality and an emotional impact that it had lacked for much of the previous decade. Allied bombers perform the same service for his late invocation of Malatesta's *tempio* that is again under siege, in Pound's own century (LXXVI/459/479), having been severely damaged by bombs in late 1943 and early 1944. Like the sacrificial blood in Canto I, the Second World War brings the past back into the present.[24]

The apotheosis of Pound's epic lies in this paradox: that the poem increases in aesthetic and emotional force and makes more compelling claims on its readers as its subject turns to what, from Pound's point of view, must in significant respects be understood as his poem's failures. Had Pound's attempt at an epic ended with his *Draft of XXX Cantos*, or with the summaries of history and the assorted lessons on economics and government in the thirties cantos, or had circumstances allowed it to conclude with the triumphant establishment of a fascist state in Italy after the war, the *Cantos* would be less substantial, his place in the history of modern poetry less assured. Pound's often anguished assessment of his project ('Many errors, / a little rightness', CXVI/797/817) generates much that is best and most enduring in the *Pisan Cantos* and the three volumes and the fragments that follow. His painful introspection on the wheel of fire to which he has condemned himself – 'the mind as Ixion, unstill, ever turning' (CXIII/790/810) – carries him and his reader into human failure, remorse, anger at himself and others; it also generates some of the most gorgeous poetry of the poem.

Pound, writing the last cantos of his poem when he is in his seventies and eighties, considering his achievements but also dwelling on his intemperance, his credulous embrace of violent political programmes, his anti-Semitism, his 'pride, jealousy and possessiveness' (CXIII/787/807), finds he has much to atone for. He subjects himself, late in his life, to what Eliot, in 'Little Gidding', calls 'the rending pain of re-enactment' (another inflection for the phrase 'a second time', this one forced upon us by age). And he finds that, with a host of memories collected around him, much blood having flowed in the fosse since he began his epic in 1915, he would do best now simply to let go of all that he has gathered into this poem:

> I have tried to write Paradise
>
> Do not move
>   Let the wind speak
>   that is paradise.
>
> Let the Gods forgive what I
>   have made
> Let those I love try to forgive
>   what I have made. (CXX/803/822)

Depending on which edition of the *Cantos* we are reading, these may be the last lines of the poem, or the volume may end with the tellingly titled 'Notes for CXVII et seq.', which is filled with observations and blessings of nature and ends with a prayer for a goal only occasionally achieved in human history: 'To be men not destroyers'. The third conclusion to this long poem, used in the most recent American edition, is titled 'Fragment (1966)'. Pound sent it to James Laughlin, at New Directions Press, in 1966. After a homage to his mistress, Olga, Pound adds a note, also in poetry, that instructs editors and readers to keep his beloved's name at the end of whatever collection of poetry the *Cantos* comprise at any point in the future:

>   That her acts
>   Olga's acts
>   of beauty
>   be remembered.
>
>   Her name was Courage
>   & is written Olga
>
> These lines are for the
>   ultimate CANTO
>
> whatever I may write
>   in the interim. [24 August 1966] (824)

By writing this proleptic conclusion, Pound has solved a problem that variously vexes all modern epics: given the lack of cultural, theological, and political coherence in the world, and given a prevailing disbelief in forms of intervention that would stop or rearrange time and reveal pattern instead of mere motion, how can a long poem including history be brought to a satisfactory conclusion? Pound's other two endings are, beautifully, cantos of prayer and self-renunciation. This ending for Olga also turns our attention away from Pound. And it ties a knot in time, suturing one specific moment, '24 August 1966', to the point when each of us reaches the end of a book we have been reading, its contents not quite settled, called *The Cantos of Ezra Pound*. Pound might be said to have taken the second clause of Elpenor's epitaph from the first canto – 'and with a name to come' – and given it, in this testament, to his beloved. Meanwhile, Pound and the rest of us write and read and live in the interim, the unredeemed time, during which we follow the uneven but compelling rhythms of memory and desire, sometimes asking our own versions of a question Pound poses in one of his late cantos, 'How came beauty against this blackness . . .?' (CXVI/796/816).

NOTES

1 *The Cantos of Ezra Pound* (New York: New Directions, 1995). Passages from Pound's *Cantos* are cited by canto number and page number. From the *Pisan Cantos* forward, because of the addition of cantos LXXII–LXXIII to this most recent edition of the *Cantos*, the page numbers have changed from the hardback edition (1972). For citations of the later cantos, I include page references to both currently available editions of Pound's poem (1972/1995).

2 T. S. Eliot, *Selected Essays* (New York: Harcourt Brace Jovanovich, 1950), 6.

3 William Wordsworth, *The Prelude, or Growth of a Poet's Mind*, ed. Ernest de Selincourt, revised by Helen Darbishire, 2nd edn (Oxford: Oxford University Press, 1959), xxxv. Quotations from the poem are from the 1850 text.

4 Virginia Woolf, *The Diary of Virginia Woolf*, ed. Anne Olivier Bell and Andrew McNeillie (New York: Harcourt Brace Jovanovich, 1982), vol. IV, 127.

5 W. B. Yeats, *The Poems*, ed. Richard J. Finneran, rev. edn (New York: Macmillan, 1989), 240.

6 All references to *The Waste Land* are taken from T. S. Eliot, *The Complete Poems and Plays: 1909–1950* (New York: Harcourt, Brace and World, 1971).

7 Walter Pater, *The Renaissance: Studies in Art and Poetry*, ed. Donald Hill (Berkeley: University of California Press, 1980), 186.

8 *The Letters of Ezra Pound:1907–1941*, ed. D. D. Paige (New York: Harcourt, Brace and Company, 1950), 169.

9 Edgar Allen Poe, 'The Philosophy of Composition', *Essays and Reviews* (New York: Library of America, 1984), 15.

10 Hilda Doolittle (H.D.), *Collected Poems: 1912–1944*, ed. Louis L. Martz (New York: New Directions, 1983). I cite passages from *Trilogy* by canto and page number.

11 T. S. Eliot, 'Ulysses, Order and Myth', *Dial* 70.5 (November 1923): 480–3, 483.

12 Wyndham Lewis, *Time and Western Man*, ed. Paul Edwards (Santa Rosa, CA: Black Sparrow Press, 1993), 69.

13 See Ronald Bush, *The Genesis of Ezra Pound's Cantos* (Princeton: Princeton University Press, 1976), 69–70.

14 Noel Stock, *The Life of Ezra Pound* (San Francisco: North Point Press, 1982), 76.

15 Ezra Pound, *Personae* (New York: New Directions, 1926), 187.

16 *The Odyssey*, trans. Robert Fitzgerald (Garden City, NY: Anchor Books, 1963), 11.42–3.

17 *Literary Essays of Ezra Pound*, ed. T. S. Eliot (New York: New Directions, 1954), 86.

18 Ezra Pound, *Jefferson and/or Mussolini* (London: Stanley Nott, 1935), 17.

19 'Verse is a Sword: Unpublished Letters of Ezra Pound', ed. Noel Stock, *X: A Quarterly Review* 1 (1960): 258–65.

20 Lewis, *Time and Western Man*, 68.

21 Ezra Pound, *ABC of Reading* (Norfolk, CT: New Directions, 1951), 22.

22 Carroll F. Terrell, *A Companion to the Cantos of Ezra Pound*, 2 vols. (Berkeley: University of California Press, 1980, 1984), vol. I, 248.

23 Ezra Pound, trans., *Confucius* (New York: New Directions, 1969), 99.

24 See Lawrence S. Rainey, *Ezra Pound and the Monument of Culture: Text, History, and the Malatesta Cantos* (Chicago: University of Chicago Press, 1991), 209–13.

13

ROBERT HAMNER

Derek Walcott's *Omeros*

Centuries of critical study have established a working consensus regarding the standard components of the classical epic. At the same time, centuries of writers have produced subtle changes and experimental variations so that this venerable genre turns out to be more flexible than academic purists might prefer. As early as Dante, the elevated heritage of the epic managed to survive the insertion of the poet as a participant in the action. Later the definition has been expanded in order to accommodate the prose of Melville and then Joyce, with common seamen or citizens of Dublin as protagonists. Over time the idea of heroic action has undergone serious re-evaluation, and our postmodern age questions the legitimacy of any hierarchical literary canon.

Against this fluid background, Derek Walcott published his extended West Indian narrative poem, *Omeros*, in 1990. Whereas predecessors in the epic field might depend upon a cohesive national, racial, or spiritual framework, Walcott assembles his story out of the detritus of imperial exploitation and colonial neglect. Born on the tiny island of St Lucia in the Lesser Antilles (1930), the mulatto descendant of European masters and African slaves, he writes of fragmented cultures and uprooted peoples dealing with life in their marginalized corner of the world. With such an unpromising point of departure, the initial challenge is in drawing out the relevance of their struggle. On this point Walcott is explicit. 'The conceit behind history, the conceit behind art, is its presumption to be able to elevate the ordinary, the common, and therefore the phenomenon. That's the sequence: the ordinary and therefore the phenomenon, not the phenomenon and therefore its cause. But that's what life is really like . . . it is the ordinariness, not the astonishment, that is the miracle.'[1] Elsewhere he tells interviewers that he expects his deliberate evocation of Homer in the title and multiple allusions to the *Odyssey, Iliad*, and *Ulysses* to distract scholars from his central focus. All the classical paraphernalia eventually proves an ironic point. What he wants in his poem is to recapture something of the vigour and elation, the vulgar, lurid reality of Homer's Greece before its lionization through history and art. 'The freshness, the truth of the Archipelago . . . has nothing to do with the figure that we call Homer.'[2] *Omeros* is written in homage to the islands of the Caribbean and their down-to-earth people, who live beautifully without commemoration in historical monuments or literary masterpieces.

Characterization and motive

To enact his story, Walcott offers a cast of primary characters in roughly three categories. The St Lucian peasantry is represented by a black Helen, with her two suitors, Hector and Achille. One of their companions, Philoctete, recalls Homeric Philoctetes in the incurable festering sore that often leaves him in isolation. Walcott makes it clear that his is a racial wound, a communal affliction that requires spiritual as well as physical healing. In this circle is also the shopkeeper, Ma Kilman, who, because of her powers in sorcery, is associated with St Lucia's cloud-topped Mount La Sorcière. A second category of characters is represented by a pair of British colonialists who settled in St Lucia shortly after the Second World War: Sergeant Major (retired) Dennis Plunkett and his wife, Maud. Yet a third category comprises two multi-dimensional figures. One is the blind, itinerant Seven Seas, or Old St Omere (Omeros). The second transcendent character is the Walcott narrator who, like Seven Seas, interacts with the islanders on occasion, travels back and forth in time, and often steps beyond the margins for intertextual commentary on the action.

Helen is the heart of this tale even more than her Greek counterpart in the *Iliad* and the *Odyssey*. Not only is she the object of the conflict between Hector and Achille on the peasant level of the story, but the plight of this beautiful black woman who once served as maid to the Plunketts inspires the immigrant Major to undertake writing the history of her island. Above all, her central role is guaranteed when the poet/narrator presents her as the embodiment of St Lucia. Island children are taught in school that St Lucia is ' "The Helen Of The West" because she was fought for so often by the French and British'.[3] Western enterprise has thus subordinated the island to foreign designs, even imposing classical names within the population. Descendants of slaves forcibly transplanted from Africa at best can claim only rootless genealogical branches. Consequently, no small part of Helen's symbolic function is to raise the complicated issue of posterity. She is pregnant, suspended between Hector and Achille, and unsure of her expected child's paternity. In undertaking her island's story, Major Plunkett wishes to right the wrongs of history, but at the same time diligent research fills a void in his marriage. As immigrants he and Maud have voluntarily severed roots with their European heritage, but more significantly their marriage has produced no offspring. Unanticipated compensation arises when records connected with Helen's history lead to the name of a young midshipman Plunkett, who died during the famous Battle of the Saints back in 1782. Thus coincidence ties the Major to the island through the blood of an 'adopted' son. Complementing this familial aspect of character motivation, Walcott introduces the ghost of his father, Warwick, who died when he and his twin brother, Roderick, were barely a year old. Through this ghostly reunion, Walcott acknowledges his rudimentary artistic inspiration: his father undertook poetry, painting, and drawing in this small island. The son now extends Warwick's ambition.

Appropriately, the ancestral thread weaves through the love triangle of Helen, Hector and Achille. While he despairs over apparently losing Helen to Hector, Achille experiences a sunstroke-induced trance returning him to an African village where he encounters Afolabe, the tribal father who has been lost in time through slavery. At first, this discovery links Achille as never before to the African-influenced culture of his native island, but it ultimately strengthens his personal attachment to Helen. At the end of the narrative, after Hector's death in an automobile accident and Helen has returned to Achille, we learn through Ma Kilman that her unborn child is Hector's. By this time, however, that uncertainty is irrelevant. Achille has been reconciled with his late rival, accepted Helen once more, and wishes to raise their child under an African name.

Obviously these unassuming villagers lack the stature usually associated with epics. Of the major characters, only one needs no lineal ancestor or offspring, because he embodies a crucial literary ancestor. The blind Seven Seas/Omeros, in keeping with Walcott's image of the vagabond Homeric poet of the Aegean, is of the peasant class; but he is a timeless figure, a sightless witness to the broad human struggle. He can materialize as an African griot (bard), a Native American shaman on a Sioux reservation in the 1890s, elsewhere as the animated statue of Homer in a St Lucian inferno. Speaking of his attachment to these assorted villagers, Walcott tells D. J. R. Bruckner, 'The whole book is an act of gratitude. It is a fantastic privilege to be in a place in which limbs, features, smells, the lineaments and presence of the people are so powerful . . . One reason I don't like talking about an epic is that I think it is wrong to try to ennoble people . . . And just to write history is wrong. History makes similes of people, but these people are their own nouns.'[4] Regardless of their marginal existence, one of Walcott's primary objectives is to demonstrate that they do not have to be heroic in stature to be significant.

Form and structure

Walcott's pointed objection to epic pretensions is in keeping with his reservations regarding history and art. As he explains in 'Reflections on *Omeros*', it is presumptuous for a writer to think that his work somehow elevates the ordinary.[5] Having denied heroic proportions to his characters, he creates a dilemma in recounting their interlocking stories. On the one hand, both the Major and the narrative persona feel inspired to exonerate Helen. On the other, that goal implies the inadequacy of her actuality. Central to the development of the poem is the resolution of this problem. In traditional order, the movement toward that essential clarification begins in the midst of things, pursues the several conflicts, and closes on a note of elemental continuity.

Omeros is composed of sixty-four consecutively numbered chapters of three cantos each, distributed over seven books. The pattern of loose hexametrical three-line stanzas resembles Dante's terza rima form without maintaining the standard interlocking rhyme scheme.[6] In fact, Walcott employs such a variety of permutations on near and multiple rhymes that Brad Leithauser concludes *Omeros* might well serve as a casebook on rhyme.[7] The lyrical play of tropes and analogies ensures a measure of sensual and imaginative unity. However, as to the larger scale of action, Walcott deliberately avoids a pattern of linear development. He chooses instead to move about geographically and chronologically, advancing various plotlines in segments. Form and content thus reinforce each other, suggesting the multifaceted and broken history of the West Indies.

The opening scene involves Philoctete, already healed of his wound, soliciting tourist money by telling about fishermen ritualistically converting trees into the pirogues (dugout canoes) that are necessary to sustain their way of life. The story then elides into the actions of fishermen cutting and shaping new pirogues back when Philoctete suffered alone, unable to accompany his friends when they leave the shore. As with his Greek namesake, Philoctete's role is communal. His wound represents the affliction of his race. His anchor-shaped lesion, located where shackles might have eaten into a man's flesh, evokes the Atlantic crossing that reduced their ancestors to slaves. Significantly, Philoctete is the centre of the only political scene in the poem. While he campaigns on behalf of Maljo versus Compton, he regrets the factions dividing his countrymen. The carnivalesque atmosphere of the contest – language flavoured with puns, wry humour, and exaggerations typical of calypso contests – cannot detract from Philoctete's concern for his island. As he travels from village to village, he longs for reconciliation:

> Why couldn't they love the place, same way, together,
> the way he always loved her, even with his sore?
> Love Helen like a wife in good and bad weather.[8]

In the sequence of healings that take place in the poem, it is significant that Philoctete's comes first. Ma Kilman discovers the lost African herb necessary to the seawater bath in which he must be baptized; and his transformation reflects not only the physical curing of his shin, but the restoration of pride, overcoming centuries of loss and pain (246–8). His is not one of the leading roles, yet after the burden lifts from his shoulders, the way is cleared for others; just as in Greek mythology Philoctetes's cure and reinstatement were necessary for victory over Troy.

Although the central struggle in *Omeros* does not pit nation against warring nation, the human scope is nonetheless expansive for being couched in personal terms. Only a few pages into *Omeros*, the fishermen about whom Philoctete began speaking are seen launching their pirogues for another day on the sea. On this particular morning, Hector picks a fight with Achille over the possession of a rusty bailing tin. The real point of contention, however, traces back to their desire to win Helen. Her elusiveness motivates both men in different directions. Although in a moment of anger she leaves Achille to live with Hector, he never feels that she belongs to him. In order to impress her, Hector gives up the sea to drive a taxi, the Comet, like a madman across the treacherous mountains of the island. His occupational change brings money, but at great cost:

> A man who cursed the sea had cursed his own mother.
> Mer was both mother and sea. (231)

The crucial event for Achille, as he yearns to reclaim Helen, takes the form of a sunstroke-induced voyage back in time to tribal Africa.

While he and his mate sail farther out than their usual fishing grounds, Achille falls into a trance. There he is drawn by a sea-swift, reversing the slavers' Middle Passage to Africa. In the crossing he envisions drowned generations of nameless brothers, then a midshipman Plunkett, and at the spectre of his father's face, 'for the first time, he asked himself who he was' (128, 130). Eventually landing before an African river village, he recognizes his own facial lineaments in Afolabe, his tribal ancestor. Afolabe asks if his newly found son knows the meaning of the name he now bears. When he cannot answer, Afolabe explains that men without names have no substance, cast no shadow:

> 'And therefore, Achille, if I pointed and I said, There
> is the name of that man, that tree, and this father,
> would every sound be a shadow that crossed your ear,
>
> without the shape of a man or a tree? What would it be?'
> (And just as branches sway in the dusk from their fear
> of amnesia, of oblivion, the tribe began to grieve). (138)

The gravity of that amnesia weighs both on the forgotten tribesmen and on their vanished children.

At this point, Walcott reverses a crucial fortune-telling scene from Virgil's *Aeneid*. Whereas Anchises in Hades foretells his son's founding of glorious Rome, Walcott's Achille, knowing what lies ahead, protectively conceals from his forefather the degrading future of slavery. As a result of his visionary dream, however, Achille now has his amnesia erased, relearning the rituals of his forgotten race, recognizing elements of his own island's dances and musical instruments:

> the same chac-chac and ra-ra, the drumming the same,
> and the chant of the seed-eyed prophet the same
> response from the blurring ankles. The same, the same. (143)

He witnesses a neighbouring tribe capture prisoners to sell as slaves, hears the village griot's doleful litany, and retraces three hundred years of the Atlantic passage to the shore he has known from childhood. In spite of the bleakness, however, Achille comes to a realization that might well provide the epigraph for *Omeros*:

> But they crossed, they survived. There is the epical splendour.
> Multiply the rain's lances, multiply their ruin,
> the grace born from subtraction . . . (149)

Out of that dream, Achille emerges more whole than he has ever been, more worthy of Helen and all she represents. During Achille's protracted absence, Helen also undergoes transformation. Her longing for Achille draws out time until she waits, 'Not Helen now, but Penelope' (153). The indecisiveness suspending her between rival suitors gives way and one must prevail. Hector, cut off from the life-giving sea, sensing Helen's true feelings, loses control of his Comet and dies off a narrow mountain road. At his funeral, Achille pays tribute to a respected companion, laying on his grave an oar and the same bailing cup over which they once almost came to blows.

The third major subplot is launched as early as the fifth chapter, as Dennis Plunkett glimpses Helen passing by in a striking yellow dress that once belonged to Maud. Her attitude, pride, had already caused her dismissal from their household:

> Her head was lowered; she seemed to drift like a waif,
> not like the arrogant servant that ruled their house.
> It was at that moment that he felt a duty
>
> towards her hopelessness, something to redress
> (he punned relentlessly) that desolate beauty
> so like her island's. He drained the foaming Guinness.

. . .

> He smiled at the mythical hallucination
> that went with the name's shadow; the island was once
> named Helen; its Homeric association

> rose like smoke from a siege; the Battle of the Saints
> was launched with that sound, from what was the 'Gibraltar
> of the Caribbean', after thirteen treaties.   (29–30, 31)

Duty is important to Plunkett, having served under Montgomery in Africa. He, like Philoctete also bears a scar, his from a head wound suffered in battle that led him to Maud, his nurse, who became his wife. Their decision to leave the metropolitan centre and settle in one of the small corners of the waning British Empire requires a delicate balancing act. One manifestation of Plunkett's old wound is another kind of racial insecurity. Guilt as well as duty prompts his obligation to Helen.

As a structural component, Plunkett's role is not only to represent the white presence in Caribbean life but to interrogate established Western values. There is no amnesia for a representative of the ruling class. His research, however, leads him to reorient the established version of history. As a Sergeant Major he expresses contempt for higher officers, and he ridicules the 'phony pukka tones of ex-patriates' at the local Victoria club (25). His being a pig farmer also affords another of Walcott's subtle epic allusions. When Odysseus finally makes landfall back in Ithaca, it is his faithful swine-herd Eumaios who gives him shelter and assists in restoring his kingdom. If there is no throne to reclaim for Helen, Plunkett can still assemble the facts about the British victory in the Battle of the Saints to establish her broader significance. His enthusiasm can be sweeping when he imagines 'Homeric coincidence'. On one occasion he calls to Maud:

> 'Look, love, for instance,
> near sunset, on April 12, hear this, the *Ville de Paris*

> struck her colours to Rodney. Surrendered. Is this chance
> or an echo? Paris gives the golden apple, a war is
> fought for an island called Helen?' – clapping conclusive hands.   (100)

Moreover, there is his Plunkett namesake among the recorded fatalities to give him a blood tie with her island's history.

Just as Plunkett's England, Maud's Ireland, and Achille's African roots suggest disparate sources of West Indian culture, their story lines regularly feed into each other. Midshipman Plunkett, before his duty in the Caribbean, had conducted reconnaissance for Admiral Rodney in the Netherlands. One of the slaves involved in fortifying St Lucia against the French was born Afolabe. It is Rodney who renames him Achilles. As simply as that, a classical allusion replaces an African name eventually to be Creolized in local pronunciation to 'A-sheel'. Late in the story – Achille and Helen rejoined, Philoctete now healed – Achille shares with Helen from his dream the African meanings behind the island ceremonies they have been practising in ignorance for generations (275). When Maud dies, her funeral unites the community across racial lines. In attendance at the service, the authorial persona wonders at Achille's obvious empathy for the stricken Plunkett: 'Where was it from, this charity of soul . . .?' (265). In the depths of his suffering, the Major seeks Ma Kilman's spiritual intervention. At their séance, when Ma Kilman assures him Maud is now in a green place near a silver lake, he imagines Glen-da-Lough in her beloved Ireland, and knows 'That moment bound him for good to another race' (307). His lingering wound eases, he appreciates a new closeness to his workmen and, most significant for the narrative core of *Omeros*, he recognizes the fallacy of his attitude toward Helen. She certainly needs no historical validation: 'when he thought of Helen / she was not a cause or a cloud, only a name / for a local wonder' (309). Her existence is sufficient without reference to another culture's monuments or achievements.

For much of the coalescence of movements in *Omeros*, Ma Kilman is a major force. As with the rest of her countrymen, fragmented cultures drift through her mind. When she overhears the unintelligible mutterings of Old St Omere, the words 'were Greek to her. Or old African babble' (18). Although she regularly attends Mass, remnants of lost African gods retain their subtle influence beneath the rituals and teaching of Catholicism. Her concern for Philoctete's suffering draws her mind back to ancient African folk remedies, but the ingredients elude her until on the way to Mass one evening a trail of ants draws her off course and into the mountains. They lead her to a foul-smelling, anchor-shaped plant, the seed of which had been carried by a swift from Africa and ejected onto the island's soil (239). Reverting to lost homeopathic arts, Ma Kilman performs the rites necessary to claim the power of the transplanted herb. In the scene, generations are conjured up as she is thrown into gyrations eliciting both the obeah-women of the New World and the sibyl of ancient Cumae (245). Newly attuned to the curative influence of her forgotten predecessors, Ma Kilman proceeds to release Philoctete from his affliction as she would later minister to the needs of Dennis Plunkett. As the poem draws to a close, many of the villagers gather in her No Pain Café. There Ma Kilman reveals that Helen's child comes from Hector; there Seven Seas/Omeros promises 'We shall all heal' (319). The grace note of the final scene evokes transcendence within the ordinary. After a long day of fishing, when Achille cleans up his equipment before returning home to Helen we are assured, 'When he left the beach the sea was still going on' (325).

Narrative perspective

An epic comprises more than performers of feats and unfolding action. Regardless of Walcott's insistence that his authorial intrusions disqualify *Omeros* as an epic, a storyteller's perspective, no matter how 'objective' or remote, must have its place.[9] In *Omeros*, the shaping voice rises to the surface early, is explicit, and integral to the overall experience of the poem. In time-honoured fashion, Walcott has points to make. If *Omeros* has elements of didacticism, it is simply in a more secular mode than the *Divine Comedy* or *Paradise Lost*, where the ghost of Virgil or an angel materializes to guide Dante or Milton's Adam towards enlightenment and salvation. It is significant, because of his frequent epic denials, that in his first authorial intervention, Walcott introduces a West Indian etymology for his title. After his Greek lover instructs him in the authentic pronunciation for Homer's name, 'O-meros', he muses:

> and O was the conch-shell's invocation, *mer* was
> both mother and sea in our Antillean patois,
> *os*, a grey bone, and the white surf as it crashes
>
> and spreads its sibilant collar on a lace shore.   (14)

Walcott first steps among his peasant characters when he simultaneously witnesses with Major Plunkett Helen's momentous entrance on the beach (23). Subsequently, both men launch their tributes to this striking woman – one historical, the other literary, the very poem we are reading. Providing background for Plunkett also brings the first intertextual aside regarding the author's creative intention:

> This wound I have stitched into Plunkett's character.
> He has to be wounded, affliction is one theme
> of this work, this fiction, since every 'I' is a
>
> fiction finally. Phantom narrator, resume.   (28)

The account he resumes integrates elements of his putative autobiography into the design of the poem and occasionally into his representative characters. His is another of the journeys to be undertaken toward healing and deeper understanding.

Chapter 12 introduces one of the most basic influences on Walcott's career, the remnants of verse and painting left behind by his late father.

The appearance of Warwick's ghost, frozen at the age of his death, presents a conundrum. With a son twice Warwick's age carrying on his avocation, the question arises, whose verse, whose calling does he follow. The answer: ' "Sir" – I swallowed – "they are one voice" '. Affinities carry over in their shared appreciation for coincidences and puns. Warwick toys with the fact that his name is the same as William Shakespeare's home county; his 'Will' left to Derek is the 'foreign machinery known as Literature'. Moreover, Warwick died on Shakespeare's birth date, of a disease 'like Hamlet's old man's spread from an infected ear . . . Death imitating Art, eh?' (68, 69). Of greater consequence for the advancement of the poem, Warwick's ghost duplicates the role Anchises served his son Aeneas: enunciating his calling. Conjuring up images from Walcott's childhood of remarkable black women hauling baskets of coal up gangways of merchant ships in the harbour of Castries, Warwick delivers his charge:

> Kneel to your load, then balance your staggering feet
> and walk up that coal ladder as they do in time,
> one bare foot after the next in ancestral rhyme.
>
> . . . and your duty
>
> from the time you watched them from your grandmother's house
> as a child wounded by their power and beauty
> is the chance you now have, to give those feet a voice.   (75–6)

Pointedly, Walcott's mission is not to serve an empire, but to give utterance to the overlooked worthiness of the disenfranchised upon whose backs empires have been built.

The African bloodline is only half of Walcott's mulatto heritage. He editorializes during Achille's African dream that half of him is with Achille, the other half with Midshipman Plunkett in the Netherlands (135). St Lucia's location in the New World also prompts acknowledgment of the influence of North American history. Life and the poem explicitly follow parallel paths as Book 3 ends with the poet departing for Boston; below his plane is Achille's lateen sail bearing for Gros Islet village (168). Book 4 opens in Brookline, Massachusetts, where Walcott lived while teaching at Boston University. His persona is suffering the pangs of divorce, so that grief and loneliness eventually find imaginative outlet in the plight of Native Americans and Catherine Weldon, a sympathizer who abandoned her white privileges in the east to cast her lot with Sitting Bull and his starving Sioux people in the Dakotas.[10] In keeping with his other characters, the poet is also afflicted, bearing his own wounds from divorce, but he retains a sense of proportion. In his mind the many government treaties broken with the tribes and his own tattered marriage vows materialize as falling snow on the western plains.

Walcott's odyssey turns eastwards at the close of Book 4, prompted by the second appearance of Warwick's shade. Having previously verbalized his son's artistic obligations, Warwick now directs him to tour the storied sites of the Old World, Lisbon, London, Dublin, the Aegean. His objective is pointed:

> 'Once you have seen everything and gone everywhere,
> cherish our island for its green simplicities,
> . . .
> . . . The sea-swift vanishes in rain,
>
> and yet in its travelling all that the sea-swift does
> it does in a circular pattern. Remember that, son'.   (187–8)

The advice bears fruit. Upon his return to the island, his perspective undergoes a crucial change. His conversion anticipates that of Dennis Plunkett as he begins to recognize self-centredness in his devotion to Helen. He wonders,

> . . . Didn't I want the poor
> to stay in the same light so that I could transfix
> them in amber, the afterglow of an empire . . .?   (227)

He and Plunkett were both wrong in imposing their designs on Helen (271). Their kinship is deeper than ideological, as well. Among the figures he has created, Walcott confides that there are vestiges of Plunkett in his father, Maud in his mother, and Telemachus in him (263). Embedded in the elaborate fictional expressions is a core of reality. At last, the epic paraphernalia must be cleared away in order to seize the authentic properties of Caribbean life. This growing conviction is reinforced during an encounter with the animated statue of Omeros. Walcott's reincarnation of Homer is sage but amiable, and conversant in the local patois. In discussing the underlying motive of heroic poetry, his mentor admits the Trojan War was an excuse for an epic, and while the love of a woman is good, 'the love of your own people is greater' (284). Furthermore, Omeros informs him that his life has pursued two journeys: one carrying him through great cities of the world while the other remained motionless involving a desk, paper, and pen:

> 'Therefore, this is what this island has meant to you,
> why my bust spoke, why the sea-swift was sent to you:
> to circle yourself and your island with this art'.   (291)

The walking statue then leads the narrator through the purgatorial inferno of volcanic Soufrière's crater on the west coast of the island, so that his vision is finally clarified.

In the end, the poet admits the vanity of his objectification of Helen. Achille will never be able to read this poem, but he lives an inoffensive, fruitful life, and that is sufficient. No matter what Walcott can give to his native island as son and artist, all pales in comparison with what the archipelago has given him. For his purposes, Walcott attempts neither to copy nor to parody Homeric tradition. Gregson Davis convincingly argues that his rhetorical disavowal of epic formulae is itself a classical ploy: setting the reader 'a generic foil to the poet's articulation of his/her project'.[11] Regardless of the fact that the status of *Omeros* as an epic may be questioned, the poem arises from a remarkable people and gives utterance to their place in the world.

NOTES

1 Derek Walcott, 'Reflections on *Omeros*', *South Atlantic Quarterly* 96 (1997): 233.
2 Robert Brown and Cheryl Johnson, 'An Interview with Derek Walcott', *Cream City Review* 14 (1990): 216.
3 Walcott, 'Leaving School', *London Magazine* 5 (1965): 4.
4 D. J. R. Buckner, 'A Poem in Homage to an Unwanted Man', *New York Times* (9 October 1990): 13.
5 Walcott, 'Reflections', 233.
6 J. P. White, 'An Interview with Derek Walcott', *Green Mountain Review* ns. 4 (1990): 36.
7 Brad Leithauser, 'Ancestral Rhyme', *New Yorker* (11 February 1991): 93.
8 Walcott, *Omeros* (New York: Farrar, Straus and Giroux, 1990), 108. Hereafter cited by page number in text.
9 Bruce King, *Derek Walcott: A Caribbean Life* (Oxford: Oxford University Press, 2000), 519; and White, 'Interview', 36.
10 King, *Derek Walcott*, 519.
11 Gregson Davis, '"With No Homeric Shadow": The Disavowal of Epic in Derek Walcott's *Omeros*', *The South Atlantic Quarterly* 96 (1997): 324.

14

PAUL MERCHANT

Epic in translation

Like so many other terms associated with epic, the term 'translation' itself presents varied facets, leading to questions of definition. In its most obvious sense, there is the long sequence of English renderings of epics, presenting their own form of literary history. Then, from the perspective of two and more millennia, we can see that a main characteristic of the original epics is the ability to generate successors. They translate their predecessors in the sense of carrying them forward into new territories. Not only do we recognize influences and lines of descent from epic into other genres (lyric, theatre, novel, opera), but almost without exception both major and minor practitioners of epic have themselves operated with an unusual sense of their ancestors, an acknowledged *pietas*. This has not only been true of the long line of literary, or secondary, epics. It was true also for the performers of the primary epics, most of whom looked back from their own 'dark' ages to a heroic period many hundreds of years earlier when the tales had originated, at the start of an oral transmission spanning many generations of bards. Those who transmitted the *Iliad, Odyssey, Aeneid, Beowulf,* and *Mahabharata* were both literally and figuratively singing to an Iron Age audience the lays of a lost Bronze Age, with behind it the even more shadowy myths of a Golden Age. Their poems were symbolized in the golden bough, 'so long unseen', that served to unlock a buried past.

A further application of the term 'translation' might return to its Latin root for the notion of transfer, expressing continuity through the persistent motif of travel, symbolic of a search for identity. For Greeks, this was the journey to and from Asia in the Argonautic and Trojan expeditions; for Romans, their founding myth out of Troy; for the English of Offa's Mercia, the dragon's gold in a distant Danish tumulus; for Dante, the downward and upward gyres of sin and redemption; for the Genesis poet and for Milton it was exile from the garden; for Joyce, the odyssey of Leopold Bloom through a Dublin recalled from the easternmost edge of Europe. This motif of cultural transfer is famously symbolized in Aeneas as he carries his father and his household gods from Troy to Italy, following a western star that was also a folk motif in the almost contemporary Nativity story. It seems likely that the earliest such exploratory songs would have recorded the spirit journeys of tribal shamans, still sung in today's aboriginal cultures. Perhaps more important, almost every European culture expressed its version of *translatio imperii,* the tracing of authority back to an imagined eponym – for example Aeneas's son Iulus, first of the Julian line; Brutus, the Trojan founder of Britain; or Hector's son Francus, ancestor of the Frankish emperor Charlemagne.

A third kind of translation is represented in epic's ever-increasing variety. The genre repeatedly translates into new narrative modes, every time reminding us that 'translation' is itself a literal rendition of the Greek 'metaphor'. Once again, this combination of strangeness and familiarity is present throughout the tradition. Epic poets aim at invention while remaining faithful to the demands of telling the tale of the tribe. They sing as they choose, but their stories' antiquity obliges them to stay within certain bounds set by the expectations of their audience. In no other literary form is originality of invention so clearly tempered by fidelity to a tradition. As Milman Parry and Albert B. Lord have established, the oral bard expresses invented material in a mixture of new phrases and ancient inherited formulas.[1] The basic tradition remains stable, but the definition of epic is stretched with every new example. And this fluidity of definition begins to seem the key quality of epic, with each successful assault on the form breaking the mould.

Translation into English

The high-water mark of epic translation into English was surely at its beginning in the reign of Queen Elizabeth, herself a translator. The first target was Virgil, rendered by the spirited Scots dialect of Gavin Douglas and the cooler measures of Thomas Phaer and the Earl of Surrey. The *Pentateuch* became available in the Geneva Bible, Ovid's *Metamorphoses* in Arthur Golding's translation, Homer in George Chapman's *Iliad* and *Odyssey,* the first book of Lucan's *Pharsalia* as rendered by Christopher Marlowe, and Ariosto's *Orlando Furioso* in the witty version of John Harington, the queen's godson, commissioned by her as a penance.

The task of finding a satisfactory response to hexameter verse in English was tackled differently by the three Tudor translators of Virgil. Douglas composed rhymed couplets, in a vigorous and fast-moving metre of four stressed syllables, Phaer attempted a more leisurely solution in rhymed fourteeners (the ballad measure), and Surrey's strongly end-stopped iambic pentameter (introducing blank verse to English poetry) is a clumsy first pass at what would very soon be a versatile narrative and theatrical medium. The strengths of Douglas's version are the lively muscularity of his language and the rapidity of his four-stress line, the shortest measure used by any translator discussed here. The line's brevity, in appearance a far cry from Virgil's hexameter, is filled out by the richly consonantal vocabulary, which English readers (and especially listeners) from south of the Scottish border have presumably always taken at a leisurely pace. The best of the Homeric translators, Chapman, also presented readers and listeners with a bristling and intractable style, with an ample store of invented words to parallel Douglas's dialect usages. As for metre, Chapman chose rhymed fourteeners for his *Iliad*, but rhymed iambic pentameter (as established in Chaucer's *Canterbury Tales*) for the *Odyssey*, where he was perhaps looking for a more rapid and discursive narrative style. Paradoxically, the shorter line seems too narrow a compass for Chapman's rhetorical instincts, with the result more often of obscurity than of speed. His *Iliad,* however, comes at us with all the verbal power of a highly litigious age trained in *disputatio,* an age when one might hear Marlowe, Shakespeare, and Webster as well as Chapman in the theatre, and John Donne and Lancelot Andrews (one of the translators of the *Pentateuch* for the King James Bible) from the pulpit. Chapman's version, perhaps the only complete translation of Homer that matches the rhetorical energy of the original, must be read aloud to experience the full force and inventiveness of his language. Keats (who like all the Romantic poets loved to hear poetry declaimed) felt he had not experienced the true Homeric voice 'Till I heard Chapman speak out loud and bold'.[2]

Chapman's translations of epic were not confined to Homer's two major poems and the *Batrachomyomachia* and Homeric Hymns. He also completed Marlowe's minor epic, *Hero and Leander,* translated Musaeus's short poem on the same subject, and made a version of Hesiod's philosophical epic, *Works and Days.* This interest in a wide range of major and minor epic types was natural in an age of discovery and turbulent change. An appendage to the most interesting vernacular epic of the period, Spenser's *Faerie Queene,* offered a debate between Mutabilitie and Nature. 'Nothing', says Mutabilitie, 'doth firme and permanent appeare, / But all things tost and turnèd by transverse'.[3] Spenser would have found an apt source for this judgement in Arthur Golding's version of Ovid's *Metamorphoses,* which the translator called a 'dark Philosophie of turned shapes'.[4] After challenging the Augustan moral code with amatory instructions in infidelity, Ovid had next taken the even greater risk of exploring change, a risk avoided by Virgil, who praised the stability of the new order. Ovid celebrated the instability inherent in the myths, their impermanence, and was rewarded with exile. Shakespeare spoke directly to an equivalent sense of uncertainty when he allowed Titus to quote the loss of Justice in the Iron Age: '*Terras Astrea reliquit*; / Be you rememb'red, Marcus, she's gone, she's fled.'[5] Among other uses of the *Metamorphoses* to illustrate changes of fortune, Shakespeare made comic use of the fatal misunderstanding of Pyramus and Thisbe in *A Midsummer Night's Dream*, and finally had Prospero echo the incantations of Medea when giving up his craft at the end of *The Tempest*.

Ovid had himself abandoned his trademark witty elegiacs for the epic measure of continuous hexameters in his *Metamorphoses*, and Golding's brisk fourteeners provide the perfect complement in English. The ballad metre was an inspired choice for a poem that most English readers would have read as a collection of tales like Boccaccio's or Chaucer's. Like the other great translating success of the period, Chapman's *Iliad*, Golding's fourteeners read rapidly and fluently, while (also like Chapman) enjoying the chance to display newfangled vocabulary – in this case, in response to Ovid's delight in surprises and eccentric psychological experiences. Almost all the Elizabethan epics, but most obviously Spenser's *Faerie Queene*, Chapman's *Iliad* and *Hero and Leander* continuation, and Golding's Ovid, carry clear allegorical messages. Golding's allegorical intent fortunately does not overshadow the pervasive ironic humour in Ovid's text. This pleasing combination, of a witty narration and an underlying moral force, made it one of the most admired of all translations into English. The *Metamorphoses* have translated easily into the twentieth century, first as a co-partner with the *Odyssey* and *The Divine Comedy* as avatars of Pound's early *Cantos*, and at the end of the century in Ted Hughes's well-received *Tales from Ovid*. A translator's inventiveness may be limited by respect for the target work, or a rare miracle may take place: the stimulus of a great original generates pure poetry in response. Hughes was the master of quirky metaphors and (in the minor epic *Crow* and elsewhere) an explorer of psychological states through myth. 'The act of metamorphosis', he writes, 'which at some point touches each of the tales, operates as the symbolic guarantee that the passion has become mythic, has achieved the unendurable intensity that lifts the whole episode onto the supernatural or divine plane.' The book is a selection, not a full translation, and the order of the stories has been rearranged, to end, for example, with the tale of Pyramus and Thisbe. In the telling some elements are expanded, others abbreviated. Page after page we experience original, instantly recognizable, poetry. Golding's was the Elizabethan Ovid. For Hughes, Ovid expressed 'what it feels like to live in the psychological gulf that opens at the end of an era'.[6] His alert, laconic version speaks to a similar moment in history.

If the *Iliad* and *Metamorphoses* carried allegorical implications for the Elizabethan world, Lucan's *Pharsalia* and Ariosto's *Orlando Furioso* speak to other aspects of the time. The *Pharsalia* is the obverse of the *Aeneid* medal. It is a poem of loss. David Quint comments that the eventual victors in the civil war 'experience history as a coherent, end-directed story told by their own power; the losers experience a contingency that they are power-less to shape to their own ends'.[7] The dissident, anti-heroic strain in Lucan's epic would have had an application to the political uncertainties of late Elizabethan England, and would have appealed especially to Marlowe, one of the age's great dissidents. Marlowe's Lucan was published in 1600, after his death, when the Essex rebellion was a fresh memory, in the disillusioned climate of Donne's and Guilpin's satires and of the anti-heroic *Troilus and Cressida*. A later dissident, Alexander Pope, also translated *Pharsalia*'s first book, no doubt relishing, as Marlowe and Jonson had earlier, the fantastic turns and idiosyncrasies of Lucan's style. Closer to our own day a fourth poet, Robert Graves, made a prose translation of *Pharsalia* for the Penguin Classics series in 1956. Graves, another notable controversialist, confessed to a strong distaste for Lucan, whose 'impatience with craftsmanship, digressive irrelevancies, emphasis on the macabre, lack of religious convic-tion, turgid hyperbole, inconsistency, appeal to violence, and occasional flashes of real brilliance – have been rediscovered by this new disagreeable [modernist] world'. He translated him because 'he anticipated so many of the literary *genres* dominant today that it would be unfair not to put him in modern dress for the admiration of the great majority whose tastes differ from mine'.[8] One of the idiosyncrasies of the translation is the decision by this erudite writer to include explications of the poem's obscurities as expansions of the text, rather than in explanatory notes. The result is something between a translation and a commentary, with the feeling more of a historical novel than of a poem. Graves was unfailingly interesting in everything he touched, but on this occasion once again the Englishing of Lucan had taken an irreverent turn.

Harington's Elizabethan translation of *Orlando Furioso* delivered another kind of irreverence, in response to Ariosto's sprawling romance from the world of chivalry. The Italian poem is a *tour de force* of varied episodes, fantastic locations, and erotic suggestiveness, and the witty cour-tier Harington translated one of its racier scenes to amuse the queen's ladies in waiting. His punishment from the queen was to translate the whole epic. The result was popular as a story-book and as a satire on contemporary manners in the increasingly ironic climate that would soon welcome Beaumont's *Knight of the Burning Pestle* and Cervantes's *Don Quixote*. The Elizabethan translators of epic played a significant role in describing the age to itself. We should add that in many cultures the weight, prestige, and popularity of the great literary epics and their analogues would have been instrumental in stabilizing that culture's vernacular. Dante's *Commedia* helped to define the standard dialect of Italy, and Chaucer performed a similar task in England. Another example, although a more special case, is the Bible, in the translations of Luther into German, of Tyndale into English, and of William Morgan (published by Christopher Barker, the royal printer) into Welsh, and in the Irish New Testament by many hands, promoted by Queen Elizabeth early in her reign.

The next great period of epic translation, that of Dryden and Pope, resulted in versions that were again most ideally suited to their own times. Dryden's *Aeneid* and Pope's *Iliad* and *Odyssey* illustrate one of the golden rules of translation: that each new version should compete with the original as a poem. Only the best poets can keep pace with Homer and Virgil, and only then (as was also true of Gavin Douglas and of Chapman) by building poems in their own manner. Virgil assembles paragraphs of uninterrupted rhythms, each one a completed architecture; Homer's oral method brings together verbal units that become increasingly familiar by repetition, but only over time. Neither of these narrative styles is ideally served by the rhymed heroic couplets of Dryden and Pope, but one should look rather to the qualities that both of these poets brought to their versions, their sharpness of observation, and their ability to bring a complex thought into a brief compass. The problem of judging epic translations by their inadequacies rather than by their contributions is well illustrated in Matthew Arnold's 1860 lectures on translating Homer. Arnold proposed four qualities in Homer's style that a translator should reproduce: his rapidity, plainness, and directness of style and ideas, and his nobleness. His immediate, all too easy, targets were Ichabod Charles Wright, somewhat more successful as a translator of Dante, and Francis William Newman, brother of the cardinal. Surveying their translations along with other previous versions, Arnold found Cowper and Wright deficient in rapidity, Pope and Sotheby in plainness and directness of style, Chapman in plainness and directness of ideas, and Newman in nobility.

It is at once obvious that the criteria are cunningly composed so as to make all translations defective in some respect. To the extent that Homer is rapid (though the Homeric poems are of course often leisurely and discursive) that quality, and those of plainness and directness, will be presumably counteracted by nobility – a characteristic, incidentally, that Arnold sees no need to define. With hindsight we see that these four adjectives (rapid, plain, direct, noble) were chosen in direct opposition to Newman's stated mission to transmit Homer's particular qualities. Newman had been sceptical that any translation of Homer could reproduce Homer as a modern poem, to 'rear a poem that shall affect our countrymen as the original may be conceived to have affected its original hearers'. He proposed instead 'precisely the opposite: to retain every peculiarity of the original'. Arnold made short work of this position in his scornful response: 'we cannot possibly tell *how* the *Iliad* "affected its original hearers". It is probably meant merely that he should try to affect Englishmen powerfully, as Homer affected Greeks powerfully; but this direction is not enough, and can give no real guidance.'[9] But Newman (whatever his defects as a translator) had struck to the heart of the problem: while attempting to create a genuine new poem, a translator must preserve at least some sense of the original's idiosyncrasies. In establishing mutually exclusive Romantic and Victorian criteria for Homer, a Wordsworthian lucidity and a Tennysonian sonority, perhaps, Arnold had established safe ground for his attack on Milton's high style and Pope's elegance.

Arnold had made his own forays into epic poetry, in *Sohrab and Rustum* and *Balder Dead*. Of these, the former seems far the most successful both in its choice of subject, an episode from Sir John Malcolm's *History of Persia*, and in its execution. His Rustum is an Achilles keeping to his tent, only reluctantly drawn into single combat, and there is a Homeric feel to the boasting challenges and the many similes from nature. The story is more sentimentally told than any similar episode in Homer, but it preserves something of the oral tradition. In 1862, after the death of his friend Arthur Hugh Clough, Arnold ended his final thoughts on Homer (in the essay 'Last Words') with a generous reference to his friend's humorous minor epic, *The Bothie of Tober-na-Voulich*, commenting that it has 'some admirable Homeric qualities – out of doors freshness, life, naturalness, rapidity'.[10] Clough's *Bothie* is indeed, in style if not in subject, the most Homeric poetry of the nineteenth century, and its hexameters are perhaps the only examples in English with any true ease and fluency: colloquial, witty, varied, inventive, unpretentious. And they are assembled in close imitation of the oral manner, with almost formulaic repetitions, occasional extended similes, and a frequent recourse to direct speech. The effect is close to pastiche, even to parody, but the poem's purpose is mock-heroic, and it succeeds admirably, as the most amusing and subversive poem since *Don Juan*.

The emphasis to this point on metrics (fourteeners, blank verse, hexameters, rhyming couplets) reflects the challenge of choosing a form that can be sustained over the length of an epic poem. The original bards had no such challenge, since the metre in which they sang had been developed over time into the perfect medium for their material. But a translator, even when approaching a lyric poem, faces formal questions – whether to preserve rhyme, exact lineation, metre. These questions are daunting in the case of epic. And perhaps the most daunting case is that of *Beowulf*, whose mouthfuls of consonants, clanging alliterations, and oblique kennings (compound words) cannot easily be duplicated in the smoother accents of modern English. The poem was not rendered satisfactorily in the nineteenth century, with William Morris's false medievalism as a dire example. In his translation of *The Seafarer*, whatever may be said about its accuracy, Ezra Pound left a gritty model for future translators of *Beowulf*. In his earliest writings Pound had his own Pre-Raphaelite medievalisms, but by 1912 he could present Anglo-Saxon with vivid clarity and force, the monosyllables, alliteration, and internal rhymes making a fine music: 'May I for my own self song's truth reckon, / Journey's jargon, how I in harsh days / Hardship endured oft'.[11] Later poets were able to learn from this model, notably Basil Bunting in the Northumbrian epic *Briggflatts*, and Tony Harrison in his translation of *Oresteia*, but modern translators of *Beowulf* (who include Edwin Morgan, Michael Alexander, and Seamus Heaney) have preferred to moderate the language of the original for the sake of telling the story.

In the years following the First World War three talented writers turned to the *Odyssey*. Ezra Pound began his *Cantos* with a Homeric fragment that both moves adroitly and still has time for vivid word-choices: 'And then went down to the ship, / Set keel to breakers, forth on the godly sea, and / we set up mast and sail on that swart ship'.[12] T. E. Lawrence chose prose for his *Odyssey* translation, the work of a master storyteller. His version is notable for his solution to the problem of the formulas. Having decided to narrate the poem as a modern adventure novel, Lawrence varied the formulas instead of repeating them. The result is no longer Homer's poem, but it represents a translation into a new medium. Meanwhile Joyce was turning Homer's poem book by book into the chapters of *Ulysses*. All three writers had ventured far from their homes, but all were drawn to the *Odyssey* by more than nostalgia. The hero's difficult return journey to security had psychic value in the chaos following the war, as did Eliot's use of the Grail Legend in *The Waste Land*. And the inter-war exhaustion and disillusion discouraged translators from attempting an *Iliad*. These promising experiments, however, were followed by two ultimately retrogressive developments: the publication of E. V. Rieu's *Odyssey* in 1946, as the first in the new Penguin Classics Series, and the enormous post-war boom in translations for use in university literature classes. We have already noted the prose Lucan of Robert Graves, with its assumption that modern readers prefer their poetry served up in a more accessible narrative form. The huge success of Rieu's *Odyssey* (with sales of three million copies) encouraged prose renderings of other epic poems, establishing the novel rather than narrative verse as the model for under-standing the great oral poems. Another unfortunate result was the narrowing of the canon to those works selected for this influential series, so that the epic poet Statius, so admired by Dante, is now read only by specialists. An even more disastrous side-effect is that modern translators of the classics began to feel free, even when presenting their translations as verse, essentially to render the originals as prose. Very few modern translations of the long poems have much poetic quality. Poets after all have their own work to do, so the task is often left to hired professional translators with aspirations to no more than literal accuracy, as if that were not already provided by the Loeb series. It is time, perhaps, for a new Pope to begin on a modern *Dunciad*. There are honourable excep-tions: Robert Fitzgerald's *Odyssey* is the work of a poet with a real feel for the idiom of the folk tale. And Christopher Logue's vivid free render-ings of portions of the *Iliad* for delivery on BBC radio (a medium that had hosted Dylan Thomas's *Under Milk Wood* and Louis MacNeice's *The Dark Tower*) showed what could still be achieved through oral delivery.

Carrying forward: the theme of travel

Summarizing two centuries of scholarly work on the distribution of myths and folk tales, Stith Thompson noted that many, though by no means all, of the motifs were collected and disseminated from India, perhaps the great early clearing house of oral narratives.[13] Indeed, our earliest surviving epic, the *Mahabharata*, has been recited on the subcontinent for two if not three thousand years. In 1893 Andrew Lang, who had earlier wittily demolished prevailing theories of myth as universally derived from celestial events by proving Gladstone to have been a solar deity, proposed a parallel descent of heroic epics and *Märchen* from a common origin in primitive tales, as medi-ated through folk storytelling. In many cultures only folk tales survive as evidence of the original primitive oral narratives. The *Mahabharata* and its somewhat younger literary sister, the *Ramayana*, stand as models for two kinds of territorial myths that establish boundaries of influence. The dynastic conflicts of the *Mahabharata* look forward to the power struggles described in the *Iliad* and in *War and Peace*, and we remember that the last heroic action of Turnus in the *Aeneid* is to hurl a boundary stone. The *Ramayana* traverses great tracts of territory, in the course of which Rama builds a bridge from the continent to the island of Sri Lanka to win back his stolen wife, Sita. The epic contains motifs found in both Homeric poems, for example feats of archery exemplifying cowardice, like that of Paris, and of skill, like that of Odysseus.

The motif of the journey is important also in a quite different sense, and from another source with a long history: the spirit-journey of the shaman, ascending into the sky or under the earth or water to bring back messages from the other world. For the primitive mind, it is likely that our separation from the dead was one of the greatest mysteries, one that many myths were developed to explain. In the descent to the underworld, the shaman illustrates the connection of the mortal world with an eternal Elysium or Hell, and conducts the soul from one world to the other, in some cases returning the soul to the world of the living. Later myth and literature, including epics, show these beliefs in various forms: the scattering of the limbs of Osiris and his reign over the dead must have a distant relationship with the search by Lemminkäinen's mother for her son's scattered limbs in the lake of Tuonela, as also with the three-day descent of Christ into Hell and his Easter resurrection. The underworld journey of Gilgamesh in search of the dead Enkidu is paralleled in the stories of Orpheus and Eurydice, Admetus and Alcestis, and Demeter and Persephone.

In the final episode of the *Iliad*, Hermes leading Priam to beg his son's body from Achilles echoes his mythic role as guide of souls and (in the case of Eurydice) recoverer of the dead. Hermes performs another shamanic function in the *Odyssey* Book 10, providing the hero with the protective herb *moly* when he visits Circe, a modified queen of the dead who can change humans to swine. Following Circe's instruction, Odysseus (a descendant of Hermes) soon risks the shaman's journey to talk with the dead, as does Aeneas in the *Aeneid* Book 6. Beowulf swims a day's journey underwater to do battle with a personification of death, Grendel's mother. Dante, in the most complex literary enactment of a shaman's journey both under the earth and into the sky, is accompanied by a magician of contemporary repute, Virgil, as he interrogates the dead. His Ulysses is buried deep in the *Inferno*, but for Ezra Pound at the start of the *Cantos* the symbolism of Odysseus, as he wrote to his father on 11 April 1927, is the shaman's ability to link the worlds: 'live man goes down into world of dead . . . The "repeat in history". . . moment of metamorphosis, bust thru from quotidien into "divine or permanent world". Gods, etc'.[14] Mutated versions of this original spirit journey can be seen in the trials of the Argonauts and the parallel tales of Sinbad, in the Irish *Tain*'s raid and return, in the Grail Quest narratives and in native American vision quests, in all too human tales told on a pilgrimage to Canterbury, and in Leopold Bloom's perambulation of Dublin and Clarissa Dalloway's parallel one-day journey through London.

The surviving epics contain another widespread evidence of a shared shamanic origin, in the shadowy presence of bears, as guides to the underworld and animal spirit-helpers in life. One obvious case is the name of

Beowulf, who is Bee-wolf, or the honey-eating bear. In the Norse sagas this name relates to the bear-warriors, Bodvar Bjarki and his father Bjorn, from the *Saga of King Hrolf Kraki*, and to other berserkers. Elsewhere in the tradition we find a bear-hero lurking behind Odysseus in Rhys Carpenter's account, and the bear (Welsh *arth*) concealed in the name of Arthur. Bear ceremonial can even be seen in the cult of Artemis, whose girl acolytes in Brauron were called bears. Mircea Eliade has collected evidence of bear ceremonialism across the entire shamanic culture area.[15] Reverence for the bear (including ritual feasts under the patronage of a bear skull) can be documented from the tribes of the northwest coast of America through Finland and Siberia to the Ainu of Hokkaido.

The Aarne-Thompson folk tale and folk motif indexes summarize a huge body of stories derived from primitive lore, much of it surely derived from the earliest oral narratives. Sometimes, in order to establish the original oral traditions of a culture, one has to assemble from folk material, from prose summaries, from myth collections, a shadowy sense of the poems that originally carried those elements, a vanished archetype that can still be imagined. An excellent example can be seen in the surviving poetry and prose descended from the great oral narratives of the Vikings, the pre-eminent explorers and raiders of the post-Roman world. By the time the oral tradition of the Vikings was written down, by the Icelander Snorri Sturluson in the prose *Edda* of the early thirteenth century, the myths had separated into individual stories. Snorri's book is a compendium, a collection of myths for poetic use, but lacking the epic coherence and organizing pattern of a *Metamorphoses*. The great epics in which these materials had originally been sung are lost, although they would presumably have included the exploits of Sigurd the Volsung (the *Nibelungenlied*'s Siegfried), now known to us through the prose sagas of the Volsungs and of Hrolf Kraki. The Old English *Beowulf* is a close cousin of these lost Viking epics. The myths can also be seen presenting a pale remnant of their original form in the *Völuspá*, a short verse narrative on the birth and death of the universe written near the start of the tenth century. The poem is a summary told by a female shaman, who describes the golden age of the Norse gods and prophesies their twilight and destruction, the *ragnarök*. Taken together with the prose *Edda* and other sagas, and with the German *Nibelungenlied*, these poetic and prose narratives can be viewed as the end point of a long transmission handing down significant parts of the original Norse oral epic cycle.

Every culture has its foundation myths that express the relationship between gods and mortals and the representative feats of its heroes in this world and in the afterlife. Creation may be in the hands of benign beings (as in Genesis, the *Metamorphoses* and the Australian Aborigine Djanggawul Cycle) or the product of genial tricksters such as the West African Anansi, the native American Coyote, or Ted Hughes's Crow. Or a culture may find its own distinctive form of national narrative. Modern Greek poets, for example, from Costis Palamas in *The Twelve Lays of the Gipsy*, through Nikos Kazantzakis in his *Odyssey*, and Yannis Ritsos in his great cycle of mythological narrative poems, to Odysseas Elytis in *Heroic and Elegiac Song on the Lost Second Lieutenant of Albania* and the *Axion Esti*, Takis Sinopoulos in *Deathfeast*, and Eleni Vakalo in *Genealogy*, have found a means to continue the ancient epic tradition into the present with an intriguing mixture of original mythology with later folk motifs, memories of Ottoman occupation, and even modern historical narrative. A similar means of defining an emerging culture has been the response of contemporary Latin American writers to their cultures' mixed indigenous and Hispanic heritage. The magical realism in novels by the Colombian Gabriel García Márquez, the Peruvian Mario Vargas Llosa, and the Mexican Carlos Fuentes, with their mixture of fantasy and accurately observed political history, can be paralleled in poetry on an epic scale by Chilean Pablo Neruda (*The Heights of Macchu Picchu*), and by Nicaraguan Ernesto Cardenal (*Homage to the American Indian*). These poems combine rich and often surreal imagery with a leisurely poetic manner, infused with a sardonic political and social wit that can be seen in the tradition as far back as Cervantes. Meanwhile, we observe a quite different epic tradition in the East. There, the Japanese *Heike Monogatari*, the Turkish *Book of Dede Korkut*, the Chinese *Water Margin* and *Journey to the West*, the Vietnamese *Kim van Kieu*, and the Mongolian/Tibetan *Gesar* now survive as collections of folk or historical narratives strung into lengthy presentations – in the case of *Gesar*, probably the longest epic still in performance. Whatever the original forms of these tales, they have been handed down within the last thousand years more as chronicles than as single-subject epic poems.

Finally, we can trace two distinctive traditions in the English-speaking cultures of Britain and America. The 'Matter of Britain' is a continuous record of Celtic myths seen in narrative form in the Welsh *Gododdin*, the earliest heroic poem to mention Arthur, and the same culture's *Mabinogion*, the Irish *Tain*, Malory's *Morte d'Arthur*, and Spenser's *Faerie Queene*. In its development of the concept of *translatio imperii*, the Tudor court with its Welsh connections had enthusiastically endorsed the suggestions of antiquarians like John Dee of a joint heritage in the Trojan Brut and the Celtic Arthur. Sidney had first meditated his *Arcadia* as an Arthuriad, as later did Milton his *Paradise Lost*. The line continues through Tennyson's *Idylls of the King* and Joyce's *Finnegans Wake* to the *Anathemata* of David Jones, Geoffrey Hill's *Mercian Hymns*, John Arden's *Island of the Mighty*, and Howard Brenton's *The Romans in Britain*. The common element at every stage of the tradition is the distinctive, often otherworldly, quality of the native Celtic myths. The tales characteristically leap from episode to episode with the intricate movement exemplified in the Celtic interlacing of the Lindisfarne Gospel decorations. And when the Volsung saga describes a magic sword destined to be drawn by one hero alone (in this case Sigurd), we glimpse the common ancestry of the Arthurian and Norse mythologies.

The American epic tradition begins in two long poems published in 1855. The first draft of Whitman's *Leaves of Grass* followed Emerson's 1844 pronouncement that 'America is a poem in our eyes' by establishing the leisurely form of a long line and irregular stanza lengths, capacious enough to 'contain multitudes'.[16] Beginning as a personal testament set against the largeness of America, the record of an individual's omnivorous experience somewhat in the tradition of the growth of a poet's soul in Dante or Wordsworth, the poem is transformed by Whitman's experiences in the Civil War into the epic of that national trauma, America's *Iliad*. On the other hand, Longfellow was inspired by Elias Lonnröt's great collection of Finnish folk tales in his epic *Kalevala* to borrow stories from Henry Schoolcraft's collections of Obiway legends and weave them into the single, not entirely seamless, narrative of *Hiawatha*. The influence of *Kalevala* is not only seen in Longfellow's imitation of its four-stress line, but also in its anthropological intention. Longfellow created a series of tales centred on a single hero, with a narrative arc from youth to age, marriage to death, but at the same time creating a tribal journey from innocence to experience, beginning in harmony and ending in the arrival of the missionaries and Hiawatha's departure, a kind of inverted *Odyssey*.

These two epic impulses, on the one hand to chart the growth of a poet's understanding and on the other to establish a distinctly American anthropological and historical record, can be seen in the twentieth-century successors of Whitman and Longfellow: in Ezra Pound's *Cantos*, in the five books of *Paterson* by William Carlos Williams and in the six sections of Charles Olson's *Maximus* poems. And these same, paired traditions have been carried into the next generation, in Allen Ginsberg's *Howl*, Gary Snyder's *Mountains and Rivers Without End*, and Jerome Rothenberg's poetic explorations into his European ancestry and adoption into the Seneca tribe in the trilogy *Poland 1931*, *A Seneca Journal*, and *Vienna Blood*. The investigation of cultural roots in the American epics takes the form of creating large canvases to hold such assemblages as the indigenous culture of a continent distinct from Europe, and the many forms of immigrant experience. The epic line in Britain, while harking back to a more distant past, seems focused on a world before Romans, before Saxons, before Normans, in an unspoiled land. Both impulses lead in the same direction, towards a cultural model that could invigorate (in the spirit of a Holy Grail or a spear of summer grass) a disillusioned present.

Translation into new modes

Every age presents its expanded definitions. While specialists in the field of epic continue to find useful the established categories (ancient and contemporary oral narratives, secondary epic, the allusive tradition, etc.), a more flexible critical vocabulary develops to accommodate the diversity of new epic modes. Almost inevitably in the hands of modern poets, new epic genealogies are likely to be determined by different kinds of DNA. Large and varied segments of later theatre have been indebted to epic origins, from Aeschylus's 'slices from Homer's great banquet' (according to Athenaeus) through Shakespeare's histories, with their type-characters and pre-battle dawn invocations, to the Epic Theatre of Piscator and Brecht and their successors.[17] Parts of the great novel tradition may also be traced back to epic. One of the most successful reworkings of Homer is Fénelon's *Adventures of Telemachus*, viewing the *Odyssey* as an instruction manual in moral leadership by following the untold story of Telemachus and Mentor. Ursula le Guin has recently taken a parallel approach to the *Aeneid* in her *Lavinia*, which views the marriage of Latin and Trojan from the indigenous, and female, perspective. And the *Ethiopica* of Heliodorus, one of the earliest novels, refers constantly back to the Homeric poems, but also, in establishing a line of romantic histories, became a likely source for Verdi's *Aida*. Indeed, the very first opera was on an epic subject (Monteverdi's *Marriage of Aeneas and Lavinia,* now lost), as was his first surviving work, *The Return of Ulysses to his Homeland.* Many of the finest operas found libretti of high intensity in the same tradition: Purcell's *Dido and Aeneas,* Handel's *Messiah,* Haydn's *Creation,* Berlioz's *The Trojans at Carthage,* Wagner's *The Ring of the Nibelung,* Strauss's *Electra,* and Tippett's *King Priam.*

And what is the future of the philosophical epic? At the start of the tradition the *Bhagavad Gita* stands out from its place in the *Mahabharata* as an extended discussion between that epic's Achilles, Arjuna, and his charioteer, the god Krishna, concerning the nature of the self and its struggle with evil. The influence of this great poem, perhaps once an independent epic, has been compared with the Mosaic Law in the Hebrew Exodus, and it had a particular impact on the nineteenth-century American Transcendentalists. Read enthusiastically by Emerson, it proved also a major influence on Thoreau and Whitman, both of whom admired its noble philosophy. In the Greek tradition both Homer and Hesiod's *Works and Days* and *Theogony* were valued for their metaphysical content, similar in impact to Plato's Myth of Er at the close of the *Republic*. Lucretius used epic form (invoking in his first line Venus as patroness of Aeneas) to convey the atomism of Epicurus. In a kind of response, Ovid put into the mouth of Pythagoras the concluding statement in *Metamorphoses* of change and rebirth into new forms.

Later examples abound. Donne's fragmentary *Progress of the Soul* continues the Pythagorean theme into a satiric mode. In the next century William Cowper's poem *The Task* must surely be the only epic poem composed by accident. Cowper was the translator of both Homeric epics, into stiff versions that have not found modern readers, but *The Task* deserves to be more widely read. Cowper's prefatory note describes the process of composition: 'A lady, fond of blank verse, demanded a poem of that kind from the author, and gave him the Sofa for a subject. He obeyed; and having much leisure, connected another subject with it; and pursuing the train of thought to which his situation and turn of mind led him, brought forth at length, instead of the trifle which he at first intended, a serious affair – a Volume.'[18] The 'trifle', which was his first response to Lady Austen, is a mock-epic genealogy of seats, from the joint stool to the sofa, but this greatly underrated poem soon abandons the sedentary mode for excursions along country lanes during which the linked thoughts of the author follow a similar winding route. The tone is a little like one of Horace's satires or epistles, genial and intelligent, but the eventual growth of the poem into six books gives Cowper the philosophical scope of a Hesiod or a Lucretius, with room for sharp attacks on failures in education and religion, and with a strong sympathy for traditional ways. Cowper turns a fine epigrammatic phrase – 'God made the country, and man made the town', 'There is a pleasure in poetic pains / That only poets know', 'God never meant that man should scale the heavens / By strides of human wisdom', 'Who loves a garden loves a greenhouse too' – but the poem's chief merit is a general warm-hearted discursiveness, the perfect medium for a rambling conversation.[19] Stylistically, *The Task* owes an obvious debt to Milton, but in its sinuous movement of gradually unfolding ideas it looks both back at Pope's epistles and forward to Byron's *Don Juan* and Wordsworth's *Prelude*. By a pleasing coincidence, in the same year Erasmus Darwin was putting Linnaean ideas into rhymed couplets in his long poem *The Botanic Garden*, showing a similar confidence that the long poem remained a suitable vehicle for serious philosophical ideas. Fortunately, the concept is still alive in our time, as can be seen in Hugh McDiarmid's challenging *On a Raised Beach*, full of scientific vocabulary, and in the use of the extended verse epistle by W. H. Auden (*A Letter to Lord Byron*), and by the American Tom McGrath (*Letter to an Imaginary Friend*). It is not that one would claim most, or even any, of these philosophical poems as true epics, but they may enable us to revisit key moments in our epic tradition, such as Achilles's statement to Priam on the good and evil urns dispensing human fortune, or Anchises's speech on the purposes of Rome with a somewhat enlarged context. At the same time, considerations of this kind open up avenues of encouragement to future experiments in the long poem.

One concluding lateral perspective on epic is provided by the history of fragments in the nineteenth and twentieth centuries. Delight in the fragmentary was itself a part of the eighteenth-century fashion for Gothic follies, hermitages, and ruins. Snippets of ancient writings had long been extracted from mummy bindings, unreadable cuneiform tablets had been brought back to Europe from the early seventeenth century, and Greek and Roman sculptures were a growing import into Western Europe, but with Napoleon's Egyptian expedition and the puzzle of the Rosetta Stone, interest quickened. The fragment became both a powerful metaphor and a literary form in its own right in the hands of the Romantic poets. One definitive response was Shelley's ironic sonnet 'Ozymandias'. Others were Keats's wonder at seeing the Elgin Marbles, that mingling of 'Grecian grandeur with the rude / Wasting of old Time' and Blake's proverbs in *The Marriage of Heaven and Hell*.[20] And, in the same year as Coleridge's celebrated announcement of his *Kubla Khan* as 'a Vision in a Dream. A Fragment', appeared Friedrich Schlegel's fragment 20: 'The fragment, like a small art work, should be quite separate from the world around it, self-sufficient, like a hedgehog'.[21] Two years earlier Friedrich August Wolf had published his *Prolegomena to Homer*, the first systematic disintegration of the text into separate lays, and Coleridge had already begun amassing the brilliant sentences and aphorisms that would fill his seventy notebooks. In the middle of the century Coleridge's grandson Herbert started to assemble the thousands of file cards that would result in the *Oxford English Dictionary*, and at Nineveh the explorer Austen Henry Layard uncovered Ashurbanipal's huge library of cuneiform tablets that included the text of the Gilgamesh epic. Around the same time one of the greatest epic novels, Melville's *Moby-Dick*, was prefaced with a collection of 'Extracts (Supplied by a sub-sub-librarian)' describing whales. The world was beginning to be seen as an assemblage from disparate parts, and epics had started to be flamboyantly episodic, like Goethe's *Faust* or Byron's *Don Juan*. Soon Browning would stumble across the *Old Yellow Book* in Florence and would tease out the varied psychologies of the principals in a long-forgotten murder trial. The resulting six-book poem, *The Ring and the Book*, builds its case patiently from small details, as in the new genre of detective tale pioneered by Poe and soon to be popularized in England by Wilkie Collins and Arthur Conan Doyle.

At the start of the twentieth century a more certain sense of disintegration followed the indiscriminate slaughter of the First World War. It was obvious that the old certainties had been illusions. In the physics of matter itself, Einstein declared that the atom, named for its absolute unity, could be split, and Heisenberg announced his principle of uncertainty. In the world of art, painting and music experienced the spatial divisions of Cubism and the atonality of serial composition, and the Dadaists experimented with absurd verbal relationships. Now epics began to be collections of disparate personal records, like Proust's great series of novels recovering a vanished world, Pound's *Cantos* ('As a lone ant from a broken ant-hill / from the wreckage of Europe, ego scriptor'), Eliot's *Waste Land* ('These fragments I have shored against my ruins'), and David Jones's *Anathemata* ('I have made a heap of all that I could find').[22] The term 'bricolage' introduced by Claude Lévi-Strauss in *The Savage Mind* could as easily describe the box assemblages of Joseph Cornell or Walter Benjamin's vast *Arcades Project*, unfinished at his death, but gathering into a single shifting pattern thousands of individual observations from nineteenth-century Paris.

Epic is still, in its scale and particularity, an excellent medium for analysis of our times, but it may now be a pattern of minutiae rather than a single heroic vision. One of the most successful of recent examples would be Derek Walcott's *Omeros*. Among its many pleasures is the great circular journey taken by the narrator, starting and ending in the Caribbean and moving through Holland, Africa, New England, Lisbon, London, Dublin, the Aegean, and Istanbul. The effect is simultaneously of a multinational inclusiveness and a postmodern rootlessness. Something similar can be seen in the four diverging narrative perspectives in Lawrence Durrell's *Alexandria Quartet*, and in the multivalent novels of W. G. Sebald. Finally, there are even deeper uncertainties in such explorations of instability as Alan Halsey's *The Text of Shelley's Death,* which gathers the widely divergent contemporary accounts into a kaleidoscopic and deeply untrustworthy narrative. And most transgressively, we have the texts of British artist Tom Phillips excised from earlier works (*A Humument* and *The Inferno*), and American poet Ronald Johnson's long poem *Radi Os* chiselled from *Paradise Lost*. It is a fine circumstance that epic, which began as poetry stitched together from inherited materials handed down from a heroic age, should return to its roots, but this time by stitching together random evidences of a broken world.

NOTES

1 Milman Parry, *The Making of Homeric Verse*, new edn (Oxford: Oxford University Press, 1987); Albert B. Lord, *The Singer of Tales* (Cambridge, MA: Harvard University Press, 1960).

2 Keats, 'On First Looking Into Chapman's Homer', in *The Complete Poems*, ed. John Barnard, 2nd edn (Harmondsworth: Penguin, 1977).

3 Spenser, *The Faerie Queene*, ed. Hiroshi Yamashita, Toshiyuki Suzuki, and A. C. Hamilton, rev. edn (London: Longman, 2007), VII.vii.56.

4 Arthur Golding, trans., Translator's Epistle, *Ovid's Metamorphoses*, ed. Madeleine Forey (London: Penguin, 2002), 7.

5 *Titus Andronicus* IV.iii.4–5, in *The Riverside Shakespeare*, ed. G. Blakemore Evans *et al.*, 2nd edn (Boston: Houghton Mifflin, 1997).

6 Ted Hughes, *Tales from Ovid* (London: Faber and Faber, 1997), x, xi.

7 David Quint, *Epic and Empire: Politics and Generic Form from Virgil to Milton* (Princeton: Princeton University Press, 1993), 9.

8 Robert Graves, trans., *Pharsalia: Dramatic Episodes of the Civil Wars* (London: Penguin, 1956), 23–4.

9 Matthew Arnold, *On Translating Homer* (London: Macmillan, 1893), 142–3.

10 *Ibid.*, 300.

11 *The Seafarer*, lines 1–3, in *The Translations of Ezra Pound*, ed. Hugh Kenner (New York: New Directions, 1953).

12 *The Cantos of Ezra Pound* (New York: New Directions, 1995), Canto I, 1–3.

13 Stith Thompson, *The Folktale* (Berkeley: University of California Press, 1977).

14 *The Letters of Ezra Pound 1907–1941*, ed. D. D. Paige (New York: Harcourt, Brace and Company), 210.

15 See Mircea Eliade, *Sharmanism* (Princeton: Princeton University Press, 1964).

16 Ralph Waldo Emerson, 'The Poet' (1844), in *Selected Essays*, ed. Larzer Ziff (Harmondsworth: Penguin, 1982), 281.

17 Athenaeus, *The Deipnosophists*, ed. C. B. Gulick (Cambridge, MA: Harvard University Press, 1927), 8.347e.

18 *The Task*, preliminary Advertisement, in *The Poems of William Cowper*, ed. John D. Baird and Charles Ryskamp, 2 vols. (Oxford: Clarendon Press, 1980).

19 *The Task*, I.748; II.285–6; III.220–1; III.566.

20 Keats, 'On Seeing the Elgin Marbles for the First Time'.

21 August Wilhelm Schlegel and Friedrich Schlegel, *Athenaeum*, I, part 2, fragment 20 (my translation).

22 Pound, *Cantos*, Canto LXXVI; T. S. Eliot, *The Waste Land*, line 430, in *The Annotated Waste Land*, ed. Lawrence Rainey (New Haven: Yale University Press, 2005); David Jones, *The Anathemata: Fragments of an Attempted Writing*, 2nd edn (London: Faber and Faber, 1972), Preface, line 1.

GUIDE TO FURTHER READING

General

Beissinger, Margaret, Tylus, Jane, and Wofford, Susanne, eds., *Epic Traditions in the Contemporary World: The Poetics of Community*, Berkeley, University of California Press, 1999

Bowra, C. M., *From Virgil to Milton*, London, Macmillan, 1945
  Heroic Poetry, London, Macmillan, 1952

Foley, J. M., *The Theory of Oral Composition: History and Methodology*, Bloomington, IN, Indiana University Press, 1988

Greene, Thomas, *The Descent from Heaven: A Study in Epic Continuity*, New Haven, Yale University Press, 1963

Hainsworth, J. B., *The Idea of Epic*, Berkeley, University of California Press, 1991

Hatto, A. T., gen. ed., J. B. Hainsworth, ed., *Traditions of Heroic and Epic Poetry*, 2 vols., London, The Modern Humanities Research Association, 1980–9

Johns-Putra, Adeline, *The History of Epic*, London, Palgrave Macmillan, 2006

Koljević, Svetozar, *The Epic in the Making*, Oxford, Clarendon Press, 1980

Lord, Albert B., *The Singer of Tales*, 2nd edn, ed. S. Mitchell and G. Nagy, Cambridge, MA, Harvard University Press, 2000

Merchant, Paul, *The Epic*, London, Methuen, 1971

Miller, D. A., *The Epic Hero*, Baltimore, Johns Hopkins University Press, 2000

Nuttall, A. D., *Openings: Narrative Beginnings from the Epic to the Novel*, Oxford, Clarendon Press, 1992

Parry, Milman, *The Making of Homeric Verse*, new edn, Oxford, Oxford University Press, 1987

Quint, David, *Epic and Empire: Politics and Generic Form from Virgil to Milton*, Princeton, Princeton University Press, 1993

Wofford, Susanne, *The Choice of Achilles: The Ideology of Figure in the Epic*, Stanford, Stanford University Press, 1992

1 The Epic of Gilgamesh

Damrosch, D., *The Buried Book: The Loss and Rediscovery of the Great Epic of Gilgamesh*, New York, H. Holt, 2007

Foster, B. R., *The Epic of Gilgamesh*, New York, Norton, 2000

George, A. R., *The Epic of Gilgamesh: The Babylonian Epic Poem and Other Texts in Akkadian and Sumerian*, London, Penguin Classics, 1999

The Babylonian Epic of Gilgamesh: Introduction, Critical Edition and Cuneiform Texts, 2 vols., Oxford, Oxford University Press, 2003

Leik, G., ed., *The Babylonian World*, London, Routledge, 2007

Tigay, J., *The Evolution of the Gilgamesh Epic*, Philadelphia, University of Pennsylvania Press, 1982

2   Greek epic

Cohen, Beth, ed., *The Distaff Side: Representing the Female in Homer's Odyssey*, Oxford, Oxford University Press, 1995

Davies, Malcolm, *The Epic Cycle*, Bristol, Bristol Classical Press, 1989

Doherty, Lillian Eileen, *Siren Songs: Gender, Audiences, and Narrators in the Odyssey*, Ann Arbor, MI, University of Michigan Press, 1995

Finley, M. I., *The World of Odysseus*, 2nd edn, Oxford, Clarendon Press, 1979

Foley, John Miles, ed., *A Companion to Ancient Epic*, Oxford, Blackwell, 2005

Fowler, Robert, ed., *The Cambridge Companion to Homer*, Cambridge, Cambridge University Press, 2004

Griffin, J., *Homer on Life and Death*, Oxford, Clarendon Press, 1980

Homer: The Odyssey, 2nd edn, Cambridge, Cambridge University Press, 2004

Katz, Marilyn A., *Penelope's Renown: Meaning and Indeterminacy in the Odyssey*, Princeton, Princeton University Press, 1991

Kim, Jinyo, *Achilleus' Pity: Oral Style and the Unity of the Iliad*, Oxford, Rowan and Littlefield Publishers, 1997

Louden, Bruce, *The Odyssey: Structure, Narration, Meaning*, Baltimore, Johns Hopkins University Press, 1999

Morris, I., and Powell, B., eds., *A New Companion to Homer*, Leiden, E. J. Brill, 1997

Murray, Gilbert, *The Rise of the Greek Epic*, 4th edn, London, Oxford University Press, 1934

Page, D. L., *The Homeric Odyssey*, Oxford, Oxford University Press, 1955

Folktales in Homer's Odyssey, Cambridge, MA, Harvard University Press, 1973

Parry, Milman, *The Making of Homeric Verse*, ed. Adam Parry, Oxford, Oxford University Press, 1971

Pucci, Pietro, *Odysseus Polutropos: Intertextual Readings in the Odyssey and the Iliad*, Ithaca, Cornell University Press, 1995

The Song of the Sirens: Essays on Homer, Lanham, MD, Rowan and Littlefield Publishers, 1998

Schein, S. L., *The Mortal Hero: An Introduction to Homer's Iliad*, Berkeley, University of California Press, 1996

Reading the Odyssey: Selected Interpretive Essays, Princeton, Princeton University Press, 1996

Silk, Michael, *The Iliad*, 2nd edn, Cambridge, Cambridge University Press, 2004

Stanford, W. B., *The Ulysses Theme: A Study in the Adaptability of a Traditional Hero*, rev. edn, Oxford, Blackwell, 1992

Suzuki, Mihoko, *Metamorphoses of Helen: Authority, Difference and the Epic*, Ithaca, Cornell University Press, 1989

Thalmann, W. G., *The Odyssey: An Epic of Return*, New York, Twayne Publishers, 1992

The Swineherd and the Bow: Representations of Class in the Odyssey, Ithaca, Cornell University Press, 1998

Willcock, Malcolm, *A Companion to the Iliad*, Chicago, University of Chicago Press, 1976

Wright, G. M., and Jones, P. V., eds., *Homer: German Scholarship in Translation*, Oxford, Clarendon Press, 1997

de Yong, I. J. J., ed., *Homer: Critical Assessments*, 4 vols., London, Routledge, 1999

3   Roman epic

Bertolín-Cebrián, Reyes, *Singing the Dead: A Model for Epic Evolution*, New York, Peter Lang, 2006

   Comic Epic and Parodies of Epic: Literature for Children and Youth in Ancient Greece, Spudasmata, Georg Olms, 2009

Boyle, A. J., *Roman Tragedy*, London, Routledge, 2006

Conte, Gian Biagio, *The Poetry of Pathos: Studies in Virgilian Epic*, trans. Elaine Fantham and Glenn Most, ed. Stephen Harrison, Oxford, Clarendon Press, 2007

Crump, M. Marjorie, *The Epyllion: From Theocritus to Ovid*, Oxford, Blackwell, 1931

Fantham, Elaine, *Ovid's Metamorphoses*, Oxford, Oxford University Press, 2004

Feeney, D. C., *The Gods in Epic: Poets and Critics of the Classical Tradition*, Oxford, Clarendon Press, 1991

Ganiban, Randall T., *Statius and Virgil: The 'Thebaid' and the Re-interpretation of the 'Aeneid'*, Cambridge, Cambridge University Press, 2007

Hardie, Philip, *The Epic Successors of Virgil: A Study in the Dynamics of a Tradition*, Cambridge, Cambridge University Press, 1993

Harris, W. V., *Restraining Rage: The Ideology of Anger Control in Classical Antiquity*, Cambridge, MA, Harvard University Press, 2001

Henderson, John, *Fighting for Rome: Poets and Caesars, History and Civil War*, Cambridge, Cambridge University Press, 1998

Hershkowitz Debra, *The Madness of Epic: Reading Insanity from Homer to Statius*, Oxford, Clarendon Press, 1998

   Valerius Flaccus' Argonautica: Abbreviated Voyages in Silver Latin Epic, Oxford, Clarendon Press, 1998

Keith, A. M., *Engendering Epic: Women in Latin Epic*, Cambridge, Cambridge University Press, 2000

Martindale, Charles, ed., *The Cambridge Companion to Virgil*, Cambridge, Cambridge University Press, 1997

Masters, Jamie, *Poetry and Civil War in Lucan's 'Bellum Civile'*, Cambridge, Cambridge University Press, 1992

Miles, Gary B., *Virgil's 'Georgics': A New Interpretation*, Berkeley, University of California Press, 1980

Miller, John F., *Ovid's Elegiac Festivals: Studies in the 'Fasti'*, Frankfurt am Main, Peter Lang, 1991

Nagy, Gregory, *The Best of the Achaeans: Concepts of the Hero in Archaic Greek Poetry*, Baltimore, Johns Hopkins University Press, 1979

O'Hara, James, *True Names: Vergil and the Alexandrian Tradition of Etymological Wordplay*, Ann Arbor, University of Michigan Press, 1996

O'Loughlin, Michael, *The Garlands of Repose: The Literary Celebration of Civic and Retired Leisure: The Traditions of Homer and Vergil, Horace and Montaigne*, Chicago, University of Chicago Press, 1978

Otis, Brooks, *Virgil: A Study in Civilized Poetry*, Oxford, Clarendon Press, 1964

Perkell, Christine G., *The Poet's Truth: A Study of the Poet in Virgil's 'Georgics'*, Berkeley, University of California Press, 1989

Putnam, Michael C. J., *The Poetry of the 'Aeneid': Four Studies in Imaginative Unity and Design*, Cambridge, MA, Harvard University Press, 1965
  Virgil's Poem of the Earth: Studies in the 'Georgics', Princeton, Princeton University Press, 1979

Quinn, Kenneth, *Virgil's 'Aeneid': A Critical Description*, London, Routledge and Kegan Paul, 1968

Ross, David O., *Virgil's Elements: Physics and Poetry in the 'Georgics'*, Princeton, Princeton University Press, 1987

Sullivan, J. P., *The 'Satyricon' of Petronius: A Literary Study*, London, Faber and Faber, 1968

Thomas, Richard F., ed., *Virgil: Georgics*, 2 vols., Cambridge, Cambridge University Press, 1988

Toohey, Peter, *Reading Epic: An Introduction to the Ancient Narratives*, London, Routledge, 1992
  Epic Lessons: An Introduction to Ancient Didactic Poetry, London, Routledge, 1996

Vessey, David, *Statius and the Thebaid*, Cambridge, Cambridge University Press, 1973

Wilkinson, L. P., *Ovid Recalled*, Cambridge, Cambridge University Press, 1955
  The Georgics of Virgil: A Critical Survey, Cambridge, Cambridge University Press, 1969

Williams, Gordon, *Technique and Ideas in the 'Aeneid'*, New Haven, Yale University Press, 1983

4   Heroic epic poetry in the Middle Ages

Bjork, R. E., and J. D. Niles, eds., *A Beowulf Handbook*, Lincoln, NE, University of Nebraska Press, 1996

Bostock, J. Knight, *A Handbook on Old High German Literature*, Oxford, Clarendon Press, 1955

Brault, G. J., ed. and trans., *The Song of Roland: An Analytical Edition*, 2 vols., University Park, PA, Pennsylvania State University Press, 1978

Brodeur, A. G., *The Art of Beowulf*, Berkeley, CA, University of California Press, 1959

Chickering, Howell D., Jr., ed. and trans., *Beowulf*, New York, Doubleday, 1977

De Chasca, E., *The Poem of the Cid*, Twayne's World Authors Series, 378, Boston, Twayne, 1976

Dronke, U., ed. and trans., *The Poetic Edda. I. Heroic Poems*, Oxford, Clarendon Press, 1969

Duggan, J. J., *The 'Cantar de mio Cid': Poetic Creation in its Economic and Social Contexts*, Cambridge, Cambridge University Press, 1989

Fenik, B., *Homer and the Nibelungenlied: Comparative Studies in Epic Style*, Cambridge, MA, Harvard University Press, 1986

Foley, J. M. *Traditional Oral Epic: The 'Odyssey', 'Beowulf', and the Serbo-Croatian Return Song*, Berkeley, University of California Press, 1990

Fulk, R. D., Bjork, R. E., and Niles, J. D., eds., *Klaeber's Beowulf and the Fight at Finnsburg*, with a foreword by H. Damico, 4th edn, Toronto, University of Toronto Press, 2008

Harris, J., 'Eddic Poetry', in *Old Norse – Icelandic Literature: A Critical Guide*, ed. C. J. Clover and J. Lindow, Islandica, 45, Ithaca, Cornell University Press, 1985, 68–156

Hatto, A. T., trans., *The Nibelungenlied*, rev. edn, Harmondsworth, Penguin, 1969

Joy, E. A., and Ramsey, M. K., eds., *The Postmodern 'Beowulf': A Critical Casebook*, Morgantown, VA, West Virginia University Press, 2006

Kay, S., *The Chansons de Geste in the Age of Romance: Political Fictions*, Oxford, Clarendon Press, 1995

Michael, I., ed., Hamilton, R., and Perry, J. trans., *The Poem of the Cid*, Harmondsworth, Penguin, 1984

Momma, H., *The Compositon of Old English Poetry*, Cambridge, Cambridge University Press, 1997

Niles, J. D., *Beowulf: The Poem and its Tradition*, Cambridge, MA, Harvard University Press, 1983

Reichl, K. *Singing the Past: Turkic and Medieval Heroic Poetry*, Ithaca, Cornell University Press, 2000

5 Dante and the epic of transcendence

Auerbach, Erich, *Dante, Poet of the Secular World*, trans. Ralph Mannheim, Chicago, University of Chicago Press, 1961

Bloom, Harold, ed., *Odysseus/Ulysses*, New York: Chelsea House Publishers, 1991

Curtius, E. R., *European Literature and the Latin Middle Ages*, New York, Routledge and Kegan Paul, 1953

Freccero, John, *Dante: The Poetics of Conversion*, ed. Rachel Jacoff, Cambridge, MA, Harvard University Press, 1986

Freccero, John, ed., *Dante: A Collection of Critical Essays*, Englewood Cliffs, NJ, Prentice Hall, 1965

Lamberton, Robert, *Homer the Theologian: Neoplatonist Allegorical Reading and the Growth of the Epic Tradition*, Berkeley, University of California Press, 1986

Singleton, Charles S., *Journey to Beatrice*, Cambridge, MA, Harvard University Press, 1958

Thompson, David, *Dante's Epic Journeys*, Baltimore, Johns Hopkins University Press, 1974

Wetherbee, Winthrop, *The Ancient Flame: Dante and the Poets*, Notre Dame, IN, University of Notre Dame Press, 2008

6 Italian Renaissance epic

Ascoli, Albert, *Ariosto's Bitter Harmony: Crisis and Evasion in the Italian Renaissance*, Princeton, Princeton University Press, 1987

Brand, C. P., *Torquato Tasso: A Study of the Poet and his Contribution to English Literature*, Cambridge, Cambridge University Press, 1965

Cavallo, Jo Ann, *Boiardo's 'Orlando Innamorato': An Ethics of Desire*, London, Associated University Presses, 1993
   The Romance Epics of Boiardo, Arisoto and Tasso: From Public Duty to Private Pleasure, Toronto, University of Toronto Press, 2004
Everson, Jane E., *The Italian Romance Epic in the Age of Humanism*, Oxford, Oxford University Press, 2001
Marinelli, Peter V., *Ariosto and Boiardo: The Origins of 'Orlando Furioso'*, Columbia, University of Missouri Press, 1987
Murrin, Michael, *The Allegorical Epic: Essays in its Rise and Decline*, Chicago, University of Chicago Press, 1980
Quint, David, *Epic and Empire: Politics and Generic Form from Virgil to Milton*, Princeton, Princeton University Press, 1993
Zatti, Sergio, *The Quest for Epic*, trans. Sally Hill and Dennis Looney, Toronto, University of Toronto Press, 2006

7   Camões's 'Os Lusíadas': the first modern epic

Bacon, Leonard, trans., *The Lusiads*, New York: Hispanic Society of America, 1950
Bell, Aubrey F. G., *Luis de Camões*, Oxford, Oxford University Press, 1923
Hart, Henry Hersch, *Luis de Camoens and the Epic of the Lusiads*, Norman, University of Oklahoma Press, 1962
Monteiro, George, *The Presence of Camões: Influences on the Literature of England, America, and Southern Africa*, Lexington, University Press of Kentucky, 1996
Pierce, Frank, ed., *Os Lusíadas*, Oxford, Clarendon Press, 1973
Subrahmanyam, Sanjay, *The Career and Legend of Vasco da Gama*, Cambridge, Cambridge University Press, 1997
Taylor, L. C., ed., *Luís de Camões: Epic and Lyric*, trans. Keith Bosley, Manchester, Carcanet, 1990
White, Landeg, trans., *The Lusiads*, Oxford and New York, Oxford University Press, 1997
Woodberry, George Edward, *The Inspiration of Poetry*, New York, Macmillan, 1910

8   'The Faerie Queene': Britain's national monument

Bellamy, Elizabeth J., *Translations of Power: Narcissism and the Unconscious in Epic History*, Ithaca, Cornell University Press, 1992
Berger, Harry, Jr., *Revisionary Play: Studies in the Spenserian Dynamics*, Berkeley, University of California Press, 1988
Biow, Douglas, *Mirabile Dictu: Representations of the Marvelous in Medieval and Renaissance Epic*, Ann Arbor, MI, University of Michigan Press, 1996
Borris, Kenneth, *Allegory and Epic in English Renaissance Literature: Heroic Form in Sidney, Spenser, and Milton*, Cambridge, Cambridge University Press, 2000
Burrow, Colin, *Epic Romance: Homer to Milton*, Oxford, Clarendon Press, 1993
Cook, Patrick J., *Milton, Spenser and the Epic Tradition*, Aldershot, Ashgate, 1996
Fichter, Andrew, *Poets Historical: Dynastic Epic in the Renaissance*, New Haven, Yale University Press, 1982

Goldberg, Jonathan, *Endlesse Worke: Spenser and the Structures of Discourse*, Baltimore, Johns Hopkins University Press, 1981

Helgerson, Richard, *Forms of Nationhood: The Elizabethan Writing of England*, Chicago, University of Chicago Press, 1992

Kaske, Carol K., *Spenser and Biblical Poetics*, Ithaca, Cornell University Press, 1999

Murrin, Michael, *The Allegorical Epic: Essays in its Rise and Decline*, Chicago, University of Chicago Press, 1980

Nohrnberg, James, *The Analogy of 'The Faerie Queene'*, Princeton, Princeton University Press, 1976

Warner, Christopher J., *The Augustinian Epic, Petrarch to Milton*, Ann Arbor, MI, University of Michigan Press, 2005

Watkins, John, *The Specter of Dido: Spenser and Virgilian Epic*, New Haven, Yale University Press, 1995

Wofford, Susanne, *The Choice of Achilles: The Ideology of Figure in the Epic*, Stanford, Stanford University Press, 1992

9 Seventeenth-century Protestant English epic

Achinstein, Sharon, *Milton and the Revolutionary Reader*, Princeton, Princeton University Press, 1994

    Literature and Dissent in Milton's England, Cambridge, Cambridge University Press, 2003

Bennett, Joan S., *Reviving Liberty: Radical Christian Humanism in Milton's Great Poems*, Cambridge, MA, Harvard University Press, 1989

Corns, Thomas N., *Regaining 'Paradise Lost'*, London, Longman, 1994

Davies, Stevie, *Images of Kingship in 'Paradise Lost': Milton's Politics and Christian Liberty*, Columbia, MS, University of Missouri Press, 1983

Fallon, Robert T. *Divided Empire: Milton's Political Imagery*, University Park, Pennsylvania University Press, 1995

Gregerson, Linda, *The Reformation of the Subject: Spenser, Milton, and the English Protestant Epic*, Cambridge, Cambridge University Press, 1995

Hill, Christopher, *The Experience of Defeat: Milton and Some Contemporaries*, New York, Viking Penguin, 1984

Knoppers, Laura L. *Historicizing Milton: Spectacle, Power, and Poetry in Restoration England*, Athens, GA, University of Georgia Press, 1994

Lewalski, Barbara K., *Milton's Brief Epic: The Genre, Meaning, and Art of 'Paradise Regained'*, Providence, Brown University Press, 1966

    'Paradise Lost' and the Rhetoric of Literary Forms, Princeton, Princeton University Press, 1986

Lim, Walter S. H. *John Milton, Radical Politics, and Biblical Republicanism*, Newark, University of Delaware Press, 2006

Loewenstein, David, *Representing Revolution in Milton and his Contemporaries: Religion, Politics, and Polemics in Radical Puritanism*, Cambridge, Cambridge University Press, 2001

    Milton: Paradise Lost, 2nd edn, Cambridge, Cambridge University Press, 2004

Miller, Shannon, *Engendering the Fall: John Milton and Seventeenth-Century Women Writers*, Philadelphia, University of Pennsylvania Press, 2008

Norbrook, David, *Writing the English Republic: Poetry, Rhetoric, and Politics, 1627–1660*, Cambridge, Cambridge University Press, 1999

Quint, David, *Epic and Empire: Politics and Generic Form from Virgil to Milton*, Princeton, Princeton University Press, 1993

Radzinowicz, Mary Ann, *Toward 'Samson Agonistes': The Growth of Milton's Mind*, Princeton, Princeton University Press, 1978

Turner, James Grantham, *One Flesh: Paradisal Marriage and Sexual Relations in the Age of Milton*, Oxford, Clarendon Press, 1987

Webber, Joan W., *Milton and his Epic Tradition*, Seattle, University of Washington Press, 1979

Wilding, Michael, *Dragons Teeth: Literature in the English Revolution*, Oxford, Clarendon Press, 1987

10 Mock-heroic and English poetry

Bond, Richmond P., *English Burlesque Poetry 1700–1750*, Cambridge, MA, Harvard University Press, 1932

Broich, Ulrich, *The Eighteenth-Century Mock-Heroic Poem*, trs. D. H. Wilson, Cambridge, Cambridge University Press, 1990

Brower, R. A., *Alexander Pope: The Poetry of Allusion*, Oxford, Clarendon Press, 1959

Clark, A. F. B., *Boileau and the French Classical Critics in England (1660–1830)*, Paris, Champion, 1925

Griffin, Dustin, *Satire: A Critical Reintroduction*, Lexington, University Press of Kentucky, 1994

Lord, George de F., *Heroic Mockery: Variations on Epic Themes from Homer to Joyce*, Newark, University of Delaware Press, 1977

Maresca, Thomas E., *Epic to Novel*, Columbus, Ohio State University Press, 1974

Rawson, Claude, *Order from Confusion Sprung: Studies in Eighteenth-Century Literature from Swift to Cowper*, London, George Allen and Unwin, 1985
   Satire and Sentiment, 1660–1830, Cambridge, Cambridge University Press 1994

Selden, Raman, *English Verse Satire 1590–1765*, London, George Allen and Unwin, 1978

Terry, Richard, *Mock-Heroic from Butler to Cowper*, Aldershot, Ashgate, 2005

11 Romantic re-appropriations of the epic

Abrams, M. H., *Natural Supernaturalism: Tradition and Revolution in Romantic Literature*, New York, Norton, 1971

Curran, Stuart, *Poetic Form and British Romanticism*, New York, Oxford University Press, 1986

Kucich, Greg, *Keats, Shelley, and Romantic Spenserianism*, University Park, PA, Pennyslvania State University Press, 1991

Sperry, Stuart M., *Keats the Poet*, Princeton, Princeton University Press, 1973

Tucker, Herbert F., *Epic: Britain's Heroic Muse 1790–1910*, Oxford, Oxford University Press, 2008

Vogler, Thomas, A., *Preludes to Vision: The Epic Venture in Blake, Wordsworth, Keats and Hart Crane*, Berkeley, University of California Press, 1971

Wilkie, Brian, *Romantic Poets and Epic Tradition*, Madison, University of Wisconsin Press, 1965

Wu, Duncan, ed., *Romanticism: An Anthology*, 3rd edn, Oxford, Blackwell, 2006

12 Ezra Pound, T. S. Eliot, and the modern epic

Bakhtin, M. M., *The Dialogic Imagination*, ed. Michael Holquist, trans. Caryl Emerson and Michael Holquist, Austin, University of Texas Press, 1981

Bernstein, Michael, *The Tale of the Tribe: Ezra Pound and the Modern Verse Epic*, Princeton, Princeton University Press, 1980

Bush, Ronald, *T. S. Eliot: A Study in Character and Style*, New York, Oxford University Press, 1984

Casillo, Robert, *The Genealogy of Demons: Anti-Semitism, Fascism, and the Myths of Ezra Pound*, Evanston, IL, Northwestern University Press, 1988

Eksteins, Modris, *Rites of Spring: The Great War and the Birth of the Modern Age*, New York, Anchor Doubleday, 1989

Eliot, T. S., *The Waste Land: A Facsimile and Transcript of the Original Drafts Including the Annotations of Ezra Pound*, ed. Valerie Eliot, New York, Harcourt Brace Jovanovich, 1971

   The Annotated Waste Land, with Eliot's Contemporary Prose, ed. Lawrence Rainey, New Haven, Yale University Press, 2005

Kenner, Hugh, *The Pound Era*, Berkeley, University of California Press, 1971

Lukács, Georg, *The Historical Novel*, Lincoln, NB, University of Nebraska Press, 1983

Makin, Peter, *Pound's Cantos*, London, George Allen and Unwin, 1985

Marcus, Laura, and Nicholls, Peter, eds., *The Cambridge History of Twentieth-Century English Literature*, Cambridge, Cambridge University Press, 2004

Menand, Louis, *Discovering Modernism: T. S. Eliot and his Context*, New York, Oxford University Press, 1987

Moretti, Franco, *Modern Epic: The World-System from Goethe to Garcia Marquez*, New York, Verso, 1996

Nicholls, Peter, *Ezra Pound: Politics, Economics, Writing*, London, Macmillan, 1984

North, Michael, *Reading 1922: A Return to the Scene of the Modern*, New York, Oxford University Press, 1999

Rainey, Lawrence, ed., *A Poem Including History: The Cantos of Ezra Pound*, Ann Arbor, University of Michigan Press, 1996

Redman, Tim, *Ezra Pound and Italian Fascism*, Cambridge, Cambridge University Press, 1991

Sherry, Vincent, *Ezra Pound, Wyndham Lewis, and Radical Modernism*, New York, Oxford University Press, 1993

Sieburth, Richard, ed., *Ezra Pound: The Pisan Cantos*, New York, New Directions, 2003

Surette, Leon, *Pound in Purgatory: From Economic Radicalism to Anti-Semitism*, Urbana, University of Illinois Press, 1999

13 Derek Walcott's 'Omeros'

Baer, William, ed., *Literary Conversations with Derek Walcott*, Jackson, MS, University Press of Mississippi, 1996

Baugh, Edward, *Derek Walcott*, Cambridge, Cambridge University Press, 2006

Bloom, Harold, ed., *Derek Walcott*, Philadelphia, Chelsea House, 2003
Breslin, Paul, *Nobody's Nation: Reading Derek Walcott*, Chicago, University of Chicago Press, 2002
Brown, Stewart, ed., *The Art of Derek Walcott*, Bridgend, Seren Books, 1991
Hamner, Robert, *Epic of the Dispossessed: Derek Walcott's 'Omeros'*, Columbia, University of Missouri Press, 1996
Henrikson, Line, *Ambition and Anxiety: Ezra Pound's 'Cantos' and Derek Walcott's 'Omeros' as Twentieth-Century Epics*, Amsterdam, Rodopi, 2006
Ismond, Patricia, *Abandoning Dead Metaphors: The Caribbean Phase of Derek Walcott's Poetry*, Kingston, Jamaica, University of West Indies Press, 2001
King, Bruce, *Derek Walcott: A Caribbean Life*, Oxford, Oxford University Press, 2000
Pollard, Charles W., *New World Modernisms: T. S. Eliot, Derek Walcott, and Kamau Braithwaite*, Charlottesville, VA, University of Virginia Press, 2004
Thieme, John, *Derek Walcott*, Manchester, Manchester University Press, 1999
Wilson-Tagoe, Nana, *Historical Thought and Literary Representation in West Indian Literature*, Gainesville, University Press of Florida, 1998

14 Epic in translation

Benjamin, Walter, *The Arcades Project* [Das Passagen-Werk], Cambridge, MA, Harvard University Press, 1999
Bernstein, Michael, *The Tale of the Tribe*, Princeton, Princeton University Press, 1980
Bowra, C. M., *Primitive Song*, London, Weidenfeld and Nicolson, 1962
Campbell, Joseph, *The Hero With a Thousand Faces*, Princeton, Princeton University Press, 1949
Eliade, Mircea, *Shamanism*, Princeton, Princeton University Press, 1964
Finnegan, Ruth, ed., *The Penguin Book of Oral Poetry*, Bloomington, Indiana University Press, 1978
Green, Peter, trans., *The Argonautika*, Berkeley, University of California Press, 1997
Lévi-Strauss, Claude, *The Savage Mind*, London, Weidenfeld and Nicolson, 1966
Lord, Albert B., *The Singer of Tales*, Cambridge, MA, Harvard University Press, 1960
Magoun, Francis Peabody, Jr., *The Kalevala*, Cambridge, MA, Harvard University Press, 1963
McCullough, Helen Craig, *The Tale of the Heike*, Stanford, Stanford University Press, 1988
Philippi, Donald L., *Songs of Gods, Songs of Humans*, Princeton, Princeton University Press, 1979
Ramsay, Jarold, *Coyote Was Going There*, Seattle, University of Washington Press, 1977
Reardon, B. P., *Collected Ancient Greek Novels*, Berkeley, University of California Press, 1989
Thompson, Stith, *The Folktale*, Berkeley, University of California Press, 1977

INDEX

Cambridge Companions to ...

AUTHORS